WHISPERS OF REVOLUTION

WHISPERS OF REVOLUTION

Jesus and the coming of God as king

Michael F. Bird

Published in Great Britain in 2025

Apollos
Studio 101, The Record Hall, 16–16A Baldwin's Gardens, London EC1N 7RJ
ivpbooks.com

Text copyright © Michael F. Bird 2025
This edition copyright © Inter-Varsity Press 2025

Michael F. Bird has asserted his right under the Copyright, Designs and Patents Act, 1988, to be identified as Author of this work.

All rights reserved. No part of this book may be reproduced or transmitted in any form or by any means, electronic or mechanical, including photocopying, recording, or by any information storage and retrieval system, without permission in writing from the publisher.

Unless otherwise noted, Scripture quotations are taken or adapted from the New Revised Standard Version Updated Edition. Copyright © 2021 National Council of Churches of Christ in the United States of America. Used by permission. All rights reserved worldwide.

EU GPSR Authorised Representative
LOGOS EUROPE, 9 rue Nicolas Poussin, 17000, La Rochelle, France
Email: Contact@logoseurope.eu

British Library Cataloguing-in-Publication Data
A catalogue record for this book is available from the British Library

ISBN 978-1-78359-952-3
eBook ISBN 978-1-78359-953-0

10 9 8 7 6 5 4 3 2 1

Typeset by Fakenham Prepress Solutions, Fakenham, Norfolk NR21 8NL
First printed in Great Britain by Clays Limited, Bungay, Suffolk

eBook by Fakenham Prepress Solutions, Fakenham, Norfolk NR21 8NL

Produced on paper from sustainable sources

Inter-Varsity Press publishes Christian books that are true to the Bible and that communicate the gospel, develop discipleship and strengthen the church for its mission in the world.

IVP originated within the Inter-Varsity Fellowship, now the Universities and Colleges Christian Fellowship, a student movement connecting Christian Unions in universities and colleges throughout Great Britain, and a member movement of the International Fellowship of Evangelical Students. Website: www.uccf.org.uk. That historic association is maintained, and all senior IVP staff and committee members subscribe to the UCCF Basis of Faith.

For Isaiah, Courtney, Bethany and Heidi

Contents

List of tables	x
Preface	xi
List of abbreviations	xiv
Introduction	xxi
1 The problems of studying the historical Jesus	**1**
The possibility of the historical Jesus	1
The pay-off in studying the historical Jesus	11
2 Jesus of Nazareth and his early life	**20**
Jesus' birth and early years	20
Baptism by John	26
3 Jesus and the kingdom of God	**30**
Jesus as kingdom-proclaimer	30
The kingdom of God in the Old Testament and early Judaism	31
The kingdom of God in the message of Jesus	41
Subjects of the kingdom	50
Jesus and his kingdom	53
4 Jesus and the restoration of Israel	**55**
God's kingdom as a restored Israel	55
Israel's restoration: a neglected topic	56
Jewish hopes for restoration	59
Jesus, a Jewish prophet of Israel's restoration	61
Jesus, Israel and the kingdom	66
5 Who was Jesus?	**68**
Jesus according to Jesus	68

Jesus as prophet	69
Jesus as seer	71
Jesus as sage	74
Jesus as rabbi	78
Jesus as exorcist, healer and miracle-worker	78
Jesus as God's envoy and embodiment	82
An ancient holy man	104
6 The teaching of Jesus	**106**
A new teaching – with authority	106
Parables	107
Ethics	119
Piety	122
Wealth and riches	128
Torah	130
Prophetic warnings	144
Jesus as messianic teacher	153
7 Jesus and his contemporaries	**155**
Jesus as others saw him	155
Jesus among the people	157
Jesus among rivals	162
Jesus among family and disciples	200
Jesus and Gentiles	207
Jesus between anonymity and charisma	216
8 Jesus' last days in Jerusalem	**217**
'Surely no prophet can die outside Jerusalem'	217
Triumphal entry	225
Jesus and the Jerusalem temple	228
Courting controversy with sayings and stories	251
Final (Passover) meal	263
A destiny in death	272

9 The death and resurrection of Jesus — 274
    The death of the Messiah — 274
    The resurrection of the Lord — 294

Postscript — 298
    The indisputable historical facts about Jesus — 298
    'Who then is this?' — 299
    Where to next? — 302

Bibliography — 305
Index of Scripture references and ancient sources — 342
Index of modern authors — 350

Tables

5.1	The so-called 'Johannine Thunderbolt'	86
5.2	'Son of Man' sayings functioning as indirect self-reference for Jesus	93
6.1	Themes of exile and repentance in the prayer of Solomon	146
8.1	The words of institution in the New Testament	266
9.1	Confrontations between Pontius Pilate and the chief priests of Judea	285

Preface

According to Dale Allison, 'Big books on Jesus are like the clouds: no matter how large, imposing, and beautiful they may be, they never last for long. There will never be any definitive non-canonical edition of his life.'[1] That's a pessimistic thought with which to begin a book about the historical Jesus! I concede, though, that it is generally true: books on the historical Jesus are either failures from the beginning or short-lived successes – their impact fleeting and soon forgotten. So why bother? To answer that, I have to respond with the words of Dr Tobias Funke from the US sitcom *Arrested Development*, who proposes to his wife a plan to rescue their marriage, a plan that inevitably fails for every couple who tries it, but to paraphrase Tobias for our purposes: 'It might just work for me.' So, in contrast to the several hundred books on the historical Jesus that have been dismantled by reviewers or discontinued in print, perhaps my historical Jesus book will succeed where others have failed. That is probably too ambitious, so I know to keep my aims quite modest. Thus, I am not proposing to write a Fifth Gospel or the definitive life of Jesus that becomes the basis for a hit musical. Nor do I imagine that this book will warrant me being awarded the F. C. Burkitt medal for biblical studies, let alone getting a place on the *New York Times* bestseller list, an invitation onto Joe Rogan's podcast, lunch with the Pope and the Obamas, an invited lecture at the Smithsonian, and a professorship at Oxbridge University in Jesus studies. But I do want to ask two important questions: can we move the conversation forward on the study of the historical Jesus, and does anybody know how to make those things happen for me? In reality, I'm hoping this book is more than a passing cloud, that it joins an ongoing conversation on who Jesus is, in both the academy and the church, and that it remains worthy of consideration for those in the conversation long after me.

---

1 Allison 2009: 10.

This book was due in the publisher's email inbox in 2013 and I only delivered the manuscript in 2024. However, I think the delay has given me time to produce a more mature and measured book on the historical Jesus than I would otherwise have written. If I had completed this book back in the early 2000s, it would have been very different from the book I offer here. Back then, I was very much writing on the historical Jesus with N. T. Wright's *Jesus and the Victory of God* open on one side of my desk and John P. Meier's *A Marginal Jew* open on the other side of the desk, with myself largely trying to walk a line between them (Wright and Meier were two leading scholars of the 'Third Quest' for the historical Jesus). While my indebtedness to Wright and Meier will be obvious, as well as others such as Dunn and Sanders, I feel freer and more independent now, able to pave my own path when it comes to telling the story of Jesus. I should add that historical Jesus scholarship has been in a bit of a lull since 2010, with very few 'lives' of Jesus written in the last fifteen years. That said, the *Journal for the Study of the Historical Jesus* has continued to publish outstanding articles on the historical Jesus, several major reference works about the history of Jesus research have been written,[2] there is continued interest in social memory theory in relation to the Jesus tradition,[3] and the publication of books on the historical Jesus is beginning to pick up steam.[4] We also stand on the precipice of a 'Next Quest' for the historical Jesus,[5] or a 'Fourth Quest',[6] but who knows, maybe it is about to happen, and heaven knows if I will inadvertently find myself press-ganged into it by chronological proximity or family resemblance to what other scholars are currently doing.

Some of my friends, such as Scot McKnight, have abandoned the historical Jesus project, instead preferring, in the tradition of Martin Kähler, the Jesus of the canonical Gospels. That is an approach I sympathize with, but one I cannot go along with, because I think we need to wrestle with the Jesus who stands behind the Gospels, not to draw a stark contrast to them or to give succour to conspiracy theories about

---

2 Notably Brown 2022.
3 E.g. Butticaz and Norelli 2018.
4 See recent works by David Wenham (2021) and Craig Blomberg (2023).
5 Crossley 2021.
6 Anderson 2021; Blomberg 2023.

Christian origins, but because Jesus as a figure of history still matters immensely for the study of history, religion, theology, faith and discipleship.[7] The slight pause in the intensity of historical Jesus scholarship will positively enable us to take stock of the past, evaluate prior scholarship, find new methods, reassess the problems and chart fresh approaches. For a start, I am no longer using the criteria of authenticity in my own Jesus research. Those tools were too clunky, blunt and heavy-handed to produce the results that were expected of them. Instead, I'm merely interested in reconstructing and telling the story of Jesus insofar as it helps us to make sense of Jesus, the Gospels and the early church in the context of Second Temple Judaism and the wider Greco-Roman world. You could call this criterion the 'veracity of the vibe': attempting to approximate the truth about Jesus through a compelling, albeit not infallible, historical narration, or at least grasping the gist of what his life and death were all about in a way that appears to many as historically persuasive.

Finally, I'm grateful to Philip Duce who commissioned this book for Apollos and to Tom Creedy for seeing it to completion. In addition, many friends, colleagues, staff and students at Ridley College and the Australian University of Theology continued to assist and support me in the completion of this project, for which I am most grateful. It's my hope that such a volume helps us to dig deeper into the questions of who Jesus of Nazareth was, and why a movement that sprang from him still endures to this day.

---

7 Dahl 1974: 85; Wright 1999: 14; Bird 2004; Allison 2009: 7.

Abbreviations

Journals, lexica, etc.

Aram.	Aramaic
AYBRL	Anchor Yale Reference Library
BAR	British Archaeological Reports
BAR	*Biblical Archaeology Review*
BBR	*Bulletin for Biblical Research*
BDAG	Danker, F. W., W. Bauer, W. F. Arndt and F. W. Gingrich, *Greek–English Lexicon of the New Testament and Other Early Christian Literature*, 3rd edn, Chicago, 2000
BIS	Biblical Studies
BJRL	*Bulletin of the John Rylands University Library of Manchester*
BRev	*Bible Review*
BSL	Biblical Studies Library
CBQ	*Catholic Biblical Quarterly*
CBR	*Currents in Biblical Research*
CEB	Common English Bible
CIJ	*Corpus inscriptionum Iudaicarum*
CITM	Christianity in the Making
COQG	Christian Origins and the Question of God
CONBNT	Coniectanea biblica: New Testament Series
CSB	Christian Standard Bible
EC	*Early Christianity*
EQ	*Evangelical Quarterly*
ExpT	*Expository Times*
FS	Festschrift
Gk	Greek

Heb.	Hebrew
HBM	Hebrew Bible Monographs
HTKNT	Herders theologischer Kommentar zum Neuen Testament
HTR	*Harvard Theological Review*
HTS	*Hervormde Teologiese Studies*
ISV	International Standard Version
JBL	*Journal of Biblical Literature*
JBT	*Jahrbuch für biblische Theologie*
JJS	*Journal of Jewish Studies*
JQ	*Jewish Quarterly*
JSATS	*Journal of the South African Theological Seminary*
JSHJ	*Journal for the Study of the Historical Jesus*
JSHJSup	Journal for the Study of the Historical Jesus Supplement Series
JSJ	*Journal for the Study of Judaism in the Persian, Hellenistic, and Roman Periods*
JSNT	*Journal for the Study of the New Testament*
JSNTSup	Journal for the Study of the New Testament Supplement Series
JSP	*Journal for the Study of the Pseudepigrapha*
JTS	*Journal of Theological Studies*
KJV	King James Version
Lat.	Latin
LHJS	Library of Historical Jesus Studies
LNTS	Library of New Testament Studies
LXX	Septuagint
NIGTC	New International Greek Testament Commentary
NIV	New International Version
NovT	*Novum Testamentum*
NRSV	New Revised Standard Version
NRSVUE	New Revised Standard Version Updated Edition
NS	new series
NSBT	New Studies in Biblical Theology

NT	New Testament
NTM	New Testament Monographs
NTS	*New Testament Studies*
NTTS	New Testament Tools and Studies
OT	Old Testament
PIBA	*Proceedings of the Irish Biblical Association*
PSI	Papiri greci e latini (Pubblicazioni della Società Italiana per la ricerca dei papiri greci e latini in Egitto)
PTM	Paternoster Theological Monographs
SJT	*Scottish Journal of Theology*
SNTSMS	Society for New Testament Studies Monograph Series
TynB	*Tyndale Bulletin*
TZ	*Theologische Zeitschrift*
WBC	Word Biblical Commentary
WUNT	Wissenschaftliche Untersuchungen zum Neuen Testament
ZNW	*Zeitschrift für die neutestamentichle Wissenschaft und die Kunde der älteren Kirche*

Ancient texts

1QapGen	*Genesis Apocryphon*
1QH	*Thanksgiving Hymns*
1QM	*War Scroll*
1QpHab	*Pesher Habakkuk*
1QS	*Community Rule*
4Q174	*Florilegium*
4Q246	*Aramaic Apocalypse*
4Q400	*Songs of the Sabbath Sacrifice*
4Q504	*Words of the Luminaries*
4Q521	*Messianic Apocalypse*
4QMMT	*Halakhic Letter*
11QMelch	*Melchizedek*

Abbreviations

11QT	*Temple Scroll*
Acts John	*Acts of John*
Acts Phil.	*Acts of Philip*
Apoc. Jas	*Apocalypse of James*
Arist.	*Letter of Aristeas*
Aristotle	
Virt. et Vit.	*Virtues and Vices*
Ass. Mos.	*Assumption of Moses*
b.	Babylonian Talmud
2 Bar.	*2 Baruch*
3 Bar.	*3 Baruch*
Barn.	*Barnabas*
Batra	*Bava Batra*
Ber.	*Berakhot*
CD	Cairo Genizah copy of the *Damascus Document*
Cicero	
Nat. Deo.	*On the Nature of the Gods*
Verr.	*Against Verres*
1 Clem.	*1 Clement*
2 Clem.	*2 Clement*
Dem.	*Demai*
Did.	*Didache*
Dio Chrysostom	
Orat.	*Orations*
Ep. Diogn.	*Epistle to Diognetus*
Eusebius	
Hist. Eccl.	*Ecclesiastical History*
Gen. Rab.	*Genesis Rabbah*
Gos. Eb.	*Gospel of the Ebionites*
Gos. Heb.	*Gospel of the Hebrews*
Gos. Naz.	*Gospel of the Nazarenes*
Gos. Pet.	*Gospel of Peter*
Gos. Thom.	*Gospel of Thomas*

Hag.	*Hagigah*
Herm. Sim.	*Shepherd of Hermas, Similitudes*
Horace	
Ep.	*Epistles*
Ignatius	
Eph.	*To the Ephesians*
Magn.	*To the Magnesians*
Phild.	*To the Philadelphians*
Rom.	*To the Romans*
Smyrn.	*To the Smyrneans*
Trall.	*To the Trallians*
Jos. Asen.	*Joseph and Aseneth*
Josephus	
Ant.	*Jewish Antiquities*
Apion	*Against Apion*
Life	*The Life*
War	*The Jewish War*
Jub.	*Jubilees*
Justin	
1 Apol.	*First Apology*
Dial.	*Dialogue with Trypho*
Juvenal	
Sat.	*Satires*
Kel.	*Kelim*
Ker.	*Kerithot*
Lucian	
Peregr.	*The Passing of Peregrinus*
m.	Mishnah
Mart. Isa.	*Martyrdom of Isaiah*
Meg.	*Megillah*
Mid.	*Middot*
Ned.	*Nedarim*
Od. Sol.	*Odes of Solomon*

Abbreviations

Origen
   C. Cels.   *Against Celsus*
P. Egert.   Egerton Papyrus
P. Oxy.   Oxyrhynchus Papyri
Pesah.   *Pesahim*
Philo
   Abr.   *On the Life of Abraham*
   Dec.   *On the Decalogue*
   Flacc.   *Against Flaccus*
   Hypoth.   *Hypothetica*
   Leg. Gai.   *On the Embassy to Gaius*
   Migr.   *On the Migration of Abraham*
   Quod Omn.   *That Every Good Person Is Free*
   Praem. Poen.   *On Rewards and Punishments*
   Somn.   *On Dreams*
   Spec. Leg.   *On the Special Laws*
   Vit. Cont.   *On the Contemplative Life*
   Vit. Mos.   *On the Life of Moses*
Pliny the Elder
   Nat. Hist.   *Natural History*
Pol. *Phil.*   Polycarp, *To the Philippians*
Ps.-Clem. Recogn.   Pseudo-Clementine Recognitions
Ps.-Phil, *Bib. Ant.*   Pseudo-Philo, *Liber antiquitatum biblicarum*
Ps.-Phoc.   Pseudo-Phocylides
Pss Sol.   *Psalms of Solomon*
Quintilian
   Decl.   *Declamations*
Shab.   *Shabbat*
Sanh.   *Sanhedrin*
Seneca
   Dial.   *Dialogues*
Sib. Or.   *Sibylline Oracles*
Sot.   *Sotah*

Suetonius
    Vesp. — *Vespasian*
t. — Tosefta
T. Abr. — *Testament of Abraham*
T. Benj. — *Testament of Benjamin*
T. Dan — *Testament of Dan*
T. Job — *Testament of Job*
T. Jud. — *Testament of Judah*
T. Iss. — *Testament of Issachar*
T. Levi — *Testament of Levi*
T. Mos. — *Testament of Moses*
T. Naph. — *Testament of Naphtali*
T. Zeb. — *Testament of Zebulun*
Taan. — *Taanit*
Tacitus
    Ann. — *Annals*
    Hist. — *Histories*
Tatian
    Diat. — *Diatesseron*
Tertullian
    Adv. Marc. — *Against Marcion*
    Spect. — *The Shows*
Tg. Exod. — *Targum Exodus*
Tg. Isa. — *Targum Isaiah*
Toh. — *Tohorot*
y. — Jerusalem Talmud
Yad. — *Yadayim*
Zeb. — *Zevahim*

Introduction

The underlying rationale for this volume is that a study of the historical Jesus is a necessary preliminary phase for a New Testament (NT) theology. Just to be clear, NT theology is indeed my real purpose, and this volume is kind of an extended throat-clearing exercise for that larger task. I am trying to line up my ducks on Jesus in this volume and then (perhaps) on the Jerusalem church in a later volume, so that I can then prosecute a concerted investigation of the theological texture of the NT.

I do not think that study of the historical Jesus is part of NT theology proper. That is because NT theology gives its attention to the historical context and theological substance of the actual texts of the NT with a view to attaining a normative expression of Christian faith. Nonetheless, I find it simply unimaginable to expound the NT's central subject, namely God, Jesus and faith, without first saying something about the historical figure of Jesus, a man who gathered disciples, disciples who founded a movement which became the church, a church that composed, copied and eventually canonized the NT. The NT is, then, part of the effective history of the man Jesus of Nazareth and constitutes the literary legacy of the first Christian generations. Although Jesus wrote no books, the NT is a library of books that are a singular testimony to his momentous impact on his disciples and through his disciples on subsequent generations in the wider Mediterranean theatre. NT theology cannot proceed or succeed without first studying its roots in the life of the historical Jesus and in the emergence of the early church. Jesus and the early church are the reason why the NT even exists.

My point is that researching the history of Jesus and the Jerusalem church is a kind of necessary and preliminary exercise before delving into a concerted study of the NT and exploring its message. Ultimately, *if* we are trying to explain what the NT is about, what animated its authors and audiences, why it was written and treasured, which topics of interest occur repeatedly within it, and what accounts for the patterns of devotion that the first Christians expressed, *then*, sooner or later, we are going to have to say something about the historical Jesus, the kingdom of God, Jerusalem during one fateful Passover in AD 30, Jesus' death, belief in Jesus' resurrection, the survival of the disciples in the aftermath, the formation of the church in Jerusalem, the spread of the church into non-Jewish territory, and how a Jewish message of a crucified Messiah found fertile soil in the Greco-Roman world. There is simply no other way. Before launching into an NT theology, we must inevitably and inescapably come to some sort of conclusion about Jesus of Nazareth and the early church. Who was Jesus? What did he do and say? Why was he crucified? How did the early church begin and why did it take the shape that it did? In other words, why are there Christians and who is this Christ of theirs?

1
The problems of studying the historical Jesus

The possibility of the historical Jesus

Study of the historical Jesus is an important prolegomenon for exploration of the theology of the NT.[1] Yet that conviction does not guarantee that the task is possible and that it will deliver anything beneficial. Which brings us to our first two topics of enquiry: (1) Can we truly excavate a historical Jesus beneath the text of the NT and other sources adjacent to it? (2) What are the pay-offs or dividends that accrue if one incorporates the historical Jesus into an NT theology?

Is the study of the historical Jesus possible given the habits of modern interpreters and the problems posed by our sources?

Is the 'historical Jesus' merely a mirror of the interpreter?

Concerning modern interpreters, one could say that after nearly three centuries of questing after the historical Jesus we still have the problem of readers projecting images of themselves onto Jesus.[2] Liberal theologians

---

[1] See more fully Wright and Bird 2019: 169–185.
[2] Martin Kähler (1988 [1882]: 57) noted that when it comes to authors who write books on Jesus, 'what is usually happening is that the image of Jesus is being refracted through the spirit of these gentlemen themselves'. Albert Schweitzer (1945 [1906]: 396) could state that the portrait of Jesus that emerged in the eighteenth- and nineteenth-century quests was 'a figure designed by rationalism, endowed with life by liberalism, and clothed by modern theology in an historical garb'. Of course, Schweitzer's own apocalyptic Jesus has been called 'the Superman of Nietzsche in Galilean robes' (Court 2006: 21), so that door swings both ways! George Tyrell (1909: 44) said: 'The Christ he [Harnack] sees looking back through nineteen centuries of Catholic darkness is only the reflection of a liberal Protestant face, seen at the bottom of a deep well.' Sanders (1985: 330) chides: 'It is amazing that so many New Testament scholars write books about Jesus in which they discover that he agrees with their own version of Christianity.' John Dominic Crossan (1991: xxviii) notes how many scholars 'do theology and call it history, do autobiography and call it biography' (which is the biggest self-own in Jesus scholarship if you ask me). Similar is Dale C. Allison (2009:

find a liberal Jesus, and evangelical theologians find an evangelical Jesus. Sadly, in the hands of many practitioners, the historical Jesus becomes an allegory for one's own religious values and provides religious capital for preferred political visions. The collection of scholars who formed the Jesus Seminar and who met in the 1980s and 1990s represent a useful morality tale. The Jesus Seminar offered a portrait of Jesus as a person more Hellenistic than Jewish in ethos, someone opposed to Jewish purity scruples, committed to a kingdom of socio-economic equals, and against imperialism and patriarchy, whose beliefs were conveniently shorn of Jewish apocalyptic hopes[3] and who dropped countercultural aphorisms like a Beatnik poet slamming 'the man'.[4] This Jesus was, as Crossan calls him, a Cynic hippie in an age of Augustan yuppies.[5] Alas, the Jesus of the Jesus Seminar was mostly a projection of American west coast liberal values onto Jesus, so much so that its findings are now mercilessly mocked for fabricating the 'California Jesus'.[6] In brutal honesty, it

---

24), who wonders if in modern Jesus research, '[m]aybe we have unthinkingly reduced [the] biography [of Jesus] to autobiography'. Knight (2004: 2) notes: 'The quest in many ways reveals the presuppositions and interests of the questors.'

3 A tendency of liberal theology that Cadbury (1937: 26) first noticed: 'Thus the apocalyptic element in the gospels has been frequently laid almost exclusively to the account of the evangelists, not because there is any real evidence that Jesus also did not share it, but mainly because it is uncongenial to the present day critic.'

4 The chief achievement of the seminar was the book *The Five Gospels* (Funk and Hoover 1993).

5 Crossan 1991: 421.

6 Theissen and Merz (1998 [1996]: 11) comment: 'The "non-eschatological Jesus" seems to have more Californian than Galilean local colouring.' Richard Burridge (Burridge and Gould 2004: 32) declares that the Jesus Seminar 'has produced a Jesus who is not Jewish in his teaching, but more like a Greek wisdom teacher or philosopher, and he's against sexism, imperialism and all the oppressiveness of the Roman empire. In other words, he's a Californian.' Crossley's short manifesto for a 'Next Quest' for the historical Jesus, which is interesting and provocative (2021), perhaps calling for the change of course that is needed, in the very least a more diverse range of historical Jesus research of cross-disciplinary expertise, is a welcomed move (Crossley and Keith 2024, 13). But Crossley's proposal for the future of historical Jesus research is explicitly concerned with Jesus in relation to colonialism and capitalism, race and ethnicity, gender and sexuality, and class and slavery, which makes me fear that it is going to end up with 'The California Jesus Makes a TikTok Video about Critical Theory'. My cynicism may well be premature, but it will entirely depend on whether such as a project, as Crossley himself nobly says, attempts to bring us closer to 'establishing the earliest ideas associated with the historical Jesus' (2021: 261). Postscript: Just as I was about to submit the manuscript for this book, I received a copy of Crossley and Keith 2024, *The Next Quest for the Historical Jesus*, which is something of a mixed bag. Crossley's introduction anticipates the criticism that 'we can't do historical Jesus study; it's too tied up with discourses and agendas' (2004: 9), and yet that is precisely what some contributors argue in the book, abandoning a reconstruction of the life and person of Jesus and preferring instead to deconstruct historical Jesus scholarship. One contributor, Wongi Park (2024), though making salient points about race, ethnicity and whiteness in historical Jesus research, contends that Markan priority is antisemitic, anti-Catholic and racist, and

beggars belief as to why anybody ever took the Jesus Seminar seriously in the first place.[7] Of course, conservative interpreters are not immune from creating Jesus in their own image. If the historical Jesus looks as though he is about to start a big-tent revival or announce tax breaks for rich Romans, or if he carries a rosary and a copy of the *New York Post*, then maybe your Jesus is less historical and more ideologically embedded. American news pundit Bill O'Reilly co-wrote *Killing Jesus*, a book about Jesus' life and last days, which according to one reviewer depicts 'A Tea Party Son of God'.[8] This tendency towards anachronism, allegory and trying to ally Jesus to one's own religion or politics is a temptation that many fall into. So one might have to finally concede that the historical Jesus is just a mirror of oneself.

At the end of the day, having presuppositions and projecting our biases, whether secular or sacred, is inevitable in the study of Jesus. 'We always bring with us a story, formed or half-formed,' says Allison, 'a story about Jesus, a story made up of expectations and presuppositions that tacitly guide us' in what we think is plausible and probable about him.[9] Even so, I do not think that trying to map Jesus within ancient Judaism or trying to plot him in a genetic relationship to the early church is purely a mirror for our own dispositions. There is a real history to be found, and real insights can be made when scholars and readers of this history exchange notes and trade observations. I have read things about Jesus that I think ring true from the Jesus Seminar, Jesuit priests, Jewish scholars and religiously invested Jesus-followers. I know I have had to change my mind about certain things pertaining to Jesus when confronted with overwhelming evidence, even when it had certain flow-on effects in my own religious devotion. Maybe the study of the historical Jesus is not so much a mirror as a dark windowpane. Although we can see our reflection on the glass, hopefully we can also see through it, however imperfectly, however clouded, and see Jesus in his own time.

---

should be abandoned (360). Such a claim is a genetic fallacy as it conflates the wrongful ideology of advocates of Markan priority with the case for Markan priority itself (see Wright and Bird 2019: 686–694).

7 See critiques of the Jesus Seminar in Wright 1996: 28–82; Witherington 1997: 42–57; Dunn 2003: 58–65; Keener 2009: 14–32.
8 O'Reilly and Dugard 2017; reviewed by O'Grady (2013).
9 Allison 1998: 36.

Thus, one cannot claim neutrality, disinterest or independence as a Jesus-researcher. There is no epistemological Switzerland that one can occupy and no hermeneutical court of The Hague to which one can appeal for impartial judgment.[10] The best we can do is critically read the sources, offer hypotheses, and submit our findings to peer review in the hope that we are persuasive in the global community of researchers when it comes to describing the historical Jesus. That, I think, is adequate, and is what I am endeavouring to do in this book: offer a portrait of Jesus that is persuasive to other readers. I have embarked on this project with no claim to scholarly independence or privileged position. I am, after all, an Australian Anglican priest, a moderate evangelical, in the business of historical study and theological analysis, and my contemporaries can haggle over where I have gone wrong. I certainly have no desire to peddle my presuppositions, but rather to conduct a sort of open and detailed enquiry that will either vindicate them or lead me to abandon them.[11] I want to engage in the kind of critical labour concerning Jesus and ancient

---

10 See McKnight (2005: 20–21) on not succumbing to the cynicism (or narcissism) of postmodern interpreters who believe that the object of study is swallowed up by the subject doing the study. Bauckham (2017: 3) notes: 'All history – meaning all that historians write, all historiography – is an extricable combination of fact and interpretation, the empirically observable and the intuited or constructed meaning.' For Hengel and Schwemer (2019 [2007]: 281–282), '[p]erhaps both sides, "conservative" and "radical" critics, need to be more modest and acknowledge that they both often work with hypotheses that can be grounded only in a limited way'. Schröter (2014 [2012]: 17) believes that Jesus research moves in a 'fuzzy sphere' since our sources do not mediate an unambiguous account of the past. Therefore, the 'goal cannot be to reach the *one* Jesus *behind* the texts but to reach a conception grounded on the weighing of plausibilities, which as an abstraction from the sources always moves *in front* of the sources' (emphasis original).

11 Chilton 1978a: 85. Jonathan Rowlands (2023) has done a global exposition of the significance of metaphysical presuppositions in the study of the historical Jesus and calls for greater openness and plurality of perspectives in scholarly studies. Craig Evans (1994: 133) suggests that religious disposition does not necessarily 'invalidate historical Jesus research [any more] than the love of art invalidates the work of an art critic or the love of science invalidates the research of a scientist'. Joel Willitts (2005) urges scholars not to try to escape their presuppositions but to embrace them as bringing fresh perspectives to Jesus research. Dunn (2003: 121) is right that merely stating one's presuppositions does not vindicate them, because everyone has presuppositions: 'The point is rather that as the exegete moves round the hermeneutical circle between pre-understanding and text, the text reacts back upon pre-understanding, both sharpening it and requiring of it revision at one point or another, and thus enabling a fresh scrutiny of the text, necessitating in turn a further revision of pre-understanding, and so on and on.' Allison (2009: 19–20) adds some optimism: 'While we inevitably read ourselves into the texts, we can at the same time come to conclusions that neither arise solely from our expectations nor simply confirm our wishes.' Mitzi Smith (2024: 382) encourages researchers to embrace 'epistemological vulnerability and hermeneutical humility', which requires a willingness to be found wrong and a willingness to change one's mind.

history that includes an interpretative element, so as to bring coherence, clarity, colour and even creativity to the task of answering the questions: who is Jesus, what did he do and say, why did he die, why did people claim that he rose from the dead, and how did the church begin and expand?[12] That is my objective when it comes to studying the historical Jesus.

Can we access reliable history about Jesus from the Gospels?

Concerning our sources, there is the preliminary problem of feasibility. Is the historical Jesus even accessible to us? The canonical Gospels are not secular histories; they are deliberate and self-conscious Christian proclamations of Jesus, and their narrations of Jesus are theologically freighted and imbued with faith-convictions about Jesus as Lord. The four evangelists have skin in the game of who Jesus is and what he means for their audiences. Even the evangelists' sources, whether people or parchments, possess an angle on Jesus that they wish to push, or an axe against certain groups that they wish to grind. How does one separate the history of Jesus from the interpretation, theology, faith, bias and partisanship of those who carried the tradition and composed the Gospels?

Well, to negotiate that challenge, in the industry of Jesus studies, a saying or story of Jesus was normally deemed historically 'authentic' if and only if it met certain criteria, that is, scholarly indices used to separate history from theology in the Gospels. The criteria included multiple attestation across sources, coherence with other accepted traditions, dissimilarity from Judaism and the early church, or potential to cause embarrassment to the early church, among others.[13] I used these criteria in my own earlier forays into historical Jesus research;[14] it was the toolbox I inherited from the academy. The criteria were designed to find history underneath the interpretative layers of the Gospels. Yet we are now conscious that these so-called 'criteria of authenticity' are not really

---

12 See Cadbury (1937: 191): 'That is the task of all history; the evangelic episode is no unique one. First the labor of criticism and research, and then the artistic, poetic reconstruction.'
13 See survey in Porter 2000.
14 Bird 2006a; 2009.

capable of separating the Christ of faith from the Jesus of history.[15] I'm not convinced they are completely useless, like trying to perform open-heart surgery with a paperclip; but I have to admit that they are not going to deliver what they promised, namely a historical Jesus shorn of faith in Jesus as Lord. A reality check is necessary: there is no history, tradition, memory or knowledge of Jesus independent of the followers, interpreters and worshippers who wrote about him.[16] Consequently, and as I've said more than once before, trying to separate history and theology in the Gospels is like trying to separate red and blue from the colour purple. They are both there, but you are daft if you think you can surgically separate one from the other.[17]

---

15 See Hooker 1972; Porter 2000; Theissen and Winter 2002 [1998]; Allison 2008; 2009: 54–60; 2010b; Rodríguez 2009; 2010; Keith and Le Donne 2012; Keith 2014; 2016; Bernier 2016; Bock and Komoszewski 2019; Barber 2023: 16–42. Crossley (2021: 261) is nakedly honest: 'The criteria of authenticity have all but been demolished.' That said, Anderson (2021: 29–31) has proposed new criteria based on corroboration (over multiple attestation), primitivity (over dissimilarity and embarrassment), critical realism (over dogmatic naturalism) and open coherence (over closed portraiture), yet still believes that they can yield a percentage-calculated gradation of historical certainty.

16 Allison (2008: 94; cf. 2009: 61–66) puts it eloquently: 'Jesus' identity cannot be sundered from a whole constellation of post-Easter circumstances: somebody attributed to him the remarkable Sermon on the Mount, and somebody else remembered his death by creating Mark's stark and moving passion narrative, and somebody else penned Luke's beautiful and human Gospel, and somebody else produced the symbolically rich and mystically charged Gospel of John, and somebody else composed the paean to love in 1 Corinthians 13 and declared there to be no difference between Jew and Gentile. Jesus wrote none of this, but without him none of it would have been written; and if his character had been different, the character of these texts would be too.' Watson (2008: 107, 114) is similar: 'At every point Jesus is filtered through early Christian tradition; at no point do we encounter him face to face... Even from a historical point of view, however, it is not at all easy to detach Jesus from his first followers. Their caption of him is also his impact on them.' Schnelle (2009 [2007]: 67) expands on the same point: 'The quest for Jesus cannot be reduced to the "historical Jesus" or the "real Jesus," for if Jesus is accessible to us only in the narratives that present him, and therefore already interpret him, research cannot distinguish between a "purely historical" and a theological approach. There is a historical quest for Jesus, but not a quest for the historical Jesus. Because Jesus of Nazareth has never been accessible apart from his significance for faith, research must also pose the pre-Easter questions of his consciousness of his own mission and the theological significance of his work.' Social memory theory probably offers the most promising paradigm for studying Jesus as a figure of history whose memory was both preserved and refracted in the recollection, performance and literization of the Jesus tradition. A good entrée to that discussion is Keith 2011. On the whole quest for the remembered Jesus, see Havukainen 2020; Graeig 2024: 90–176.

17 Dahl (1974: 67) noted: 'In no case can any distinct and sharp separation be achieved between genuine words of Jesus and construction of the community. We do not escape the fact that we know Jesus only as the disciples remembered him. Whoever thinks that the disciples completely misunderstood their Master or even consciously falsified his picture may give his phantasy free rein.' Watson (2008: 102–103) observes: 'From a purely historical point of view, the problems encountered in trying to distinguish primary from secondary material have a simple explanation: they reflect the considerable area of overlap between what mattered to Jesus and what mattered to the early communities of his followers over

The problems of studying the historical Jesus

One response is to be sceptical and say that the four Gospels – our primary sources about Jesus – are just so shot through with bias, myth, theology, literary tropes, and internecine polemics among Jews and Christians that there is no access to a historical Jesus: at best you might find a faint whisper of his message, or else a record of what people believed about Jesus.[18] Let's be honest: scepticism of this order is a great way to tout one's scholarly credentials, and to get clicks, views and downloads. Scepticism provides a platform to elevate oneself over and against naive, optimistic, fideistic or churchly approaches to historical questions about Jesus.

However, not all scepticism is scholarly! Most self-professed sceptics have predilections and agendas that make them want to believe certain things about Jesus and the early church, either because it keeps their disgust fresh or because it emboldens their narrative about the hidden origins of Christianity. For a case in point, Jesus mythicism, the belief that Jesus did not exist, is not a product of scholarly scepticism; it is not even marginal in the academy. Jesus mythicism is an anti-religious dogma located in the bounded beliefs of certain (online) atheist communities. This is scepticism, but it is not scholarly![19]

In addition, not all scepticism is consistent. Cadbury noted the inherent irony of so much scholarship about the historical Jesus. He wrote:

> When I read a life of Christ that in the most careful approved fashion describes at length the unhistorical character of the gospels and the aspects of their viewpoint which are to be rejected as late

---

the next few decades.' Allison (2009: 22–23) is similar: 'I must confess . . . that, with every year of further contemplation, I become more uncertain about anyone's ability, including my own, cleanly to extricate Jesus from his interpreters.' Schröter (2021: 222; cf. 2014 [2012]: 16) comments: 'History and theology in the gospels are not opposed to each other. Instead, the gospels are a mixture of both. They refer to a historical past that is represented by their story worlds, and they claim to provide reliable portraits of that past by their own narratives.' Hengel and Schwemer (2019 [2007]: 184) state: 'We can no more separate Jesus' words and deeds from the church than we can imagine a plant without roots.' See too Allison 2009: 25–29, 54.

18 See e.g. Bultmann 1963 [1921]: 373; Henaut 1993; Hollander 2000; cf. discussion in Theissen and Merz 1998 [1996]: 94–124.

19 For a critique of Jesus mythicism, see Byrskog 2011; Ehrman 2013; Casey 2014; Gullotta 2017; Gathercole 2018. More sympathetic to Jesus mythicism is Meggitt 2019.

and secondary, but then proceeds to construct a portrait of the Master shot through with modern standards of value, I feel like saying, 'Why beholdest thou the mote that is in thy brother's eye, but considerest not the beam that is in thine own eye?'[20]

It is comical when you think about it. So much scholarship can be like: 'We all know that the Gospels are not historically reliable – they aren't even interested in a "historical Jesus"; they are saturated with bias and theology; they are only interested in the Christ of faith, bashing on Jews and other Christian groups, oppressing women and marketing Jesus to Gentiles. By the way, let me tell you the secrets of the historical Jesus that the Vatican and Baptist fundamentalists don't want you to know about! Turn with me to the Gospel of Mark chapter one where you'll see that the real Jesus is basically Che Guevara speaking Yiddish.' For scholars like that, who deny the historical value of the Gospels and then proceed to use the Gospels as their primary source to reconstruct the secret, hidden, real Jesus of history, I have no words, only gifs expressing exasperation.[21]

I am persuaded that the early church was indeed interested in the earthly and pre-Easter Jesus.[22] Maybe not the 'historical Jesus' of a Discovery Channel documentary; but the questions of who Jesus was, what he said and did, and what he was like were not questions that first emerged in the 1700s. The life, teaching, mission and identity of Jesus was intrinsic to the church's faith in Jesus from the very beginning. The evangelists, even as they locate Jesus in Israel's sacred history, even as they record fantastic tales of healings and exorcisms, even as they are saturated in scriptural allusions, even as they use biographical genres and literary forms of the time, even as they embellish details, even as they tinker with timelines, even as they imprint something of themselves

---

20 Cadbury 1937: 46–47.
21 The worst offender here is Bart Ehrman, who has argued that the NT manuscripts are corrupted (2005), as is the memory and oral tradition about Jesus behind the Gospels (2016), and that the Gospels are full of contradictions (2009), and yet he is still able to write a book about the historical Jesus using the Gospels as his main source (1999).
22 Schröter (2014 [2012]: 9) distinguishes the 'earthly Jesus', the Jew who lived and was active in Galilee in the first century but is no longer accessible to us, from the 'historical Jesus', who is a product of the evaluation of sources made by the interpreter (even earlier was Hahn [1969]). McKnight (2005: 29) defines the historical Jesus as 'a narrative representation of the existential facts about Jesus that survive critical scrutiny'.

in the telling, are still trying to communicate the back-then-ness of Jesus and are not writing a narrative commentary about their own faith.[23]

An honest appraisal of our sources means that we cannot arrive at a historical Jesus who can be clinically separated from the devotion of his later followers, but we can attain a portrait of Jesus who was remembered even as he was reinterpreted by successive generations. It is undoubtedly true that, on the one hand, the Jesus traditions lying underneath the Gospels have been shaped by the interpreters and custodians of that tradition; but on the other hand, the shapers of that tradition were themselves originally shaped by the historical Jesus.[24] The Gospels convey the impact that Jesus had on his first followers and the early church, an impact that extends even to their creative literary activity and interpretative accents. Accordingly, the Gospels emanate both bias and biography, authenticity and artistry, fact and faith, history and hermeneutic. What the Gospels produce is not the Christ of faith superimposed onto the historical Jesus. Rather, the Gospels offer a striking representation, much like a docudrama, of Jesus' actions in the past and his voice for the present made available through the church's corporate memory of Jesus, a memory shaped by living eyewitnesses, tradents of a tradition concerned with truth and testimony, beside a burgeoning literary culture of Christological exegesis and aetiological development, and deployment of stories from Jesus and about Jesus for sectarian ends.[25] We certainly cannot excavate a Jesus *behind* our sources, but only a Jesus who appears *through* them.[26] Our reconstruction of a *remembered* Jesus is not identical to the *historical* Jesus, but we proceed on the assumption that they do overlap sufficiently to be possible in the theatre of historical study.[27]

An abrupt decision must be made! Do you think the Gospels are, at least generally, a reliable guide to the life and teaching of Jesus, or not? Sean Freyne posed the issue bluntly: 'Either we accept that the early followers of Jesus had some interest in and memory of the historical

---

23 As I've argued extensively in Bird 2014b: 21–72. For other works on the general historical reliability of the Gospels, see Eddy and Boyd 2008; Blomberg 2016; Bauckham 2017; Williams 2018; Keener 2019.
24 See Allison 2009: 22–30.
25 Bird 2014b: 110–111.
26 Schröter 2018a: 85.
27 Schröter 2018a: 85.

figure of Jesus as they began to proclaim the good news about him, or we must abandon the process entirely.'[28] Dale Allison is equally dichotomous:

> Either they [the Gospels] tend to preserve pre-Easter memories or they do not. In the former case, we have some possibility of getting somewhere. But in the latter case, our questing for Jesus is probably pointless and we should consider surrendering to ignorance. If the tradition is seriously misleading in its broad features, then we can hardly make much of its details.[29]

As you can tell, I support the former view, that the Gospels are, with caveats and qualifications, reliable guides to the historical Jesus. The Gospels and adjacent sources at the very least 'preserve details about the geographical region and individual places of Jesus' activity, information and characterizations about his family, followers and adversaries as well as biographical episodes'.[30]

What is perhaps needed is to approach study of the historical Jesus with an epistemology of *critical realism* (history is knowable, but never independently of the knower),[31] a type of *believing criticism* for the religious reader (Christian faith requires historical study of Jesus)[32] and a genuine *commitment to the truth* (the necessary condition for an open and honest enquiry into any topic). The materials before us warrant, says Tuomas Havukainen, neither 'naïve apologetic trust nor hyperskepticism'.[33] I'm convinced that all one can do is read the primary sources at our disposal, listen to conversations in secondary literature, have an honest and self-critical reflection of one's own presuppositions, and then sketch out a story of the Galilean prophet named Jesus of Nazareth, who preached the kingdom of God, was crucified under Pontius Pilate, was acclaimed as

---

28 Freyne 2005: 4.
29 Allison 2008: 84–85. Allison (2010b: 9 n. 47), who is hardly an apologist or conservative in his view of the authenticity and transmission of the Jesus tradition, says: 'I do not contend that the evangelists were, in effect, amnesiacs.'
30 Schröter 2018b: 99.
31 Wright and Bird 2019: 50–59, largely dependent on Wright 1992: 81–120. See too Bernier 2016.
32 Wright 1999: 14; Bird 2014b: 67–72.
33 Havukainen 2020: 297; cf. Barber 2023: 32–35.

resurrected and exalted, fits credibly within Second Temple Judaism and stands in organic continuity with the early church.[34] The task is to draw a picture of the man Jesus that makes sense within the context of first-century Roman Judea, a man who plausibly excited hopes and faith as we have them in Paul's letters and the Gospels, and whose effective history yielded the spread of the Jesus movement into the Trans-Jordan region and the eastern Mediterranean.[35] Moreover, to do that in such a way as to garner some measure of agreement from scholarly peers and religious practitioners.[36] If this quest has a name, it's the quest for the (admittedly underwhelming) *plausible* Jesus[37] using a method focused on the narratival veracity of any version of the Jesus story that a historian constructs.

The pay-off in studying the historical Jesus

Changing hats from historian to theologian, I want to explore here the place of the historical Jesus in an NT theology and the pay-off in engaging in a study of the historical Jesus.

---

34 Cf. Meyer 1979: 83; Sanders 1985: 3, 18, 22; Wright 1996: 132; Becker 1998: 14; Theissen and Winter 2002 [1998]: 211–212; Pitre 2015: 44–46; Klausner 2025: 369.

35 I like how Theissen and Winter (2002 [1998]: 212) put it: 'What we know of Jesus as a whole must allow him to be recognized within his contemporary Jewish context and must be compatible with the Christian (canonical and noncanonical) history of his effects.' Allison (1998: 35–36) comments wisely: 'As historians of the Jesus tradition we are storytellers. We can do no more than aspire to fashion a narrative that is more persuasive than competing narratives, one that satisfies our aesthetic and historical sensibilities because of its apparent ability to clarify more data in a more satisfactory fashion than its rivals.' Stuhlmacher (2018 [1999]: 53) asserts that '[n]o biography of Jesus can be drawn from this material but only a historically plausible picture of Jesus's messianic mission'. Schnelle (2009 [2007]: 28) says: 'All that one can do is to declare in the present one's own interpretation of the past.' Sanders (1985: 58, 229) writes: 'One is looking for a hypothesis which explains more (not everything), which gives a good account (not the only one) of what happened, which fits Jesus realistically into his environment, and which has in view cause and effect', which leads us to 'looking for a Jesus who makes the most sense of the available facts and what we otherwise know of Judaism and nascent Christianity'. Feldmeier and Spieckermann (2021: 220) put it this way: 'The aim is to form with the greatest possible historical plausibility a picture that can explain how the early Christian interpretations of the Christ event did not superimpose something completely different upon the history of the earthly Jesus but instead, precisely from their post-Easter perspective, attempted to do justice to the life and the suffering of the earthly Jesus.' Barber (2023: 234) asks, 'Which interpretations of Jesus likely bring us closest to history?'

36 Dahl (1974: 63–64) contended that '[s]cholars with different starting points co-operate and are able mutually to correct each other. For that reason also, it is not desirable that non-Christian scholars remain aloof from this work. In certain respects even antipathy can be illuminating; Jewish scholars, e.g., can have a clear eye for what is characteristic of Jesus.'

37 Cf. Theissen and Winter 2002 [1998], esp. 172–225.

The place of Jesus in a New Testament theology

It helps if we remember that the NT was written by the first generations of believers, and is largely about what the God of Israel had accomplished in Jesus in the totality of his life, death and resurrection, a totality which included his person, message, identity and promises, all relating to God's kingdom.[38] It would be odd to think that the first way one encounters Jesus in an NT theology is through an analysis of Christological titles or articulations of the atonement. Surely, Jesus the man, his mission and message, not just the Christologies of Luke or Hebrews, must have a proximate place in an NT theology. It is Jesus, earthly, exalted, and eschatological consummator, who is the alpha and omega of NT thought.[39] Furthermore, with a few exceptions, most NT theologians seem to have thought so too.[40]

On the exception side, Rudolf Bultmann, who had little interest in the historical Jesus, said that '[t]he message of Jesus is a presupposition for the theology of the New Testament rather than a part of that theology itself'.[41] There was no question for Bultmann of recovering Jesus' personality or psychology; that was inaccessible.[42] But the message of Jesus was still faintly echoed in the Gospels, and that was the assumed foundation for an NT theology. Bultmann accordingly devoted thirty pages to Jesus as a preface to his *Theology of the New Testament*. I contend that Bultmann was partly right to be allergic to including Jesus in an NT theology proper. In NT theology we are concerned with the theological message of the individual books and the whole corpus with a view to sketching a normative account of Christian faith, ethics, ministry, devotion and discipleship. The historical Jesus is not a text or an artefact, but something of a scholarly construct, fallible and artificial, and cannot

---

38 Wright and Bird 2019: 178.
39 Witherington 2009–10: 1:63.
40 Treatments of Jesus within an NT theology include *inter alia* Kümmel 1974 [1972]: 22–95; Schnelle 2009 [2007]: 61–162; Witherington 2009–10: 1:63–170; Stuhlmacher 2018 [1999]: 51–184; Blomberg 2018: 17–100; Schnabel 2023: 71–260. No section on Jesus is given in Ladd 1993 [1974]; Marshall 2004; Thielman 2005; Matera 2007. Stauffer (1955: 25–29) has only a brief and vague section on Jesus' teaching about the Son of Man as the link between John the Baptist and the primitive church. Strecker (2000 [1996]: 227–263) gets as far as 'Early Christian Traditions to the Composition of the Gospels'.
41 Bultmann 1952–55: 1:3.
42 Bultmann 1958: 8.

be accorded the authority of the biblical canon. Further, if we make the hypothetical historical Jesus part of an NT theology, then why not other hypothetical subjects too, such as Q and a Q community, Antiochene theology, the Johannine community?

Even so, contra Bultmann, I think that the historical Jesus is more than a presupposition of NT theology and that it deserves more than some brief prefatory remarks in an NT theology.[43] If the Christ of faith in his earthly manifestation is not in some sense 'historical' – leaving aside what 'historical' means for the moment – what is the jolly point of the whole thing? Here is where Ernst Käsemann's insight rings true: as long as the early church believed that its exalted Lord was also the crucified Jesus, then the early church never lost interest in the historical Jesus as properly basic for faith![44] The Gospels are not about the early church's faith in Jesus; they are about Jesus, the Galilean prophet from Nazareth. The Gospels assume a continuity between Jesus back then and Jesus as he was later proclaimed, and so demand that we explore the historical back-then-ness of Jesus as a precondition for any further contemporizing of Jesus now.[45]

Thus, we have arrived at a problem: the historical Jesus is important to NT thought, and the historical (or earthly) Jesus is more than a presupposition to NT theology, but study of the historical Jesus does not constitute a formal part of an NT theology.[46] So, then, where precisely does the study of the historical Jesus belong?

I think a sketch of the historical Jesus needs to be part of the prolegomena to an NT theology. That is because, first, it explains in historically nuanced terms who Jesus is and what he did; and second, it allows us to begin plotting the continuities and discontinuities between Jesus and those in the Jesus movement who wrote the NT. As such, I'm inclined towards the approach of Joachim Jeremias, who made the

---

43 Cf. Hengel and Schwemer (2019 [2007]: 185): Jesus' activities and suffering are not the presupposition 'but are the root and foundation – we could also say, *the historical and theological origin* of early Christianity' (emphasis original).
44 Käsemann 1964b; cf. Bird 2014b: 23–26.
45 Cf. Meyer 1979: 252; Witherington 1990: 1–2; Wright 1992: 418–427; Bockmuehl 1994: 8, 167; Barnett 1997: 34–35; Hahn 2002: 1:30–32, 40–43; Dunn 2006: 26–27; Watson 2008: 108–109; Schnelle 2009 [2007]: 43–44.
46 I would also add, following Witherington (1990: 2), that while Christian faith requires a historical Jesus, it is not dependent on our abilities or findings on a historical Jesus.

first volume of his incomplete NT theology about the proclamation of Jesus, and similarly Joachim Gnilka, whose volume on Jesus is a handy precursor to his NT theology.[47] What is required, then, is not a historical Jesus study to function as a kind of Fifth Gospel either beside or above the canonical Gospels. Also, what is needed is more than a Gospel harmony, a synthesis of the canonical testimony that is neither historically sensitive nor respectful of the distinct theological activity of each of the evangelists.

Study of the historical Jesus is necessary because the NT is – in the end – really about Jesus: his life, death, resurrection, message and influence, and the emergence of an ancient religious movement. Schnelle is correct: 'Jesus of Nazareth is a historical figure, and the New Testament is testimony to his historical impact.'[48] Consequently, studying the NT requires saying something historically about the figure of Jesus, for without a historical Jesus there would be no NT, and the NT would not be worth studying without a historical Jesus. So, concerning the task of researching the historical Jesus, it is difficult, debated, but ultimately indispensable for religious scholarship and the life of Christian faith.[49]

---

47 Jeremias 1971; Gnilka 1997 [1993].
48 Schnelle 2009 [2007]: 27.
49 On the theological–dogmatic necessity of a study of the historical Jesus, see Jeremias 1971: 1–17; Dahl 1974: 74–89; Morgan 1987; Meier 1991–2016: 2:198–200; Bird 2004; 2006c: 309–310; Watson 2008; Wright 1999: 14; Wright and Bird 2019: 173–176. Stuhlmacher (2018 [1999]: 53, 60–61) is aware that the historical Jesus can be 'an artificial scholarly construct' and accepts Martin Kähler's preference for the Christ of faith, but Stuhlmacher still insists that historical Jesus study is dogmatically necessary because: (1) God reveals himself savingly in history and climactically in Jesus; (2) irrespective of whether you are pursuing the historical Jesus or the biblical Jesus, both require doing business with the biblical tradition at a historical level; and (3) answering why Jesus was crucified and why he was later proclaimed as Lord means we cannot evade historical investigation. See too Gnilka (1997 [1993]: 12), who notes: 'The aim of the historical work is to investigate the relationship between Jesus and the NT witness of faith, between his proclamation and that of the post-Easter community, as presented in the NT and especially in the Gospels.' Allison (2009: 7) is right too: 'God became incarnate not in a text, but in a human life, from which it follows that Christians are obligated to inquire beyond and behind the canonical texts, impelled to learn all that they can about a first-century Galilean Jew.' Finally, note the concluding remarks of Jens Schröter (2020: 296): 'From a hermeneutical and epistemological perspective, the historical Jesus and the Christ of faith should not, therefore, be played off against one another, nor should they be regarded as two separate, unrelated views of Jesus. Instead, the quest for the historical Jesus should be regarded as a hermeneutical enterprise of substantial importance for Christian theology and faith. Research into the historical figure of Jesus does not lead us to a unified, unambiguous portrait of the man. It does, however, offer historical-critical depictions of Jesus that can serve as a historical orientation of Christianity in its various cultural circumstances.'

The dividends of studying the historical Jesus

There are several benefits that accrue from prefacing an NT theology with an extended investigation of the historical Jesus in relation to early Christianity.

First, the historical Jesus contributes to the church's theological formation. Jesus is the church's primal theologian. One should not regard Jesus as a messiah and martyr who inspired subsequent theological formulations about God, the kingdom and his own person, as if to say that while Jesus was a rabbi and a prophet, it is Paul, Luke and John who are the real theological giants of the New Testament. I, for one, remain absolutely perplexed as to why the theological and interpretative insights in the Gospels are always attributed to the evangelists and their communities while Jesus is relegated to being the mere muse who inspired their theological artistry and hermeneutical imaginations. Why is Mark rather than Jesus the one who married together Daniel's 'one like a son of man' and Isaiah's 'servant of the Lord'? Why should we think that it was Luke's insight rather than Jesus' to use Psalm 110 to describe his own status and authority? Why should we think it was John's creative expression to regard Jesus as a new temple when Jesus clearly opposed the temple and staked himself as the builder of a new one? The failure to attribute theological acumen to the historical Jesus is all the more astounding when we consider that he was clearly a prophetic figure with a scripturally shaped mind, who thought and acted creatively within the Jewish tradition. It was Jesus who excited hopes about Israel's restoration, who elicited faith in himself as a divine agent, who taught with memorable idioms and images. It was Jesus who provocatively antagonized both the Pharisees and the priestly leadership, whose magnetism, mighty works and message drew together crowds, and who launched a movement that survived well beyond his death and migrated beyond Judea. Surely such an individual could furnish creative, surprising and unforgettable teachings about God, the kingdom, Israel and himself that in turn inspired the storytelling, epistle-writing and apocalypse-authoring of the early church. Jesus was the first theologian of the Jesus movement (duh!), and his is the creative mind behind so much of the church's generative tradition (ta-dah!).[50] That is not to make Jesus into a 'religious genius' in the Romantic sense, venerated by so many eighteenth-century scholars. Instead, it is simply to state that the theology of the NT should find (?) its impetus not exclusively but initially on the lips of Jesus of Nazareth, whose creative mind inspired those who followed after him. Thus, NT theology will be enhanced by looking first to Jesus, the prophet of Israel's renewal.

Second, the study of the historical Jesus contributes to the exploration of Christology. One of the ultimate questions in NT theology is Christology, namely, who is Jesus? The individual witnesses, from Matthew to Revelation, each contribute something to that question. However, surely we must also interrogate our sources to ask and answer: who did Jesus think he was? What was the Christology of Jesus? Any summary of the NT's testimony about Jesus must, at some point and in some way, take into account Jesus' own declarations about himself as far as we are able to reconstruct them. A summative statement about the person, work and identity of Jesus must leave room to accommodate Jesus' own testimony concerning himself.

Now, from a confessional point of view, let me add an important caveat. I do not think that Jesus needed to do and claim everything ascribed to him in the Gospels in order for the Gospels to be historical or for Christological confessions to be valid. It is not an all-or-nothing game. Even if Jesus never said, 'Amen, I say to you, before Abraham was born, I am' (John 8:58, MFB trans.), he said and did things that made people think that he was to be identified with God in an astounding and unprecedented way that made them attribute sayings like that to him. Again, Jesus might not have strictly said, 'I was sent only to the lost sheep of the house of Israel' (Matt. 15:24), but that is still the impression he created among his disciples and it's a good summation of his mission

---

[50] Schweitzer (1945 [1906]: 348) put it well: 'For, after all, why should not Jesus think in terms of doctrine, and make history in action, just as well as a poor Evangelist can do on paper, under the pressure of the theological interest of the primitive community.' Wesley inspired the Wesleyans; the Wesleyans did not invent Wesley in their own image out of thin air! Cf. too Wright 1996: 478–479 and very much the main point of Allison 2009. Keith (2024: 110) agrees: 'Labeling interpretive categories as "theological" does not change the fact of the categories' historical emergence, production, and acceptance. And somewhere at the beginning of that reception history is the person of Jesus, inaccessible but responsible at least in part for a reception history that is accessible.'

to restore Israel. Similarly, I don't need Jesus to have claimed himself to be the 'leader' (*archēgos*) of a renewed Israel in order to justify the church's ascription of the title to him.[51] Who Jesus *is* and *will be* is not constrained by who the historical Jesus claimed to be or is reconstructed to be.[52] While the church's Jesus will always be more than the historical Jesus, my point is that the church's Jesus must in some sense not be less than an historical Jesus.[53] Thus, the historical Jesus will be a contributing part of NT theology's explanation and exposition of who Jesus was, is and will be. The workflow that one might adopt is comprised of the excavated Jesus (the appraisal and analysis of sources), the reconstructed Jesus (placing the data in interpretative paradigms for the explanation of Christian origins) and then the theologized Jesus (a contemporary statement of the key findings and their significance for wider global communities interested in faith and history).[54]

Third, study of the historical Jesus is a reminder that the 'Word became flesh'. Jesus inspired several Christologies, but he is not the sum of those Christologies. 'Jesus' is not a religious philosophy, a system of religious beliefs or a scheme of ethical ideals. Jesus is a human person, flesh like our flesh, who knows the full suite of human emotions and experiences, who participates in everything that is true of other human beings.[55] It is in Jesus that God is enfleshed, and it is his glorified flesh that is assumed

---

51 Acts 3:15; 5:31; Heb. 2:10; 12:2.

52 This was Bultmann's point: it is the Christ of the kerygma, not the historical Jesus, that matters for faith. I think Bultmann took this distinction in unhelpful directions, so that history was mostly irrelevant when it came to Jesus apart from the fact of his crucifixion. Nonetheless, Bultmann was correct that historical judgments about Jesus are not the same as, equal to, or required to square with theological convictions about Jesus. Better is Dunn (1989: 254), who comments: 'Christianity's claims regarding Jesus have never depended solely on Jesus' own testimony regarding himself, let alone on its accessibility or otherwise. On the other hand, a complete discontinuity between Jesus' own self-assertions and the subsequent claims about him would constitute a fatal flaw at the foundation of the whole superstructure of subsequent christology, not least the doctrine of the incarnation.'

53 Similar is Watson (2008: 106, 114): 'The Jesus of faith comprehends the historical Jesus but is not to be reduced to him . . . The concrete traits of the historical Jesus belong *within* an account of the "historic, biblical Christ" and should not be allowed to take on an independent life of their own. The distinction is inevitable, but it exists only in order to be transcended. The Gospels assume that we are to speak not of Jesus alone but of Jesus in relation to God and of God in relation to Jesus; and there is no good reason not to take that assumption seriously' (emphasis original).

54 Cf. Boring 1998: 243.

55 Heb. 2:17.

into heaven and exalted at God's right hand.⁵⁶ In which case, study of the historical Jesus makes it very hard to be a docetist and makes it easier to affirm the Chalcedonian formula that Jesus was consubstantial with our humanity. In addition, given that the narrative unity between the earthly life of the man Jesus and his status as exalted Lord is one of the primary fixtures in NT Christology,⁵⁷ study of the historical Jesus anchors one half of that unity, ensuring that Jesus is never articulated as 'Saviour' or 'Revealer' apart from the story of his earthly existence. It also gives us a criterion to evaluate the living voice of Jesus in subsequent experiences and in prophetic speech. For, however Jesus speaks to the churches, between Easter and the eschaton, those words must be adjudicated as to how they relate to the earthly message of Jesus as the church remembered him. For instance, we can evaluate the words of the 'living Jesus' in Revelation 2 – 3 and in the *Gospel of Thomas* against the Jesus tradition and its reception. Thus, the historical Jesus enables us to affirm a key creedal conviction that Jesus' humanity, his Jewish humanity, was real and necessary for his redemptive mission.⁵⁸ Plus, Jesus' teaching retains

---

56 John 1:14; Acts 1:9–11.

57 See Käsemann 1964b; Hurtado 1988: 116; Bockmuehl 1994: 167; Stuhlmacher 1995: 83; Barnett 1997: 56; Matera 1999: 27; Dunn 2006: 369; Hays 2008: 182.

58 Thoma (1980: 107) puts it like this: 'Christians have torn Jesus from the soil of Israel. They have de-Judaized, uprooted, alienated, Hellenized, and Europeanized him. The consequences of these manipulations and whitewashings are hopeless confusion about the person of Jesus, the nature and tasks of Christianity, and the meaning of Judaism in religious history.' Adele Reinhartz (2024: 53) opines how 'from the late first century until the mid-twentieth century, most Christian exegetes, theologians, historians, and storytellers have attempted to dissociate Jesus from Jewishness'. Cf. Bockmuehl 1994: 119–124; Wright 1996: 83–124 (esp. 91–98); Tomson 2001: 40; Dunn 2003: 85–92; Keener 2009: 178; Casey 2010: 59; Meier 1991–2016: 4:7, on the necessity of situating Jesus in Judaism if only to avoid horrible anachronisms and turning Jesus into a mirror of oneself. Hengel and Schwemer (2019 [2007]: 200) correctly note that Jesus did not 'relate' to Judaism, 'but lived and acted exclusively within it'. Wright (1996: 98) comments that 'Jesus cannot be separated from his Jewish context, but neither can he be collapsed into it so that he is left without a sharp critique of his contemporaries'. The point stands, but the danger is of course that the 'sharp critique of his contemporaries' morphs into the Christian critique of Judaism as essentially ritualistic, nationalistic or legalistic. The result can be, as Crossley (2015: 18) warns, the idea that Jesus was 'Jewish . . . but not Jewish'. Indeed, the scholarly language describing Jesus as a 'radical' or 'subversive' is often meant to imply that he was proposing a radical departure from Judaism or undermining Judaism for not being what would soon become Christianity (see Myles 2016). Thus, Vermes (1973; 2003) and Levine (2006b) make for good reading against Christian propensities to Christianize Jesus. To be avoided is Elliott's suggestion (2007) that Jesus is best viewed not as a Jew or even a Judean but as an ancient Israelite, as this gives far too much over to deconstruction debates about *Ioudaioi*; see in response Crossley 2013: 124–129.

a certain authenticating function to discern the living voice of Jesus in subsequent experiences and ecstatic utterances thereafter.

Evidently, then, we need more than a Gospel harmony (making a historical Jesus by putting the Gospels in a blender) and an alternative to scholarly reconstructions of the 'real' Jesus (a peculiar mix of sensationalism, anachronism and autobiography). Accordingly, in the sections that follow, I discuss several aspects of the historical Jesus, not covering everything there is to be explored, but focusing on those aspects of Jesus' life that are generally agreed upon by historians, putting them into a coherent historical framework, and striving to succinctly describe the historical figure who would be the catalyst for the emergence of the church and would influence world history far more than any figure has since.

My aim is not to weigh up the authenticity of the many words attributed to Jesus; rather, the task is more like trying to trace the whisper of a voice heard amid the cacophony of a busy café. A whisper that dared to declare that God was king and that his kingly power had been launched afresh upon a land ravaged by war and weighed down by the yoke of slavery. Did I hear rightly? Who said it? What did he mean? To whom was it spoken? And what was the response? We can no longer see the person who said it, but the echoes of that whisper have reverberated down the corridors of history. The words, once whispered, throbbed with news of victory, declaring the conquest of villains, and hopes for things to be on earth as they are in heaven. We search for that whisper now beneath the stones of Galilee, under the sands of the Judean desert, within the pages of torn papyri, and in the memory of many who went to martyrdom because they had the courage and conviction to turn the whisper into a story that everyone would live by.

2
Jesus of Nazareth and his early life

Jesus' birth and early years

The early life of Jesus is shrouded in partial silence and overall mystery. It was a period that was ripe for legendary elaboration by later interpreters. Some would say that the legendary embellishment began with the Matthean and Lukan infancy narratives, but in any case it had certainly crystallized by the time one gets to the various *Infancy Gospels*. I am going to avoid discussion of the virgin birth or virgin conception, because, irrespective of its historicity or lack thereof, it is undoubtedly intended as a clarification of Jesus' divine sonship and not the basis for his prophetic ministry. Jesus was obviously born; the 'how' need not concern us for now, especially if we are keen to avoid getting involved in lengthy discussions about Augustan fiscal reforms, Christianity and pagan mythology, and Matthean midrash, and making brisket from the sacred cow that Mary and Joseph were turned away from the Bethlehem Holiday Inn. There are bigger fish to fry as we explore Jesus' geographical and cultural background, the family he was born into and his relationship to John the Baptist.[1]

Jesus was probably born around 7–4 BC,[2] on the eve of the death of

---

1 On the virgin birth or conception in relation to Christian doctrine, see Bird 2020: 416–429. What we can say is that there was a tradition and/or allegation that Jesus may have been illegitimate, i.e. a *mamzer* or 'bastard' (see John 8:41; *Gos. Thom.* 105; Tertullian, *Spect.* 30.6; *Protoevangelium of James* 13–16; *Acts of Pilate* 2.3; Origen, *C. Cels.* 1.28, 32). Such an allegation does not prove a virgin conception (there are other explanations for why this smear arose), but the virgin conception is at least consistent with it. It seems probable that Jesus' paternity was enigmatic from the start (Bockmuehl 1994: 33). The best historical and theological reflections on Jesus' birth are Brown 1993; Crisp 2009; Lincoln 2013.

2 Jesus began his ministry during the governorship of Pontius Pilate (c. AD 26–36) and during the fifteenth year of Tiberius's reign (c. AD 14–37), which brings us to c. AD 26–28, depending on calculations, and we are told that Jesus was 'thirty years old' when he began his work (Luke 3:1–2, 23; *Gos. Eb.* 5).

Herod the Great, and he grew up in the Galilean village of Nazareth,[3] his mother Mary's ancestral home.[4] Jesus came to be specifically known as 'the prophet Jesus from Nazareth in Galilee' (Matt. 21:11) and as 'Jesus son of Joseph from Nazareth' (John 1:45); in short, as 'Jesus of Nazareth'.[5] The association of Jesus and Nazareth was strong enough that the early church could be called 'the sect of the Nazarenes' (Acts 24:5).

Galilee was among the most fertile regions of Syro-Palestine and supported an agrarian society.[6] The Jewish population of Galilee (i.e. those committed to the Judean way of life and oriented towards the Jerusalem temple) increased during the Maccabean period, with many Jews settling in the region as Seleucid power and influence diminished. It was called 'Galilee of the Gentiles', not because it was filled with Gentiles, but because it was surrounded by Gentile populations with Syria to the north, the province of Gaulanitis to the east, the Decapolis to the southeast, Samaria to the direct south, and the cities of Tyre and Sidon to the west. Prior to AD 70, the degree of Hellenization was modest, though it increased with the founding of the cities of Sepphoris and then later Tiberias. There is no evidence that the urbanization of Sepphoris and Tiberias pauperized the surrounding countryside.[7] That said, it is likely that Herodian family members and retainers, as well as Jerusalem's elite echelons including those belonging to the high priest and his extended family, had substantial land holdings in Galilee, leading to inequalities between absentee landlords and resident peasant farmers.

At the time of Jesus, ancient Nazareth was located on a ridge overlooking the Jezreel Valley, not far from a highway linking Tiberias to Ptolemais. It had a population of a few hundred people, covered some 5 hectares (12 acres) and was singularly insignificant.[8] Excavations reveal the existence of private dwellings constructed from fieldstones and mud, often built into caves, accompanied by small-scale agriculture with vineyards, olives, presses and grain silos, plus local industry based on stone

---

3 Matt. 2:23; Luke 2:39; 4:16.
4 Luke 1:26.
5 Mark 10:47; Luke 24:19; John 18:5, 7; Acts 2:22; 6:14.
6 Cf. Josephus, *War* 3.42–43, 517–519.
7 Jensen 2010 [2006]: 162–186.
8 Cf. John 1:46.

masonry and presumably livestock-farming and tanning. Depending on harvests, taxation and turmoil, economic existence was agrarian, staple, subsistence. For a Galilean peasant, the staples were bread, olives, olive oil, wine, beans, lentils, seasonal vegetables, nuts, fruits, cheese and meats – the latter only on festive occasions.[9] The village had *miqvaot* (ritual baths), stone vessels common to Jewish homes, typical Jewish burial chambers and a synagogue,[10] and generally reflects the 'distinctively Jewish character of the domestic space of Jesus' Galilee'.[11]

Quite important is the proximity of Nazareth to the city of Sepphoris, which was 4 miles (6.5 km) north-west of Nazareth. Prior to AD 70, Sepphoris had a population of about 10,000, and the city exhibited a degree of Greek and Roman influences evident in its orthogonal grids, mosaics and architecture, even while the city was quintessentially Jewish in other ways; for example, no evidence has been found for pork consumption or the use of coins with imperial and pagan images, while the presence of stone vessels and ritual baths indicates adherence to Jewish purity scruples.[12] Sepphoris came to prominence under the Romans, who in 63 BC organized the city as the provincial capital of one of five Jewish districts.[13] Herod the Great took control of the city from Antigonus, and subsequently built a palace there and installed an armoury. Upon the death of Herod the Great in 4 BC, Judas the Galilean (son of the brigand chief Hezekiah, whom Herod had earlier executed) launched a popular uprising against the Herodian regime by capturing Sepphoris, seizing the weapons from the armoury, and leading a revolt against Roman taxation, a practice viewed as a violation of God's rule over Israel.[14] Varus, the Roman legate of Syria, arrived with his legions and auxiliaries and crushed the insurrection, destroying Sepphoris and selling the

---

9 Crossan and Reed 2001: 54.
10 Crossan and Reed 2001: 65–70; Evans 2012: 13–15.
11 Reed 2006: 41.
12 Reed 2006: 49–50; Evans 2012: 24–30. The degree of Hellenization and Romanization of Galilee in general and Sepphoris in particular at the time of Jesus is debated. Many overstate the case and envisage Jesus going to the Sepphoris theatre (whether it existed pre-AD 70 is disputed) to watch the Greek plays of Sophocles and hearing Cynic philosophers rant on the street corners. It was not the 'semi-pagan, despised Galilee' of Bornkamm 1960 [1956]: 53. See esp. Chancey (2005), who says (225): 'All Judaism was Hellenistic Judaism, but not all Judaism was affected by Hellenism in the same ways or to the same extent.'
13 Josephus, *Ant.* 14.91; *War* 1.170.
14 Josephus, *Ant.* 17.271–272; 18.23; *War* 2.56, 118.

inhabitants into slavery.¹⁵ The city now passed into the possession of the tetrarch Herod Antipas, who promptly began rebuilding and refortifying the city, renaming it 'Autonomous' (*Autocratēs*) and making it the capital of Galilee; Josephus called it the 'ornament of all Galilee'.¹⁶ Antipas then built Tiberias and moved his administrative apparatus there in AD 20. The inhabitants of Sepphoris, despite the sallies of Josephus, did not want to join the Judean revolt against Rome in AD 66–70 and mostly escaped the 'fire and blood' that filled all of Galilee.¹⁷

Jesus thus grew up amid the rebellion, desolation and rebuilding of Sepphoris, where physical signs and traumatic memories of Roman imperial violence were palpable. A Roman army had swept through the region and brought with it carnage, destruction, death, rape, plundering and enslavement.¹⁸ In his adolescence, Jesus took up Joseph's trade as a *tektōn*, a stonemason or woodworker,¹⁹ and while we cannot say for certain, it is possible that the sons of Joseph found occasional or even regular employment as builders in Sepphoris, and they probably traded in the city or at least with its people. Interesting too is the theory that the urban language that one detects in the Gospels – much talk about courts, prisons, agoras, wide and narrow streets, gates, a city on a hill, rich men and day labourers – owes something to Jesus' experience of Sepphoris. However, the Gospels never once mention the place, and Jesus seems to have deliberately avoided the large Galilean urban centres of Sepphoris and Tiberias, perhaps to evade Herod Antipas's security forces or because of rural antipathy towards the local urban inhabitants.²⁰ Such avoidance of Galilean cities is 'curious' because Jesus entered the Judean cities of Jericho and Jerusalem.²¹

If Jesus did spend time in Sepphoris²² then he would have been exposed to non-Jews, including Syrians, Arabs, Phoenicians, Romans

---

15 Josephus, *Ant.* 17.288–289; *War* 2.68–69.
16 Josephus, *Ant.* 18.27.
17 Josephus, *War* 3.30–34, 59–61; *Life* 30, 124.
18 Cf. Josephus, *Ant.* 17.285–291; *War* 2.68–71.
19 Mark 6:3/Matt. 13:55.
20 Josephus (*Life* 374–384) reports that the rural Galileans detested the cities of Tiberias and Sepphoris and plundered and burned them at the first opportunity.
21 Evans 2012: 30.
22 Schnelle (2009 [2007]: 138 n. 235) comments: 'A personal note: anyone who has once walked the 3.5 miles from Nazareth to Sepphoris can hardly imagine, with the best will in the world, that Jesus was never there.'

and Greeks, among the city's merchants, slaves, soldiers and administrators. The village of Nazareth cannot be reduced to the outer suburbs of Sepphoris. Yet the urban populace of the city shaped the economic and social climate of the region. Although Sepphoris and Galilee were not cosmopolitan by any stretch of the imagination, they were not isolated from non-Jewish people and cultures. Jesus may even have known some Greek, a possibility enhanced by the fact that he had two disciples with Greek names in Philip and Andrew.

Jesus was raised in an extended family with his mother Mary and his putative father Joseph. Jesus had brothers (James, Joseph, Simon and Jude) and sisters (unnamed),[23] and patristic debates revolved around whether these siblings were born through Joseph's procreation with Mary, were stepbrothers/sisters from a previous marriage on the part of Joseph, or were a mixture of both. Jesus' family was widely associated, via Joseph, with Davidic ancestry.[24] Davidic motifs appear in Jesus' ministry,[25] and the early church amplified the connection of Jesus with Davidic lineage as part of seeing him as the Davidic deliverer.[26]

We know practically nothing of Jesus' upbringing and childhood. The *Infancy Gospels* are late, legendary and often tendentious in their details. The infancy narratives of Matthew and Luke depict Jesus as born into a pious Jewish family, Torah-observant, hoping for Israel's deliverance and making regular pilgrimages to the Jerusalem temple. This accords with what we know about Galilee in general: the populace was committed to the Jewish way of life laid out in the Torah, conscious of purity scruples (hence the presence of stone vessels and *miqvaot* – ritual baths),[27] following a *halakhah*[28] that with some variation approximates to that of the Pharisees, and devoted to the Jerusalem cultus, with some priests living in Galilee as local Torah-interpreters.[29] Jesus grew up speaking Aramaic, probably acquiring some proficiency

---

23 Mark 3:31–35; 6:3; John 7:3–5.
24 Matt. 1:6, 20; Luke 1:27, 69; 2:4.
25 Mark 10:47–48; 11:20; 12:35–37.
26 Rom. 1:3–4; 2 Tim. 2:8; Rev. 3:7; 5:5; 22:16; Ignatius, *Eph.* 18.2; 20.2; *Trall.* 9.1; *Rom.* 7.3; *Smyrn.* 1.1; *Did.* 9.2; 10.6; Eusebius, *Hist. Eccl.* 3.20.
27 On purity and immersion in Jewish practice, see Sanders 1992: 224–229.
28 One's 'walk', or one's precise way of interpreting and living out the Torah.
29 See Mark 1:44; Luke 2:41–43; 13:1; John 7:8–10; Josephus, *Ant.* 20.43–44; *Life* 198.

Jesus of Nazareth and his early life

in Hebrew and perhaps, as mentioned above, some facility in Greek. The impression one gets from Jesus' sermon in Nazareth[30] is that Jesus was literate, which accords with Josephus's remark about the high importance that Jews placed on educating children.[31] Meier is right to say:

> If we take into account that Jesus' adult life became fiercely focused on the Jewish religion, that he is presented by almost all the Gospel traditions as engaging in learned disputes over Scripture and halaka[h] with students of the Law, that he was accorded the respectful – but at that time vague – title of rabbi or teacher, that more than one Gospel tradition presents him preaching or teaching in the synagogues (presumably after and on the Scripture readings), and that, even apart from formal disputes, his teaching was strongly imbued with the outlook and language of the sacred texts of Israel, it is reasonable to suppose that Jesus' religious formation in his family was intense and profound, and included instruction in reading biblical Hebrew.[32]

Jesus, then, probably learned a trade from his father and was taught how to read Torah by his father, relatives or a local priest.

It is likely that Joseph died before Jesus began his itinerant prophetic work, whereas Mary was alive during Jesus' prophetic years and can be later found among the members of the Jerusalem church.[33] Jesus' family, including his brothers, exhibited sardonic contempt for his ministry[34] and even attempted to intervene to stop him at one point.[35] However, the Easter experience transformed his brothers, enabling them to become leaders in the burgeoning church.[36] They were revered as *desposynoi* ('belonging to the master') according to Sextus Julius

---

30 Luke 4:16–21.
31 Josephus, *Apion* 1.60; 2.204. Ancient literacy rates were probably higher than is normally recognized; see Wright 2017.
32 Meier 1991–2016: 1:276. Cf. too Foster 2006.
33 Mark 2:21; John 2:1–12; 19:25; Acts 1:4.
34 John 7:3–10.
35 Mark 3:21, 31–35.
36 Acts 12:13; 15:13–21; 21:18; Gal. 1:9; Jas 1:1; Jude 1.

Africanus,[37] and Jude's grandsons were allegedly summoned to appear before Emperor Domitian.[38] It would be hard to deny that James became the leading elder of the Jerusalem church not only due to the flight and mission of the disciples but also on account of his blood connection to Jesus.

In sum, Jesus was born into an agrarian–artisan peasant family in rural Galilee who had seen first-hand the brutality of Roman military power and were religiously devoted as they etched out a subsistence living.

Baptism by John

John the Baptist is a subject worthy of historical investigation in his own right and, in relation to him, we are confronted with numerous questions and problems that we cannot go into now. By way of summary,[39] from our sources we can infer that John was probably born into a priestly family settled in Galilee.[40] Around AD 27/28, he appeared in the Judean wilderness at the River Jordan as an ascetic holy man dressed like Elijah,[41] preaching a message of God's judgment largely drawn from Malachi 3 and preparation for deliverance largely rehearsing Isaiah 40.[42] The location by the Jordan was quite intentional,[43] as the Baptizer was inviting people to become part of a purified Israel, and to symbolically re-enter the land along the lines of a new exodus (Exod. 7 – 19) or a new conquest (Josh. 3 – 4). This makes even more sense if the Baptizer saw himself, as per Ezekiel's prophecy, as among the first of those to come out of exile, to be cleansed, and to be on the cusp of covenant renewal through the pouring out of the Holy Spirit:

> I will take you from the nations and gather you from all the countries and bring you into your own land. I will sprinkle clean

---

37 Eusebius, *Hist. Eccl.* 1.7.11–14.
38 Eusebius, *Hist. Eccl.* 3.20.1–7.
39 See my summary in Bird 2011 and extended studies by Webb (1991); Taylor (1997); Murphy (2003); Dapaah (2005); McGrath (2024).
40 Luke 1:5.
41 2 Kgs 1:8.
42 Matt. 3:1–12/Luke 3:1–18; John 1:23–27; Josephus, *Ant.* 18.117.
43 Cf. John 1:28; 3:3.

water upon you, and you shall be clean from all your uncleannesses, and from all your idols I will cleanse you. A new heart I will give you, and a new spirit I will put within you, and I will remove from your body the heart of stone and give you a heart of flesh. I will put my spirit within you and make you follow my statutes and be careful to observe my ordinances.
(Ezek. 36:24–27)

This is precisely what the Qumranites, living in settlements beside the Dead Sea, believed would be fulfilled in the last days when, on the one hand, God's visitation would bring an end to falsehood and wickedness, but on the other hand the Spirit was to be poured out as purifying waters to cleanse people of sin. At that time, Israel would witness the wisdom of the Most High abounding and Israel would experience the establishment of an everlasting covenant.[44] John, then, was a prophet of both judgment and restoration.[45]

The description 'the Baptist' or 'the Baptizer' (*bapistēs*) was appended to John's name because of his distinctive practice of offering water baptism to devotees of his teaching. For those who underwent this baptism, it functioned as a sign of turning away from past sins and as a symbol of cleansing and release from moral impurity through the Spirit, and it conveyed a commitment to live in an upright manner thereafter. The practice was related to John's message of repentance and judgment, as it was a necessary rite of preparation ahead of the 'Day of the Lord'. The baptism of water symbolized and anticipated what the baptism of the Spirit would bring about: a purification of the people.[46] For the Baptizer, a person's ethnicity and election was no safeguard from divine judgment; only an interior transformation would suffice, an inner renewal ahead of covenant renewal. John, then, was a preacher of righteousness and repentance announced in the light of the imminent coming of Yahweh's eschatological wrath upon the wicked (rendering

---

44 1QS 4.18-23. Cf. Joel 3:1-5 and *Jub.* 1.23.
45 Horsley (2012: 25) argues that the Baptist does not evidence 'an apocalyptic judgment of a vengeful God, but prophetic declarations of God's coming in judgment and deliverance as sanctions on the covenant renewal of the people of Israel'.
46 Meier 1991-2016: 2:35-40, 81-84.

moot any debates as to whether the Baptist was about eschatology or ethics). John was not a preacher of apocalyptic vengeance and cosmic meltdown; more properly, he was one declaring a prophetic lawsuit against a nation, against its elites and its expendables, for failing to exercise the righteousness required for national redemption and renewal.[47] John was also a self-conscious forerunner of a future eschatological agent, the 'coming one', a quasi-messianic figure who would bring his own baptism of spirit and fire, resulting in either purification or perdition.

Jesus' baptism by John is historically solid and is simply assumed in later Christian sources.[48] What is more, given that the baptism could imply the subordination of Jesus to John, the event was *potentially* embarrassing to the evangelists, which is why the tendency of the tradition was to emphasize the Baptizer's unworthiness to baptize Jesus,[49] or in the case of the Gospel of John to omit the baptismal episode altogether. Jesus' baptism appears to have occasioned a visionary experience whereby he saw the heavens torn open, sensed God's Spirit descend upon him, and heard a heavenly voice that commissioned him for Isaianic mission and messianic office.[50] We cannot say whether this initiated self-knowledge in Jesus or reaffirmed something he already knew of himself, but the experience was so powerful and palpable that he immediately removed himself to the wilderness, there to be tested by the elements and by the Satan.[51] This was an ordeal from which Jesus believed he had emerged victorious, and in his triumph he saw Satan fall.[52]

We can infer a few things from this. First, whatever relationship Jesus had with John (was John a mentor or a relative?), after his baptism Jesus seems to have hived off and begun his own prophetic work and gathered his own disciples. It is likely that Jesus initially operated in a way similar

---

47 Horsley 2012: 25.
48 Mark 1:9–12; cf. *Gos. Eb.* 4–5; *Gos. Heb.* 6.
49 Matt. 3:14–15.
50 Echoing Isa. 42:1 and Ps. 2:7.
51 Luke 1:12–13; Matt. 4:1–11; Luke 4:1–13.
52 Luke 10:18.

to John by administering baptism.[53] He drew followers from the Baptist's circle,[54] and the continuity was such that many thought Jesus was John *redivivus* or was deliberately imitating John's Elijah-esque prophetic work.[55] In any case, the sources are clear: Jesus' work began after his baptism.[56]

Second, Jesus was committed to John's programme of covenant renewal and warning of divine judgment, but with a different method and different message. Whereas John was location-bound, Jesus would be itinerant; whereas John preached preparation, Jesus would preach a proleptic fulfilment of God's coming kingship; whereas John saw the template of Israel's rescue in Malachi, Jesus saw the template in Isaiah; whereas John's vision of the restoration of all things meant creating a remnant,[57] Jesus saw restoration as signified by the Isaianic signs of deliverance.[58]

Third, John's message lacked the egocentrism of Jesus. Jesus appears as one uniquely commissioned for a special task: to hasten Israel's restoration and to inaugurate a new exodus, which would play out not only in Israel but also in the realm of demonic powers. God's kingship was to be announced, for sure, but it was more than that; it was to be embodied and enacted, with Jesus as its central actor. God's kingship was mysteriously connected to the identity and work of Jesus of Nazareth. Soon the Galilean hamlets and hinterland were filled with rumours and mutterings: people said a prophet had arisen among them who was declaring that God's kingship was on the cusp of arriving.

---

53 John 4:1–3.
54 John 1:37–40.
55 Mark 6:14; 8:28. On continuity between John and Jesus, see Meier 1991–2016: 2:7; Allison 2010a: 204–219. McKnight's verdict remains correct (1999: 4): 'Jesus' vision, message, and tactics were shaped by John.' More recently, McGrath 2024: 105–151.
56 Acts 1:22; 10:37; 13:24–25; 19:4–5; Ignatius, *Eph.* 18.2; *Smyrn.* 1.1; Justin, *Dial.* 50.1.
57 Mark 9:12.
58 Luke 7:22–23/Matt. 11:4–5.

3
Jesus and the kingdom of God

Jesus as kingdom-proclaimer

There is no doubt that Jesus' central message pertained to the kingdom of God. Indeed, '[n]owhere in the literature of ancient Judaism does the kingdom of God stand in such a central place as in the message of Jesus'.[1] Thus, it is here that we must spend considerable time unpacking the meaning of the kingdom of God and its relationship to Israel's restoration in Jesus' teaching.

The history of Gospel interpretation and Christian theology has placed the kingdom of God on numerous horizons. The kingdom has been conceived as something ethical, ecclesial, spiritual, economic or apocalyptic-cataclysmic. Checking through the files of my mental lexicon, I can recall scholars and theologians who have described the kingdom in assorted ways: God's sphere of sovereignty, divine government, the church as a spiritual kingdom, God in strength, God's reign over God's people in God's place, the love of God and the brotherhood of man, a military triumph over Rome, pure theocracy, a brokerless society of equals, economic liberation. All these proposals tend to have some anchor point either in Scripture or in certain interpretative traditions, but they all tend to be overly selective or somewhat reductionist in trying to restrict the meaning of God's kingdom to a single conceptual frame.

---

1 Camponovo 1984: 444 ['Nirgends in der frühjüdischen Literatur steht die Herrschaft Gottes jedoch so im Zentrum der Verkündigung wie bei Jesus']. Cf. Bultmann (1952–55: 1:4): 'The dominant concept of Jesus' message is the *Reign of God*' (emphasis original); Jeremias (1971: 96): 'Our starting point is the fact that the central theme in the public proclamation of Jesus was the kingly reign of God'; Perrin (2019: 25): 'When the Galilean began his ministry some two thousand years ago, he began by preaching the kingdom of God (Matt. 4:17). In his departing words to his disciples as the risen Lord, he is again talking about the kingdom (Acts 1:6–8). And in between these inaugural and climactic events, we have a plethora of parables, sayings, and enacted dramas all explicitly or implicitly relating to the kingdom. The kingdom of God was not simply at the heart of Jesus's agenda; it *was* his agenda' (emphasis original).

The kingdom of God is never just one thing; rather, the term refers to a cohort of semantic domains, several conceptual connotations and a cluster of interpretations.

Jesus probably proclaimed in Aramaic the gospel of the *malkutha di elaha* ('the kingdom of God'). The word *malkutha* ('kingdom/kingship') pertains to divine sovereignty, dominion, power and greatness[2] with possible connotations of victory if analogous to the Hebrew words *malukah* and *melek*.[3] Such language could obviously be related to God's reign in a spatial and territorial sense,[4] whether a heavenly realm or an earthly domain where God is king. However, understood more specifically, it can pertain to God's sphere of sovereignty over creation, the nations, his people, and history. For Bruce Chilton, this is all about *regnum Dei Deus est*, that is, God's kingdom is God himself; it is God's personal and dynamic presence, God's kingly power and saving activity, in the present and in the future.[5] Similarly, for Hans Kvalbein, we are dealing with a '*nomen actionis* denoting God's function as a king, his Reign or Rule'.[6] In any case, Jesus' proclamation of the kingdom is undoubtedly shot through with language and imagery drawn from the Hebrew Bible and its interpretation within Second Temple Jewish literature, so it is here, in the fields of Jewish hopes, that we must look.[7]

The kingdom of God in the Hebrew Bible and early Judaism

First, in the Hebrew Bible, Yahweh is uniquely king of Israel by virtue of his deliverance of the Hebrews from Egypt.[8] In the words of John Goldingay: 'A king [Pharaoh] confronts Israel, so Yhwh becomes a king in order to confront this king and play him at his own game, as king

---

2 Cf. esp. Dan. 7:27.
3 Exod. 15:16–20; Pss 20:9; 44:1–4; Obad. 21.
4 Rightly emphasized by Allison (2010a: 201).
5 Chilton 1978b; 1987; 1996.
6 Kvalbein 1998: 204.
7 See surveys in Camponovo 1984; Collins 1987; Hengel and Schwemer 1991; Meier 1991–2016: 2:237–288; Duling 1992; Allison 2010c; Green 2013. On keeping Jesus' kingdom 'Jewish' in scope and contents, see Levine 2006b: 51–52.
8 Exod. 15:17–18; Num. 23:21; 1 Sam. 8:7; 12:12; Pss 47:1–9; 98:1–9; 114:1–2; cf. Jos. *Ant.* 6.60; *Sib. Or.* 5.499.

delivering Israel from Egypt with powerful decisive acts.'[9] Similarly, Yahweh's kingship is then expressed with respect to his continuing and/or projected rescue of Israel,[10] and to his establishing of justice for Israel and in Israel and even against Israel.[11] Yahweh appears here as both warrior-king and merciful judge, so that Israel's exodus entailed his enthronement, just as Israel's restoration from exile will be proof that Yahweh (again!) reigns over the earth.[12] Yahweh's kingship is, then, bound up with a mixture of sovereignty and salvation.

Second, Yahweh's kingship was absorbed in various ways into Israel's social, political and religious life. In the Israelite monarchy it became possible in some instances to speak of a Davidic ruler appointed as king over the 'kingdom of Yahweh' (*malkut Yahweh*).[13] Yahweh's kingship and kingdom were thereafter closely related to the Davidic covenant and inspired hope for a coming Davidic deliverer who would usher in a restored Israelite kingdom of Yahweh.[14] While Israel adapted Near Eastern notions of 'divine kingship' for its earthly king,[15] Yahweh and the king were never identical since Yahweh appointed the king;[16] therefore, Yahweh was superior to and sovereign over any earthly monarch.[17] The Jerusalem cultus celebrated Yahweh's kingship in ways that venerated divine actions and attributions in association with Yahweh's eternal reign: 'Yours, O LORD, are the greatness, the power, the glory, the victory, and the majesty; for all that is in the heavens and on the earth is yours; yours is the kingdom, O LORD, and you are exalted as head above all' (1 Chr. 29:11). The exilic and post-exilic prophets are permeated with the promise that Yahweh will again manifest his kingly power to deliver Israel from exile and to establish a new kingdom. Consequently, Israel's cultural memory of Yahweh's deliverance and covenant generated the

---

9 Goldingay 2003: 331.
10 Pss 10:16; 24:8–10; 89:19; 145:11–13; Isa. 33:22; 43:1–8, 15; 44:6; Mic. 2:12–13; 4:9.
11 Ps. 99:1–9; Isa. 6:5; Ezek. 34:16–20; Mal. 1:14; Ezek. 20:33.
12 Cf. esp. Exod. 15:17–18; Isa. 52:7.
13 1 Chr. 28:5; 2 Chr. 13:8.
14 2 Sam. 7:12–16; 1 Chr. 17:14; Ps. 89:1–52; Isa. 9:1–7; 11:1–5; Jer. 23:5; 30:9; Ezek. 34:23–24; 37:24–26; Amos 9:11–12; Mic. 5:1–5; 1 Macc. 2:57.
15 Cf. e.g. Ps. 45:1–9.
16 Cf. e.g. Ps. 2:7.
17 Duling 1992: 4:50.

cultic acclamation *Yahweh malak* ('Yahweh has become king!') and the prophetic pronouncement *Yahweh yimlok* ('Yahweh will reign as king'). Such a view can be summed up in Balaam's second oracle:

> The LORD their God is with them,
>   acclaimed as a king among them.
> (Num. 23:21)

Yahweh's kingship was instantiated in king, cultus and covenant.

Third, Yahweh's kingship was never limited to Israel's territory or confined to its temple, but was eternal, universal, cosmological and eschatological. The dominion of Yahweh over Israel was extended to include the cosmos, which meant identifying Yahweh as king of creation and king over the nations[18] so that Yahweh appointed kings over other kingdoms.[19] In that case, Yahweh's reign over the world and the nations is tantamount to Yahweh's reign from Israel over the world.[20] Finally, Yahweh's kingship/kingdom also endures throughout the ages in an eternal reign.[21]

Importantly, prophetic literature depicts the future day of deliverance as the coming of Yahweh as king to rescue Israel:

> I myself will be the shepherd of my sheep, and I will make them lie down, says the Lord GOD. I will seek the lost, and I will bring back the strays, and I will bind up the injured, and I will strengthen the weak, but the fat and the strong I will destroy. I will feed them with justice . . . I will set up over them one shepherd, my servant David, and he shall feed them; he shall feed them and be their shepherd.
> (Ezek. 34:15–16, 23)

> How beautiful upon the mountains
>   are the feet of the messenger who announces peace,

---

18 2 Kgs 19:15; 1 Chr. 16:31; 29:11; Pss 22:28; 29:10; 47:1–9; 93:1–2; 95:1–7; 96:10; 97:1; 103:19; Jer. 10:10; cf. Add. Esth. 14:12; 1 Macc. 2:24; *Pss Sol.* 2.30; *Sib. Or.* 5.499; *1 Enoch* 84.2.
19 Dan. 2:37, 47; 4:17, 32; Jer. 46:18; Hag. 2:20–23; Wis. 6:1–5; cf. Pr. Azar. 33; Rom. 13:1–6; *1 Enoch* 63.2–4.
20 Goldingay 2003: 332.
21 Exod. 15:18; Pss 10:16; 29:10; 103:19; 145:13; Dan. 2:44; 6:26; 7:27; cf. Tob. 13:1–2, 6–11; Sir. 51:12; *Pss Sol.* 2.29–30; 17.1; *1 Enoch* 12.3; 25.1, 7; 27.3; 84.2.

who brings good news,
   who announces salvation,
   who says to Zion, 'Your God reigns' . . .
The L ORD has bared his holy arm
   before the eyes of all the nations;
and all the ends of the earth shall see
   the salvation of our God.
(Isa. 52:7, 10)

And the L ORD will become king over all the earth; on that day the L ORD will be one and his name one.
(Zech. 14:9)

On that day, says the L ORD,
   I will assemble the lame
and gather those who have been driven away
   and those whom I have afflicted.
The lame I will make the remnant,
   and those who were cast off, a strong nation,
and the L ORD will reign over them in Mount Zion
   now and for evermore.
(Mic. 4:6–7)

Those who have been saved shall go up to Mount Zion
   to rule Mount Esau;
   and the kingdom shall be the L ORD's.
(Obad. 21)

Sing aloud, O daughter Zion;
   shout, O Israel!
Rejoice and exult with all your heart,
   O daughter Jerusalem!
The L ORD has taken away the judgments against you;
   he has turned away your enemies.
The king of Israel, the L ORD, is in your midst;
   you shall fear disaster no more.

> On that day it shall be said to Jerusalem:
> 'Do not fear, O Zion;
>   do not let your hands grow weak.
> The LORD, your God, is in your midst,
>   a warrior who gives victory;
> he will rejoice over you with gladness,
>   he will renew you in his love;
> he will exult over you with loud singing
>   as on a day of festival.'
> I will remove disaster from you,
>   so that you will not bear reproach for it.
> I will deal with all your oppressors
>   at that time.
> And I will save the lame
>   and gather the outcast,
> and I will change their shame into praise
>   and renown in all the earth.
> At that time I will bring you home,
>   at the time when I gather you;
> for I will make you renowned and praised
>   among all the peoples of the earth,
> when I restore your fortunes
>   before your eyes, says the LORD.
> (Zeph. 3:14–20)

> And in the days of those kings the God of heaven will set up a kingdom that shall never be destroyed, nor shall this kingdom be left to another people. It shall crush all these kingdoms and bring them to an end, and it shall stand for ever.
> (Dan. 2:44; cf. 4:3, 34–35; 7:14, 18, 27)

> See, I am sending my messenger to prepare the way before me, and the Lord whom you seek will suddenly come to his temple. The messenger of the covenant in whom you delight – indeed, he is coming, says the LORD of hosts.
> (Mal. 3:1)

This view of God's kingship as something to be revealed persisted and was intensified in the Second Temple period and even into the rabbinic era:

> Their kingdom will be an eternal kingdom, and all their paths will be righteous. They will judge the land justly, and all nations will make peace. Warfare will cease from the land, and all the nations shall do obeisance to them. The great God will be their help, he himself will fight for them, putting peoples into their power, overthrowing before them all before them. God's rule will be an eternal rule and all the depths of [the earth are his].
> (4Q245 ii 5–10)

> For he will honor the pious upon the th[ro]ne of his eternal kingdom, setting prisoners free, opening the eyes of the blind, raising up those who are bo[wed down] . . . The Lord shall do glorious things which have not been done, just as he said: For he shall heal the critically wounded, he shall revive the dead, he shall send good news to the afflicted.
> (4Q521 2.7–12)

> After these, two divisions of infantry shall . . . bring down the slain by the judgment of God, to subdue the battle line of the enemy by the power of God, and to render recompense for their evil for all the vainglorious nations. So the kingship shall belong to the God of Israel, and by the holy ones of his people he shall act powerfully.
> (1QM 6.4–6; cf. 12.15; 19.7)

> But when Rome will also rule over Egypt guiding it toward a single goal, then indeed the most great kingdom of the immortal king will become manifest over men. For a holy prince will come to gain sway over the scepters of the earth forever, as time presses on.
> (*Sib. Or.* 3.45–49; cf. 3.767)

> Therefore when you turn back to the Lord, you will receive mercy, and he will lead you into his holy place, proclaiming peace to you.

And there shall arise for you from the tribe of Judah and (the tribe of) Levi the Lord's salvation. He will make war against Beliar; he will grant the vengeance of victory as our goal. And he shall take from Beliar the captives, the souls of the saints; and he shall turn the hearts of the disobedient ones to the Lord, and grant eternal peace to those who call upon him. And the saints shall refresh themselves in Eden; the righteous shall rejoice in the New Jerusalem, which shall be eternally from the glorification of God. And Jerusalem shall no longer undergo desolation, nor shall Israel be led into captivity, because the Lord will be in her midst [living among human beings]. The Holy One of Israel will rule over them in humility and poverty, and he who trusts in him shall reign in truth in the heavens.
(*T. Dan* 5.10–17)

Then his kingdom will appear through the whole creation. Then the devil will have an end. Yea, sorrow will be led away with him.
(*T. Mos.* 10.1)

Restore our judges as of old and our leaders as at the beginning and reign over us – you alone.
(*Amidah* 11)

For His (= the Holy One's) is the crown of kingship; and He is the King of kings in this world, and His is the kingship in the world to come. And His it is and shall be for ever and ever.
(*Tg. Exod.* 15.18)[22]

Thus, in the Hebrew Bible, in Second Temple literature and beyond, Yahweh was, is and will be king.[23] Yahweh is king of creation from all ages and for the ages. Yahweh is the king who made a covenant with

---

22 Cited in Duling 1992: 53.
23 Ladd (1993 [1974]: 58) puts it well: 'This leads to the conclusion that while God is the King, he must also become King, i.e., he must manifest his kingship in the world of human beings and nations.' Perrin (2019: 46) notes the tension in Ps. 47 in that Yahweh is the 'great king over all the earth' (v. 2) and yet Yahweh is also enthroned in the submission and in-gathering of the Gentiles (vv. 3, 5, 9). According to Perrin, 'Yahweh becomes king of the cosmos in the fullest sense on the universal recognition of his right to take that throne.'

Israel, whom he delivered from slavery to be his royal and priestly people who would worship him as king in the Jerusalem cultus. So it was hoped that Yahweh would again show himself as king by rescuing Israel from her plight, often through a Davidic ruler, sometimes defeating pagan nations and/or Satan, and yielding an eternal kingdom. So, beyond general descriptions of Yahweh as sovereign over Israel and the cosmos, we find specific articulations that Yahweh is and will be king: Yahweh will establish his kingdom, and when he does, it will mean deliverance for Israel.[24]

There were many different views as to what Yahweh's kingdom was and would look like when brought to expression. Yahweh's kingship/kingdom could be given various interpretations, and while many of these overlap, they rehearse several basic ideas about the kingdom.

Heavenly

Given that Yahweh was king of heaven[25] and heaven was his throne,[26] it was natural to think of God's kingdom in heavenly dimensions, even as a heavenly counterpart to Jerusalem.[27] The *Songs of the Sabbath Sacrifice* describe angelic worship in heaven where '[God's] kingdom [is] among the utterly holy', and heaven as a temple realm inhabited by '[angelic] leaders of each and every holy kingdom belonging to the holy King, who serve in all the exalted temples of his glorious realm' (4Q400 1 ii 1; 4Q404 23 ii 11). Elsewhere, the archangel Michael was said to have the keys to the kingdom of heaven, which consists of heaven itself.[28] It was also possible to imagine that the conflict between God's angels and Satan in a heavenly realm mirrored the battle between the Judeans and the Greeks in an earthly realm.[29] These two realms could intersect in the future so that angelic warriors could be portrayed as joining an Israelite army to 'exalt the authority of Michael among the gods and the dominion of Israel among all flesh' (1QM 17.7–8).

---

24 See similarly McKnight 2014: 45.
25 Dan. 4:34; *T. Abr.* 7.7.
26 Ps. 103:19.
27 Gal. 4:26.
28 *3 Bar.* 11.2.
29 Dan. 7:10–12; Rev. 12.

Paradise

Common was the notion of God's kingdom as paradisal, characterized by peace, blessing, agricultural fecundity and other dividends. One finds language such as 'in those days', referring to an era where good things are found, for example justice, an end to suffering and war, and even animals living in harmony with one another.[30] The kingdom is tantamount to 'the new creation' or the 'coming age'.

Priestly–cultic

Hopes for a new Jerusalem with a new temple loom large, sometimes in tandem with a messiah as temple-builder.[31] The Apocalypse of Weeks in *1 Enoch* specifically links together a glorified realm where 'a house and kingdom shall be built'.[32] In Hasmonean ideology there was a close connection between God's salvation and the reinstitution and amalgamation of kingly and priestly offices, with the temple's purification as the first step towards ending the Judean dispersion.[33] The Qumran scrolls, taking their cue from Zechariah 4:14, envisage an eschatological duumvirate of Davidic (royal) and Aaronic (priestly) messiahs leading the sons of light into God's kingdom.[34] Accordingly, in the Qumran scrolls the kingdom of God is associated with Israel's 'reign' over the surrounding nations, allowing the creation of a temple state complete with a vindicated remnant, a renewed covenant, peace and prosperity, a purified cultus and an angelic presence.[35] According to *Jubilees*, a form of rewritten Scripture, the sabbath is dedicated as a day 'for the holy kingdom for all Israel'.[36] It is through monolatry and sabbath observance that faithful Judeans experience God's kingly rule and in due time become 'a kingdom and a priesthood and a holy people'.[37]

---

30 Isa. 11:6–8; 65:25; *Sib. Or.* 3.667–695; *1 Enoch* 22.1–7; 91.8–11; Rev. 21:1–4; 22:1–5; *2 Bar.* 73.1–7; Philo, *Praem. Poen.* 85–90.
31 Cf. Ezek. 40 – 48; *Sib. Or.* 3.285–290, 772–774; *T. Dan* 5.11–13; Mark 14:58; John 2:19; *1 Enoch* 91.13.
32 *1 Enoch* 93.7.
33 *2 Macc.* 2:17–18; Josephus, *War* 1.68.
34 CD 14.19; 1QS 9.11; 1QSa 2.11–20; 4Q254 iv.
35 1QM 12:3–17; 19.8; 1QSb 3.1–7; 4.22–26; 5.20–21.
36 *Jub.* 50.9.
37 *Jub.* 16.18.

Theophanic

Elsewhere, God's kingdom appears abruptly, displacing local or universal pagan kingdoms.[38] God 'the eternal king' suddenly 'descends to visit the earth with goodness'.[39] This transpires, without any human agents, when God comes from his kingly throne to establish his kingdom by wreaking vengeance on the nations and their idols and then exalting Israel to heavenly heights.[40] God often arrives in Zion with salvation for the captives and oppressed.[41] Some scribes saw Torah as pointing to a theophanic theocracy where God was the father of Israel and would suddenly appear as king upon Mount Zion, subsequently reigning in the sanctuary for ever and ever.[42]

Political–prophetic liberation

Several Jewish resistance movements, from the followers of Judas the Galilean to the Sicarii, emphasized God as their sole ruler and king over Israel, and envisaged something along the lines of a new Israelite kingdom free from pagan hegemony.[43] Josephus also refers to several 'deceivers' who attempted to produce signs that God's liberation of the nation was at hand;[44] these we call the Judean 'sign prophets', such as Theudas and 'the Egyptian'.[45]

Messianic

A messianic kingdom is apparent in the *Psalms of Solomon*: 'The Lord himself is our king forever more.' The author places hope in 'God our saviour' and in the 'kingdom of our God' which is to be manifested in the kingly reign of the 'Lord Messiah' through whom God overthrows sinners and the nations.[46] In the Similitudes of *1 Enoch*, the 'Lord of Spirits' installs on his throne of glory the 'Son of Man', a messianic agent with supernatural

---

38 Dan. 2:44–45.
39 *2 Enoch* 25.3.
40 *T. Mos.* 10.1–1.
41 Isa. 51:1–11; 59:16; Zeph. 3:16–18; Sir. 36:19; Rom. 11:26; *4 Ezra* 13.35–36.
42 *Jub.* 1.28.
43 Josephus, *Ant.* 18.4, 23–24; *War* 7.410.
44 Josephus, *War* 2.258–260; *Ant.* 20.167–168.
45 Acts 21:38; Josephus, *War* 2.261–263; Acts 5:36; Josephus, *Ant.* 20.97–99.
46 *Pss Sol.* 17.3, 7, 32, 46.

powers, filled with wisdom and acting in righteousness, who sees that the elect are vindicated and exalted, shines as a light to the Gentiles, heals the sick, vanquishes evil, judges the wicked, and deposes the earthly kings of the nations, who are forced to do obeisance before him.[47]

Interregnum

Some Jewish seers forecast a temporal earthly kingdom ahead of a universal kingdom, a view which shaped Christian tradition concerning a 'millennium'.[48]

Sapiential

For many, God's kingdom was found in the possession of a wisdom fit to make one wise enough to reign and to enjoy an afterlife.[49]

Spiritual

In later rabbinic writings, the sociopolitical connotations of the kingdom are displaced by ethical horizons so that the 'kingdom of heaven' could be equated with accepting the yoke of Torah and its profession of God's oneness.[50] In the *Gospel of Thomas*, the kingdom could even be reduced to some kind of internalized self-knowledge.[51] There were Christian accounts that emphasized the nature of the kingdom as very much otherworldly and of a purely spiritual texture.[52]

The kingdom of God in the message of Jesus

As we will see, Jesus' message of the kingdom was equally diverse and variegated in the ways it could be articulated and how it could be constructed before an audience (something exploited in the redactional

---

47 *1 Enoch* 46.1–8; 48.1–10; 52.4; 62 – 63; 69.29.
48 1 Cor. 15:24–25; Rev. 20:4–6; *4 Ezra* 7.26–44; *2 Bar.* 29.1–8; 39.7 – 40.2; 70.9 – 74.4.
49 Wis. 3:1–8; 6:4, 19–21; 10:10; Philo, *Somn.* 2.243–244; *Spec. Leg.* 4.164; *Abr.* 261; 1 Cor. 4:8; *4 Macc.* 2.23.
50 *m. Ber.* 2.2; *b. Ber.* 2.2; 13b; *Pirkē Abot* 3.7.
51 *Gos. Thom.* 3.
52 Often leaning on John 18:36 (KJV), 'My kingdom is not of this world.' See Eusebius, *Hist. Eccl.* 3.19; Justin, *1 Apol.* 11.

activity of the evangelists themselves).[53] Scholars rightly see Jesus' kingdom message as 'multivalent' or 'polyvalent',[54] as it touches upon notions of God's dominion and deliverance. It is a domain of power, authority, kingship; benefaction and blessing; economic and political liberation; the present and future; justice and judgment; people and place. It is transcendent yet immanent; something supernatural though terrestrial; capable of abstraction in parables and yet brutally confronting when its demands are laid upon individuals.[55]

Jesus appears to have been shaped principally by Isaiah, Daniel and Zechariah in his discourse about God's kingdom. At the same time, while Jesus was semantically and intertextually rehearsing well-known themes about God's kingship, we might want to consider that the reason he spent so much time teaching about the kingdom is that he meant by it something that his contemporaries did not. That is not to make Jesus idiosyncratically unique within Second Temple Judaism, but it alerts us to the danger of assuming that merely finding the right background, whether in the Qumran scrolls or among wisdom traditions, somehow unlocks all of Jesus' kingdom proclamation.

In reality, Jesus' message of the kingdom was an appropriation of Israel's sacred traditions even while it challenged and undermined competing notions of God's kingship vis-à-vis Israel and the world. Jesus' message had eschatological content and apocalyptic energy,[56] as it was oriented towards the advent of a future kingdom, the coming of God as king.[57] This

---

53 For a catalogue of sayings and verses about the kingdom of God in early Christian literature, see Wright 1996: 663–670; Allison 2010c: 164–204.

54 Witherington 2009–10: 81; Schnelle 2009 [2007]: 109. Perrin (1976: 29–30, 33, 40) of course famously regarded the 'kingdom of God' as neither an idea nor a concept but rather as a 'tensive symbol', which is an entity that cannot be exhausted or adequately expressed by any single description. In that case, God's kingship invokes 'the myth of the activity of God as king on behalf of his people' and projects 'the expectation of a final eschatological act of God on behalf of his people'.

55 A good example of a broad definition of the kingdom is Chilton (1994b: 280): 'The phrase [the kingdom of God] appears to convey the ways in which God rules – today and tomorrow, with force and immanently, righteously and in judgment, gathering the pure and yet standing alone, in Zion and everywhere.'

56 Meier (1991–2016: 1:317) comments: 'A completely un-eschatological Jesus, a Jesus totally shorn of all apocalyptic traits, is simply not the historical Jesus, however compatible he might be to modern tastes, at least in middle-class American academia.' Similar is Allison (2010a: 46–47): 'our choice is not between an apocalyptic Jesus and some other Jesus; it is between an apocalyptic Jesus and no Jesus at all.'

57 On the kingdom as God coming *as* king, see Meyer 1979: 136; Wright 1996: 615–624; 2012;

forward-looking and transcendent view of the kingdom, along the lines of a future dominion–domain–deliverance in which Jesus himself played a key role, was thoroughly imbibed by the early church. This is evident in Paul's letters with the coalescing of Jesus' parousia and God's kingdom,[58] and is also extant in the Jewish Christian texts of James and Jude and John the Seer's apocalypse, which draw together the coming kingdom with the coming of Jesus as king.[59] The church knew the 'kingdom' as something experienced in the present as a triangulation of *power, persecution* and *patience*.[60] The kingdom was something to be paradoxically awaited as much as anticipated! The very mention of 'kingdom' could function as an abbreviation for the church's ethics[61] and for its royal-priestly vocation in the world.[62] The early church was a kingdom movement because Jesus was a kingdom-proclaimer who, as we will see, envisaged a determinative role for himself as the arbiter of God's kingly rule.

The first aspect of the kingdom of Jesus' proclamation that stands out to us is its orientation towards the future. Disciples are told to pray, 'Your kingdom come.'[63] Jesus placed tremendous emphasis on the necessity and difficulty of 'entering' the kingdom. Entering this kingdom can only be done with the openness and vulnerability of a child,[64] through an eschatological purification,[65] with a righteousness greater than that of the Pharisees,[66] without being seduced by possessions,[67] and if necessary without eyes or limbs if they entice one into sin.[68] Mere confession of Jesus as Lord does not qualify one to enter,[69] and exalting oneself

---

Meier 1991–2016: 2:299, 452; Chilton 1978b; 1987; 1996. Note esp. Isa. 26:21; 35:4; 40:9–10; 66:16; Zech. 14:5; Mic. 1:3–4; Mal. 3:2; *Jub.* 1.22–28; *T. Mos.* 10.1–12; *T. Levi* 5.2; *1 Enoch* 1.3–9.

58 1 Thess. 1:9–10; 2:12; 1 Cor. 15:24–28, 50; Phil. 3:20–21; Col. 1:13.
59 Jas 5:9; Jude 21; Rev. 11:15; 12:10.
60 Acts 14:12; 1 Cor. 4:20; 15:24; Rev. 1:9.
61 Matt. 5:20; 6:33; Rom. 14:17.
62 1 Pet. 2:9; Rev. 1:6; 5:10.
63 Luke 11:2/Matt. 6:10.
64 Mark 10:15; Matt. 18:14.
65 John 3:5.
66 Matt. 5:20.
67 Mark 10:23–25.
68 Mark 9:47.
69 Matt. 7:21.

disqualifies one from entering.[70] Indeed, one must seek or strive after the kingdom.[71] In the coming age, only those blessed by the Father will inherit the kingdom of God.[72] At the last supper, Jesus promised not to drink the fruit of the vine until he could enjoy it afresh in the kingdom of God.[73] In this future kingdom there will be a patriarchal banquet with a renewed Israel and even Gentiles in attendance,[74] and the disciples will preside over a restored Israel as judges.[75] Such a kingdom would be equated with eternal life,[76] the renewal of all things,[77] an inversion of social power making the first last and the last first,[78] and resurrection.[79] Jesus, then, like some of his contemporaries, was awaiting, hoping for or anticipating the kingdom of God,[80] albeit referring to signs of its coming rather than narrating a precise schedule for its appearance.[81]

In sum, the overwhelming impression that Jesus created was that the 'kingdom' was God's present reign ahead of its expression in a future realm, one that was supernatural and spatial, something to be entered by discipline and desperation, where there would be the life, renewal, blessings and justice that the prophets had announced. It is this emphasis on the kingdom as a hybrid of God's forthcoming dominion–domain–deliverance[82] that arguably had the biggest influence on the kingdom language of the early church.[83]

---

70 Matt. 23:12; Luke 14:11; 18:14.
71 Luke 12:31/Matt. 6:33.
72 Matt. 25:34.
73 Mark 14:25.
74 Luke 13:28–29/Matt. 8:11–12.
75 Luke 19:28–29/Matt. 22:29–30.
76 Mark 10:29–30; John 3:3, 15–16.
77 Matt. 19:28.
78 Mark 10:31; Matt. 20:16; Luke 13:30.
79 Mark 12:26–28; Luke 14:14; John 5:29.
80 On Jesus' contemporaries looking ahead for the kingdom of God, see Mark 10:37; 15:43; Luke 14:14; 23:42; and the Jewish *Amidah* and *Kaddish* prayers.
81 See Meier 1991–2016: 1:336–348; Allison 1998: 130; Witherington 1999: 261–265, 291; Horsley 2012: 34–64; Hengel and Schwemer 2019 [2007]: 438.
82 See Kvalbein (1998: 205), who refers to Jesus' kingdom as focused on 'the gift of salvation, the place of salvation and the time of salvation'. Allison (2010a: 201) believes that *basileia tou theou* designates 'a realm as well as a reign; it is a place and time yet to come in which God will reign supreme'.
83 See Acts 14:22; 1 Cor. 6:9–10; 15:24, 50; Gal. 5:21; Eph. 5:5; 1 Thess. 2:12; 2 Thess. 1:5; 2 Tim. 4:1; Jas 2:5; 2 Pet. 1:11; Rev. 11:15, 17; 12:10; 20:4; 22:5; *1 Clem.* 42.3; 50.3; *2 Clem.* 9.6; 11.7;

Jesus and the kingdom of God

The second prominent aspect of Jesus' kingdom is the way in which Jesus regarded the kingdom as, in some sense, a partially realized reality, something already intruding on the present, even if only in embryonic form. While we know that many Jews could describe their future hopes, whether construed as eternal life or as national liberation, as God's coming kingdom, Jesus 'was the only Jew of ancient times known to us who preached not only that people stood at the threshold of the end time, but that the new age of salvation had begun'.[84]

Mark's programmatic summary of Jesus' message is: 'The time is fulfilled, and the kingdom of God has come near; repent, and believe in the good news' (Mark 1:15).[85] This is the message that Jesus rehearsed from place to place[86] and instructed his disciples to replicate.[87] This is more than 'God is king; long live the king'; it is meant to be the spark that lights a new empire. The mood of announcement is that 'something dramatic and unprecedented has begun to unfold'.[88] The fulfilment here is probably to the effect that the largely Isaianic promises of Israel's restoration are beginning to come true.[89] The hint that we should think in Isaianic coordinates derives from the language of 'gospel' or 'good news', which appears to be a deliberate throw-back to Isaiah 52:7 with its 'glad tidings' (*mebasser*) of Yahweh's coming as 'king' (*malak*) to liberate the exiles and to usher in Israel's renewal.[90] Jesus also, like Josephus later, urged people to repent, that is, to give up their way of being Israel and

---

12.1–6; Ignatius, *Phild.* 3.3; Pol. *Phil.* 5.3; *Barn.* 4.13; *Herm. Sim.* 9.15.3; *Gos. Thom.* 27, 44, 49, 99.

84 Flusser and Notley 2001: 110.

85 Concerning the kingdom's nearness, much ink has been spilt on the meaning of *ēngiken* as 'drawn near' or 'has already come' (see Palu 2012). I would aver that irrespective of any underlying Aramaic, the perfect-tense form of the Greek verb certainly indicates prominence. The issue of what is prominent depends on what one thinks of the perfect-tense form in general: past event with ongoing signification (the kingdom is here, but not yet fully realized); stative (the kingdom is in the state of nearness); or heightened proximity (the kingdom has spatially come near or is near in a heightened sense). Most likely, the time of fulfilment relates to the proximity of the kingdom spatially in terms of Jesus' person and temporally in terms of the future kingdom's power being exercised in the present.

86 Matt. 4:23; Luke 4:43; 8:1.

87 Matt. 10:7/Luke 9:2; Luke 10:9.

88 Allison 2010c: 39.

89 Though see too Dan. 7:22: 'until the Ancient One came; then judgment was given for the holy ones of the Most High, and *the time arrived* when the holy ones gained possession of the kingdom' (emphasis added).

90 Cf. similar echoes of Isa. 52 in 11Q13 2.14–16, 23–25; *Pss Sol.* 11.1.

to entrust themselves to his vision for the nation's rescue.[91] Israel was called to faith – trust, fidelity and allegiance – at times of great crisis.[92] At this coming day of reckoning, Israel was again called to have faith in her God, more precisely Israel's God working through Jesus.[93] Jesus' announcement is something of a cross between Father Hidalgo's Cry of Dolores which launched the Mexican revolt against Spanish rule in 1810 and Beaver's joyous whisper to the Pevensie children that Aslan has returned in *The Lion, the Witch and the Wardrobe*. The great rescue that Israel's covenant God had promised is now, at last, beginning! God's victory is on the horizon, and is already here!

Central to this 'nowness' of the kingdom was Jesus' belief that he had won, and was continuing to win, a dramatic victory over Satan. The figure of Satan grows and develops in the intertestamental period from angelic tempter to divine adversary pitted against Israel.[94] Many strands of Jewish expectation looked ahead to the vanquishing of the Satan at the end of the age.[95] Jesus reports a vision of some kind in which he saw 'Satan fall like lightning',[96] perhaps referring back to his triumph over satanic temptation in the wilderness.[97] Or else, this victory was established by his exorcisms of demonic spirits to the point of expelling the satanic ruler out of the world.[98] Jesus considered himself to be the 'strong man' who plunders and ransacks the demonic realm as empowered by the Spirit/finger of God.[99] Jesus appears here like a figure presented in the *Testament of Daniel*: 'And there shall arise for you from the tribe of Judah and (the tribe of) Levi the Lord's salvation. He will make war against Beliar; he will grant the vengeance of victory as our goal.'[100] So, '[i]n short', says Craig Evans, 'for Jesus and his followers, the exorcisms

---
91 Wright 1996: 250–251.
92 Cf. e.g. Pss 9:10; 26:1; 31:6; 40:1–4; Isa. 12:2; 26:4; Jer. 17:7; Hab. 2:4; 2 Macc. 7:40; 15:7.
93 Wright 1996: 261–262. However, I admit that Wright's claim (274) that Jesus was replacing adherence to Torah and temple with allegiance to himself needs to be heavily qualified.
94 Josephus, *Life* 110; cf. 1 Chr. 21:1; Job 1 – 2; Zech. 3:1–2; *T. Dan* 5.10–13; 1QS 3.19–25.
95 Cf. Isa. 24:21–22; *Jub.* 23.39; 1QS 4.18–19; *T. Mos.* 10.1; *T. Levi* 18.12; *T. Jud.* 25.3; Jude 6; Rev. 20:2–3.
96 See Luke 10:18.
97 Mark 1:12–13.
98 Mark 1:34; John 12:31.
99 Mark 3:27; Luke 11:20/Matt. 12:28.
100 *T. Dan* 5.10.

offered dramatic proof of the defeat and retreat of Satan's kingdom in the face of the advancing rule of God'.[101] What distinguishes Jesus from other seers, observes Bornkamm, is that

> he himself enters the battlefield; God's victory over Satan takes place in his words and deeds, and it is in them that the signs of this victory are erected. In Jesus himself is to be found the stronger man who puts an end to the rule of Satan and takes his booty from him.[102]

Jesus is the Spirit-anointed prince who fights against the prince of the powers of darkness.

Another indication of the presence of the kingdom is provided by the demonstrable signs of Israel's restoration.[103] In one episode with good claim to historical authenticity (because, let's face it, who would invent a story where John had second thoughts about Jesus?), disciples of John the Baptist relay to Jesus a question from John: 'Are you the one who is to come, or are we to wait for another?'[104] You can hardly blame John for his doubts. Sitting as he was in Herod Antipas's dungeon, awaiting probable execution, it did not feel to him as though the kingdom of God or Israel's day of liberation had arrived. So had John backed the wrong horse of the apocalypse? Was Jesus procrastinating before unleashing whatever it was that he, as 'the one', was supposed to unleash? Jesus' answer to John might sound evasive, but it is in fact quite pointed:

> Go and tell John what you have seen and heard: the blind receive their sight; the lame walk; those with a skin disease are cleansed; the deaf hear; the dead are raised; the poor have good news brought to them. And blessed is anyone who takes no offence at me.
> (Luke 7:22–23/Matt. 11:4–6)

---

101 Evans 2005a: 75; cf. Witherington 1990: 203–204; Meier 1991–2016: 2:416–417; Allison 2010a: 112.
102 Bornkamm 1960 [1956]: 68.
103 Thus, for Wright (1996: 307), the kingdom is 'the action of the covenant god [sic], within Israel's history, to restore her fortunes, to bring to an end the bitter period of exile, and to defeat, through her, the evil that ruled the whole world'.
104 Luke 7:20/Matt. 11:3.

At one level, Jesus is telling John not to mistake the reception of the kingdom with its reality. Yes, Herod Antipas is still in his palace, Caesar is still safely ensconced in Rome, the new temple has not arrived, Israel is still in slavery, the land is hardly overflowing with milk and honey; but beyond that, the signs of the new exodus, the true end of exile, God coming as king, are there for those with eyes to see it. Jesus' list of his deeds does not consist of random quotes from his prophetic CV; it deliberately echoes Isaiah's prophecy about what happens when God's reign comes – when the end of exile begins and deliverance is manifested.[105] Even more astoundingly, in Qumran's messianic apocalypse, these are precisely the same deeds that it was thought that the Messiah – or maybe God through the Messiah – would do in the future:

> He will honor the pious upon the th[ro]ne of His eternal kingdom, setting prisoners free, opening the eyes of the blind, raising up those who are bo[wed down] . . . He shall heal the critically wounded, He shall revive the dead, He shall send good news to the afflicted. (4Q521 2.7–12)

If we correlate this with the 'Nazareth Manifesto',[106] then Jesus is the messianic herald of salvation, Isaiah's Spirit-anointed prophet, and the coming Davidic deliverer who ushers in God's kingdom by expressing the prophetic signs of Israel's rescue.

There are further indications that Jesus announced the presence of the kingdom. For a start, many of the parables portray the kingdom as something that appears insignificant and inert, like a mere seed, but then grows of its own accord into an immense harvest.[107] Or else it is like a mustard seed, something tiny which soon sprouts and takes over everything in its path like an infesting weed;[108] or else it is like yeast, something that works itself through everything it touches.[109] These

---

105 Cf. Isa. 26:19; 29:18–19; 35:5–6; 42:7, 19; 53:4; 61:1.
106 Luke 4:16–21.
107 Mark 4:26–29.
108 Mark 4:30–32; *Gos. Thom.* 20.
109 Matt. 13:33; *Gos. Thom.* 96.

Jesus and the kingdom of God

extended metaphors depict the kingdom as a present reality which, while seemingly inauspicious, is nevertheless destined to dominate all before it.

In addition, the enigmatic verses in Luke 17:20-21 show Jesus rebuking the Pharisees, when they demand a sign or timetable for the kingdom, with a response that 'the kingdom of God is among you [or: in your midst / within your grasp]'. The Greek *entos hymōn* is notoriously opaque, and such words were susceptible to internalized interpretations by later Christians, hence the Vulgate's rendering of *regnum Dei intra vos est* as 'the kingdom of God is inside you', and *Gospel of Thomas* 3 with 'the kingdom is within you and it is outside you'.[110] Whereas the Pharisees wanted an answer to 'When is the kingdom coming?' Jesus responds in effect with 'What do you think is in front of you?' The kingdom is here, powerful and palpable; yes, the Son of Man and his judgment are yet to come, but in the 'here and now' the kingdom's sphere of operation is active and within your reach. All this is to say: the royal rescue and the drama of deliverance have begun.

Important too is how the kingdom of God orbits around Jesus.[111] It remains truly perplexing to me that scholars of Christian origins can still insist that Jesus proclaimed the kingdom and that thereafter the church abandoned Jesus' kingdom project and proclaimed him as a Hellenistic deity who promised followers the immortality of the soul. The obvious problem here is that Jesus' message always had an element of self-reference:[112] it is the Spirit acting through Jesus that manifests the kingdom: 'But if it is by the Spirit/finger of God that I cast out demons, then the kingdom of God has come to you.'[113] It is Jesus' mighty deeds that enact the new exodus that Isaiah spoke about.[114] To be close to Jesus is to be close to the kingdom.[115] Jesus is the 'strong man' who raids the

---

110 See the variant tradition/interpretation in *Gos. Thom.* 113: 'His disciples said to him: "The kingdom – on what day will it come?" [Jesus replied:] "It will not come by watching and waiting for it. They will not say: 'Look, here!' or 'Look, there!' Rather, the kingdom of the Father is spread out upon the earth, and people do not see it."'
111 Chilton (1994b: 256) is right to warn of the danger of collapsing the kingdom into Christology, since the kingdom is theocentric, but such a caveat should not be pressed into making Jesus a mere messenger of the kingdom.
112 Rightly recognized by a diverse assortment of scholars, including Bultmann 1952-55: 1:7; Sanders 1985: 153; Meier 1991-2016: 1:453-454; Wright 1996: 222; Schreiner 2008: 51.
113 See Luke 11:20/Matt. 12:28.
114 Luke 7:22-23/Matt. 11:4-6.
115 *Gos. Thom.* 82.

demons' kingdom and establishes his own.¹¹⁶ Jesus is also the Son of Man around whom the disciples will gather as the leaders in charge of a restored Israelite monarchy which the Father will confer on Jesus.¹¹⁷ Those who witness Jesus' deeds and hear his words are 'blessed' because they see what many prophets and kings of Israel's sacred history longed for but did not experience, namely, the fulfilment of God's promises to reveal his kingly power precisely in Jesus.¹¹⁸ It is one's response to Jesus that determines entrance to the kingdom.¹¹⁹

When it comes to the kingdom, Jesus was no onlooker and no forerunner. To the contrary, he believed that he was at the centre of it as its chief agent. This is why, presumably, the early church correlated Jesus and the kingdom, yielding expressions such as 'the kingdom of God and the name/teaching of Jesus',¹²⁰ 'the kingdom of the son of his love'¹²¹ and the 'kingdom of Christ',¹²² believing that '[Jesus] must reign until he has put all his enemies under his feet', destroying 'every ruler and every authority and power', and that '[t]hen comes the end, when he hands over the kingdom to God the Father'.¹²³ One day, the church would declare: 'The kingdom of the world has become the kingdom of our Lord and of his Messiah, and he will reign for ever and ever.'¹²⁴ God's kingdom entails the reign of Jesus!

Subjects of the kingdom

One aspect of the kingdom that needs consideration, one that might seem banal but is often neglected, is that a kingdom is a people ruled by a king.¹²⁵ As such, it is natural that attention is drawn towards people in relationship to the kingdom. The kingdom will have people who are

---

116 Mark 3:27.
117 Luke 22:28–30/Matt. 19:28.
118 Matt. 13:16–17/Luke 10:23–24; cf. *Pss Sol.* 17.44; 18.6.
119 Mark 8:38; 9:37; Matt. 12:30/Luke 11:23; Luke 10:16; John 10:9; 12:44–45; 13:20.
120 See Acts 8:12; 28:31.
121 Col. 1:13 (MFB trans.).
122 Eph. 5:5.
123 1 Cor. 15:24–26.
124 Rev. 11:15; 12:10.
125 A point emphasized by McKnight (2014: 65–79).

'least' and 'great'.[126] Some of Jesus' interlocutors are told that they are 'not far from the kingdom',[127] and others are warned they will be locked out.[128] The kingdom is a possession to which one belongs,[129] it is something one must strive with urgency to 'enter',[130] yet it is also 'inherited'[131] or 'received'.[132] Jesus, then, seems to offer the kingdom as something like a pilgrimage, or a journey out of slavery, knowing that many will scoff from the outset, some will start and then soon turn back, while others will reach the end and receive a gift if they persevere in covenant faithfulness. The kingdom is not a realm of lofty religious ideals, nor is it immortal bliss in a hereafter; it is a restored creation, a renewed covenant, redemption wrought by God's kingly power, and a reconstituted Israel.

The subjects of the kingdom, the ones to whom the kingdom belongs, then, are naturally the people of Israel. However, Jesus' specific articulation of the kingdom, what it is and is not, its cultic and political corollaries, creates division within Israel. Ultimately, it comes down to a cluster of issues. Whose way of being Israel will prevail? How does the kingdom come – by priestly purification, military rebellion or angelic invention? Messiah or no Messiah? How does one enter this kingdom? What does God require of his people? Is this the true temple or should we expect or build a bigger and better one? What does one do under the Romans or about the Romans? Jesus lamented, in various warnings and woe oracles, that not all of those who belonged to Israel would enter the kingdom of God;[133] something John the Baptist also declared.[134] Although the kingdom is for Israel, Jesus announced – just like other leaders of Jewish renewal movements – that not all Israel would receive it. If people rejected this kingdom, then it would be given to others; not

---

126 Cf. e.g. Matt. 5:19; 18:1–4; Luke 7:28/Matt. 11:11.
127 Mark 12:34.
128 Luke 13:28–29/Matt. 8:11–12.
129 Mark 10:14; Matt. 5:3/Luke 6:20; Matt. 5:10.
130 Mark 10:23–25; Luke 9:59–62; 16:16; John 3:5.
131 See Matt. 5:5; 25:34.
132 See Mark 10:15.
133 Matt. 11:21/Luke 10:13; Matt. 8:11–12/Luke 13:28–30; Matt. 23:2–39; Luke 4:25–29; 11:42–54; 13:23–27; 13:34–35; 19:41–44.
134 Luke 3:8/Matt. 3:9.

to people other than Israel, but to 'others' within Israel.¹³⁵ This, of course, raised the question: who would enter the kingdom?

The advent of the kingdom meant that the boundaries of Israel were being redrawn around a different set of commitments and proffered a different test of covenantal loyalty from those ordinarily posed by the Pharisees (the unofficial leaders of Judaism) and the priestly class (the official leaders of Judaism). It was no longer commitment to Torah and the temple that marked out those destined to inherit the kingdom: these two pillars of Judaism were not absolute, but were either relativized or retooled in the light of the eschatological crisis facing Israel. Instead, it was those who followed the praxes related to Jesus' kingdom message, who joined the new exodus that was happening, and who embarked on the road literally with Jesus, who would reach their destination. What Jesus demanded of people was to repent of sins and renounce other socio-religious agendas, to trust in him/God, and to turn towards true covenant justice, embracing Israel's covenantal vocation as the light of the world and putting the kingdom at the centre of their lives. Those who took on this 'yoke' would enter the kingdom.¹³⁶

Jesus' call, 'Follow me', was not, then, an invitation to try a new religion the way one might sample a new yoga class.¹³⁷ Jesus was calling people within Israel to join a new way of being Israel. Jesus was inviting people from all tiers of life, agrarian and urban, to be part of a strange revolution, to see God become king, to join the pilgrimage in the new exodus, to perfect their love for Torah into a Torah of love.¹³⁸ Jesus called people to be part of something both supernatural and snowballing; not a revolution of swords and siege engines, but not merely an interior awakening either. Jesus offered people the chance to participate in the kingdom revolution with its liberation from oppression and renewal of the covenant. To be part of this movement was to see Israel's destiny on the horizon and to experience God's kingly power in Jesus' words and works. This explains why Jesus believed that the marker of belonging to the kingdom was not the adoption of a certain style of *halakhah*, a

---

135 Cf. Mark 12:9; Matt. 21:31; Luke 4:25-27; 14:12-24.
136 Matt. 11:29-30.
137 Mark 1:17; 2:14; 8:34; 10:31; Luke 9:59-61.
138 McKnight 2004: 53-54.

distinctive way of obeying the Torah, but devotion to himself as the chief agent and actor of the kingdom's manifestation.[139]

Jesus' message was not restricted to a segment of society, whether rural versus urban, rich versus poor, or Galilean versus Judean. Jesus attracted followers from a wide range of geographical and social positions within Israel. However, he did seem to have an intense concern for the poor, those who were economically destitute, socially disempowered and of marginalized status. That concern itself was not peripheral to Jesus' kingdom aims, as if it were some philanthropic project on the side; rather, the kingdom's advent meant a return to covenant justice, a reversal of privileges and a reordering of power – a state where, to use the language of Isaiah:

> you shall see and be radiant;
> your heart shall thrill and rejoice,
> because the abundance of the sea shall be brought to you;
> the wealth of the nations shall come to you.
> (Isa. 60:5)

> My servants shall eat,
> but you shall be hungry;
> my servants shall drink,
> but you shall be thirsty;
> my servants shall rejoice,
> but you shall be put to shame;
> my servants shall sing with gladness of heart,
> but you shall cry out in pain of heart
> and shall wail in anguish of spirit.
> (Isa. 65:13–14)

Jesus and his kingdom

Jesus' proclamation of God's kingdom consisted of combining and amplifying a cluster of themes involving Satan's defeat, rescue of the oppressed

---

139 Sanders 1985: 225; Wright 1996: 302.

people, recompense against the wicked, return from exile, new exodus, redemption of prisoners, release from debts, respite for the poor, reversal of privileges, covenant righteousness, a radical reordering of power and the renewal of all things. In its future orientation the kingdom appears to be principally – though not exclusively – spatial: it is something entered into or obtained, a place of eternal life, and of resurrection![140] Yet the kingdom is also a sphere of sovereignty that invades and interrupts the present moment, ahead of any eschatological dénouement, seen principally in the Spirit's powerful manifestation through Jesus.[141] But in many ways I have to insist that any definition of the kingdom – as present and future, dynamic and spatial, immanent and transcendent, reign and realm – can simply miss the point if the kingdom is not tied to the story of Israel and its sociopolitical situation in the first century. Ultimately, as John Meier says, '[t]he kingdom of God does not have a definition; it tells a story'.[142] It is to the story of the kingdom that we must now turn!

---

140 The spatial element of the kingdom has been marginalized in recent decades, so on its importance see Kvalbein 1998: 204–214; Meier 1991–2016: 2:240; Schreiner 2016.

141 In German, we might say that this entails both *Gottesherrschaft* ('God's reign') and *Reich Gottes* ('God's kingdom').

142 Meier 1991–2016: 2:241.

4
Jesus and the restoration of Israel

God's kingdom as a restored Israel

The story of God's kingship, evoked by the appellation 'kingdom of God', refers to a great many things: God's creation of and sovereignty over a good and ordered cosmos; the creation of human beings as viceroys; human disobedience and rebellion. Then, the call of Abraham as the beginning of the divine plan to return humanity to its place of vice-regency; the deliverance of the Hebrews from Egypt in the exodus; God's covenant with the Hebrews, his vassal; the giving of the commandments; the land of Canaan as a new type of Eden. Then, later, under the Davidic monarchy and its covenant, God promises to provide Israel with an anointed king to be always at the helm of Israel's future, even when less than ideal kings emerge, when the Israelites are divided or fall into idolatry, and when prophetic warnings to turn back are ignored. When covenantal judgments are imposed, through the Assyrian and then the Babylonian invasion, resulting in exile and the temple's destruction, God promises a new exodus, a future restoration, including the regathering of the dispersed tribes, a new Jerusalem, a new temple, a new covenant, a new David, and even new heavens and a new earth. The pagan world is set to experience judgment for its ignorance and violence, but will then find its own restoration as the nations cease raging against Israel and her king and instead worship the God of Israel with them. Thereafter is peace, blessing, banqueting – in brief, paradise regained. The shorthand way of referring to all the hopes outlined in this story, with its twists and turns and alternative endings, was the 'kingdom of God' or: 'The Lord is King; he will save us.'[1]

Despite the return of a remnant of exiles to Judah from Babylon, things did not look or feel very much like a new exodus as far as the Jewish

---
1 See Meier 1991–2016: 2:241–242.

people were concerned. Even the liberation from Syrian rule under the Hasmoneans turned out to be a false crest towards the arrival of God's reign on earth, since the Hasmonean dynasty was, to some degree, ruined by their usurpation of the priesthood, and then completely undermined by the Roman conquest of Syro-Palestine. Even with a new temple built by Herod the Great (a Roman puppet and a half-Jew at that!), the bright promises of restoration given in the prophets were not materializing. There was no regathering of the dispersed Israelite tribes, no glorious Davidic king, no defeat of the pagan nations, no pilgrimage of the Gentiles to worship God in Zion, no glorious new temple and no renewal of the covenant. As far as it looked, it was the Son of Augustus, not the Son of David, who was running the world's affairs. Prophetic protestors and those daring enough to take up a sword were always put back in their place with ruthless displays of brutality. Israel, then, was still in slavery, still in 'exile', or at least waiting for the full restoration after exile.[2]

In any case, God was clearly not reigning as king in the way his kingship had come to be imagined, and no one was saying that he was. That is, until Jesus of Nazareth steps onto the stage of Judean history and declares the good news that God is king and that his kingdom is about to be dramatically and powerfully revealed. It was a declaration that meant that those prophetic promises of Israel's restoration were now under way, the new exodus had been launched, prophesies were being fulfilled, God was becoming king! In other words, the restoration of the Jewish nation was at hand.

Israel's restoration: a neglected topic

The notion that Jesus was a prophet of Jewish restoration eschatology is, lamentably, disputed in some quarters. Yet it provides the key to understanding Jesus' mission, aims, self-understanding and hope.[3]

---

[2] See Sanders 1985: 80; Meier 1991–2016: 2:247–248; Wright 1992: 302–307; 1996: 202–209; Perrin 2019: 56.

[3] Meyer (1979: 221) went so far as to say: 'In sum, once the theme of national restoration in its full eschatological sweep is grasped as the concrete meaning of the reign of God, Jesus' career begins to become intelligible as a unity.'

First, for some evangelical interpreters, the story of Israel is strangely irrelevant to the story of Jesus. Some envisage Jesus' career as comprised of a sinless birth, a sin-bearing death, and a mixture of revivalist preaching and family-values campaigning in between. By hearing Jesus preach, the Jews got first bite of the apple, so to speak, which they promptly rejected, so then the real and proper mission to the Gentiles began with Paul and his gospel of justification by faith. Protestant Christianity is really about Paul, with Jesus as Paul's own John-the-Baptist-style forerunner.[4]

Second, there are German existentialists who cannot for the life of them believe that Jesus was remotely interested in Israel's restoration or any debates about the Jerusalem cultus. For such persons, Jesus is consumed with thoughts of a coming cosmic catastrophe (which Jesus was sadly deluded about, poor guy, but that's incarnation for you – you take on human flesh and you're gonna be prone to human errors). To compensate for that, Jesus' message gets filtered into existentialist categories. Here Jesus did not aim to renew the Jewish religion with its icky rituals and legalistic laws! No, instead, Jesus intended to establish a new orientation for faith, a new way of relating to God, a new I–Thou relationship, a new way of approaching God in grace.[5] For these interpreters, the story of Jesus might well have been set in Narnia or Westeros or Middle Earth for all it matters, since Israel's plight and its resolution seems to matter relatively little.

Alternatively, in the light of Jewish restoration eschatology, I would aver that Jesus was challenging his contemporaries to make a 'decision', but it was not a call to accept him as Lord and Saviour of their heart (evangelical option) or to stake their personal claim for faith in God (existential option). Rather, as George Caird said:

> [Jesus] believed that Israel was at the cross-roads, that she must choose between two conceptions of her national destiny, and that the time for choice was terrifyingly short. This explains why, in his instructions to his disciples, he speaks of 'towns where they receive you' and 'towns where they do not receive you'. He seems to

---

4 See Wright 1996: 13–16 (esp. 14); McKnight 2011.
5 See e.g. Bultmann 1952–55: 1:4, 6; Schnelle 2009 [2007]: 99–104, 145–146.

have expected not individual but mass response. 'It shall be more tolerable for Sodom and Gomorrah in the judgment than for that town.' The disciples were not evangelistic preachers, sent out to save individual souls for some unearthly paradise. They were couriers proclaiming a national emergency and conducting a referendum on a question of national survival.[6]

Thus, with Caird again, 'Jesus believed that Israel was called by God to be the agent of his purpose, and that he himself had been sent to bring about that reformation without which Israel could not fulfil her national destiny'.[7] Or more fully:

> Jesus believed that Israel had been called to be God's saved and saving nation, the agent through whom God intended to assert his sovereignty over the rest of the world, and that the time had come when God was summoning the nation once for all to take its place in his economy as the Son of Man. His teaching was something more than individual piety and ethics, it was a national way of life through which alone God's purpose could be implemented. The nation must choose between the way of Jesus and all other possible alternatives, and on its choice depended its hope for a national future. For nothing but the thoroughgoing change of heart which Jesus demanded and made possible could in the end keep the nation out of disastrous conflict with Rome. If the nation would not listen to him, it must pay the consequences; but he at least, and anyone else who would share it with him, must fulfil the destiny of the Son of Man. But so deeply does he love his nation, so fully is he identified with its life, so bitterly does he regret what he sees coming upon it, that only death can silence his reiterated and disturbing appeal. He goes to his death at the hands of a Roman judge on a charge of which he was innocent and his accusers, as the event proved, were guilty. And so, not only in theological truth but in historic fact, the one bore the sins of the many, confident that in

---

[6] Caird's view (1965: 9–10) contrasts with that of Bultmann (1952–55: 1:9, 25), who saw Jesus' call for 'decision' as being personal and individual, not national and eschatological.
[7] Caird 1965: 20.

him the whole Jewish nation was being nailed to the cross, only to come to life again in a better resurrection, and that the Day of the Son of Man which would see the end of the old Israel would see also the vindication of the new.[8]

The career of Jesus, including his proclamation and prophetic praxes, his opposition to the temple, his warning of judgment, and the events surrounding his death, should all be situated in a context where many Jews were looking for a day when Israel's covenant God would come again to liberate his people from bondage and establish his kingly power over them by undoing once and for all the residual effects of their forced migration and foreign domination; namely, the end of exile. The exile was a type of national death, and its salvation would be a miracle on a par with resurrection.[9] If exile meant punishment for sins, dislocation from the land, the destruction of the temple and the demise of the Davidic family, then the end of exile would mean the forgiveness of sins, homecoming, a new temple and a new David, among other things. Locating Jesus within the coordinates of Jewish restoration eschatology not only illuminates individual sayings and episodes in his career, but also has this profound effect: the link between Jesus, Israel, his followers and the Gentiles suddenly becomes explicable. For, in the prophetic promises, a transformed Israel would transform the nations;[10] this was something Jesus anticipated in his encounters with Gentiles,[11] and it explains the missionary thrust of the early church to carry Israel's royal and priestly vocation into the world.[12]

Jewish hopes for restoration

It needs to be acknowledged that Jewish restoration eschatology was not monolithic. It was variegated in its form and substance, but there

---

8 Caird 1965: 22; cf. McKnight 1999: 237.
9 Ezek. 37.
10 Cf. e.g. Isa. 2:2–4; 42:6; 49:6; Mic. 4:1–4; Zech. 8:23. See Manson 1964: 6–7, 22–23.
11 Mark 7:24–30; Matt. 8:5–12.
12 Matt. 28:19–20; Luke 24:47; Acts 1:8; Rom. 15:7–13; Rev. 1:6; 5:10; 20:6. Cf. Manson 1964: 23–24. See also Sanders 1985: 212–221; Wright 1996: 308–310; Bird 2006a.

was a broadly shared expectation that Yahweh would again rescue and restore Israel in dramatic fashion. In the end, not only would the lingering effects of Israel's exile be reversed, but also, according to some accounts, the restoration would be positively cosmic. A cursory reading of the exilic prophets Jeremiah, Ezekiel and Isaiah; the royal ideology of the Psalter; writings of the Persian period such as Zechariah and Malachi; the final form of the book of Daniel; combined with a wide array of intertestamental writings, all point ahead to Yahweh coming as king, with certain priestly, angelic or messianic agents, to bring Israel's restoration.[13] Time and space prohibit a lengthy exposition of Jewish restoration eschatology, yet we may note its most salient expressions:[14]

- Yahweh coming to Zion to deliver the people of Israel from political domination and to forgive their national sins;
- the advent of 'anointed' figures, including a royal Davidic ruler and/or a priestly figure, to lead a renewed Israel;
- the regathering of dispersed Jews to Judea in a reconstituted twelve-tribe federation;
- the rebuilding of the Jerusalem temple;
- the renewal of the covenant;
- agricultural fecundity and prosperity;
- triumph over the Gentiles and/or their pilgrimage to worship Yahweh in Jerusalem;
- the defeat of Satan and evil spirits;
- a final judgment of the wicked and sinners;
- the resurrection of the dead;
- a future paradisal state.

---

13 A useful sampler would be Amos 9:11–12; Isa. 40 – 55; Jer. 30 – 31; Ezek. 34; Dan. 2:44–45; 12:1–2; Tob. 14; Sir. 36; *Pss Sol.* 11, 17–18; 4Q521; 1QM; *T. Dan* 5; *Sib. Or.* 3.265–294, 767–795; and Philo, *Praem. Poen.*, which illustrate several recurring themes associated with Israel's restoration.

14 See Schürer 1973–87: 2:514–547; Sanders 1992: 289–298; Wright 1992: 299–338; Dunn 2003: 393–396.

Jesus, a Jewish prophet of Israel's restoration

One does not detect in the Gospels all of the motifs of Jewish restoration eschatology in every instance of hopes for the future. However, they do reappear, and get reinterpreted and reapplied in new settings. The theme of Israel's restoration after a protracted state of exile through a new exodus wrought by God manifests itself at several points in Jesus' career.

First, the Isaianic vision of Israel's restoration is prominent. Jesus' 'gospel of the kingdom'[15] has clear ties to Isaiah 52:7–10, a passage that speaks about the 'glad tidings' (MFB trans.) of Yahweh's return to Zion to set Israel free from exile in a new exodus. Further, it remains highly probable that Jesus took the Isaianic script for restoration to be part of his own mission statement as the Spirit-anointed prophet who was heralding the very signs of Israel's restoration.[16] Again, the fact that Jesus believed that through his own work many would be 'coming from the east and the west'[17] indicates that he had in mind Isaianic imagery for the return of the dispersed tribes to Israel, with Gentiles in their entourage, to share a great eschatological banquet on the holy mountain.[18]

Second, it is fascinating to consider how Qumran's 11QMelch 2 could be regarded as an epitome of Jesus' restoration campaign. In it, the 'Day of Visitation/Salvation'[19] is announced by the prophets, who proclaim that Yahweh reigns;[20] the messenger is the anointed one who will be cut off,[21] and who yet declares divine vengeance and comforts mourners;[22] Belial is defeated, and the sons of righteousness are delivered to become the Zion of the new age. We can easily map this onto the Jesus tradition: Jesus proclaimed a time of God's 'visitation';

---

15 See Mark 1:15.
16 Luke 4:16–21; Matt. 11:4–5/Luke 7:22–23; Isa. 35:5–6; 26:19; 29:18–19; 61:1–2.
17 See Matt. 8:11/Luke 13:29.
18 Isa. 2:2–4; 25:6; 27:12–13; 43:5; 66:19–23; cf. Zech. 8:7–8; Bar. 4:37; 5.5; Tob. 14:1–7; *Pss Sol.* 11.1.
19 Cf. Isa. 49:8.
20 Isa. 52:7.
21 Dan. 9:26.
22 Isa. 61:2.

he was the anointed prophet declaring the year of the Lord's favour; he would be cut off; he would defeat Satan; and his community would be the eschatologically restored people and temple.[23] The struggle in which Jesus' ministry takes place is not one of grace versus religion, not oppressed versus colonizers, not egalitarianism versus patriarchy, but the struggle of God and his people against the powers of darkness, disobedience and deprivation. The revelation of God's kingship for Israel would mean the revolution of the sociopolitical order of the entire world to the point where the only language appropriate for it would be a new empire, a renewal of all things, or even eternal life. If that constituted Jesus' aims, then he was undoubtedly engaged in an 'eschatological vocation' as an anointed figure proclaiming the dawning age of Israel's restoration.[24]

Third, Jesus appointed twelve disciples,[25] not because a dozen is a good number, but because these twelve men symbolized the restored Israel that he was forming around himself.[26] He subsequently promised them that they would become leaders of a restored Israelite tribal league.[27] Jesus' institution of the twelve conveys a theocentric and specifically messianic reconstitution of Israel under the authority of the disciples, acting as tribal leaders, and Jesus as their putative king.[28] In an analogous way, the council of the Qumran community contained twelve persons who signified each Israelite tribe, and three priests who represented the Levitical clans, thus forming a microcosm of the restored Israel.[29] For Jesus, as for the Qumranites, the twelve persons not only symbolized the hope of restoration, but also represented an embryonic fulfilment of that hope, which had become partially realized in their own circle. Put concisely, the twelve are the symbol of a hope, a mission and a reality

---

23 Drawing from Luke 19:44; Mark 1:15; Luke 4:18–21; 10:18; 19:44; Mark 14:58.
24 Meyer 1979: 136.
25 Mark 3:13–16.
26 See the significance of the number twelve in Gen. 35:22–26; 49:28; Exod. 15:27; 24:4; 28:21; 39:14; Josh. 3:12; 4:2–4, 8–9; 1 Kgs 18:31; Ezra 8:24, 35; Ezek. 47:13.
27 Matt. 19:28/Luke 22:30. Cf. Jeremias 1971: 234; Sanders 1985: 98–106; Wright 1996: 299–300; Theissen and Merz 1998 [1996]: 216–217; McKnight 2001; Dunn 2003: 507–510; Horsley 2012: 120–121.
28 Witherington 1990: 65; Theissen and Merz 1998 [1996]: 235–236; Bockmuehl 2008: 71–72.
29 1QS 8.1.

Jesus and the restoration of Israel

– the restoration of Israel – which Jesus and his followers were intending to proclaim and embody.[30]

Fourth, the claim that Jesus said, 'I will destroy this temple that is made with hands, and in three days I will build another, not made with hands' (Mark 14:58), is remarkable.[31] For a start, it coheres with Jesus' other pronouncements of judgment against the temple.[32] The early church is unlikely to have invented such a saying for several reasons: it was the Romans, not Jesus, who destroyed the temple; they burned it but did not raze it; and Jesus had not by the evangelists' day established a new physical temple.[33] Such a logion also meant that Jesus understood himself as a new David destined to build a new temple. It had been the role of Israel's king, ever since the time of Solomon, to build God's temple.[34] This is precisely why Herod the Great invested so much effort in rebuilding the Jerusalem temple: he wished to ostensibly legitimize his (contested!) claim to be the king of the Jews. Jesus, much like Jeremiah, sees either God or himself destroying the temple; and, like Ezekiel, he looks forward to a new temple.

Fifth, Jesus identified the Baptist's message and death within a particularized account of Jewish restoration eschatology. Jesus was faced with a question from his disciples as to how the Son of Man's resurrection, which I take as a coded reference to Israel's restoration, could be close at hand when the scribes said that 'Elijah must come first'.[35] Jesus responded that the Baptist was the returning Elijah who had come 'first to restore all things',[36] which meant that the Baptist was indeed the eschatological Elijah who would announce the coming 'Day of the Lord'.[37] However, in some accounts this returning Elijah was 'destined to calm the wrath of God before it breaks out in fury, to turn the hearts of parents to their children, and to restore the tribes of Jacob' (Sir. 48:10). Yet Jesus seems to reject such a strand of restoration tradition that equated Israel's

---

30 Bird 2006a: 130–134.
31 Cf. Mark 15:29–30; John 2:19; Acts 6:14; *Gos. Thom.* 71.
32 Mark 13:2; Matt. 23:38/Luke 13:35; Luke 19:43–44.
33 Theissen 1976: 145; Bockmuehl 1994: 63.
34 1 Kgs 8; 2 Chr. 7.
35 Mark 9:9–11.
36 Mark 9:12.
37 See Mal. 4:5–6.

reconstitution with the advent of the eschatological Elijah. Jesus affirmed instead another tradition whereby the eschatological Elijah's role was a preliminary form of restoration prior to a time of tribulation and judgment. The Baptist, by virtue of his formation of a repenting remnant, and the fact that he himself participated in the travails that preceded the kingdom, was the returning Elijah.[38]

It is important to note the impact that Jesus' restoration eschatology had on the early church which, in the transformed post-Easter context, carried forward Jesus' appropriation of Israel's sacred traditions about the restoration of Israel and the inclusion of the nations in God's saving purposes. It is in Luke–Acts that we observe how this story of Jesus as the agent of Israel's restoration was taken up into the preaching and praxes of the first Christians. The Magnificat and Benedictus touch on the themes of divine strength, Israel's redemption and rescue from enemies, covenant mercy, forgiveness, a reversal between the poor and rich, fecundity and food, a Davidic deliverer, the establishment of an age of holiness, righteousness and peace, and patriarchal promises fulfilled.[39] The righteous Simeon was waiting for the 'consolation of Israel' and saw in the infant Jesus the long-promised 'salvation' and 'a light for revelation to the Gentiles and for glory to [God's] people Israel', as he was 'the Lord's Messiah'.[40] Similarly, the prophetess Anna saw in the child Jesus hope for those 'looking for the redemption of Jerusalem'.[41] These Lukan songs, rooted in the memory and piety of the Palestinian churches, are as clear a summary of Jewish hopes as one could imagine.

In the Lukan narrative, Jesus himself enacts this restoration programme as specifically laid out in the Nazareth Manifesto, which in many ways is a miniature summary of the entire plot of Luke–Acts.[42] The two travellers on the road to Emmaus were lamenting Jesus' execution, not entirely based on grave injustice and personal loss but because 'we had hoped that he was the one to redeem Israel'.[43] The debris of failed

---

38 Bryan 2002: 88–129, 238–239.
39 Luke 1:46–55, 67–79.
40 Luke 2:25–26, 30, 32.
41 Luke 2:38.
42 Luke 4:16–30.
43 Luke 24:21.

expectations was then transformed and intensified by meeting the risen Jesus, so much so that later the disciples could ask the risen Jesus, 'Lord, is this the time when you will restore the kingdom to Israel?'[44] The underlying assumption is, of course, that Jesus' resurrection was not a stand-alone event; it surely required, in whatever time span, Israel's full rescue as the next item on the divine agenda. The Messiah's resurrection entailed, in whatever form, Israel's restoration and resurrection. Israel's restoration could be conceived as a metaphorical resurrection,[45] or include a literal one as its climax.[46] The Lukan Peter's speech in Solomon's Portico to the Jerusalemites puts Israel's restoration of the people of Israel at the front and centre of who Jesus is and what his exaltation means for them:

> Repent, therefore, and turn to God so that your sins may be wiped out, so that *times of refreshing* may come from the presence of the Lord and that he may send the Messiah appointed for you, that is, Jesus, who must remain in heaven until the time of *universal restoration* that God announced long ago through his holy prophets. (Acts 3:19–21, emphasis added)

Then, at the Jerusalem Council, James cites Amos 9:11–12 (LXX) to justify the inclusion of Gentiles in the church without their having to first become proselytes to Judaism; such a text expresses the view that after the restoration of the Davidic kingdom the Gentiles will be called to be part of God's own people within or beside a renewed Israel.[47] Paul combines national restoration and national resurrection in his appeal to Agrippa II:

> And now I stand here on trial on account of my hope in the *promise made by God to our ancestors, a promise that our twelve tribes hope to attain*, as they earnestly worship day and night. It is for this

---

44 Acts 1:6.
45 Hos. 6:1–3; Isa. 26:16–19; Ezek. 37.
46 Dan. 12:1–2; *Pss Sol.* 3.11–12.
47 Acts 15:13–18.

hope, Your Excellency, that I am accused by Jews! Why is it thought incredible by any of you that *God raises the dead*?
(Acts 26:6–8, emphasis added)

In Luke's telling – and I suspect that Luke is at least reflecting something of his sources here – Israel's hopes for redemption, rescue, restoration and resurrection had come to fruition, at least embryonically, through Jesus. This was evident chiefly in Jesus' resurrection–exaltation, the offer of forgiveness and the pouring out of the Spirit – all given as proof that the day of 'salvation' was here. But such blessings were more than advance notice of the end or a foretaste of good things still to come. The narrative of Jesus as Israel's kingdom-bringer,[48] and the good news of Israel's restoration realized in Jesus' resurrection and exaltation,[49] meant that the church now had the task of carrying forward the story of Israel, to be Israel-for-the-sake-of-the-world, to be, just like Jesus himself, 'a light for the Gentiles, so that you may bring salvation to the ends of the earth'.[50] This is, however, not a uniquely Lukan motif. The notion that Jesus came to 'serve' Israel for the sake of making the patriarchal promises a reality was a stable feature in Christian discourse from Paul to Justin.[51] The early church, in other words, saw itself as living out the hopes of what would happen when Israel's new exodus began to take root among the Jews and Gentiles of the eastern Mediterranean. What they believed and how they behaved is indicative of a conviction that God's kingdom had embryonically arrived in the person of Jesus.

Jesus, Israel and the kingdom

So there we are! Jesus' proclamation of the kingdom cannot be abstracted into the heavenly realm; nor can it be squeezed into a message of personal salvation condensed down to something like a pre-Easter version of 'justification by faith'. More properly, Jesus' message of the kingdom was implicitly claiming that the story of God's creational purposes for the

---

48 Acts 8:12; 28:23, 31.
49 Acts 13:32–33.
50 Isa. 49:6; Acts 13:47; 26:23; cf. *Barn.* 14.7–8; Justin, *Dial.* 121–122.
51 Cf. Gal. 3:13–14; Rom. 15:7–13; Justin, *Dial.* 134.4.

world and his specific covenantal purposes for Israel was *now* coming to a head *and would soon be* fully implemented. Of course, that raises the question as to what kind of person claims to be doing such a thing. Who announces that the kingdom is at hand and hints that he has a place of particular authority in that very kingdom? In other words, what is the Christology of Jesus?

5
Who was Jesus?

Jesus according to Jesus

If Jesus proclaimed that the kingdom was here and yet near, if he had a distinctive charisma and authority, and if he believed that Israel's regathering was already under way, then an inevitable question arises: who was he? Or, more precisely, who did people think he was?[1] When they saw Jesus praying for healing, declaring judgment, arguing with the scribes or telling parables, what type of figure did people think they were encountering? One of the problems with studying Jesus is not so much that he defies categories as that he simultaneously inhabits so many categories for a religious leader in antiquity. Among the types of religious leaders that you might find in first-century Galilee and Judea – and by no means exhaustively – are the categories of prophet, philosopher, seer, sage, healer, rabbi, exorcist, miracle-worker, mystic and priest.[2] It is these roles that either Jesus deliberately acted out or others identified him as matching. We get a whisper of the type of rumours and speculations centred on him: he was a prophet from Nazareth,[3] an Elijah-like prophet, John the Baptist *redivivus*,[4] a Moses-like prophet,[5] a Galilean

---

1 Cf. Theissen 1987: 138–139; Witherington 1990: 267–268; Levine 2006a: 12–14.
2 Hengel (1981 [1968]: 66, 69) comments: 'Whether we describe Jesus as a "rabbi" or as a wisdom teacher and prophet we shall equally fail to do justice to this unheard of self-confidence which cuts across all the analogies in the field of *Religionsgeschichte* which are known to us from contemporary Judaism . . . he remains in the last resort incommensurable, and so basically confounds every attempt to fit him into the categories suggested by the phenomenology or sociology of religion.' For Hengel, though, Jesus was best described as an 'eschatological charismatic' with a particular 'messianic' type of authority.
3 Matt. 21:11; Luke 24:19.
4 Mark 6:14–16; 8:27.
5 John 6:14.

Hasid,[6] a potential king,[7] an eschatological agent or a holy man of some variety.[8] The many categories are by no means mutually exclusive, even though historians habitually tend to stress one category over others.[9] But before considering who Jesus believed he was, we must consider who others thought he was and what categories they might have used to understand his message and mission. A survey of these leadership categories will enable us to better understand Jesus' role as the agent of the kingdom of God for a restored Israel.[10]

Jesus as prophet

Jesus emerged in Galilee around AD 27/28 and gave the impression to observers that he was carrying the prophetic mantle of the prophet Elijah[11] and was like one of the many 'sign prophets' of the first century who formed movements of national renewal, often invoking scriptural themes of exodus and conquest, and claiming to offer portents of Israel's deliverance.[12] Whereas the NT epistles, in their diverse array of Christologies, never recall Jesus as a prophet, the prophetic category turns out to be the primary description for him in the Gospels. Jesus is regarded as a prophet like Elijah, Jeremiah and John the Baptist.[13] In Matthean tradition, Jesus is heralded during his entry into Jerusalem as 'the prophet Jesus from Nazareth in Galilee',[14] and the chief priests were fearful of moving against him because the people 'regarded him as a prophet'.[15] Jesus' miracles elicited explicit acclamations: 'A great

---

6 Vermes 2003: 10.

7 Mark 14:61; John 6:15.

8 Cf. McKnight and Modica 2008; Hurtado and Keith 2011.

9 Keener (2009: 187) is right: 'It is unlikely that Galilean Jews who saw themselves as faithful to God's law would have made a hard-and-fast distinction among categories like charismatic sage, teacher of wisdom and teacher of Scripture.'

10 I have reserved the discussion for Jesus as 'Messiah' for later since it intersects with wider themes related to Jesus' self-understanding, his opposition to the temple, his role in the kingdom and his decision to embrace the cross.

11 Mark 6:15; 8:28.

12 Hence the demand for a 'sign' in Mark 8:11–12; John 2:18; 6:30. For a good exposition of the Judean sign prophets, see Eve 2002: 296–325.

13 Mark 6:14–16/Matt. 14:1–2/Luke 9:7–9; Mark 8:28/Matt. 16:14/Luke 9:19.

14 Matt. 21:11.

15 Matt. 21:46.

prophet has arisen among us!'[16] and in another episode the Pharisees were scandalized that Jesus, a so-called prophet, did not know that he was allowing a licentious woman to invade his personal space.[17] The Pharisees, according to John, rejected Jesus since 'no prophet is to arise from Galilee'; they evidently had not heard of Jonah and Nahum, who were both from northern Israel.[18]

In another sense, it is precisely Jesus' prophetic vocation that destines him for his passion. Jesus engaged in a prophetic protest against the priestly leadership, pronounced judgment against the temple, and brought against the Pharisees a mixture of challenge and contest over who spoke for God, yielding a coalition of deadly designs against him. Episodes of verbal and physical rejection drew Jesus' proverbial utterance: 'Prophets are not without honour, except in their home town and among their own kin and in their own house.'[19] Jesus declared, in response to news of Herod Antipas's pursuit of him, that 'it is impossible for a prophet to be killed outside of Jerusalem'.[20] Jesus lamented that Jerusalem kills the prophets and stones those who are sent to it;[21] a sentiment rehearsed in the parable of the tenants[22] and in the logion about the killing of the prophets even at the Jerusalem altar.[23] At his trial, Jesus was accused of being a false prophet who was leading the nation astray,[24] and was cruelly mocked and tormented as a prophet.[25] Jesus knew, like other prophets before him, that he was playing with fire and that people were already preparing to kill him: a fate that it turns out would be the fulcrum on which the kingdom actually turned.

In the Jerusalem church, Luke tells us that there was a strong memory of Jesus as 'a prophet mighty in deed and word', no less than 'a man attested to you by God with deeds of power, wonders, and signs that God

---

16 Luke 7:16; cf. John 4:19; 9:17.
17 Luke 7:37–39.
18 John 7:52; cf. 2 Kgs 14:25; Nah. 1:1.
19 Mark 6:4; cf. Luke 4:24; John 4:44; *Gos. Thom.* 31.
20 Luke 13:33.
21 Matt. 23:37/Luke 13:34.
22 Mark 12:1–12.
23 Luke 11:49–51.
24 Mark 14:55–59; cf. John 11:47–48; *b. Sanh.* 43a.
25 Mark 14:65.

did through him among you', and even as the eschatological prophet-like-Moses (forecast in Deut. 18:15) according to Peter's and Stephen's speeches.[26] The memory of Jesus as a prophet, as *the* prophet, is firm and reliable.

We do well, then, to imagine the prophet Jesus travelling itinerantly from village to village, partly to get his message out, but partly to stay ahead of any security agents on his trail. In his prophetic utterances, he gives an invitation to enter God's kingdom and likewise utters oracles of judgment if this invitation is refused. The result is something of a cross between a political campaign speech and a warning that a wildfire is coming down the hill. Jesus combines moral instruction with exorcisms and healings, with cryptic stories of God's kingship, with open table fellowship and with words of woe. He discourses about love and laments the nation's blindness. Jesus deliberately invokes the memory of prophets ancient and recent. Like Micaiah ben Imlach, he grieves over Israel as a nation of scattered sheep without a shepherd.[27] Like Elijah, he performs mighty deeds as he speaks truth to power. Like Amos, he announces a judgment that will not only crush the nations but also land on Jerusalem. Like Isaiah, he looks ahead to God's kingship being revealed and announces to the Jewish people that God is truly becoming king in their midst. Like Ezekiel, he predicts that the temple will be abandoned but a new one will be made. Like Jeremiah, he runs the risk of being called a traitor to the national cause because he dares to challenge its official and unofficial leaders, even while he claims to speak for God. Like Zechariah and Daniel, he explains in symbols and stories Israel's coming tribulation, reconstitution and vindication. Like John the Baptist, he calls faithless people back to covenant fidelity in the light of God's judgment.[28]

Jesus as seer

Jesus was a seer in the sense that – like certain other Jews – he was a recipient of visions about the supernatural realities operating behind

---

26 Luke 24:19; Acts 2:22; 3:23; 7:37; cf. 1QS 9.9–11; 4Q17.
27 Mark 6:34/Matt. 9:36.
28 In this paragraph, I'm highly indebted to Wright 1996: 164–168.

earthly affairs and also of cryptic forecasts about the future. Israel's sacred traditions were filled with accounts of dreams, visions and hopes – each given its own literary arrangement – about what was truly happening and how heavenly realities impinged on the present; accounts telling of divine promises, bringing portents of judgment, sometimes including stories of otherworldly journeys led by an angelic guide, often enigmatic and metaphoric, and expressing hope for the righteous to be redeemed.[29]

For example, there is Jacob's dream of a ladder between heaven and earth with angels ascending and descending upon it;[30] Isaiah's vision of the Lord in his temple and his own commission to prophesy to the people;[31] Ezekiel's visions of four living creatures and the throne chariot.[32] The book of Zechariah records eight visions that anticipate Israel's restoration.[33] In the book of Daniel, there are dreams interpreted to be about God's kingdom in relation to the Babylonian Empire,[34] and multiple visions pertaining largely to the rise of the Persian and Macedonian empires, the persecution of the saints by the Seleucids and Israel's subsequent salvation.[35] Daniel was much celebrated as a prophet of God's providence over imperial history,[36] and his visions were rehearsed in the composite Enochic texts, in book 3 of the *Sibylline Oracles* and in apocalyptic works such as *4 Ezra*.[37] Similarly, Ezekiel's throne vision was to prove very influential on the burgeoning tradition of *Merkabah* mysticism as reflected in Qumran's angelic liturgies,[38] later in the post-AD 70 era in the apocalypse *2 Enoch*, and in the *Hekhalot* literature about rabbis ascending to the heavenly throne room. Visions were common to Jewish religious experience and expression in the first century. Josephus describes Simon the Essene interpreting a vision

---

29 Cf. Witherington 1999.
30 Gen. 28:11–12.
31 Isa. 6.
32 Ezek. 1.
33 Zech. 1 – 6.
34 Dan. 2; 4.
35 Dan. 7 – 12.
36 Josephus, *Ant.* 10.267–280.
37 See Allison 2010a: 76–77.
38 4Q405.

that had appeared in Archelaus's dream just before Archelaus was deposed by Emperor Tiberius.[39] Even among the members of the early church, visionary experiences were prevalent, as evidenced by Ananias of Antioch's vision of Jesus;[40] Peter's vision of a white sheet filled with unclean animals;[41] the apostle Paul's own account of his vision of a seventh heaven,[42] his multiple visions of Jesus,[43] and his dream of a Macedonian man calling him;[44] and of course the experiences of John of Patmos, who received the *revelation* of Jesus Christ.[45]

There are several indications that Jesus experienced visions and revelations, and saw apparitions.[46] First, Jesus' baptism is reported to have included what sounds very much like a vision, with a portent of the heavens being torn open, the Spirit descending upon him like a dove, and a voice calling him 'my Son, the Beloved'.[47] Second, we read how the Spirit then drove Jesus into the wilderness where he fasted for forty days and was tempted by Satan,[48] an account which is expanded by Luke and Matthew in a way that is suggestive of a visionary experience concerning Jesus' resistance of satanic temptation.[49] The combination of asceticism,[50] Spirit-ecstasy, temptation, and visual and audible experiences provides the ingredients of a visionary phenomenon. Third, in a Lukan logion, Jesus responds to the missionary successes of his disciples in their exorcisms with the words, 'I watched Satan fall from heaven like a flash of lightning' (Luke 10:18). Such a statement may represent not only confidence

---

[39] Josephus, *Ant.* 17.345–347.
[40] Acts 9:10–11.
[41] Acts 10:9–16.
[42] 2 Cor. 12:1–7.
[43] Acts 18:9–10; 26:12–23.
[44] Acts 16:9–10.
[45] Rev. 1:1–2.
[46] The question of whether these were subjective or objective revelatory experiences is moot; they could have been either, and we have little way of knowing most of the time. Even if they were subjective, that does not lessen their reality; they were very real for Jesus and shaped his ministry.
[47] Mark 1:10–11.
[48] Mark 1:12–13.
[49] Matt. 4:11/Luke 4:1–13.
[50] Fasting and acts of self-denial are often the precondition for visionary experiences; see Dan. 9:3; 10:203; *4 Ezra* 5.13, 20; *2 Bar.* 9.2.

in victory over Satan through the exorcisms of his disciples, but also something of Jesus' own unique visionary experience in seeing the primordial expelling of Satan from the heavens,[51] which is replicated in his exorcisms as a plundering of the satanic realm.[52] Fourth, there is the so-called 'Johannine Thunderbolt', which appears in different contexts in Luke (as a post-missionary discourse) and Matthew (as woes declared on Galilean towns), and depicts Jesus thanking God for the divinely given revelation that has been hidden from the wise, the unique Father–Son relationship and the blessedness of the disciples to witness this moment.[53] Fifth, the transfiguration – once thought to be a misplaced resurrection story – might well be a type of group vision among Jesus and his disciples of a visitation by renowned figures of Israel's sacred history.[54] Sixth, while it is disputed, one could argue that the Olivet discourse is not only a prophetic oracle of judgment on the temple, but is also partly based on a vision of coming tribulation and trauma, of a symbolic world dying by literal warfare, looking ahead to the church's preaching and its persecution, married to images of Jesus' vindication as the prophet who stood against the temple.[55]

Jesus thus appears as a seer – a recipient and relator of revelatory experiences, a dispenser of unveiled knowledge from heaven – who fits perfectly within the religious culture of both ancient Judaism and the nascent church. Like others before him, Jesus combined prophetic activities with the symbolic universe of apocalypticism and its seers.[56]

Jesus as sage

The category of sage is pertinent for describing Jesus because of his resourcing of Israel's sacred sapiential traditions and his use of aphorisms or pithy sayings. Witherington observes:

---

51 Cf. Rev. 12:9.
52 Mark 3:27.
53 Matt. 11:25–27/Luke 10:21–24.
54 Mark 9:2–8. Cf. Allison (2009: 72–78), who warns about prematurely dismissing the transfiguration as 'myth'.
55 Mark 13; Matt. 24 – 25; Luke 21.
56 Cf. Theissen and Merz 1998 [1996]: 248–249; Witherington 1999: 194.

> Those who collected, edited, and passed on the Jesus tradition ... seem to have gone out of their way to emphasize the Wisdom element in Jesus' teaching, for no other literary type receives anywhere near the representation of the teaching material in the Synoptics. By even a conservative estimate, at least 70% of the Jesus tradition is in the form of some sort of Wisdom utterance such as an aphorism, riddle, or parable.[57]

Jesus was undoubtedly remembered as a teacher of proverbial wisdom.[58]

Jesus delivered beatitudes[59] which drew on the Psalter[60] and apocalyptic writings.[61] His preferred mode of communication included short, provocative and often witty aphorisms; for example, memorable sayings about asking and receiving,[62] the pipe-dance/dirge-cry comparison,[63] observations of the first being last and the last being first,[64] or the image of a camel going through the eye of a needle.[65] Jesus could also regard himself as a type of 'wisdom' to be vindicated by his actions.[66] The famous statement 'Come to me, all you who are weary and are carrying heavy burdens, and I will give you rest'[67] rehearses a similar invitation issued by Lady Wisdom herself in some writings.[68] Or else Jesus can compare himself to other sages, seeing himself as like, or even greater than, Solomon, the paradigm and paragon of the wise king.[69] According to the Similitudes of *1 Enoch*, the 'Elect One/Son of Man' is indwelt by the 'spirit of wisdom'[70] and himself reveals 'secrets of wisdom'.[71] Let us not

---

57 Witherington 1994: 155–156.
58 See Winton 1990: 22–25.
59 Matt. 6:3–11/Luke 6:20–22; Matt. 13:16/Luke 10:23; Matt. 16:17; Luke 11:28; 12:37–38.
60 Pss 1:1; 84:4–5.
61 *1 Enoch* 58.1–2; *2 Enoch* 42.6–14.
62 Mark 11:24; Matt. 21:22; John 16:24.
63 Matt. 11:16–17/Luke 7:32.
64 Mark 9:35; 10:31.
65 Mark 10:25.
66 Matt. 11:19/Luke 7:35.
67 Matt. 11:28–30.
68 Prov. 9:3–5; Sir. 24:19–22; 51:23, 26.
69 Matt. 12:42.
70 *1 Enoch* 49.1–4.
71 *1 Enoch* 51.3. See Witherington 1994: 201–202; 1999: 278, 283.

forget either that Josephus in his famous *Testimonium* called Jesus a 'wise man' (*sophos anēr*), a benign statement that is unlikely to be a Christian interpolation.[72] In the late second century, Lucian referred to Christians as worshippers of a 'crucified sophist'.[73]

The notion of Jesus as a sagacious teacher of wisdom utterances was thought to dominate the hypothetical sayings-source, called 'Q', that allegedly underlies the Gospels of Matthew and Luke, while Jesus' sayings were also purportedly collected and given an esoteric interpretation in the *Gospel of Thomas*. For many researchers, this collection of Q and Thomasine sayings was the earliest and most reliable layer of the Jesus tradition. When this theory of the Jesus tradition is combined with a view of Galilee as a thoroughly Hellenistic environment, it is possible to identify Jesus as a type of Cynic philosopher (an approach that was once popular), who adopted a vagabond lifestyle and uttered counter-cultural maxims against the brokers of a hierarchical society. Viewed this way, Jesus was neither an apocalyptic prophet nor a messianic claimant, but rather a popular philosopher engaging in a Cynic-style act of socio-political resistance among the villages of Galilee and Judea.

Cynicism was a philosophical movement beginning with Diogenes of Sinope in the fourth century BC. The Cynics were so named not because they indulged in a dour kind of pessimism, but because they were like dogs (*kynos*) nipping at the heels of the well-to-do and flouting social mores by defaecating, masturbating and fornicating in public. The Cynics were typified by a simple and countercultural lifestyle which emphasized owning minimal possessions, embracing freedom, living according to nature, forming itinerant movements and renouncing social norms.[74]

The similarities between Jesus and Cynic philosophers are not hard to notice;[75] for instance, the prescribed way of dressing and the meagre provisions that Jesus commanded for his disciples in the mission discourse[76] mirror in some respects the Cynic garb and attitude to possessions.[77]

---

72 Josephus, *Ant*. 18.6.
73 Lucian, *Peregr*. 13.
74 See Fiore 2000.
75 Hengel 1981 [1968]: 54; Theissen 1978: 14–15; Crossan 1991: 72–88, 338–341, 421–422; Seeley 1997.
76 Mark 6:8-9; Matt. 10:9-10; Luke 9:3; 10:4; 22:35-36.
77 Diogenes Laertius 6.13.

Likewise, many logia in the Jesus tradition exhibit commonalities with Cynic utterances.[78] Consequently, several scholars argue that Jesus was a hybrid Jewish Cynic, who announced a social critique against religious, economic and patriarchal inequalities and espoused his own radical egalitarianism in the face of Roman power.

There are, however, several devastating criticisms that have been levelled against the 'Cynic Jesus' hypothesis.[79] Quite detrimental to the hypothesis is the fact that Galilee was not the liberally Hellenized and urbanized environment that it was alleged to be, and also we have no evidence of Cynic penetration into Galilee at the time of Jesus.[80] Jonathan Reed wisely comments:

> In this context it should be stressed that, lacking a substantial component of gentile inhabitants, having only two Jewish cities in their infancy of Hellenization, and lacking much evidence for inter-regional trade, notions of Cynic itinerants influencing Jesus or his first followers make little sense. Though the scholarly comparison of Jesus's teaching with that of Cynicism merits attention as an analogy, any genealogical relationship between Jesus and Cynics is highly unlikely.[81]

The promotion of the 'Cynic Jesus' looks like a deliberate attempt to remove Jesus from Jewish, prophetic and apocalyptic traditions which certain liberal interpreters of the historical Jesus themselves find distasteful.

A more pressing issue is the relationship between the wisdom sayings and prophetic discourse in the Jesus tradition. Are these different strands of the Jesus tradition or different layers of the Jesus tradition? Is one component authentic and the other component a later invention

---

78 Cf. e.g. Mark 2:17/P. Oxy. 1224 and Dio Chrysostom, *Orat.* 8.5, about doctors and the sick. Compare too Matt. 8:22/Luke 9:60 with Lucian's *Demonax* 65 about the saying 'Let the dead bury their own dead'.
79 Witherington 1994: 117–145; Wright 1996: 66–74; Rhodes 1996; Aune 1997; Keener 2009: 14–32.
80 See e.g. Chancey 2005: 6–7.
81 Reed 2000: 218.

ascribed to Jesus?[82] It helps if we remember that wisdom, prophecy and apocalyptic discourse were not neatly insulated or siloed away from one another either in the Hebrew Bible or in Second Temple literature. We do better to imagine that Jesus employed something of a blend of sapiential sayings, apocalyptic traditions and prophetic motifs.

Jesus as rabbi

Jesus was addressed by his disciples and others as *rabbi*, which simply means 'teacher'.[83] The title was an honorific form of address for a teacher whom one revered. The title was appropriate for Jesus as one who taught from Scripture, who called and received disciples, and whose words were of lasting memory for his followers. There are many points of contact between the Jesus tradition and the rabbinic tradition when it comes to prayers, parables, preaching, ethics, election and eschatology.[84] A comparison of the *Amidah* prayer and the Lord's Prayer is the prime example, but others abound, such as the virtue of 'giving alms in secret'.[85] Of course, Jesus was not a rabbi in the sense that he called followers to join with him in the study of Torah and was concerned with the creation of a distinctive stream of *halakhah*. Jesus' authority was, at least as far as Matthew was concerned, charismatic and messianic rather than rabbinic.[86]

Jesus as exorcist, healer and miracle-worker

There is no doubt that Jesus was known as an exorcist and miracle-worker, since the Jesus tradition is saturated with miracle stories.[87] The

---

82 Rightly asked by Schmithals (1998 [1994]: 5).
83 Mark 9:5; 10:51; 11:21; 14:45; John 1:38, 49; 3:2; 4:21; 6:25; 9:2; 11:8.
84 See esp. Young 1995; 2007; Chilton 2000.
85 Matt. 6:3–4, compared with *b. Batra* 9b where Rabbi Eliezar declares that the man who gives alms in secret is greater than Moses.
86 Matt. 23:8–10. See Hengel 1981 [1968]: 42–57, contrasted with Young (2007: 29–37) who notes the similarities between Jesus and the rabbis when it came to raising up disciples.
87 Meier (1991–2016: 2:970) doesn't pull his punches: 'Any historian who seeks to portray the historical Jesus without giving due weight to his fame as a miracle-worker is not delineating this strange and complex Jew, but rather a domesticated Jesus reminiscent of the bland moralist created by Thomas Jefferson.' The eminent studies remain Twelftree 1993; 1999.

Lukan Peter treats it as matter of public knowledge that Jesus of Nazareth was 'a man attested to you by God with deeds of power, wonders, and signs that God did through him among you, as you yourselves know',[88] which accords with Josephus's testimony that Jesus was a 'performer of astounding deeds'.[89] Judea and Galilee had their own phenomenon of holy men, hermits, prophets and diviners who claimed that they were a conduit of God's power to dispel demons or to perform powerful deeds. Josephus refers to a Jewish exorcist named Eleazar who expelled demons from people in the presence of the Roman general Vespasian and his officers.[90] The existence of other Jewish exorcists contemporary with Jesus is assumed by Jesus' response to the charge by the Pharisees that he casts out demons by the power of Beelzebul, when he asks: by what power/authority 'do your own exorcists [lit. 'sons'] cast them out?'[91] Luke also introduces us to some itinerant Jewish exorcists in Ephesus, the comical 'seven sons of Sceva', who thought they could cash in on Jesus' name in exorcisms only to have themselves beaten to a pulp by a very bemused demoniac.[92] Josephus also knows the tradition of Honi the Circle-Drawer, who broke a drought with prayer and was stoned to death for refusing to offer imprecatory prayers against Aristobulus II.[93] A hero of the rabbinic tradition was the first-century rabbi and sage Hanina ben Dosa, who was known for his effective prayers for the sick and for ending drought.[94] Although Jesus did not use incantations, amulets, roots or other paraphernalia when it came to exorcisms, as others did, nonetheless he does demand that demons give him their name,[95] he uses his saliva in one instance,[96] and he refers to the necessity of prayer for some exorcisms.[97] In other words, Jesus looks like an ancient exorcist, healer and miracle-worker; yet his supernatural abilities do not derive

---

88 Acts 2:22.
89 Josephus, *Ant.* 18.63.
90 Josephus, *Ant.* 8.46–49.
91 Matt. 12:27/Luke 11:19.
92 Acts 19:13–17.
93 Josephus, *Ant.* 14.22–24; cf. *m. Taan.* 3.8.
94 *m. Abot* 3.9–10; *m. Sot.* 9.15; *m. Ber.* 5.5.
95 Mark 5:9.
96 Mark 8:22–23.
97 Mark 9:29.

from secret techniques but rather draw from 'immediate contact with God'[98] or display him operating as an 'immanent bearer of numinous power'.[99]

Whether one can countenance miraculous events in the career of any historical figure is obviously a matter of considerable debate (as a theist, I'm obviously open to the prospect).[100] What is certain is that Jesus was widely regarded by disciples, crowds and even enemies as a successful exorcist, an effective healer and a powerful miracle-worker.[101] Rabbinic tradition about Jesus and pagan assessment of Jesus alleged that he practised 'sorcery' or 'magic', an allegation which assumes a supernatural power operative in him but transforms it into a mode of religious deviancy.[102] Miracles are maligned as magic when they are performed with apparent malice, are manipulative, and are committed outside the normal circles of recognized authority.[103] Of course, a reputation for miraculous deeds was not unique to Jesus; others too were acclaimed as miracle-working holy men, both in Judaism and in the Greco-Roman world. Where Jesus is 'unique' is in associating his miraculous works with the manifestation of God's kingdom, the sign of the Isaianic new exodus, and the defeat of Satan.[104] Distinctive too is how faith is the condition for miracles, never its consequence. The intersection of Jesus' healing and exorcistic ministry, his kingdom message and his mighty deeds is, declares Udo Schnelle, 'unparalleled in the history of religions'.[105]

To tease that out further, first, Jesus' miracles were not only acts of compassion for those suffering and oppressed, but also powerful symbols of Israel's restoration and liberation from bondage. It might be hard for us to understand, but in a world without antibiotics and antiviral drugs and with poor hygiene, infested with infectious diseases such as malaria,

---

98 Vermes 1973: 69.
99 Eve 2002: 378–379.
100 See Meyer 1979: 99–104; Meier 1991–2016: 2:509–645; Wright 1996: 186–191; Twelftree 1999: 17–53; 2017; Keener 2011; Johnson 2018; Hengel and Schwemer 2019 [2007]: 520–526.
101 Mark 3:22; 6:2–3, 14; 8:11–13; Matt. 11:2–6/Luke 7:18–23; Luke 13:32.
102 *b. Sanh.* 43a; 67b; Origen, *C. Cels.* 1.38.
103 See Reimer 2002: 3–15 for an introduction to the magic-versus-miracle debate, as well as Horsley 2014 for a survey and deconstruction of modern scholarship.
104 See esp. Twelftree 1999: 276.
105 Schnelle 2009 [2007]: 127.

tuberculosis and dysentery, most people died before the age of 30.¹⁰⁶ Illness and death were ubiquitous and inevitable forces that only a divine power could keep at bay; hence the popularity of healing gods such as Asclepius, magic spells for health, and other remedies. Accordingly, Jesus' healings of the blind, mute, crippled and 'unclean' brought relief from suffering and also meant that a divine power inhabited him. In addition, for supplicants with ailments involving skin conditions or impurities such as *lepra*,¹⁰⁷ healing restored them to inclusion in the community. Jesus was not running a mobile health clinic so much as demonstrating that God was present to save and heal, eager to welcome the poor and afflicted. The common result of the healings was an outpouring of praise as people glorified the God of Israel who was operating through Jesus.¹⁰⁸

Second, most important of all is how Jesus associated his mighty deeds with the signs of Israel's restoration as described in Isaiah.¹⁰⁹ Jesus' mighty deeds are billboards declaring that God's reign is coming and has come, God is liberating his people, the exile is ending, the new exodus is happening. In this sense, we can say that Jesus' message and his 'miracles' were part of one and the same programme.¹¹⁰

Third, the exorcisms are proof that God's kingdom is present¹¹¹ and that Jesus is fighting against Israel's true enemy – not Rome, but Satan.¹¹² With regard to Jesus, '[i]t was he', declares Twelftree, 'who associated the notion of the cosmic, supernatural battle against the kingdom of Satan in the eschaton with the very act of an ordinary exorcism'.¹¹³ These weren't just private triumphs; more properly, they were victories in the battle against the Satan.¹¹⁴

---

106 Cf. Luff 2019: 114–144.
107 The medical condition *lepra* is not leprosy, since leprosy (or Hansen's disease) was normally described as *elephantiasis*, not as *lepra*. The disease of *lepra* is probably a scaly skin condition such as psoriasis or one of various fungal infections. See Vermes 1993: 18; 2003: 5; and esp. Thiessen 2020: 43–68.
108 Matt. 15:31; Luke 18:43.
109 Isa. 35:5–6; 26:19; 29:18–19; 58:6; 61:1, alluded to in Luke 4:18–19; Matt. 11:5/Luke 7:22.
110 Cf. Dibelius 1963 [1939]: 81.
111 Matt. 12:29/Luke 11:2.
112 Mark 3:22–27.
113 Twelftree 1993: 227.
114 Wright 1996: 195.

Jesus as God's envoy and embodiment

Is it possible to speak of the Christology of Jesus?[115] The obvious problem here is the church's Christological faith and historical anachronism. The Gospels tell us what Jesus said and did, and what happened to him, but from a post-Easter perspective, as one heralded as Messiah, Lord, the very 'form of God' and the pre-existent Son. Thus, one might suspect that any elevated or exalted status attributed to Jesus, whether on his own lips, in the thanks of supplicants or in the confession of disciples, is an invention projected into the life of Jesus. This is why Walter Schmithals said, 'Whether Jesus himself ascribed to his work or his person a special role in the coming turn of the age remains uncertain.'[116]

And yet Jesus did not gather a following, alarm Herod Antipas, provoke the ire of the Pharisees, offend the Judean priestly authorities and get sentenced to death by a Roman prefect for sermonizing about a heavenly hereafter, offering fleeting thoughts on Torah and speculating how the end times might pan out if God should intervene for Israel. E. P. Sanders is on the money when he observed how Jesus 'displayed an egocentricity which must have struck many of his contemporaries as impious'.[117]

Jesus may have taken seriously the Baptist's identification of him as the 'coming one',[118] leading to his own belief in his Spirit-anointed status and power as a holy healer and exorcist inaugurating the coming age; the personification of wisdom; both a herald of the kingdom and its messianic king; one around whom a reconstituted Israel would gather; one emboldened by an acute sense of divine sonship with a unique filial relationship to Yahweh, enacting the new exodus and embodying the return of Yahweh to Zion; a human agent and a 'divine' actor, a man destined to be victorious and vindicated, enthroned with Yahweh as the

---

115 Cf. Witherington 1990; Allison 2010a: 221–304.
116 Schmithals 1998 [1994]: 12.
117 Sanders 1985: 271. The tendency – still here, alas – to see Jesus as prophet, teacher, sage or shaman fails to reckon with the mixture of eschatology, enthusiasm and egocentricity that Jesus employed, not least in his intimate connection with Israel's God and his place in God's purposes to restore Israel and renovate creation.
118 Mark 1:7; Matt. 11:3/Luke 7:19; John 1:27.

'one like a son of man'.[119] Jesus may even have entertained upscale notions of himself of the same order as those of Mariccus of Gaul, who declared himself a god and liberator of the Gauls during the 'year of the four emperors' in AD 69;[120] or seen himself as carrying claims analogous to the divine prerogatives attributed to the mysterious figure who features in the Self-Exaltation Hymn found in the Qumran scrolls.[121] Accordingly, I wholeheartedly endorse the judgment of Dale Allison: '[A]ll the primary sources repeatedly purport that Jesus had astounding things to say about himself. One can dissociate him from an exalted self-conception only through multiple radical surgeries on our texts' and 'We should hold a funeral for the view that Jesus entertained no exalted thoughts about himself.'[122] Jesus may well have had his own 'high' Christology; the only question is precisely how high![123]

There are, however, three particular titles that we must focus on in an exploration of Jesus' identity and self-understanding: Son, Son of Man, and Messiah. I am very aware that a Christology of titles is both overdone and overblown, and that what is also required is a functional or narrative Christology, or even the comparative task of identifying the primary analogue for Jesus' claims to divine authority and ascertaining what motivated his actions. While any Christology must consist of more than mere titles, it must, however, include the labels given to Jesus and Jesus' own self-designations.

---

119 Cf. Dunn (1989: 253): 'We find one who was conscious of being God's son, a sense of intimate sonship, an implication that Jesus believed or experienced this sonship to be something distinctive and unique; but the evidence does not allow us to penetrate further or to be more explicit. We find one who may well have understood the vision of Dan. 7 to be a description or indication of his own role, as one who represented God's people at the climax of the present age, as the one who would be vindicated beyond his anticipated suffering and death and play the decisive role in the final judgment. We find one who claimed to be inspired by the Spirit of God, to be a prophet in the tradition of the prophets, but more than that, to be the eschatological prophet, the one anointed by God to announce and enact the good news of God's final rule intervention. We find one who may well have claimed to speak as the final envoy of Wisdom, with an immediacy of revelatory authority that transcended anything that had gone before.'
120 Tacitus, *Hist.* 2.61.
121 4Q419c.
122 Allison 2010a: 225, 304; cf. Allison 2009: 65–66, 88.
123 Cf. Bird 2014a; Wright and Bird 2019: 216–241.

Son of God

One of the distinctives of Jesus' ministry was devotion to the God of Israel as a fatherly figure, seen in the 'Our Father' of the Lord's Prayer[124] and his use of 'Abba'[125] as an address for God which carried over into early Christianity. The Matthean tradition accents God as 'your Father in heaven / heavenly Father',[126] while the Johannine tradition accents the unique Father–Son relationship that Jesus had with God and that believers were grafted into.[127] The corollary is that Jesus understood himself as God's 'son' and his followers too as 'sons' of God.[128] It remains to be seen whether Jesus' own sense of sonship had a particularity, whether ontological, filial or messianic. The notion of God as 'Father' was common in antiquity and not unprecedented in the Jewish tradition. A corollary is that all humans were divine offspring.[129] However, the Hebrews and Israelites were God's chosen 'son',[130] and the righteous had a particular claim to divine sonship in sapiential and apocalyptic Jewish traditions,[131] so that Jesus of Nazareth was perhaps no more a son of God than the first-century charismatic rabbis Honi the Circle-Drawer and Hanina ben Dosa, who saw themselves, too, as sons of Israel's God.[132] A democratized divine sonship attributed to Jesus stands far away, in both history and tradition, from the Johannine Jesus who claims to be sent from and sanctified by the Father and states point blank: 'I am God's Son.'[133] Yet the claim and function of sonship as it appears in the

---

124 Matt. 6:9/Luke 11:2.

125 Mark 14:36; Rom. 8:15; Gal. 4:6.

126 See Matt. 5:16, 45, 48; 6:1–32; 7:11; 10:20, 29; 11:26; 18:14, 35; 23:9.

127 Cf. the following: only the Son who is close to him has made the Father known and knows the Father (John 1:14, 18; 8:38; 10:15; 12:50; 14:6–8); the Father delegates roles and responsibilities to the Son (John 3:35; 5:17–19, 20–23, 36–37); Jesus refers to God as 'my Father' (John 2:16; 5:17, 43; 6:32, 40; 8:19, 49, 54; 10:18, 25, 36–38; 13:3; 14:2, 7, 20–23; 15:1, 10, 15, 23–24; 16:15); Jesus is sent by the Father (John 5:23, 36–37; 6:44, 57; 8:16, 18, 42; 10:36; 12:49; 14:24; 17:21, 25; 20:21); Jesus' Father is 'your Father' (John 20:17).

128 Cf. esp. Matt. 5:45/Luke 6:35 which links loving behaviour to becoming children/sons of your Father in heaven, reminiscent of Sir. 4:10: 'Be a father to orphans, and be like a husband to their mother; you will then be like a son of the Most High'.

129 Cf. Acts 17:28–29 where Paul quotes the pagan poet Aratus (c. 310–245 BC), who stated that 'we are his [Zeus's] offspring'.

130 Cf. e.g. Exod. 4:22; Hos. 11:1; Jer. 31:9.

131 Wis. 2:13, 16, 18; 5.5; Sir. 4:10; 51.10; cf. the 'sons of light' in Qumran.

132 Cf. Vermes 1973: 206–207.

133 John 10:36.

Jesus tradition rises far above the use of the term 'son' to mean human creatureliness, or to describe a participant in Israel's election, or even to refer to one of the 'sons of light' in an eschatologically chastened Israel.

To be clear, any discussion of divine sonship as meaning ontological sameness with the Father, leaving aside the fourth-century Arian controversy and its Christological nomenclature, is all good; it is part of the reception history of Jesus' divine sonship. But it belongs in an adjacent seminar room in our department of divinity. Here I think we can establish that Jesus' sense of sonship conveyed an acute sense of divine favour and filial belonging, and speaks as well to his messianic intentions.

The accounts of Jesus' baptism, temptation and transfiguration[134] are arguably the final literary form of traditions, reports and memories about Jesus' own visionary and veridical experiences that inspired him in his prophetic vocation and imparted to him a belief in his bespoke place in God's purposes for Israel's restoration.[135] Such visions, if that is what they were, place Jesus squarely at the cross-section of mysticism and messianism, since he appears to have emerged from these experiences with resolute convictions that he was God's chosen or beloved Son, endowed with a particular charisma and task, such that it was necessary to go beyond the modus operandi of John the Baptist: the coming age needed less preparation and more inauguration, and Jesus' own pivotal role in the advent of God's kingdom would even see Satan defeated and all things restored.[136]

Jesus' sonship buttressed his claims to revelation and authority as a divine emissary, as seen in the 'Johannine Thunderbolt' (see Table 5.1), a saying that sounds like a bolt of Johannine Christology out of the blue and occurs in the double tradition (i.e. material common to Matthew and Luke and not found in Mark). This saying is remarkably reminiscent of Johannine tradition,[137] and has Jesus convey that the

---

134 Baptism (Mark 1:9–11/Matt. 3:13–17/Luke 3:21–22); temptation (Mark 1:12–13/Matt. 4:1–11/Luke 4:1–13); transfiguration (Mark 9:2–8/Matt. 17:1–8/Luke 9:28–36).

135 Cf. Jeremias (1971: 56) on Jesus' authority going back to the call/experience he had when baptized by John.

136 Luke 10:18; Mark 9:12; Matt. 19:28.

137 'The Father loves the Son and shows him all that he himself is doing, and he will show him greater works than these, so that you will be astonished' (John 5:20); 'I declare what I have seen in the Father's presence' (John 8:38); 'Father, I thank you for having heard me. I knew that you always hear me, but I have said this for the sake of the crowd standing here, so

Table 5.1 The so-called 'Johannine Thunderbolt'

Matt. 11:25–27	Luke 10:21–22
At that time Jesus said, 'I thank you, Father, Lord of heaven and earth, because you have hidden these things from the wise and the intelligent and have revealed them to infants; yes, Father, for such was your gracious will. All things have been handed over to me by my Father, and no one knows the Son except the Father, and no one knows the Father except the Son and anyone to whom the Son chooses to reveal him.'	At that very hour Jesus rejoiced in the Holy Spirit and said, 'I thank you, Father, Lord of heaven and earth, because you have hidden these things from the wise and the intelligent and have revealed them to infants; yes, Father, for such was your gracious will. All things have been handed over to me by my Father, and no one knows who the Son is except the Father or who the Father is except the Son and anyone to whom the Son chooses to reveal him.'

Father's plans were hidden from the wise and intelligent (i.e. official leaders or established religious authorities) and revealed to mere infants (i.e. Jesus and his disciples). Further, Jesus has been granted exceptional and exclusive knowledge of the Father, knowledge of which the disciples too are made recipients by receiving teachings from the Son. Such a statement far exceeds the claims made by other Judean teachers such as Ben Sirach or even the Teacher of Righteousness at Qumran. Yet, elsewhere, there is also an awareness that the full extent of that mystery is still veiled, as some things are known by 'neither the angels in heaven, nor the Son, but only [by] the Father'.[138] Jesus may be the chief custodian

---

that they may believe that you sent me' (John 11:41–42); 'I have called you friends, because I have made known to you everything that I have heard from my Father' (John 15:15). Casey (2010: 389–390) believes that the similarity between the 'thunderbolt' and Johannine tradition proves that it is inauthentic, whereas I would infer that the 'thunderbolt' shows that Johannine Christology has resonances with the earliest stratum of the Jesus tradition. Or, as Manson (1935: 110) put it: 'If we can give a reasonable interpretation of this particular saying, and one that fits in with what we otherwise know from our records, there is no point in discarding it merely because the epithet "Johannine" may be thrown at it.'

138 Mark 13:32/Matt. 24:36.

of the 'mystery of the kingdom',[139] something seemingly imperceptible to others,[140] but there are limits on how far even his knowledge of such mysteries penetrates. Such a shocking statement of revelational humility is unlikely to spring from the Christological devotion of the early church. In which case, Jesus' sonship stands within the mystical tradition of knowledge in symbol and story, and the apocalyptic tradition of things veiled and partly unveiled.

In the parable of the tenants, Jesus refers to himself as the Father's 'beloved son',[141] standing in a line of earlier prophets, but also as the Father's 'heir',[142] making him something closer to God's 'final envoy'.[143] Jesus as divine son is more than a prophetic recipient of mysteries; he is a divine plenipotentiary, the divine agent par excellence, one who edges towards messianic categories.[144] Israel's Davidic king was also called God's son (e.g. Ps. 2:7), and so too was the Messiah.[145] Jesus accepted acclamations of Davidic sonship,[146] and made tantalizing remarks about the Messiah and David's son which implicated himself as something of a Son of David premium-plus.[147] A point which explains why Caiaphas asked Jesus, in accusation as much as in interrogation, whether he was 'the Messiah, the Son of the Blessed One', to which Jesus answered obliquely but affirmatively with a messianic midrash of Daniel 7:13 and Psalm 110:1 referring to the Son of Man co-enthroned with Yahweh.[148]

In effect, Jesus spoke of himself as God's 'son' in the sense of being the object of divine favour and election, the recipient of revealed mysteries, and a divine agent without peer, but also the one commissioned as Israel's messianic deliverer. This lay at the root of a sonship tradition which was

---

139 Mark 4:11/Matt. 13:11/Luke 8:10 (MFB trans.); cf. *Gos. Thom.* 62.
140 *Gos. Thom.* 113.
141 Mark 12:6/Luke 20:13, while Matt. 21:37 and *Gos. Thom.* 65 have 'my son'.
142 Mark 12:7.
143 To use the language of de Jonge 1998.
144 Dunn (2003: 722) warns about reading 'too much christological weight into Jesus's possible use of the [son] motif' but acknowledges that a sense of 'eschatological climax is evident'.
145 2 Sam. 7:14; 1 Chr. 17:13; 22:10; Pss 2:7; 89:26–27; *Pss Sol.* 17.21; *1 Enoch* 105.2; 1QSa 2.11–12; 4Q174 1.10–12; *4 Ezra* 7.28–29; 13.32, 37, 52.
146 Mark 10:47–48.
147 Mark 12:35–37.
148 Mark 14:61–62.

then expanded and elaborated in the Johannine materials according to that community's own unique memory and traditions of Jesus.

Son of man

There are a lot of intractable debates in historical Jesus scholarship, but among the most difficult and technical are those pertaining to Son of Man traditions in the Gospels.[149]

Materially speaking, the label 'Son of Man' (Gk *ho huios tou anthrōpou* [lit. 'the son of the man']) appears in the Gospels as Jesus' preferred form of self-reference. The Son of Man designation appears 69 times in the Synoptic Gospels and 13 times in the Fourth Gospel. It is found only four other times outside the canonical Gospels in the NT and never in Paul's epistles.[150] It occurs twice in the *Gospel of Thomas*, once for Jesus as a wandering vagabond, and later as a designation for insiders who have attained oneness and true faith.[151] Usage in the Synoptic Gospels is generally stratified into three categories:[152] an authoritative figure,[153] a suffering figure[154] and a future exalted eschatological figure.[155] In John's Gospel, the Son of Man is a pre-existent heavenly figure who is the nexus

---

149 A small minority of scholars insist that the Son of Man sayings in total or the vast majority are not authentic; see e.g. Borg 1998 [1984]: 221–227; Crossan 1991: 238–255. I prefer the measured statement of de Jonge (1998: 88–89): 'We cannot vouch for the authenticity of each individual saying about the Son of Man, even in Mark and Q. But the fact that this unusual Greek expression is used – and is used exclusively in words of Jesus, whereas early Christians did not employ it in their own preaching (except when words of Jesus were concerned) – makes it likely that "Son of Man" belongs to the oldest layers of tradition, if not to Jesus' own vocabulary.' Cf. too Theissen and Merz 1998 [1996]: 548; Dunn 2003: 737–739. Dalman (1902 [1898]: 252) said: '[A]lthough the Gospels have proclaimed Jesus to the Church as "the Son of man" for 1800 years, yet the name has never to this day become a common title of Christ, and in books and sermons the "Son of man" is not usually spoken of save when the words of Jesus Himself are the cause.' Against Cahill (2002), who cannot imagine anybody referring to themselves in the third person.

150 Acts 7:56; Heb. 2:6 (from Ps. 8:4 LXX); Rev. 1:13; 14:14.

151 *Gos. Thom.* 86 (= Matt. 8:20/Luke 9:58); 106; and 'son of the living one' (37).

152 Bultmann 1952–55: 1:30.

153 Cf. e.g. 'the Son of Man has authority ... to forgive sins' (Mark 2:10); 'so the Son of Man is lord even of the Sabbath' (Mark 2:28). Also, Mark 9:12, 31; 10:33, 45; 14:21.

154 Cf. e.g. 'Then he began to teach them that the Son of Man must undergo great suffering and be rejected by the elders, the chief priests, and the scribes and be killed and after three days rise again' (Mark 8:31).

155 Cf. 'Those who are ashamed of me and of my words in this adulterous and sinful generation, of them the Son of Man will also be ashamed when he comes in the glory of his Father with the holy angels' (Mark 8:38); 'Then they will see "the Son of Man coming in clouds" with great power and glory' (Mark 13:26); 'I am, and "you will see the Son of Man seated at the right hand of the Power" and "coming with the clouds of heaven"' (Mark 14:62).

between heaven and earth;[156] a suffering figure to be crucified ('lifted up');[157] a man with divine authority to judge and to raise up;[158] and a man destined to be exalted.[159]

The Son of Man designation appears to have three strands of influence: in scriptural traditions, in the Aramaic language and in Jewish messianism.

First, in the Hebrew Scriptures, *ben adam* (lit. 'son of Adam') was a way of referring to human beings / humanity as a general category.

The psalmist lauds human beings as God's earthly representatives appointed to have dominion over creation: 'What are humans [Heb. *enosh*] that you are mindful of them, what are humans [Heb. *ben adam*] that you care for them?'[160] In Ezekiel, *ben adam* is repeatedly used for God's address to Ezekiel, and it seems to mean something like 'mere mortal man'.[161] Similarly, in Qumran's *Community Rule*, the term *ben adam* denotes human frailty as a clay vessel contrasted with divine glory: 'What, indeed, is the son of man, among all your marvellous deeds?'[162] Such humanizing connotations correspond nicely with Jesus' usage in healing a paralytic man and forgiving his sins: '"But so that you may know that the Son of Man has authority on earth to forgive sins" – he then said to the paralytic – "Stand up, take your bed, and go to your home." And he stood up and went to his home',[163] at which point Matthew immediately reports how the crowds were filled with awe and 'glorified God, *who had given such authority to human beings*'.[164] Elsewhere, in the saying that 'the Son of Man is lord of the Sabbath',[165] Jesus was remembered for affirming the dominion that God gave to humanity over creation, specifically authority over its cultivation and rest.[166] Such sayings about the Son of

---

156 John 1:51; 3:13.
157 John 3:14; 8:28; 13:31.
158 John 5:27; 6:27.
159 John 12:23; 13:31.
160 Ps. 8:4 (MFB trans.). Cf. CSB: 'what is a human being that you remember him, a son of man that you look after him?'
161 Cf. e.g. Ezek. 2:1–3. Similar to *1 Enoch* 60.10.
162 1QS 11.20.
163 Matt. 9:6–7/Mark 2:10–11/Luke 5:24.
164 Matt. 9:8 (emphasis added).
165 Matt. 12:8/Mark 2:27–28/Luke 6:5.
166 Cf. Dalman (1902 [1898]: 255): '[I]n the reasoning of Mark, what applies to mankind in general, applies pre-eminently to the "Son of man."' And 'Jesus called Himself אנשא בר [*bar enasha*] not indeed as the "lowly one," but as that member of the human race (*Menschenkind*),

Man's authority imply a connection with the dominion given to human beings in Jewish tradition.[167] Ignatius of Antioch called Jesus 'Son of Man' to accent his humanity over against his divinity as 'Son of God'.[168] Such 'humanizing' connotations are why several Bible translations render the strange expression as either 'Son of Adam' (Scholar's Version) or 'the Human One' (CEB).

It could be said that Jesus, as a/the Son of Man, was recovering the Adamic vocation given to human beings to exercise authority over the earth, but even more so in his own role as an anointed prophet and messianic leader of Israel.

Second, behind the Greek phrase *ho huios tou anthrōpou* was probably the Aramaic expression *bar enash* ('son of man') or *bar enasha* ('the son of man') which some scholars propose was an idiom of some kind. However, contested and technical debates revolve around what the idiom meant in the Middle Aramaic of the first century AD and how it is relevant to the varied Son of Man traditions in the Gospels. Experts in Semitic languages dispute which usages were found in eastern and western dialects of Aramaic, analyse differences between emphatic and absolute states of nouns, question whether Mishnaic and Talmudic Aramaic have first-century roots, and compare Qumran Aramaic with retroversions of the Greek of the Gospels into reconstructed Aramaic, making it all rather complex.

The Aramaic *bar enash(a)* and variations is alleged to have a generic sense of 'a man' similar to the Hebrew *ben adam*.[169] The phrase could also function as an indefinite pronoun meaning 'one' or 'someone'.[170] Or else, in direct speech, *bar enash(a)* might be an oblique form of self-reference

---

in his own nature impotent, whom God will make Lord of the world' (265), i.e. as an allusion to Ps. 8:5–6.

167 Cf. Gen. 1:26–28; Ps. 8:4–6.
168 Ignatius, *Eph.* 20.2.
169 An example provided by Casey (2007: 62) is Bardaisan, *The Book of the Laws of the Countries*, lines 11–14 (late second or early third century AD): 'This is the nature of the son of man [*bar enash*], that he should be born and grow up and reach his peak and reproduce and grow old, while eating and drinking and sleeping and waking, and that he should die.'
170 A good example here is 1QapGen 21.13: 'I will multiply your descendants like the dust of the earth which no-one [*bar enash*] can count. In the same way, your descendants will be innumerable.'

amounting to 'yours truly', '*moi*' or 'oneself'.[171] We must investigate which function of the Aramaic idiom – generic, indefinite or self-referential – we should prefer!

To begin with, as we saw above, 'Son of Man' can parallel 'human beings' or 'humanity' when it comes to the Son of Man's authority to forgive sins as a power joyously befitting humans.[172] Similarly, just as the sabbath was made for human beings, so it is that one human being, the Son of Man, is lord of the sabbath.[173] That is not to yield to the argument of Casey that *bar enash(a)* did not distinguish the emphatic and absolute states nor that its meaning was normally 'man' in a generic sense.[174] We admit only that such usage in two instances in the Gospels plays on the similarity of 'man' and 'son of man'. This last saying about the Son of Man as lord of the sabbath illustrates, against Casey, how the idiom functioned with an obvious particularity, as it was *this* son of man who was lord of the sabbath.[175]

Furthermore, *bar enasha* must have had a self-referential function too, such as when Jesus said, 'Foxes have holes, and birds of the air have nests, but the Son of Man has nowhere to lay his head',[176] where 'Son of Man' stands in for the speaker, perhaps for those with him too, and functions as 'I' or 'us'. While Vermes was anachronistic to claim

---

171 Canvassed by Dalman (1902 [1898]: 249–250). This was argued principally by Vermes (1973: 163–168; 2004: 234–235, 262–263).
172 Mark 2:10/Matt. 9:6/Luke 5:24.
173 Mark 2:27–28/Matt. 12:8/Luke 6:5.
174 Cf. Casey 2007; 2010: 358–391. For Casey's argument to work, one must assume that Aramaic was amazingly stable as a language from 750 BC to AD 1200, and that in Middle Aramaic the emphatic and absolute states of *bar (e)nash(a)* coalesced, both of which points are highly disputed (Lukaszewski 2011: 10–12; cf. Owen 2011; Shepherd 2011; Williams 2011). Middle Aramaic had several ways of making generic statements about 'man' or 'human beings', but none of them use *bar enasha* (Owen and Shepherd 2001; Owen 2011: 33, 38–39). As Dalman (1902 [1898]: 256) said long ago: 'This term . . . did not properly belong to the common language of the Palestinian Jews as a term for "man"; it was characteristic rather of the elevated diction of poetry and prophecy' – a proposition defended by Owen and Shepherd (2001).
175 An important point made by Williams (2011: 75–76) is that Jesus' usage of *bar enasha* may have been ambiguous and his hearers may not have always understood whether the reference was emphatic (the man) or absolute (a man). That said, 'if Jesus, or anyone else, wanted a reference to a "son of man" to be understood as definite he would be quite capable of indicating this, whether or not there was a definite concept of a son of man prior to his time'.
176 Matt. 8:20/Luke 9:58/*Gos. Thom.* 86.

that *bar enasha* was a technical circumlocution in Middle Aramaic,[177] it must nevertheless be acknowledged that a reading of a Gospel synopsis reveals how the evangelists can swap 'Son of Man' for 'I' or 'me' in various sayings (see Table 5.2). Thus, if 'Son of Man' in the Gospels is based on an oral Aramaic *vorlage*, then it probably did function as an indirect self-reference for Jesus.

All this is to say that, behind the Greek of the Gospels, in the Aramaic that Jesus spoke, variations of *bar enash(a)* could conceivably connote 'man', and denote 'this man', 'oneself' or 'I/us' depending on the context.

Third, the 'one like a son of man' in Daniel 7:13 (NIV) exercised wide influence on Jewish apocalyptic and messianic hopes for a heavenly deliverer. It was immensely influential on early Christology and was most probably picked up by the historical Jesus to refer to himself on select occasions.[178]

In Daniel 7, Daniel has a vision of four great beasts coming up out of the sea, each representing a powerful kingdom (i.e. Babylon, Persia, Macedon and Seleucia). The fourth beast is particularly terrifying as it is especially bestial. It has ten horns, representing ten kings, including a particularly arrogant horn: a king who utters words against the Most High, makes war on the holy people, and forcibly changes their laws and customs. Then Daniel sees a vision of the 'Ancient of Days' who judges the beasts and gives power and dominion to 'one like a son of man' who will have an everlasting kingdom. This human figure approaches the Ancient of Days. We read:

> In my vision at night I looked, and there before me was one *like a son of man* [Aram. *kebar enash*], coming with the clouds of heaven. He approached the Ancient of Days and was led into his presence.

---

[177] There is a retort by Owen and Shepherd (2001), who argue that 'son of man' is never used as an indirect form of self-reference in Middle Aramaic nor in any other phase of Aramaic during the time of Jesus. See too Andrejevs (2019: 484), who claims: 'Vermes's corpus of rabbinic sayings, frequently quoted by those scholars who adopt the non-titular hypothesis as an explanation of the New Testament's circumlocutional use, belongs to the Late Aramaic phase and is anachronistic.' Cf. Jeremias 1971: 261 n. 1.

[178] The first person to explicitly connect Jesus with Daniel's 'one like a son of man' was Tertullian in *Adv. Marc.* 4.10. However, James, via Hegesippus and Eusebius, allegedly referred to Jesus as the exalted Son of Man who was to return to bring judgment (Eusebius, *Hist. Eccl.* 2.23.13).

Table 5.2 'Son of Man' sayings functioning as indirect self-reference for Jesus

Persecution on account of the Son of Man	*Acknowledged before the Son of Man*	*Who do people say the Son of Man is?*
Blessed are you when people revile you and persecute you and utter all kinds of evil against you falsely on **my account**. (Matt. 5:11)	Everyone, therefore, who acknowledges me before others, **I also** will acknowledge before my Father in heaven, but whoever denies me before others, I also will deny before my Father in heaven. (Matt. 10:32–33)	Jesus went on with his disciples to the villages of Caesarea Philippi, and on the way he asked his disciples, 'Who do people say that **I am**?' (Mark 8:27)
Blessed are you when people hate you and when they exclude you, revile you, and defame you on **account of the Son of Man**. (Luke 6:22)	And I tell you, everyone who acknowledges me before others, **the Son of Man also** will acknowledge before the angels of God, but whoever denies me before others will be denied before the angels of God. (Luke 12:8–9)	Now when Jesus came into the district of Caesarea Philippi, he asked his disciples, 'Who do people say that **the Son of Man is**?' (Matt. 16:13)

He was given authority, glory and sovereign power; all nations and peoples of every language worshipped him. His dominion is an everlasting dominion that will not pass away, and his kingdom is one that will never be destroyed.
(Dan. 7:13–14 NIV, emphasis added)

This vision is interpreted as representing the rise and fall of powerful kingdoms and the eventual establishment of God's everlasting kingdom. The one like a son of man is perhaps the angelic representative[179] of the 'holy ones of the Most High'.[180] However, while the one like a son of man is a corporate figure representing Israel, or the faithful within Israel, he also represents God's kingship and is a king in contrast to the arrogant king. In that case, Daniel's 'one like a son of man' lent itself towards messianic interpretations.[181]

Given that many of the Son of Man materials in the Gospels are related to the assertion of Jesus' authority,[182] or predict his exaltation and judicial role,[183] it is easy to identify Jesus with this Danielic human figure who embodies divine kingship and exercises divine judgment. However, many suspect that such Son of Man sayings might be inventions of the later church, which identified Jesus with Daniel's son of man as a way of accenting his role as God's vice-regent and agent in judgment. Or else, if Jesus did speak of a 'coming Son of Man', then he too was expecting a heavenly deliverer, someone other than himself.[184]

---

179 Cf. discussion in Bird 2022: 197–198.

180 The dominion given to the one like a son of man is mirrored in the kingdom given to the holy ones in Dan. 7:18, 22, 27.

181 Cf. e.g. 4Q246; *1 Enoch* 37 – 71; *4 Ezra* 13; *Sib. Or.* 5.256–259; Justin, *Dial.* 32.1.

182 Mark 2:10/Matt. 9:6/Luke 5:25; John 5:27.

183 Mark 8:38; 13:26–27; 14:62; Matt. 10:23; 16:28; 24:27, 30, 37–39, 44; Luke 12:40; 17:22, 29–20; 21:27.

184 See Bultmann 1952–55: 1:30–32; 1963 [1921]: 152; Bornkamm 1960 [1956]: 175–178; Jeremias 1971: 257–276; Gnilka 1997 [1993]: 249–250; Andrejevs 2019. Bultmann believed that only the 'coming Son of Man' sayings were authentic because Jesus himself was looking for a heavenly deliverer, whereas Vermes (1973: 160–191; 2004: 262) and Casey (2007: 213–245; 2010: 376–377, 387–388) believe that the 'coming Son of Man' sayings are the ones invented by the early church in their own messianic elaborations. Regarding the latter view, Andrejevs (2019: 848) concludes: '[T]he residual distinction between Jesus and the Son of Man in the New Testament tradition's earliest sayings [e.g. Luke 12:8–9] strongly indicates that the phrase's pre-christological Jewish-Christian use was titular. The christological identification occurred when the human sage Jesus began to be regarded by some of his followers as the earthly representation of the heavenly Son of Man.' In counterpoint to such assertions, Allison (2010a: 295) notes that Jesus' third-person use of 'Son' in Mark 13:32 is never taken to mean that the Son of God at the final judgment was a person other than Jesus. Witherington (1990: 257–258) points out that nowhere in the Jesus tradition does Jesus expect an eschatological successor, and neither did the early Christians, who parsed Jesus' ambiguity with their own certainty that he was the eschatological agent, God's final envoy. Also, Hengel (1995: 105; Hengel and Schwemer 2019 [2007]: 568–571) complains that 'German research has here been led astray in recent decades by pseudo-radical theses. It has given far too little thought to the fact that "(son of) man", or in Aramaic, בר אנשא, was by no means a common messianic title. It first becomes a title for a relatively clearly drawn eschatological figure in the mouth of Jesus. Moreover, the early Church neither employed this

More likely, to my mind, Jesus did make deliberate and provocative allusions to Daniel 7 when discussing his exaltation as Yahweh's vice-regent and his role in the future judgment.[185] His messianic interpretation of Psalm 110:1 was mirrored in his messianic interpretation of Daniel 7:13-14; such midrashic moves are entirely congruent within Jewish messianic interpretation, resonating in particular with the Son of God scrolls (4Q246) and the Self-Exaltation Hymn (4Q419c) from Qumran, and the Enochic Son of Man (*1 Enoch* 37 – 71).[186]

But can one shift from generic (i.e. man) and indefinite (i.e. someone) usage of *bar enash(a)* towards a titular sense in connection with Daniel 7:13 so that 'one like a son of man' becomes '*the* Son of Man' in the discourse of Jesus (and not fashioned by the post-Easter churches and projected onto Jesus)? While the Aramaic may be idiomatic and function in several ways, it has nevertheless become a title in the Gospels, and we must explore how and why. The move from generic and indefinite senses to a titular usage transpired for several reasons.

First, the 'son of man' figure in Daniel 7 is more of a role than a title.[187] The 'one like a son of man' is a multivalent symbol for God's kingship, his king and his holy people. The human figure of Daniel 7:13-14 was a role that Jesus could easily identify his mission with, given that the themes of eschatological authority, enthronement, national vindication and the triumph of God's kingdom, taken from Daniel, slot naturally into his own proclamation and aims. This is all the more plausible if Jesus

---

term in a kerygmatic sense, nor took it up in confessional formulas. It remained restricted to the self-witness of Jesus.' I would add that attempts to use Luke 12:8-9 as proof that Jesus regarded the Son of Man as someone other than himself fail precisely because this text highlights how a denial of Jesus before others will result in the Son of Man denying them before angels, something that has a sharper edge if Jesus and the Son of Man are one and the same. Or, as de Jonge (1998: 90-91) puts it: 'If God's kingly rule represented by Jesus is the same as God's kingly rule represented by the Son of Man, we may ask whether we are allowed to distinguish between the two representatives. In other words: Will not Jesus' characteristic emphasis on the dynamic presence of God's kingdom have correlated with his use of "Son of Man" to designate himself?'

185 Mark 13:26 and 14:62. Cf. Dalman 1902 [1898]: 257-258.
186 Alternative theories are that Jesus' reference to a future/coming Son of Man refers to his heavenly doppelganger (Allison 2010a: 300-303) or is a collective metaphor for the vindication of God's people (Kazen 2007).
187 Hooker 1979: 167; Wright 1996: 360-367.

drew on Daniel as informing his teaching, ministry and sense of divine purpose.[188]

Second, it is highly probable that *bar enasha* could be employed with a particularizing reference whereby a specific individual, such as a speaker, is implied as *the* Son of Man.[189] For example, in the *Thanksgiving Hymns* (1QH) 12.27–37, *ben adam* implies general human frailty and wickedness, of which the speaker himself is the prime example, expressing a general class with a particular expression. Further, a definite sense of *the* Son of Man is evident in a saying about blasphemy against the Holy Spirit which we might gloss as 'everyone who speaks a word against *the man* [i.e. Jesus] will be forgiven, but whoever blasphemes against the Holy Spirit will not be forgiven'.[190] The force of 'the Son of Man has authority ... to forgive sins'[191] is not just that 'a man' can forgive sins but that one specific man has the authority to do so. Similarly, Jesus says that the 'Son of Man came not to be served but to serve and to give his life as a ransom for many', something true exclusively of Jesus and his mission.[192] Or else, it is Jesus, as Son of Man, 'who came to seek out and to save the lost'.[193] Multiple examples can be shown in which the 'Son of Man' is a self-reference to Jesus alone.[194] This interpretation is aided by the fact that many scholars argue that the only way to retrovert *ho huios tou anthrōpou* is with a definite use of *bar enasha* for 'the son of man', which in Middle Aramaic cannot be endowed with a generic or indefinite meaning.[195]

---

188 Evans 2003.
189 Cf. Bauckham 1985; Hare 1990: 241–256; Gundry 1993: 119; Hurtado 2003: 290–306.
190 Luke 12:10/Matt. 12:32/*Gos. Thom.* 44.
191 Mark 2:10/Matt. 9:6/Luke 5:24.
192 Mark 10:45.
193 Luke 19:9–10.
194 Cf. e.g. the betrayal of the Son of Man (Mark 14:41/Matt. 26:45); who is the Son of Man? (Matt. 16:13); persecution because of a relationship to the Son of Man (Luke 6:22); the Son of Man accused of gluttony and drunkenness (Matt. 11:18–19/Luke 7:33–34); those who sin against the Son of Man will be forgiven (Matt. 12:31/Luke 12:10). This is why Hengel and Schwemer (2019 [2007]: 565 n. 176) caution: 'Decisions about the original form must be made on a case-by-case basis.'
195 Andrejevs (2019: 478–479) claims that *ho huios tou anthrōpou* can only be retroverted into a definite form of *bar enasha*, which is neither a circumlocution ('I') nor indefinite ('someone') nor generic ('man'). This essentially goes back to Dalman (1902 [1898]: 256): 'The only genuine Aramaic term which suggests ὁ υἱὸς τοῦ ἀνθρώπου is בַּר אֱנָשָׁא.' So also Owen and Shepherd 2001; Lukaszewski 2011; Owen 2011; Shepherd 2011; Williams 2011; Andrejevs 2019. Cf. Williams (2011: 72–77) on expressing definiteness in Aramaic.

If, then, *bar enasha* can have (or normally has!) a definite meaning – *this man*, or *the* son of man[196] – then an association between the Aramaic idiom and Jesus' own allusions to Daniel 7:13 becomes more coherent. For instance, Mark 14:62 is probably a tacit allusion to Daniel 7:13 via Jesus' self-referential idiom. Richard Bauckham writes:

> There seems no reason why Jesus should not have exploited the coincidence between his accustomed form of oblique self-reference and the language of Dan. 7.13, so that *bar enash* in a saying alluding to Dan. 7.13 becomes the same kind of veiled hint of his own status as other authentic Son of Man sayings convey.[197]

Adela Collins concurs: 'If we conclude that Jesus alluded to Dan 7:13 in his teaching, the shift from the indefinite or generic use of the phrase "son of man" to its definite or quasi-titular use is explained.'[198] It would be wrong to detect Danielic allusions in every 'Son of Man' saying in the Gospels, since there are connotations of human authority in places (harking back to Ps. 8:4–6), and the Son of Man passion predictions do not carry Danielic echoes (functioning perhaps more as a cryptic self-reference),[199] but there is nothing inherently impossible about *bar enasha* being used in allusions to Daniel 7:13 with Jesus identifying himself as *the* Son of Man.[200]

Accordingly, while the double-articular Greek, literally '*the* son of *the* man', might seem novel or inelegant, it is nonetheless how the tradents and translators of the Jesus tradition have sought to render Jesus' own enigmatic Aramaic idiom into Greek.[201] This Greek construction cannot be derived exclusively from the Septuagintal version of Daniel 7:13,

---

196 Casey (2010: 362–368), who clearly favours a generic sense of *bar enash(a)*, still admits that in many cases the referent in such sayings is Jesus in the first instance or Jesus alone.

197 Bauckham 1985: 29–30.

198 Collins 1996: 154. Cf. Dunn 2003: 760; Allison 2010a: 294.

199 Bock (2013: 895) says: 'Regardless of the debate over idiom, the linguistic evidence shows that the term need not be a title and can make sense standing alone with an idiomatic force. Certain texts certainly have this feel to them (Mark 2:10, 28). There is no need to invoke Daniel 7 in order to make sense of the usage in these passages.'

200 Cf. too Dunn 2003: 739.

201 Casey (2010: 373–374) writes: '[T]he translation of *bar (ᵉ)nash(ā)* with *ho huios tou anthrōpou* was a brilliant creative achievement. It was rather literal, but it was not "barbaric", and *bar (ᵉ)nash(ā)* was not translated "quite wrongly", or "mistranslated". It retained the main point

which uses the anarthrous *hos huios anthrōpou* ('as a son of man'). Yet the double-articular construction, clunky as it was, was used to reflect the particular emphasis that Jesus himself attached to this expression, and its periodic connection with Daniel 7:13 which imbued the phrase with connotations of eschatological authority.[202] In which case, we are poised to grasp how the Son of Man has a messianic meaning in the Gospels, Revelation and the Enochic Similitudes.

In sum, by using the idiom *bar enasha*, Jesus took scriptural and common language for a human being but used it with forceful particularity to refer to himself, not necessarily as a concrete title but as a distinctive self-reference. Nonetheless, on some occasions, Jesus linked *bar enasha* to Daniel's 'one like a son of man', a passage that was already launched on a trajectory of messianic interpretation. Evidently, then, Jesus could on occasion employ the idiom for notions of suffering and exaltation, possibly coalescing with Isaiah 53 and Psalm 110. He thus used *bar enasha* beyond any idiomatic function to identify himself as the Messiah whose role it was to inaugurate God's kingdom as one who experiences the crucible of suffering and the triumph of exaltation. On the lips of Jesus, 'Son of Man' refers to his own distinctive yet tantalizingly cryptic form of self-reference, indicating that Israel's deliverer was a man;[203] the man among men; an anointed man who would suffer, die and then receive all authority and power, namely the Messiah. The underlying Aramaic wording, for which the Greek framers of the Jesus tradition struggled to find a Greek equivalent, translated the original Aramaic idiom into the double-articular '*the* son of *the* man' to provide emphasis and to mark Jesus out as both the true human being and arguably as the *messias designatus*.

Messiah

Any discussion of Jesus as *the* Messiah has to be prefaced with an acknowledgement of prior and ongoing discussions about royal and

---

of Jesus' original saying, that they referred particularly to himself, and it produced a major Christological title, which has served the needs of the churches since.'

202 Cf. Moule 1977: 11–16.

203 Dunn (2003: 729): 'The implication [of Dan. 7:13–14] is clear: that as "man" = the human being was climax to creation and given dominion over the rest of creation, so Israel was the climax of God's universal purpose and would be given dominion over all other nations.'

eschatological hopes in the Hebrew Bible and Septuagint, the diversity of messianic expectations in Second Temple Judaism, and whether *christos* is a title, name or honorific designation for Jesus in early Christianity. One cannot canvass those massive debates here, but we can acknowledge them.[204] Here we have to move on to the pressing issue: did Jesus claim to be the Messiah, or was this title projected onto him post-Easter as a way of intensifying the elevated titles and roles attributed to him as an eschatological deliverer? This is a question that H. J. Holtzmann over a hundred years ago described as 'the main problem of New Testament theology'.[205] It is a topic that I have addressed at length elsewhere and will briefly recapitulate now.[206]

There are three immediate problems with attributing a messianic self-understanding to Jesus. First, there is the fact that Jesus never once uses the title 'Messiah' to describe himself. At the very most, he is acclaimed as Messiah, king and Son of David by others, such as supplicants for healing, or crowds during the triumphal entry. That suggests that Jesus might have inspired messianic hopes but did not himself embrace the title as the best designation for his purpose and intentions. The second problem is that the episodes in the Gospels where Jesus accepts the messianic designation from others are thought to bear an uncanny resemblance to early Christian confessions of Jesus' identity.[207] Third, the motif of the messianic secret, where Jesus tells people not to broadcast his identity, has been alleged to be a secondary invention and not authentic. Such injunctions to silence have been regarded, since the arguments of Wrede at the turn of the twentieth century, as an invention in the tradition that Mark has amplified in order to explain why the church believed Jesus to be the Messiah when in fact it was widely known that he had never used the messianic title or had even explicitly rejected it. Consequently, some of the Gospel accounts look as if the evangelists or their sources have read their messianic faith back into stories of Jesus' pre-Easter life. It has been frequently advocated that the early church inferred Jesus' messiahship on the basis of his resurrection. Wrede argued:

---

204 Cf. Novenson 2012; 2017.
205 Holtzmann 1911: 295 ('das Hauptproblem der neutest. Theologie').
206 Bird 2009; 2013a; 2013b.
207 Mark 8:29; 14:61–62; John 4:25–26; 18:33–34.

The view that Jesus only becomes messiah after his death is assuredly not merely an old one, but the oldest of which we have any knowledge. Had the earthly life of Jesus been looked upon from the start as the actual life of the messiah, it would have been only with difficulty that, by way of supplement to this, the idea could have been hit upon of regarding the resurrection as the formal beginning of the messiahship and the appearance in glory as the *single* coming of the messiah.[208]

This argument led to the prevalent picture of an unmessianic Jesus in sections of historical Jesus scholarship, a view that has maintained some consistency in its adherents:

> For this is the truly amazing thing, that there is in fact not one single certain proof of Jesus' claiming for himself one of the Messianic titles which tradition has ascribed to him ... Not a single one of his words speaks of the *Messias designatus*.[209]

> There is no certainty that Jesus thought of himself as bearer of the title 'Messiah'. On the contrary, it is unlikely that he did so: all the gospel writers so regarded him, but they could cite little direct evidence.[210]

> Jesus never chose to call himself 'Messiah' or 'Son of God' and even when others questioned him about his Messiahship, he usually declines to give a straight answer.[211]

> The historical-critical work on the Gospels regarding the question of the work and the self-understanding of the 'earthly' Jesus leads in my opinion to the following result: Jesus did not designate himself as 'Messiah'.[212]

---

208 Wrede 1971: 218 (emphasis original).
209 Bornkamm 1960 [1956]: 172, 178.
210 Sanders 1993: 242.
211 Vermes 2004: 402.
212 Hofius 1993: 119 ('Die historisch-kritische Arbeit an den Evangelien führt hinsichtlich

Who was Jesus?

Martin Hengel commented on all this: 'Today the unmessianic Jesus has almost become a dogma among many New Testament scholars. One is tempted to describe this phenomenon as "non-messianic dogmatics."'[213] To be fair, objections to a messianic Jesus are reasonable, but they are not insurmountable, and can be assuaged or even refuted. As it turns out, postulating the historical Jesus as a messianic claimant has more merit than its alternative.

First, to begin with, the denial that Jesus thought of himself as a messianic leader creates more problems than it solves. We are stuck with the question as to why Jesus was crucified as a messianic pretender, how the messianic faith of the early church arose in the first place, and why the evangelists put the story of Jesus into a messianic matrix. The standard explanation is that the early church *inferred* Jesus' messianic identity from his resurrection. If God had raised him, then *surely* he must be the Messiah – but it is not that simple. The problem is that there is no precedent for deducing messiahship from resurrection. How does 'risen' equal 'royal' or 'Messiah'? It is unclear how belief in Jesus' resurrection would create Jesus' messianic identity in the absence of a prior messianic claim by Jesus and/or a messianic hope among his disciples.[214] The messiahship of Jesus does not figure prominently in the resurrection narratives, a context where one might expect to find a clear announcement of messiahship on the lips of Jesus or confession by one of the disciples if Jesus' messianic status was derived from Easter faith. Hengel correctly observed: 'The mere revivification of a person or, as the case may be, his translation into the heavenly realm, establishes neither messianic majesty nor eschatological mission, nor could it, of itself, supply the content of a message of salvation.'[215]

Second, in regard to the messianic secret, Jesus may well have deliberately veiled or ambiguated his messianic self-belief and intentions if it

---

der Frage nach dem Wirken und dem Selbstverständnis des "irdischen" Jesus m.E. zu den folgenden Ergebnissen: Jesus hat sich nicht selbst als "Messias" bezeichnet').

213 Hengel 1995: 16.
214 Cf. e.g. Schweitzer 1945 [1906]: 309–310; Klausner 1925: 255–256; Jeremias 1971: 255; Meyer 1979: 177–178; Meier 1991–2016: 1:219; Theissen and Merz 1998 [1996]: 540–541; Allison 1998: 67; 2010a: 242–244; Dunn 2003: 626–627; Wright 1996: 487–488; 2003: 24, 575–576.
215 Hengel 1995: 10.

was genuinely true that, as some Pharisees told him, 'Herod wants to kill you'.[216] Staking a messianic claim would be putting an even bigger target on his back and bounty on his head. But the notion that the messianic secret was developed by Mark to explain the absence of a messianic claim prior to the resurrection has always had one large painfully obvious problem that nobody ever seemed to observe: in the Markan story, what is silenced is not necessarily messianic (such as healings and exorcisms [e.g. Mark 1:44; 7:36]), while material that *is* nakedly messianic is not silenced at all (e.g. Bartimaeus calling Jesus 'Son of David' [Mark 10:47–49], Jesus' triumphal entry [Mark 11:1–10] and Jesus' enigmatic remarks about David and his Lord [Mark 12:35–37]).

Third, there are some very cogent and compelling reasons for thinking that Jesus did in fact claim to be a messianic figure. Though much could be said, I enumerate the key evidence as follows:

1 Isaiah 61, which refers to the coming of an eschatological and anointed figure, seems to have played a significant part in Jesus' own understanding of his role. There is an explicit appeal to a Spirit-anointed ministry in special Lukan material, and similarly Isaianic echoes in the sayings tradition shared by Luke and Matthew regarding John the Baptist's question as to whether Jesus really is the 'one who is to come'.[217] What makes this all the more striking and authentic is the similarity of the proof of Jesus' messianic status with a similar list of deeds expected of Israel's Messiah found at Qumran.[218]
2 It is commonly recognized that Jesus' central message pertained to the kingdom of God. What role did Jesus think he played in that kingdom, in its announcement and consummation? Jesus' choice of twelve disciples was symbolic of the restoration of Israel that he believed he was establishing.[219] There is also an eschatological saying that the twelve would sit on twelve thrones judging Israel and have a kingdom conferred on them in the same way that the Father

---

216 Luke 13:31.
217 Luke 4:18–21; Luke 7:18–23/Matt. 11:2–6.
218 4Q521 2.1–10.
219 Mark 3:13–16.

confers a kingdom on Jesus.[220] It appears that Jesus saw himself as the royal leader-to-be of the restored people of God – a king of a future kingdom.

3 We also have to take into account the prominence of allusions to David and Solomon in Jesus' teaching activities.[221] Solomon and David were both regarded as prophets and allegedly performed exorcisms, which aligns also with the pattern of Jesus' ministry. In any case, Jesus saw himself in a lineage associated with the greatest of royal figures from Israel's ancient past and viewed this as a way of explicating his eschatological role.

4 Jesus' final week was thoroughly messianic. We have a messianic action in the triumphal entry that deliberately acts out Zechariah 9.[222] There is a messianic demonstration in the temple where Jesus warns of the destruction of the temple unless Israel repents,[223] and elsewhere we are told that he predicted the rebuilding of the temple, which is a messianic task.[224] Jesus engaged the scribes on several topics, including the identity of the Messiah as David's Lord.[225] In the passion sequence, Jesus is depicted as a messianic shepherd who saves his people from the danger of tribulation by his vicarious death.[226] At his trial before Caiaphas, Jesus is asked point blank a messianic question and responds with an oblique but affirmative answer that conflates Psalm 110:1 and Daniel 7:13.[227]

5 Jesus was executed on the charge of being a messianic pretender, hence the titulus that mocked him as 'King of the Jews'.[228] As Allison comments, the 'Romans probably crucified Jesus as "king of the Jews" because he did not distance himself from that derisive epithet'.[229]

---

220 Luke 22:28–30/Matt. 19:28–30.
221 Matt. 12:42/Luke 11:31; Mark 2:23–28; 12:35–37.
222 Mark 11:1–10.
223 Mark 11:11–18.
224 Mark 14:58; John 2:19; 2 Sam. 7:11–14.
225 Mark 12:35–37.
226 Mark 14:27 = Zech. 13:7.
227 Mark 14:62.
228 Mark 15:26; Matt. 27:37; Luke 23:38; John 19:19.
229 Allison 2010a: 240.

True, Jesus did not walk around Galilee and Judea with a banner saying, 'Messiah on the March!' Jesus knew that any whiff of a messianic claim could lead to a riot or a revolution in his name (see John 6:15!). He deliberately flirted with messianic language and energy, even while playing it down or making it deliberately ambiguous, to keep the crowds, authorities and even his own disciples guessing. However, if you proclaim the kingdom of God, declare that the day of national restoration is dawning, compare yourself to David and Solomon, perform what various people considered to be signs of messianic deliverance, enter Jerusalem on a donkey with people shouting 'Hosanna to the Son of David', and end up on trial on a messianic charge and mocked in death as a Jewish king, well, you don't need a PhD in Second Temple literature to see what was going on here. Jesus deliberately acted out a messianic role, and it was this motif in his ministry that explained why the church began, how it took the shape that it did, and why it took to the language of Jesus as Messiah so quickly. The resurrection turned the debris of an apparently messianic failure into a messianic victory that inaugurated a messianic age, but resurrection alone did not turn Jesus into a messianic figure.

An ancient holy man

Peter Tomson wrote: 'The person of Jesus as he emanates from the gospels is enveloped in a cloud of enigma.'[230] That is certainly true. Jesus was an arresting figure, speaking with a sense of unmediated divine authority. He inspired hope, offended critics, acted with punctuated and provocative controversy, traversed the prophetic and scribal vocations, and claimed astounding things about the kingdom and his role within it.

Jesus consciously performed as and was publicly perceived as a holy man in whom a divine power was present. He was a prophet in word and deed, a seer claiming insights into divine secrets, a sage who discerned truth from error, a rabbi committed to the truest interpretation of Israel's Torah, an exorcist doing battle with demonic powers, a healer to the sick, and a miracle-worker able to do the seemingly impossible. He identifies himself as 'the man', one invested with and emboldened by a sense of

---

[230] Tomson 2001: 27.

divine prerogatives yet driven towards a climactic destiny to embody Israel's curse and resurrection in his own person. He was acutely aware of his own filial status, both as an anointed figure and as one who was uniquely related to Israel's God. He was also, in his mind, the Messiah – a claim he only expressed cryptically, even furtively; this was something he wanted to imply without saying, at least until his fateful and final week in Jerusalem.

This multiplicity of images is not unusual. Jesus, much like Ezekiel and Isaiah, can experience otherworldly visions as he prays and prophesies over the nation. Jesus, much like Elijah, can do wondrous deeds even as he challenges the idolatry in Israel's heart. Jesus, much like Solomon, can be a royal figure, who does exorcisms and demonstrates peerless wisdom. Jesus, like David, is a king, with a prophetic vocation and even a sense of priestly holiness.[231] The impression that Jesus made on his followers, and on crowds, competitors, supplicants and officials, required them to attach a tag of some kind to him, whether prophet or messianic pretender. One thing that forced them to do that with earnestness was hearing the gritty, arresting, memorable, witty and even offensive nature of his teaching. Who Jesus *was* was based on what he was known for, and what he was known for emerges largely from his teaching. Jesus' teaching provides the best window into the man, his mission and his ambitions.

---

231 Riffing here off Wright 1996: 166.

6
The teaching of Jesus

A new teaching – with authority

Leander Keck said: 'To a considerable degree the history of the quest [for the historical Jesus] is the quest of Jesus the teacher.'[1] Strewn across the Jesus tradition is the memory of Jesus as a teacher of arresting authority as well as the memory of his actual instruction.[2] Jesus was addressed as 'teacher' and 'rabbi',[3] and his teaching was notable for its novelty and authority in contrast to that of the scribes.[4] Jesus was a teacher of charisma and conviction. Provocative and poignant, his words courted controversy, and to his hearers they felt different from the words of many of his contemporary pedagogues.[5] Jesus' teaching was notable in his 'Amen, amen' sayings and the 'I say to you' formulas. His teaching reinforced scriptural paradigms, but also challenged the pieties of the powerful, threatened to unleash a fiery blaze and was deliberately issued to the marginalized with promises of a great reversal.

Jesus was an itinerant teacher who used his own movements, disciples, supporters, supplicants and the village rumour mill to disseminate his message far and wide. In fact, if Jesus said the same thing from place to place then the prospect of finding the 'original' form of a saying is beyond problematic; it is pointless, because every performance was an

---

[1] Keck 2000: 65.

[2] Wright (1996: 174) comments: 'There is no reason *a priori* why Jesus could not have taught in extended discourses; indeed, there is quite good reason to suggest that he did. The attempt to make one of these styles of teaching the norm, and to question the historicity of the other on that basis, stands on very thin historical ice' (emphasis original). In contrast, Allison (2010a: 305–386) regards the discourses in the Gospels as secondarily woven together from isolated aphorisms.

[3] Cf. e.g. Matt. 8:19; 23:8; Mark 9:5; 10:17; 11:21; 12:14; John 1:38, 49; 3:2.

[4] Mark 1:22, 27; 11:18, 28; 12:17; Matt. 7:28–29.

[5] Cf. Hengel and Schwemer 2019 [2007]: 534 for the *Gottesunmittelbarkeit* or 'divine immediacy' which characterized Jesus' teaching.

original! We find actual quotes from Jesus' teaching in the Corinthian letters,[6] allusions to the Jesus tradition in the Pauline letters,[7] and echoes of Jesus' instruction arguably strewn across the letter of James.[8] All of the evangelists emphasize in their own way that Jesus was an extraordinary teacher. For Mark, Jesus was the apocalyptic instructor of the last days. For Matthew, Jesus was a new Moses and the messianic teacher without rival. For Luke, Jesus was the Spirit-anointed prophetic voice of God's mercy and justice. For John, Jesus taught and embodied divine wisdom and the way to God. Even for the *Gospel of Thomas*, Jesus was a purveyor of ascetic spirituality and a dispenser of secret insights for an elite class of adherent. If Jesus' teaching had a central theme, it was God's kingdom, its meaning, and its demands upon Israel. Jesus' teaching was a mode of instruction typified by a convergence of Israel's hope (eschatology), Israel's identity (election) and Israel's behaviour (ethics) in the light of a peculiar mix of imminent national danger and immanent deliverance. Along the way, to mark himself out, Jesus addressed the burning topics of commerce and cultus, politics and purity, revolution and righteousness; he discoursed on justice and judgment; took positions on disputed points of scriptural interpretation about the sabbath and divorce; retold the story of Israel in challenging ways; and recast the meaning of fidelity to God in the light of the coming kingdom. These truths may be timeless in many ways, but they are in fact testimonies to a Galilean prophet trying to convince rural audiences of a coming danger and that the last chance to find refuge in God's reign is upon them. In what follows I shall attempt to expound the striking features of Jesus' teaching around the nodes of parables, ethics, piety, wealth and riches, Torah and prophetic warnings.

Parables

Jesus' parables[9] are a plaything for theologians and homileticians alike who (ab)use these provocative, pithy and punchy pieces of poetic

---

6 1 Cor. 7:9–11; 9:14; 11:23–25.
7 Cf. Rom. 8:15–17; Gal. 4:6–7 and Rom. 13:8, 10; Gal. 5:14.
8 Cf. e.g. Jas 1:4.
9 On the authenticity of the parables, Theissen and Merz (1998 [1996]: 33) note: 'The plausibility of both context and impact thus suggests that the parables derive from the historical

storytelling for the purpose of finding spiritual insight, moral instruction and theological construction. From Augustine to Matthew Henry, the parables are something more read into than read out, as interpreters have found in them the presenting issues, crises, villainies and values of their own time. The parables have proved to be timeless, partly because they teach things that are eminently relatable to readers across times and cultures, and partly because they can be interpreted like a Rorschach drawing onto which one can project one's own concerns. Alas, all application of the parables inevitably trades in allegory. The challenge to make the specificity of culture and context given in the parables relevant to those of us who live in a world far away from Samaritans and slaves inevitably requires interpreters to engage in a brazen and joyous eisegesis. But that is not our task here. We are concerned, rather, to hear the parables in the context of the career of the historical Jesus and his announcement that God's kingship was bursting onto the scene, with Israel's restoration already under way.

Jesus' parables are a figurative form of speech consisting of 'a narrative or saying of varying length, designed to illustrate a truth especially through comparison or simile, illustration, parable, proverb, maxim'.[10] While parables bear some similarity to Greco-Roman fables,[11] they are far more analogous to the Hebrew *mashal*, which could be a proverb,[12] taunt,[13] riddle,[14] allegory[15] or political fable.[16] We should be reminded too of famous texts such as Nathan's denunciation of David for adultery and Isaiah's allegory of God's vineyard, which certainly qualify as *meshalim*.[17] There are obviously connections with wisdom traditions, which abound in proverbs and riddles,[18] and apocalyptic texts with their metaphorical

---

Jesus; they can be derived from Jewish tradition but have an individual stamp in their present context. Primitive Christianity soon went over to other forms of figurative discourse.'

10 BDAG 759.
11 See Snodgrass 2008: 46–51.
12 Ezek. 12:23; 16:44; 18:2–3.
13 Isa. 14:3–4; Hab. 2:6.
14 Judg. 14:14.
15 Ezek. 17:2–10; 20:44–49; 21:5; 24:2–5.
16 Judg. 9:7–15; 2 Kgs 14:9–10.
17 2 Sam. 12:1–14; Isa. 5:1–7.
18 Sir. 3:29; 20:20; 39:2–3; 47:17; 4Q302; *T. Job* 18.7–8; *T. Naph.* 2.2–4; 4 Macc. 1:28–30; Ps.-Phil, *Bib. Ant.* 37.1–5; *2 Bar.* 51.1–6.

imagery.[19] The rabbinic tradition – whatever its pre-AD 200 precursors – also had a vibrant corpus of *meshalim* consisting of example stories, midrash and metaphors among the *tannaim* (rabbinic sages in the first and second centuries AD).[20] In the early church, the parables of Jesus held a special interest for Papias.[21] A couple appear in the Clementine literature,[22] while the Roman *Shepherd of Hermas* communicated using various enigmatic allegories, especially in the section on the 'similitudes'.[23] In various other Gospels, the authors interpreted or invented parabolic sayings of Jesus to be played in revelational and esoteric keys.[24]

The basic gist of a parable is *usually* available through a close reading of the content. For instance, in the parable of the good Samaritan, the point is partly undermining ethnic prejudices and religious rivalries with the prospect that an outsider such as a Samaritan could provide the type of mercy that one would normally expect only from a respected priestly leader. And, in a biting irony, it is the Samaritan, not the priest or Levite, who is exemplary for others to emulate.[25] Assuming that parables are not autonomous literary entities, the problem of interpretation does not lie in the content of the parables but rather in finding an interpretative context for them. It is one thing to read Luke 18:9–14 about the Pharisee and the tax-collector in the context of seventeenth-century debates over law and gospel, but another to imagine its meaning on the lips of Jesus on the way to Jerusalem in AD 30, or in the setting of a Gentile congregation in Achaia in AD 85 where believers are listening to Luke's travel narrative. The biggest issue with the parables is not whether they teach one, two or three points; it is what context we should we read them within. Allison puts it well:

> Jesus' parables . . . are inherently polyvalent and so exceedingly pliable, which is why an exegete's larger frame of reference typically

---

19 *1 Enoch* 1.2–3; 37–71; 89; *4 Ezra* 4.13–18, 28–32, 38–43, 47–52; 7.49–61; 8.1–3, 41–45; 9.30–37; *2 Bar.* 22 – 23.
20 Cf. e.g. *m. Abot* 1.3; *m. Sot.* 9.15; *t. Sanh.* 9.7; *t. Sot.* 5.9. Rabbi Meir was a noted parable-teller.
21 Eusebius, *Hist. Eccl.* 3.39.11–12.
22 *1 Clem.* 23.4–5; *2 Clem.* 11.2–3.
23 *Herm. Sim.* 50 – 114.
24 Cf. e.g. *Gos. Thom.* 8, 9, 20, 21, 57, 63, 64, 65, 76, 96, 97, 98, 107, 109; *Apoc. Jas* 7.24–35; 8.16–28; 12.22–30; *Acts Phil.* 135; *Acts John* 67.
25 Luke 10:37.

determines interpretation... The meaning of the parables and their metaphorical possibilities are not inherent properties of the parables as freestanding works of art but rather depend upon the narrative in which they are embedded or upon the nonliterary contexts into which we attempt to place them.[26]

Similarly, Meier declares that the parables express 'the need for an overarching interpretive framework of Jesus' ministry'.[27] But what framework should we use?

If we are looking at the historical Jesus, then we can step back from the hermeneutical mirror of our own experience and setting (valid as they may be for the pulpit) and detour around the reader-response options of feminist, queer, liberationist and ecological readings (valid as they are for religious studies seminars) as locations to read the parables. Instead, we should read them in a framework that proves to be illuminating for Jesus' career and brings coherence to the Jesus tradition. With that proviso, proposed frameworks for the parables have included: the reign of God in the human soul (Harnack), future eschatology (Schweitzer), realized eschatology (Dodd), inaugurated eschatology (Jeremias), existential decision-making (Bultmann), speech-acts declaring God's love for sinners (Fuchs), agrarian liberation (Crossan) and the end of Israel's exile (Wright). My own intuition is that Jesus' parables should be framed within Jewish restoration eschatology as sharp retellings of Israel's story with the aim of challenging an audience's view of God, kingdom, covenant membership, covenant righteousness and national deliverance. Jesus' parables combine the countercultural resources of the wisdom tradition, the midrashic texture of rabbinic parables reworking scriptural themes, the symbolic stories of Isaiah, the taunting jibes of Ezekiel, and the prophetic criticism typified by Nathan's shocking scold of David – 'You are the man!'[28] – to offer a new way of understanding the fulfilment of Israel's hope.[29]

Jesus' parables draw on agricultural imagery, daily village life, stock character-types and everyday situations to discourse on 'God, God's

---

26 Allison 2010a: 117–118.
27 Meier 1991–2016: 5:4–5.
28 2 Sam. 12:7.
29 Wright 1996: 176.

people, and God's word'.[30] They rehearse a 'collective store of Jewish imagery'[31] by utilizing Old Testament (OT) images of a farmer and a vineyard, or that of a shepherd and his sheep, which often describe God's relationship with Israel. Or else they resource common images for God and Israel such as a master and his servant, a king and his subjects, or a father and a son. They also use everyday situations: a group of day labourers waiting in the market square to be hired, the problem of weeds growing among wheat, seating arrangements at a banquet, the dilemma of showing hospitality without any bread, the danger for servants if the master catches them slacking off, a sheep that wanders off, a lost coin, an unjust steward, and more, to explain divine character, Jesus' mission, covenant faithfulness and future hope. Taking these everyday examples, the parables use surprising twists in short stories to explain God's character, kingdom imperatives and the nature of discipleship. Jesus' parables render him, in the words of Martin Hengel, 'the most impressive creator of [*meshalim*] in ancient Judaism'.[32] The shock and awe of such stories is precisely why they were preserved and transmitted by the early church.

It is because of these shocking twists that the parables are very often 'weapons of controversy'[33] akin to the parabolic declarations in the prophets which denounce Israel's leaders and intimate judgment. Parables, in the adversarial context of Jesus' ministry, retell Israel's story in startling ways, causing affront to the official and unofficial leaders of Israel. The parables redraw Israel's boundaries around tax-collectors, fishermen, prostitutes and people suffering from *lepra*; they critique those who were supposed to be above critique; they challenge things that were unchallengeable! Jesus' parables explore what it means if Israel's protracted period of exile is ending, if the new exodus is under way. What does that mean for God? Who is in and who is out? Whose way

---

30 Bockmuehl 2006: 216; cf. Snodgrass 2008: 20, 41.
31 Theissen and Merz 1998 [1996]: 343. Or for Scott (1989: 420) the parables draw on 'the repertoire of common folk – the peasant – of first-century Palestinian Judaism', while Snodgrass (2008: 25) sees Jesus resourcing 'a common fund of parables in use among Jewish teachers'.
32 Hengel 1995: 90.
33 Cadoux 1900: 13; Jeremias 1972 [1954]: 21; Meyer 1979: 163; Levine 2006b: 34–35; Snodgrass 2008: 2.

of being Israel avails? Who is in the right? What about the nations, and what are the signs of belonging to the covenant? These are not stories everyone wanted to hear if it left them off the page or put them on the wrong side of the ledger.

Parables invite hearers to nod their heads in approval until they suddenly realize that Jesus is insinuating that the stories they live by are unstable or undercut.[34] That is because parables are, as B. B. Scott suggested, a form of 'antimyth',[35] a genre which attacks and disorders resident myths, namely cultural stories about power, privilege and proximity to God. The parables make jolting claims: God loves a penitent tax-collector more than a strict Pharisee;[36] the kingdom does not come by focusing on the details of legal minutiae;[37] wealth presents a risk of judgment, not evidence of divine blessing;[38] many audiences are apathetic like people who can't be motivated for either a dance or a dirge;[39] judgment will come unexpectantly like a flood[40] or a bird caught in a snare;[41] and the members of Israel's priestly ruling class are thieving usurpers who have seized control of a vineyard that does not rightfully belong to them.[42] The parables deconstruct competing agendas for Israel's restoration and rival accounts of what it means to be God's people. The parables attack common assumptions: that God is on our side as long as the temple stands; the teaching of the elders is a fence around the Torah; Israel will tower over its neighbours like a cedar of Lebanon; God praises the honourable and casts out the shameless; the kingdom will look like Pharisees forming a phalanx; if Israel keeps but three sabbaths, the Messiah will come; separation from sinners is true holiness; and so on. This is why Jesus responds with a parable

---

[34] Cf. Wright 1996: 174–182, which remains an excellent discussion of parables that establishes this very point.
[35] Scott 1989: 39.
[36] Luke 18:10–14.
[37] Luke 17:20–21.
[38] Luke 16:19–31.
[39] Matt. 11:17/Luke 7:32.
[40] Matt. 24:37–39/Luke 17:26–27.
[41] Luke 21:34–35.
[42] Mark 12:1–12; *Gos. Thom.* 65–66.

when accused of being in league with Beelzebul,[43] of not fasting,[44] of not washing his hands according to custom,[45] of eating with sinners and tax-collectors,[46] and why parables result in plots to kill him![47] The parables use word pictures to redescribe the hope of God's kingship and to redraw Israel's identity and vocation in ways that either render all the other sects and groups irrelevant or show them up as obstacles to Israel's restoration. The parables are, in many ways, to use David Wenham's description, pictures of a revolution.[48]

Accordingly, by telling parables Jesus was doing more than delivering provocative social commentary on the establishment, or smugly saying 'It ain't necessarily so' to offend the scruples of religious conservatives. In the parables, Jesus was taking the stories that people lived by, 'truths' that they simply assumed and often cherished, and turning them on their head. Jesus declared in the parables, often cryptically, that there was another way to tell Israel's story. There was not just a problem *for* Israel but a problem *with* Israel, which required either the repentance of Israel or a rupture within Israel. Moreover, in this story of Israel's deliverance there was a big plot-twist and a stranger ending still to come. It was as though Jesus was teaching American colonial history and saying that King George III was the hero of the American war of independence and his reign over America is eternal and inviolable. Or telling a class of 4-year-olds a fairy tale where Little Red Riding Hood is devoured by the wolf, who then lives happily ever after. Or giving a sermon illustration where Methodist clergy turn away a homeless gay teenager but a Muslim family take her in. Or retelling the story of Faust, except that it turns out that Faust is the Church of England and the devil is the House of Lords. Or quoting lines from Henrik Ibsen's play *Enemy of the People* in the European parliament, and while everyone thought he was talking about Russia, he was in fact describing the European Union itself. It is the kind of thing you would hear and you'd think to yourself, 'Oh yeah, tell it like

---

43 Mark 3:23–30.
44 Mark 2:19–20.
45 Mark 7:1–23.
46 Mark 2:15–17; Matt. 21:31–32; Luke 15:1–3; P. Oxy. 1224; Justin, *1 Apol.* 15.8.
47 Mark 3:6; 11:18; 12:12.
48 Wenham 1989.

it is, brother!' then 'Wait a minute – what did he just say?' then 'OMG, is he talking about *us*?' then 'That's blasphemy and treason!' then 'Away with him – give us Barabbas!' Parables are designed to either change people's mind or cause them to look for the nearest pitchfork.

Two further aspects of the parables stand out: Jesus as a character in the parables, and hiddenness in the parables.

First, in many of the parables, Jesus is, implicitly at least, one of the characters. He is a farmer sowing the word and scattering seed in the fertile soil of Israel,[49] a shepherd sent to seek out and gather the lost sheep of Israel,[50] a doctor to the sick,[51] a strong man who plunders the satanic realm,[52] a householder who invites many guests to a great banquet,[53] a servant at a table,[54] a master returning from a wedding banquet to see if his servants are faithfully waiting for him,[55] a worker pleading for more time to render the owner's vineyard fertile,[56] a narrow door or gate that one must go through to enter the kingdom,[57] a bridegroom soon to be taken away,[58] a shepherd struck down while guarding the flock,[59] a son who was, or will be, murdered by wicked tenants.[60] Jesus furtively weaves himself into the stories he is telling, but it's no mere cameo; rather, his role ranges from prophetic voice of warning, to arbiter of judgment, to messianic martyr, to embodying Yahweh's return to Zion.

Second, Jesus' parables encode a secret about the kingdom which is not given to all hearers. The parables disclose as much as they conceal. The meaning behind the parables is not a puzzle but privileged information; not a mystery to be unravelled but a secret to be imparted.[61] The

---

49 Mark 4:3, 26.
50 Matt. 10:6; 15:24; Luke 12:32; 19:10; John 10:1–11.
51 Mark 2:17; P. Oxy. 1224.
52 Mark 3:27.
53 Luke 14:16.
54 Luke 22:27.
55 Luke 12:36.
56 Luke 13:8–9.
57 Matt. 7:13–14/Luke 13:24; John 10:1–9.
58 Mark 2:19–20.
59 Mark 14:28.
60 Mark 12:8.
61 France 2002: 196.

The teaching of Jesus

disciples have received from Jesus the 'secret of the kingdom',[62] and in Jewish texts secrets could pertain to God's knowledge of human affairs,[63] God's inscrutable ordering of creation,[64] God's hidden wisdom,[65] or deeper insights into what Scripture declares regarding God's plans.[66] In this case, the secret is how God is becoming king, how Israel's restoration is at hand, and what it means for fishermen and farmers right now. And what the reordering of power, soon to ensue, will look like. But outsiders get parabolic utterances either to facilitate their partial reception of the secret or else to harden their resolve against it. Hence the reference to Isaiah 6:9–10 where people may '"be ever hearing, but never understanding; be ever seeing, but never perceiving" . . . Otherwise they might . . . turn and be healed.'[67] The point is not that Jesus tells parables in order to deliberately obfuscate things or to render audiences jaded and judgeable.[68] Matthew's editorial remark clarifies the ambiguity with his appeal to Psalm 72:2:

> Jesus told the crowds all these things in parables; without a parable he told them nothing. This was to fulfil what had been spoken through the prophet:
>
> 'I will open my mouth to speak in parables;
>   I will proclaim what has been hidden from the
>   foundation of the world.'
> (Matt. 13:34–35 NRSV)

The parables are prophetic words that reveal something unmistakable as much as they make judgment against those who reject the message inevitable. We might say that the issue with Jesus' opponents is not stupefaction but opposition. They comprehend what Jesus teaches, but

---

62 Mark 4:11.
63 Dan. 2:18–19, 27–30, 47.
64 *2 Bar.* 48.1–5.
65 Wis. 2:22.
66 1QS 5.10–11; 9.18; 1QM 3.9; 14.14; 17.9.
67 Mark 4:12 NIV; amplified in Matt. 13:11–17; cf. 1QS 4.11.
68 Contra Marcus 1984.

their comprehension only intensifies their hostility, and consequently their culpability.[69] A good analogy is *2 Baruch*, which contrasts those who 'planted in their heart the root of wisdom' with those who 'stopped their ears that they might not hear wisdom or receive understanding'.[70]

If the secret is the meaning of the kingdom, then the parables facilitate either reception or resistance to the message and messenger.[71] In Jewish apocalyptic discourse, mysterious visions often received angelic interpretation,[72] and Jesus appears here like an angelic guide, speaking figuratively to a group, arousing attention as much as agitating audiences, and disclosing the meaning of the discourse to a more discerning group.[73] If Jesus' teaching is about the unexpected way in which the kingdom comes and is coming, what the climax of Israel's history looks like, how it affects one's daily life, then the parables seek to furnish that view with a curious mixture of enticement and unease. As if to say: 'This is what the kingdom looks like. It doesn't resemble the kingdom described by the scribes or Pharisees; it's not anything like how the revolutionary hotheads or Herodians imagine it. Rather, it's like a small mustard seed, or a branch that birds take shelter in, or a nobleman on a journey to Rome. Let those who have ears hear what I'm saying.' The parables have a dual function of drip-feeding the audience with metaphorical references to Jesus' strange retelling of the story of God and Israel to help people imagine a whole new world, while also hardening resistance to the message if the implications are grasped well enough to make them affronted.

To give a good example, the parable of the wicked tenants is a provocative, prophetic parable.[74] Much like *1 Enoch* 89, it retells the story of the wicked and faithful within Israel. As in Isaiah chapter 5, Israel is symbolized by a vineyard, and like the symbolic gestures in Ezekiel we have a symbolic story spoken against Israel's leadership.[75] The parable is

---

[69] I owe this point to a paper given by Kraig Oman at Southeastern Baptist Theological Seminary (2020).
[70] *2 Bar.* 51.1–6.
[71] Snodgrass 2008: 157–164.
[72] Dan. 7:15–28; *4 Ezra* 4.20–21.
[73] Wright 1996: 177–180.
[74] Mark 12:1–12; Matt. 21:33–46; Luke 20:9–19; *Gos. Thom.* 65–66.
[75] See Wright 1996: 497–501; Evans 2001b: 210–240.

The teaching of Jesus

Jesus' way of responding, with a biting narratival riposte, to a coalition of scribes, priests and elders who are challenging him on the source of his authority.[76] In reply, Jesus uses the familiar situation of absentee landlords,[77] and the symbol of Israel as a vineyard from Isaiah 5:1–7,[78] to present a dramatic vignette about his mission to Israel, his rejection by its wicked leadership, and God's intention of avenging his mistreatment by giving the vineyard, that is, Israel, to others. On this telling, God is the one who planted Israel like a vineyard;[79] the watchtower is most probably the temple;[80] the wine press stands for the blessings of fecundity;[81] the tenants denote the priestly leaders and their retinue; the servants are the persecuted prophets of Israel's history; the son is Jesus himself; and the new tenants, the 'others', are the vanguard of the renewed Israel that Jesus is forming around himself. As the story goes, God sends his servants to the tenants, time after time, persistently yet patiently waiting to receive his share of the harvest, while the servants are treated in increasingly violent fashion.

Note, first, that the members of the priestly leadership were themselves probably among the wealthiest landowners of Judea and Galilee, so the story ironically reverses roles and puts them in the position of being tenant farmers trying to cultivate enough crops to pay rent and taxes, and make a living.[82] Second, the parable touches on the tradition of the prophets who were rejected by Israel in violent fashion, such as Zechariah who was martyred in the temple and Isaiah who was sawn in half, according to tradition.[83] Finally, the master sends his 'beloved son', whom the tenants murder and throw outside the vineyard because he is the 'heir' and they covet the land as their own 'inheritance'. The sequel

---

76 Mark 12:1–12; Matt. 21:33–46; Luke 20:9–19; *Gos. Thom.* 65–66. For the various interpretative issues associated with this passage, see Snodgrass 1998; 2011 [1983]; Kloppenborg 2006.
77 PSI VI 594 cited from Hengel 1968; Evans 1996a.
78 Snodgrass (2008: 279) points to several rabbinic parables featuring a vineyard; the most notable is *Midrash Tanhuma Beshallah* 4.7 (on Exod. 13:17) where Israel is the orchard, the Canaanites are the tenants, and the Hebrews come and take possession of the orchard.
79 Jer. 11:17; 12:10; Ezek. 19:10; Ps. 80:8.
80 4Q500.
81 Joel 2:24; Zech. 9:17.
82 Horsley 2003: 94–95.
83 Cf. Matt. 23:30–31, 34–37/Luke 11:49–51; 13:33–34; Acts 7:52; *4 Ezra* 1.32–35.

to this violence is that the owner of the vineyard comes to 'destroy the tenants and give the vineyard to others' (in Luke's version the Jewish leaders or their sympathizers retort, 'May it never be!' while in Matthew's version the emphasis is on the fruitfulness of the new tenants). The subsequent citation of Psalm 188:22–23[84] functions as a *nimshal*, an explanatory conclusion that accents the motif of Jesus as the rejected son yet also God's chosen stone.[85]

The Christological claims of this parable can be easily glossed over, but they speak volumes about Jesus and his mission. Jesus depicts himself as not merely one more in a line of prophets but rather God's final envoy.[86] He is God's beloved son and heir, which demonstrates that Jesus' self-understanding included a mixture of messianic office and unique filial relationship to Israel's God. The Johannine emphasis on the Father–Son relationship is not far removed from what is being asserted in the parable of the tenants. The son comes to rescue the vineyard from its violent and vindictive tenants, and it is his death that prompts God to come against the wicked tenants in judgment and to rescue the vineyard. The tenants are not Jews replaced by the church, even though such a supersessionist reading became common in Christian exegesis of this passage. Rather, there is a replacement within Israel as the political and religious guardians forfeit their positions of authority and are supplanted by new tenants who make the vineyard fruitful. Ultimately, it is through the son's suffering, death and expulsion that God takes measures to save the vineyard, that is, Israel, from the wicked tenants. Bockmuehl is right that 'Jesus understands his identity as unique Son of the Father to be inextricably linked to his mission for the deliverance and renewal of Israel'.[87] The parable thus weaves together a mixture of intertextual allusions, Jesus' divine sonship, a furtive passion prediction, political critique of the

---

84 The citation could be secondary since Ps. 118:22–23 was one of the most commonly cited OT texts in the early church. However, Snodgrass (2008: 290) argues that the parable needs the citation to explain the parable and the negative reaction by the priestly leaders, while Wright (1996: 488–489) believes that Ps. 118:22–23 is especially appropriate in the light of Jesus' temple action.

85 Some see here a play on words between the Hebrew *ben* (son) and *eben* (stone); see Wright 1996: 499–501; Snodgrass 2008: 290.

86 See de Jonge 1998.

87 Bockmuehl 2006: 222.

priestly aristocracy, God's coming in judgment against the priestly class, Israel rescued, and a vision for a rejuvenated Israel under new leadership.

Ethics

Unlike nineteenth-century German scholars, one should not reduce Jesus' teaching to a system of ethics summarized in clichéd aphorisms about the love of God and the brotherhood of man.[88] Unlike twenty-first-century Western evangelicals, one should try paying attention to Jesus' ethics and perhaps even doing them! Banter aside, the kingdom constitutes a forward-looking hope for God becoming king and its many dividends. But the kingdom, a present though partial reality, also makes demands on people to behave in certain ways; ways which can conflict with human nature, tribal loyalties, cultural norms and their associated legal traditions. This brings us, of course, to complicated debates about Jesus and ethics as well as Jesus and Torah.

Jesus did not have a system of ethics; rather, God's will is the norm that Israel lives by, and the kingdom is the reality that Israel's behaviour must be conformed to.[89] Jesus' vision of the kingdom was in some ways performative in that it married eschatological vision with behavioural demands.[90] The kingdom, insofar as it is immanent, creates imperatives, and the kingdom, insofar as it looks ahead to a final judgment, requires the doing of justice. Now, one should not make the mistake of equating the kingdom with ethics – as if the kingdom is the advance expression of a social–political ideal found in old liberalism's social gospel or in the liberation theology of the twentieth century. The kingdom is very much a theocentric enterprise, something God alone does, something God establishes, and it cannot be manufactured by human effort. The kingdom is

---

[88] See critique in Cadbury 1937: 93–95. Note too Meier's (1991–2016: 4:652) warning: 'In the end, a rigorous quest for the Torah-teaching of the historical Jesus renders the Enlightenment program of surgically extracting Jesus the ethicist from the redactional overlay of the Gospels untenable.'

[89] Cf. Meier 1991–2016: 4:478–479.

[90] Chilton 1994b: 264–265; Vermes (2004: 408–410) rightly refers to Jesus' 'eschatological piety'.

a gift,[91] and yet it demands a reciprocation of righteousness.[92] Hence, 'kingdom' was an abbreviation for early Christian ethics.[93] We can, in a qualified sense,[94] speak of Jesus' 'kingdom ethics' given that the kingdom of God is the foundation and domain of Jesus' ethics.[95]

One thing that stands out in Jesus' teaching is the priority of love. When questioned by a scribe about what is the foremost commandment, Jesus responds by way of reference to love for God (Deut. 6:5) and love for neighbour (Lev. 19:18).[96] The combination of Deuteronomy 6:5 and Leviticus 19:18 is rare but hardly unknown in Jewish tradition.[97] Jesus elsewhere reiterates Leviticus 19:18, but instead of loving one's neighbours and hating one's enemies, Jesus requires followers to 'love your enemies and pray for those who persecute you'.[98] Love is the basis for the refusal to retaliate,[99] for adhering to the golden rule[100] and for showing mercy.[101] One must show love for strangers[102] and for sinners.[103] Love is the 'law of life in the reign of God' and entails an 'unlimited readiness to forgive and renunciation of expressions of hatred'.[104]

Love for one another is, of course, amplified in the Johannine tradition.[105] Jesus' love command arguably had the greatest impact on the ethos and culture of the early church, which is why its reiteration

---

91 Luke 12:32; cf. Matt. 10:8; 16:19.
92 Matt. 5:10, 20; 6:33; 13:43.
93 Rom. 14:17.
94 Kvalbein (1998: 223–224) is on to something when he says that in Jesus' ethics that kingdom is the 'powerful motivation' while Law and the Prophets explicated according to Jesus' *halakhah* are the content of ethics. But this is probably too wide a separation between the two. I'd prefer to say that in Jesus's teaching right behaviour does in some sense prepare for the kingdom, anticipate it, or even proleptically enacts the kingdom, especially as it implements healing, justice, redemption, and mercy (see Wright 2007: 218–244).
95 Harvey 1990: 190–192; Schrage 1988: 18; McKnight 1999: 156–157.
96 Mark 12:28–34.
97 Cf. *Jub.* 7.20; 20.2; 36.7–8; Philo. *Spec. Leg.* 2.63; *Dec.* 51; *T. Dan* 5.3; *T. Iss.* 5.1–2; 7.6; *T. Zeb.* 5.3.
98 Matt. 5:43–47/Luke 6:27–28, 32–33; cf. Prov. 25:21–22.
99 Matt. 5:38–39.
100 Matt. 7:12/Luke 6:31; Tob. 4.15; *b. Shab.* 31a.
101 Matt. 5:7; 18:33; Luke 6:36.
102 Luke 10:25–37.
103 Mark 2:17; Luke 7:36–50.
104 Jeremias 1971: 212–213; Hengel 1973 [1971]: 75.
105 John 13:34–35; 15:12–13.

is near ubiquitous.[106] The love command is part and parcel of Jesus' prophetic declaration of Israel's restoration and covenantal renewal. Yahweh renews the covenant to transform the people both corporately and individually;[107] the sign of embracing that renewal is love for God and love for others, love for justice and love for mercy.[108] For Jesus, love reaches out towards others, towards rivals, even enemies, working for peace and even friendship. The antithesis is hubris, hypocrisy and hardness, being concerned with externalities, status and micro-piety rather than with doing God's will.[109] In Jesus' vision, the people of a restored Israel love God with heart, mind, soul and strength, and love others by obeying the commandments with renewed intensity.[110]

The Matthean Sermon on the Mount (Matt. 5 – 7) and the Lukan Sermon on the Plain (Luke 6) are two versions of a much-loved assortment of commands revered by the religious and non-religious alike. It is a collection that has been dramatized, secularized, universalized, criticized, psychologized, politicized and radicalized by many interpreters.[111] The canonical form of the speeches reflects Matthean and Lukan redaction, evident in a contrast of the two versions. It is unlikely to have been based on a single sermon that Jesus gave, and is something closer to what we might call a collection of greatest hits.[112] That said, if Jesus did deliver sermons, aphorisms, oracles, warnings and exhortations to Galilean and Judean audiences, then there is every likelihood that he reworked and recycled materials – what preacher hasn't? – and delivered them on multiple occasions with slight variations therein. There is no reason to assume that Jesus did not teach in extended discourses, and of those discourses, delivered frequently, there was no original version, but several original performances. In the transmission of the Jesus tradition, eventually these teachings were collected and condensed into

---

106 Cf. Rom. 12:14, 17–20; 1 Cor. 4:12; Gal. 5:14; 1 Thess. 5:15; 1 Pet. 3:9; Jas 2:8; *Did.* 1.2; *Barn.* 19.5; Pol. *Phil.* 3.3.
107 Jer. 31:31–34.
108 Deut. 10 – 11, 30; Hos. 2:19; 12:6; Amos 5:15.
109 Mark 12:38–40; Matt. 7:4–5/Luke 6:42; Matt. 23:23–24/Luke 11:42; Matt. 23:25–26/Luke 11:39–41; Matt. 23:27–28/Luke 11:44.
110 McKnight 1991: 209–210; Wenham 2021: 164–165.
111 Witherington 2009–10: 129, citing Clarence Bauman.
112 Witherington 2009–10: 129.

an oral compilation, perhaps a notebook, then shared and circulated, before coming to the evangelists via 'Q' or Matthean sources (depending on which version of the Synoptic Problem one prefers). Importantly, the sermon is not a series of timeless aphorisms about ethics; rather, it is more properly a speech about covenant renewal similar to other covenant-renewal speeches that call for Israel's repentance, reform, and return to covenant fidelity.[113] It is a speech that reveres God as Israel's exclusive deity and ruler, and sets forth rigorous commands, including various blessings and curses, which lead to life and death respectively. It is obedience to these commands which proves to be not only a wise course of action, like that of a man building his house on rock,[114] but also the test for covenant loyalty and belonging to the kingdom.[115] The sermon(s) of Jesus were a challenge to his hearers to imagine and then enact a new way of being Israel ahead of the dawning of the kingdom.[116]

Piety

In the ancient world, piety (Lat. *pietas*; Gk *eusebeia*) was a cardinal virtue.[117] The Jews found admiration, and even converts from paganism, on account of the magnetic appeal of their own devotional practices.[118] The Jews of both Judea and the Diaspora stood out because of their 'inviolable piety', as Josephus calls it.[119] Adherence to piety was, of course, wide-ranging in effort, from laxity to zealotry, but generally the Jewish people were known for their dutiful diligence in keeping the customs and laws of their national way of life, even to the point of death.[120] God had chosen the Jews from all the tribes of the world, and their cultus and customs were connected to their national identity, so that loyalty to the deity meant loyalty to the community. The Jerusalem temple was a

---

113 Exod. 20; Deut. 5, 27 – 28; Josh. 24; Ezra 8; 1QS. Cf. Horsley 2012: 122–229.
114 Matt. 7:24–27/Luke 6:47–49.
115 Matt. 7:21–23/Luke 6:46.
116 Cf. Wright 1996: 288.
117 See e.g. Plato, *Protagoras* 349B; Aristotle, *Virt. et Vit.* 55.12.50; Diogenes Laertius 7.119; Philo, *Vit. Mos.* 2.216; Josephus, *Ant.* 16.176; *Apion* 2.181.
118 See e.g. Josephus, *Apion* 1.190–193; further Bird 2010a: 83–93.
119 See Josephus, *Ant.* 15.248; 16.41–44; *Apion* 2.193, 227–228, 232–233, 271, 277.
120 Dan. 11:33–35; *T. Mos.* 9.6; 1 Macc. 1:62–63; 2:19–22; 2 Macc. 6:27–28; 7:2, 9, 11, 23, 37.

prestigious symbol of God's presence with Israel, and while foreign taxes might be resented, nothing was feared more than foreign desecration of the temple.[121] To conquerors, this pious devotion was inflexibly stubborn and grossly insubordinate, while philosophers could admire the Jews for the antiquity of their religion, and their consistency and commitment in practising it.

Jewish piety consisted of general devotion to God: performing daily recitation of the Shema and prayers; obeying the Mosaic legislation, especially concerning the boundary-markers of Judaism in the form of sabbath, circumcision and food laws; paying the temple tax and participating in the temple cultus; giving alms; keeping the daily, weekly and annual rhythms of life; engaging in public reading from the Torah; showing contrition for sin; and promoting virtues such as justice and magnanimity.[122] The etymological origins of the word 'Pharisees' are found in the Hebrew word *perushim*, used for the self-styled 'pious ones' of the Maccabean and Hasmonean eras, echoing scriptural language to indicate their commitment to the Judean way of life.[123] The Pharisees were revered for their legal precision, pursuit of priest-like purity, and pious practices. Rabbi Simon the Righteous was remembered for accenting the importance of Torah, temple and acts of piety.[124]

The socio-religious world of Jesus was one where national and personal honour was bound up with public piety. Debate raged, from the technical level to the fanatical, on how to live devoutly before God. For the devout family, there were many elements of everyday life, such as daily prayers, ritual washings, meal preparations, household chores, paid labour, child-rearing, tithes and bodily discharges, that required certain rituals and were thus all affected by piety. Furthermore, since Maccabean times,

---

121 Sanders 1992: 144.
122 Sanders (1992: 237–238) refers to 'orthopraxy in worldwide Judaism' so that '[a] Jew could travel from the western most part of the empire to Mesopotamia, go to the synagogue, recognize at least aspects of the service, and perhaps even find a common language. If invited to a meal, he might find the combination of foods and the spices to be entirely new, but there would be no pork and the meat would not be bloody. On the sabbath, a few customs might be strange, but the constantly burning lamps, the absence of toil, and the service of prayer and study would be, at least in general terms, the same as the customs which he left so many miles to the west.'
123 Pss 30:5; 31:24; 37:28.
124 *m. Abot* 1.2.

questions had centred on how to negotiate the Greco-Roman world, a problem that was particularly acute for Galilee, surrounded as it was by the non-Jewish territories of Syria, Iturea, Decapolis and Samaria. How does one eat with or in proximity to Gentile guests? Can Jews go to the gymnasium or participate in athletic games? Can Jews offer sacrifices *on behalf of* the emperor rather than *to* the emperor to demonstrate loyalty to the imperial authority? Jewish piety required a constant conversation about deity, legality, purity, morality and community.[125]

Jesus is presented in our sources as a generally devout rural Galilean who is particularly committed to living under the Torah, in accordance with God's will, with an eye on the realization of Israel's hopes in God's kingship. That said, Jesus can be portrayed in Christian literature with varying degrees of adherence to, debating about, and distance from Jewish legal traditions. How Jesus exercises Jewish piety is portrayed quite differently in the Gospels of Matthew, John, *Thomas*, *Philip*, *Mary* and *the Ebionites*. Also, the danger is that Jesus' piety gets translated into culturally popular modes based on the disposition of the interpreter. Such a bias is blatant in the Romantic 'God-consciousness' of Jesus in nineteenth-century scholarship, evident too in Protestant allergies to ritual and law projected onto Jesus, and even progressive constructions of Jesus inclined towards inclusivity over boundaries and relationships over religion – all of which are obviously anachronistic. Nonetheless, Jesus should be understood as a pious Galilean whose own prophetic calling and messianic vocation was driven by a steadfast devotion to the God of his family and nation. That piety consists of putting God first, resting in God's fatherhood, and the practices of prayer, pruning sin and giving alms.

First, in Jesus' teaching, God's law, will and kingdom must be the priority. Mere profession of Jesus as 'master' or 'teacher' is insufficient; one must be committed to doing God's will.[126] Disciples are expected to 'seek first the kingdom of God and his righteousness',[127] even if it means abandoning family.[128] Their compassionate acts are pursued for God's

---

125 See, for Palestinian Jews, Sanders 1992; for Diaspora Jews, see Barclay 1996.
126 Matt. 7:21.
127 Matt. 6:33.
128 Mark 10:28–30; 13:12; Luke 9:59–62; 14:26.

The teaching of Jesus

glory.[129] Love for God is the greatest commandment.[130] God's name is to be revered in prayer.[131] They are to be perfect as their heavenly Father is perfect.[132] Jesus' followers are called to fidelity to God even in the face of persecution.[133] Faithfulness to God results in acceptance into a new fictive kinship[134] and the promise of eternal life.[135] In effect: if those who are last in society put God first, then they will be first in the reordering of power associated with God's kingdom.

Second, God's fatherhood was distinctive of Jesus' piety. This topic is teeming with scholarly assumptions and popular fictions about the status of God's fatherhood in Judaism and Jesus' unique use of *abba* prayer-language. To begin with, the notion of God as Father is not alien to Judaism. God is invoked as 'Father' in the OT, in Second Temple literature and in the rabbinic corpora, often in the context of prayer.[136] In the traditional Jewish prayer known as the *Shemoneh Esreh*, which pious Jews were meant to recite three times a day, we find the following titles of adoration: 'Lord, God of our Fathers, God of Abraham. The Holy God. Our Father'.[137] Prayer to God as Father was extant in Jesus' own day, even if Jesus adapted this language towards his specific vision of God's reign.[138]

Jesus clearly affirmed God's fatherhood to the point where the name 'Father' should be reserved for God alone.[139] That rests on the premise that fatherhood underscores God's electing love for Israel.[140] Similarly, God's fatherhood is also indicative of God's forgiveness and compassion as suggested in the Hebrew Scriptures,[141] which is why Jesus taught that

---

129 Matt. 5:16.
130 Deut. 6:4; Mark 12:30.
131 Matt. 6:9/Luke 11:2.
132 Matt. 5:48.
133 Matt. 5:10–12, 44; 10:23; Mark 4:17; 13:11–13; Luke 11:49; John 15:20.
134 Mark 3:33–34.
135 Mark 10:30.
136 Cf. e.g. Deut. 32:6; Isa. 63:16; 64:7; Jer. 3:4; 31:9; Mal. 2:10; *Jub.* 1.25, 28; *Jos. Asen.* 12.8, 14–15; 3 Macc. 6:3, 8; Tob. 13:4; Sir. 23:1, 4; 51:10; Wis. 14:3; 1QH^a 9.35; 4Q372 1.16; *m. Abot* 5.20.
137 Schürer 1973–87: 2:460–461.
138 McKnight 1999: 51–52.
139 Matt. 23:9.
140 Exod. 4:22; Deut. 14:1–2; Hos. 11:1; *4 Ezra* 1.28.
141 Ps. 103:13.

God is ever ready to forgive,[142] to provide for his children,[143] to give them good gifts[144] and to give them the kingdom.[145] For Jesus, much as it was for his contemporaries, to call God 'Father' is to speak of his authority and lordship, as well as his care, forgiveness, compassion and love.[146] Therefore, Jesus' preferred use of *abba* as a term of divine address is distinctive of him, but unlikely to be novel.

What is perhaps unique is that Jesus invites followers to enjoy the same intimate filial relationship that he himself enjoyed with God.[147] The Father of Jesus becomes the Father of his followers because Jesus calls them to a special experience of God oriented towards the manifestation of God's kingdom.[148] Note, however, that God's fatherhood is not, for Jesus, a statement of the universal human sense of dependence on God's kindness; rather, God's fatherhood is a chief symbol of God's covenant-making[149] and covenant-renewing activity.[150] God is known and experienced as the divine Father of Israel's Davidic king[151] within a restored Israelite kingdom.[152] It was, then, appropriate for Jesus to accent God's fatherly authority and love because God's kingly power and covenant love were being revealed in the beginnings of Israel's renewal. As a result, the *abba* address came to be a distinctive form of Christian prayer towards the God of Israel, used even by non-Jewish Christ-followers because they regarded themselves as the vanguard of a renewed Israel.[153]

Third, Jesus emphasizes a life of prayer through his own example and teaching. Prayer was important in Jewish life and was practised

---

142 Matt. 6:14; Luke 15:11–32.
143 Matt. 6:26.
144 Matt. 7:11/Luke 11:13.
145 Luke 12:32.
146 McKnight 1999: 54.
147 Mark 13:32; 14:36; Matt. 11:25–27/Luke 10:21–21; John 11:41–42; 17:1. According to Crump (2013: 686): 'Jesus' prayers were unique, but not because he prayed to God as *abbā*, *'ab* or *'ābî*. They were unique because Jesus, in praying to his Father, did so as the one, unique Son, a self-understanding rooted in his own religious experience . . . It was Jesus' claim to a unique identity that set his prayers apart, not an idiosyncratic vocabulary.'
148 Matt. 7:21; 25:34; Luke 12:32; 22:29.
149 Exod. 4:22–23; Deut. 14:1–2; 32:6; *4 Ezra* 1.28.
150 Hos. 11:1–4; 63:11–19; 64:8–12.
151 Ps. 2:6.
152 Luke 22:19.
153 Gal. 4:6; Rom. 8:15–16.

in the morning and evening,[154] and often with meals.[155] Prayer was associated with the temple,[156] while prayer-houses as gathering places for prayers and psalmody were possible forerunners of synagogues, which developed under Pharisaic influence.[157] The rabbinic prayers, notably the *Shemoneh Esreh* and *Amidah*, are very probably modelled on earlier patterns of prayer. Jesus grew up in a Jewish home and as part of a Jewish community where prayer was part of family and village life. In his ministry, Jesus often retreated to deserted spots to pray,[158] and he taught his disciples about prayer on more than one occasion.[159] The Johannine tradition depicts Jesus telling disciples to pray/ask in 'my name'.[160] His instructions in how to pray give a framework for petition, urge persistence in prayer and excoriate pretentiousness. Jesus' example shows that prayer is a mode of cultivating intimacy with God, especially in times of crisis.

Fourth, Jesus taught about the necessity of pruning sin from one's personal life. The Jewish world view was one cognizant of personal and national offences against God.[161] John the Baptist's message was about confessing sins as a preliminary stage of preparing for the eschatological judgment.[162] Jesus, speaking hyperbolically, told people to cut off their hand or foot or gouge out their eyes if they enticed them to sin.[163] Pruning sin and repenting of sins was necessary if one was to avoid perishing in the ordeal of judgment.[164] A person could die in and with their sins.[165] Jesus expectantly prayed, as the later rabbis did, 'Do not bring me into

---

154 Josephus, *Ant.* 4.212; *War* 2.128.
155 Deut. 8:10; Josephus, *War* 2.131; 1QS 6.4–5; *m. Ber.* 6–8.
156 Isa. 56:7; 2 Macc. 1:24–30; Acts 3:1; 22:17.
157 Acts 16:13, 16; Josephus, *Apion* 277, 280, 293. Cf. Barclay 1996: 26–27, 417; Hengel 2000: 171–195.
158 Mark 1:35; 6:46; 14:32.
159 Mark 11:24–25; 12:40; Matt. 5:44/ Luke 6:28; Matt. 6:5–11; Luke 11:1–4, 5–13; 18:1–8.
160 John 14:13–14; 15:16; 16:23–26.
161 Cf. e.g. Pss 32; 36; 51; Isa. 59:10; Jer. 15:19–21.
162 Mark 1:4–5; Matt. 3:10/Luke 3:8–9.
163 Mark 9:43–50.
164 Luke 13:5.
165 John 8:24.

the power of sin, a temptation, a shame.'[166] The sins of individuals and the nation had to be repented of ahead of the coming judgment.

Fifth, Jesus urged habits of compassion for the needy. In Second Temple Judaism a common aspect of piety was the giving of alms.[167] The Hebrew Scriptures' exhortations about caring for the poor[168] were given specific content with practices pertaining to material gifts for the destitute and other acts of kindness to the less fortunate such as burying the dead.[169] Giving alms was considered an acceptable form of sacrifice; it atoned for sins, stored up wealth before God and even delivered the giver from death.[170] Jesus declared that, in order for a person to receive a reward from God, alms should be given in secret, not in a showy fashion.[171] One could give alms to atone for sins and to make oneself clean.[172] Giving alms enabled one to store up treasure in heaven.[173] Similarly, feeding the hungry, welcoming strangers, attending to those in prison and clothing the naked were also considered forms of alms-giving that indicated true discipleship and enabled one to prevail at the final judgment.[174] Jesus is never more than, or anything other than, Jewish in his teaching about alms-giving. Unsettling as it might be to some contemporary modes of Christianity, Jesus taught that giving alms affects one's eternal destiny.

Wealth and riches

The discussion of Jesus and alms-giving is a good segue into Jesus' teachings about wealth and riches. It is true that Jesus had more to say about riches than redemption, yet that is only because one's attitude towards wealth determined one's participation in the redemptive power of the kingdom. What is more, financial matters were a significant part

---

166 *b. Ber.* 60b; cf. Matt. 6:13/Luke 11:4.
167 See Anderson 2013; Downs 2016.
168 Cf. e.g. Lev. 19:9–10; 23:22; Deut. 15:1–18; Prov. 19:17.
169 Cf. esp. Tob. 1:16–17; 4:6–16; 12:8–10; Sir. 7:10; 12:3; 17:22.
170 Dan. 4:27; Prov. 10:2; 11:4; Tob. 4:9–10; Sir. 29:11–12; 35:2; 40:17, 24.
171 Matt. 6:1–4. Note a similar link between righteousness (*dikaiosynē*) and giving alms (*eleēmosynē*) in Tob. 4:7.
172 Luke 11:41.
173 Mark 10:21; Luke 12:33.
174 Matt. 25:31–46.

The teaching of Jesus

of the early church's life, seen not least in incidents involving Ananias and Sapphira, who had withheld funds from the communal deposit,[175] the distribution of food for Aramaic-speaking and Greek-speaking widows,[176] the Jerusalem church's reminder to the Antioch church to 'remember the poor',[177] and Paul's attempt to take up and deliver a collection for the Jerusalem church.[178] Money mattered in Jesus' teaching and in the mission of the early church.

Jesus did not require all of his followers to walk out on their families and renounce possessions. Some disciples remained *in situ* and supported him in his work,[179] while others committed themselves to redistributing their goods and compensating anyone they had wronged,[180] but some disciples clearly were expected to sell their possessions, and they did.[181] For Jesus, the purpose of life is not about accruing possessions[182] as that accrues only culpability.[183] Jesus criticized the scribes for devouring widows' houses in some kind of predatory fiscal transaction.[184] He warned that one cannot serve both God and Mammon.[185] Wealth is a lure from[186] or an impediment to[187] receiving the kingdom. One must store up an imperishable wealth in terms of righteous deeds,[188] and one must be willing to give up wealth in order to gain entrance into the kingdom.[189] This resonated with the Jewish wisdom tradition where the righteous were advised: 'Lay up your treasure according to the commandments of the Most High, and it will profit you more than gold' (Sir. 29:11). Riches

---

175 Acts 5:1–11.
176 Acts 6:1–2.
177 Gal. 2:10.
178 1 Cor. 16:1–6; 2 Cor. 8:1–24; Rom. 15:25–33.
179 Luke 8:2–3.
180 Luke 18:1–10.
181 Mark 10:21–22, 28; Luke 14:33.
182 Luke 12:15.
183 Luke 16:19 31.
184 Matt. 12:40/Luke 20:47. Blomberg (1999: 145) is correct that 'Jesus is not crucified for his teaching about material possessions, but the controversies with the Jewish leaders that become increasingly pointed include items of stewardship as one prime arena in which they do not please God'.
185 Matt. 6:24/Luke 16:13.
186 Mark 4:18–19.
187 Mark 10:23.
188 Matt. 6:19–21/Luke 12:16–21, 33–34.
189 Matt. 13:44–46.

were not considered a sign of God's favour, nor did they make one rich towards God.[190] Jesus did not establish a deposit of common goods like the Qumranites, fundraise like a medieval bishop, accumulate wealth to support an army like a royal pretender, or entirely renounce possessions like a Cynic philosopher. Jesus rehearsed many scriptural and sapiential motifs about the dangers of wealth, particularly in the light of his message of the kingdom of God. In several parables, such as the story of Lazarus and the rich man, and the parable of the rich fool, wealth and status are not a sign of divine blessing; rather, they are evidence that might even damn one's soul before God's judgment.[191]

Torah

Jesus' relationship to the Torah is one of the most important and contested aspects of his ministry. To begin with, the evangelists themselves are angular on this topic. Mark writes out of what I suspect is the Pauline tradition with its view of very limited adherence to Torah for Gentiles,[192] even as the Markan Jesus in principle affirms such adherence.[193] Matthew has a tendency to rejudaize the Markan story by stressing Jesus' Jewishness and loyalty to the Torah,[194] whereby the Matthean Jesus pursues a covenantal righteousness more rigorous than that of the Pharisees,[195] even though he stresses compassion over cultus.[196] Luke in his Gospel amplifies the idea of Jesus treating the Torah as something belonging to a prior epoch of redemptive history,[197] and in Acts portrays Paul as Torah-observant, with Torah viewed as a burden not to be placed on Gentiles.[198] John treats the Torah as a prophecy of Christ, typological towards Christ and superseded by Christ.[199] Among the 'other' Gospels,

---

190 Luke 12:16-20.
191 Luke 12:13-21; 16:19-31; so Kloppenborg 2006: 47.
192 Cf. Mark 7:19; Rom. 14:14.
193 Mark 1:44; 10:19.
194 Matt. 5:17-19; 15:1-28.
195 Matt. 5:20; 23:1-29.
196 Cf. Hos. 6:6, cited in Matt. 9:13; 12:7.
197 Luke 16:16.
198 Acts 15:10, 28; 21:21-26.
199 John 1:17, 45; 3:14; 5:45-46; 12:34; 15:25. See esp. Loader 2002 [1997].

The teaching of Jesus

Thomas engages in a mixture of spiritualization and renunciation of the Torah, while the *Gospel of the Ebionites* has Jesus abolishing the temple sacrifices in total.[200] So the evangelists and later interpreters have skin in the game of Jesus and the Torah.

In addition, we must be careful to remember that we are discussing a first-century Galilean prophet talking about God's will in relation to the kingdom; not the diasporan Paul of Tarsus discoursing on how Messiah-believing Gentiles are under 'grace', not 'Torah'; and especially not Protestant concerns about the necessity of partitioning law and gospel, or the 'third use of the law'.[201] Those debates are fine, but they are happening in another seminar room. Furthermore, the root of the problem of Jesus and Torah is that Jesus appears to allow what the Torah forbids (e.g. working on the sabbath) and forbids what the Torah allows (taking oaths; retaliation; burying parents; divorce, etc.). Jesus appears to oscillate between being rigorist and liberal, intensifying some commands yet relaxing others.[202] How can Jesus possibly amplify some Mosaic regulations but seem to arbitrarily avoid others?[203]

First, if we are thinking historically, then we are constrained to think of Jesus as a Torah-observant Galilean.[204] Jesus lives a Jewish life, which entails Torah observance as the matrix for his prophetic mission and messianic identity. Bockmuehl puts it well: 'The Jesus of the Synoptic tradition approved of tithing, endorsed sacrifice and voluntary gifts to

---

200 *Gos. Thom.* 14; 53; 104; *Gos. Eb.* 6.

201 The most anti-Torah and anti-temple saying attributed to Jesus is found in the much later *Gos. Eb.* 6 where Jesus declares, 'I have come to do away with sacrifices, and if you do not cease from sacrificing, the wrath of God will not cease from you.' The second-century Valentinian teacher Ptolemy, in his letter to Flora, breaks the Torah down into three parts: what God said to Moses, what Moses said and what the elders said – a division which he attributes to the teaching of the Saviour, i.e. Jesus. Even the God-given part can be subdivided into pure law unmixed with inferiority (Decalogue), law mixed with injustice (*lex talionis*), and the allegorical and symbolic parts of the law (e.g. circumcision).

202 Theissen and Merz 1998 [1996]: 348.

203 Hence the comparison between Jesus, Philo, Qumran, rabbinic exegesis and Enochic Judaism; see Theissen and Merz 1998 [1996]: 351–353. Meier (1991–2016: 4:3) sums up the problem: 'The real enigma is how Jesus can at one and the same time affirm the Law as the given, as the normative expression of God's will for Israel, and yet in a few individual cases or legal areas (e.g., divorce and oaths) teach and enjoin what is contrary to the Law, simply on his own authority.'

204 Cadbury 1937: 146–147; Harvey 1982: 37–51; Vermes 1983: 26, 45–46; 1993: 21; Thiessen 2020. Note esp. Meier (1991–2016: 4:648): 'It is Torah and Torah alone that puts flesh and bones on the spectral figure of "Jesus the Jew."'

the temple, even paid the controversial temple tax (however grudgingly), said grace before meals, and wore tassels on his clothes.'[205] Jesus, like his contemporaries, regarded the Mosaic legislation as prescriptive and enshrining God's will for Israel, even as he disputed its precise interpretation. Anything that makes Jesus look theologically Protestant or socially progressive should be dismissed as anachronism.[206] Christian interpretation has sadly tended to negatively caricature the Torah and its practice in Second Temple Judaism whereby the Torah was absolutized to the point of legalism, interpreted in a casuistic way focused on the minutiae of detail rather than human flourishing, regarded as a means to accumulate merit and avoid recompense, had no purpose other than to be obeyed and was a yoke that Israel struggled to carry.[207] If that were indeed the case, one wonders how the psalmist could rejoice, 'Oh, how I love your law! It is my meditation all day long',[208] or how Paul could say: 'Do we then overthrow the law by this faith? By no means! On the contrary, we uphold the law' and 'the law is holy, and the commandment is holy and just and good'.[209] Statements that Jesus transcended the Torah are unhelpful. One does not transcend the Magna Carta by asking for more rights, better rights or more carefully defined rights. Jesus is not a liberal cosmopolitan; he is covenantal. He reasons within the Torah, not against it. Jesus, like Hillel, knew that love for God, love for Torah and love for other human beings were not mutually exclusive.[210] I labour the point because, as far as we know, Jesus believed in the authority and permanence of the Torah.[211] Jesus instructed people to do as Moses commanded, and he appealed to the authority of Moses concerning the resurrection of the dead.[212] Importantly, Jesus affirmed the second half of the Decalogue,[213] he upheld the statement of the Shema that God is

---

205 Bockmuehl 2006: 208.
206 Cadbury (1937: 90): 'For an age that boasts of scientific history, anachronism is a more unpardonable sin.'
207 Theissen and Merz 1998 [1996]: 359–360.
208 Ps. 119:97.
209 Rom. 3:31; 7:12.
210 *m. Abot* 1.12.
211 Matt. 5:18/Luke 16:17.
212 Mark 1:44; 7:10; 10:19; Mark 12:26.
213 Mark 12:19.

The teaching of Jesus

one,[214] and like other rabbis regarded the love command in Leviticus 19:18 as the fulfilment of the law.[215]

Second, it also helps if we remember that the intensification of some commands and the relaxation of others is a normal feature of Jewish renewal movements.[216] The Pharisees, in general, tried to extend the laws of purity for priests, first to their own circle, then second, to the whole nation, perhaps so that Israel would quite literally become a kingdom of priests à la Exodus 19:5-6. We have evidence that the Pharisaic 'associates' and the Qumran sectarians consumed their daily food in a state of ritual purity as if they were metaphorical priests.[217] The result would be that '[t]he Temple altar in Jerusalem would be replicated at the tables of all Israel'.[218] But some Pharisees also sought to liberalize certain commands to make them less burdensome to the poor, such as those pertaining to sacrifices and debts. The Qumranites followed rigorous regulations that exceeded anything proposed in the Torah for avoiding impurities, even as they ignored all the commands about celebrating festivals and offering sacrifices in the temple because they regarded the temple as corrupted. In a similar vein, Jesus can censure adultery beyond the act itself and extend it even to looking lustfully at someone[219] and also equate anger with the very act of murder.[220] Yet Jesus can also rescind prohibitions on seeking retaliation,[221] even though the Torah permitted this.[222] The point to note is that Judaism was filled with debates about which laws mattered most, which laws needed to be extended, what to do when certain laws conflicted with one another, what were legitimate exemptions to a law, and how one's view of the future impacted

---

214 Deut. 6:4 = Mark 12:29-30.
215 Mark 12:31. See Allison (2005b: 158-160) on how Mark 12:28-34 reflects Jesus' affirmation of the Decalogue.
216 Theissen 1987: 139-140; Theissen and Merz 1998 [196]: 361-372; Bockmuehl 2000: 10.
217 Himmelfarb 1997; Regev 2000; Klawans 2002: 13-14. But see doubts by Schwartz (1992), who thinks this is more of a late eighteenth-century view read back into the Pharisees.
218 Neusner 1973: 146.
219 Matt. 5:27-28.
220 Matt. 5:22.
221 Matt. 5:38-39.
222 Exod. 21:24; Lev. 24:20. Though see 1QS 10.17-18: 'I will not repay a man with an evil reward: I will pursue man with goodness. For judgment of every living being is with God and he will repay man his reward.'

Torah-keeping in the present. Jesus' remarks about Torah need to be placed in that interpretative context.

Third, in some instances, Jesus' disagreement with the Pharisees is a matter of *halakhah*; it is not questioning the legitimacy of Torah per se.[223] Halakhic interpretation derives from the premise of God's displeasure at Israel's disobedience to divine commands, combined with the need to explicate those commands in a precise and rigorous manner.[224] For example, Jesus rejected the handwashing[225] *halakhah* of the Pharisees, and he attacked their *halakhah* whereby the *Corban* regulation about gifts dedicated to the temple was used as an excuse to avoid providing for one's parents as the Decalogue commanded.[226] These are all, as it were, in-house Pharisaic debates about precisely how to obey the Torah, not abrogating the Torah. Even most of the dispute stories in the Gospels, says Meier, 'present Jesus debating with other Jewish groups or individuals about the proper interpretation and practice of the Law, not about the basic obligation of faithful Israelites to obey the Law. The Law is God's gift to Israel.'[227]

Fourth, in other cases, Jesus regards some commands as subordinated to other commands.[228] The question of what to do in ambiguous situations

---

[223] Many Jewish groups envisaged some kind of extra-scriptural tradition to help people obey Scripture. *Jubilees* is an interpretative expansion on Genesis and claims to be a transcript of an angelic recitation of heavenly tablets given to Moses on Mount Sinai in which Mosaic legislation is reiterated and also expanded into new regulations. *1 Enoch* is a composite work which claims in the astronomical section to transmit revealed law in the form of calendrical observations. Various writings from Qumran evidence a rehearsal of Mosaic laws, including their interpretation, expansion, and supplementation with additional requirements (see esp. 1QS, CD, 4QMMT, 11QT). Philo rejected purely literal and purely allegorical interpretation of the Torah, instead affirming a literal reading supplemented by allegory as a means to attaining a deeper understanding of God, wisdom and ethics from Torah (*Migr.* 89–93). In rabbinic Judaism, the teaching of the sages and rabbis was regarded as a fence around the Torah to prevent it from being violated (*m. Abot* 1.1; 3.13). One could argue that Jesus' teaching was a form of *halakhah* that engaged in dialogue with Torah and extant traditions, the difference being that Jesus was not interested in calendars, cultus or casuistic law. Even Paul's 'law of Christ' (Gal. 6:2; 1 Cor. 9:21) may represent Pauline *halakhah* on how to stay faithful to God without necessarily being under the yoke of the entirety of the Torah. Moreover, the letter to the Ephesians is replete with halakhic metaphors about one's 'walk' in good works, holiness and avoiding sexual immorality (Eph. 2:10; 4:1, 17; 5:2, 8, 15).

[224] Nickelsburg 2003: 59.

[225] On handwashing, see *Arist.* 305–306; *Sib. Or.* 3.591–593.

[226] Mark 7:1–13.

[227] Meier 1991–2016: 4:2. Or, to quote Bockmuehl (2000: 4), between Jesus and the Pharisees is the 'clash between different conceptions of halakhah, different ways of building that protective hermeneutical fence [around the Torah]'. Cf. Casey 1991: 70–73; helpful too is Kazen 2002.

[228] See Loader 2002 [1997]: 519; Vermes 2004: 104; Allison 2005b: 183–185.

occurred all the time in Judaism. Concerning the sabbath, for example, whereas Jews adhered to the day of mandated rest,[229] the Maccabeans faced the critical issue of whether they should fight the Syrians if attacked on the sabbath: to fight back was not ideal, but was deemed necessary.[230] The many sabbath controversies that Jesus was involved in reflect a similar legal concern about what was permitted by necessity on the sabbath.[231] That the sabbath belongs to humans and not humans to the sabbath is a dictum the rabbis would wholeheartedly endorse.[232] Jesus' willingness to heal on the sabbath marks him out as belonging to the camp of those who claimed that preserving life or healing an infirmity was permissible on the sabbath. In the Mishnah, 'Any matter of doubt pertaining to the saving of life supersedes the Sabbath' (*m. Yoma* 8.6), contrasts with the *Damascus Document*: 'And [if] any living person who falls into a place of water or a place of [...] Let no one bring him up with a ladder, or a rope or a tool' (CD 11.13-16, 16-17). Jesus' view was evidently more alarming than assuaging to many who scrutinized him further in order to keep their disgust at his alleged laxity on the sabbath fresh.[233] Of course, Jesus did not think of himself as disregarding the sabbath so much as working around it by necessity and as an exception in the case of hunger; a similar approach was demonstrated by the requirement to circumcise a newborn baby boy even on the sabbath.[234] Interestingly, in an agraphon, Jesus censures frivolous neglect of the sabbath,[235] and even the Thomasine Jesus claims: 'If you do not keep the sabbath as sabbath, you shall not see the Father' (*Gos. Thom.* 27). What is more, if Jesus regarded the sabbath as optional, his Galilean and Judean followers did not get the memo as they kept the sabbath.[236]

---

229 Cf. Exod. 16:23-29; 20:8-11; 31:13-16; Lev. 19:3; 30; Deut. 5:12-15; Neh. 13:15-22; *Jub.* 50.12-13; CD 10.14-11.18; Philo, *Vit. Mos.* 2.22.
230 1 Macc. 2:29-41; Josephus, *Ant.* 12.276 contrasted with *Jub.* 50.12; 4Q264ª III 8.
231 Mark 2:1-12, 23-28; 3:1-6; Luke 13:10-17; 14:1-6; John 5:1-18; 7:10-24; 9:1-17; *Gos. Thom.* 27; *Gos. Naz.* 10.
232 'The Sabbath is delivered up to you, not you to the Sabbath' (Mekhilta de R. Ishmael on Exod. 31:14) cited from Vermes 2004: 45.
233 For a fictional but realistic story of two sabbath 'police' in Capernaum, see Theissen 1987: 100-103.
234 Mark 2:23-28; John 7:23 (cf. *m. Ned.* 3.11).
235 Luke 6:5 according to Codex Bezae.
236 Cf. Mark 15:42-46; 16:1; Luke 23:56.

Fifth, Jesus was not antithetical to the purity regulations of the Torah as is often believed. Some scholars maintain the line that '[f]rom Jesus's teaching to his disciples we can infer that he considered the purity rules to be suspended'.[237] Such a view betrays an attitude somewhere between misunderstanding of and revulsion at the ancient world with its contaminants and cleansings, even more so in the case of Torah and rabbinic regulations about liquids, commodities, animals, bodies and bodily excretions. Jewish scribes and rabbis debated the nature of purity, the transference of impurity, how to avoid impurity, and how one moves from contagion to cleansing in the light of the Torah's regulations, namely: 'You are to distinguish between the holy and the common and between the unclean and the clean' (Lev. 10:10) and 'Thus you shall keep the Israelites separate from their uncleanness, so that they do not die in their uncleanness by defiling my tabernacle that is in their midst' (Lev. 15:31).[238] Jews had to avoid impurity, but only insofar as it prevented them from contacting holy things or people, such as the temple, sacrifices and priests; only by infringing such regulations did impurity become a transgression. Of course, there were different views on when the purity rules had to be carried out and how precisely to do that. According to Hannah Harrington, 'Issues of cult and purity engaged and divided Jews more so in this [Second Temple] period than at any other time in antiquity.' That is because times of crisis propel groups to erect symbolic boundaries between insiders and outsiders. Hence the prevalence of ritual baths and stone vessels throughout Galilee and Judea, the observation of ritual purity by priests and laity, and the expectation that people would consume food in a state of ritual purity.[239]

Debates about purity and impurity provide the context for understanding Jesus' contentious remarks about handwashing, food and impurities in Mark 7:1–23, in particular verse 15 (NIV): 'Nothing outside a person can defile them by going into them. Rather, it is what comes out of a person that defiles them.' I would aver that Jesus here does not

---

[237] Sacchi 1992: 130.
[238] Cf. Lev. 12 – 15; Num. 19. The secondary literature on Judaism and purity is now voluminous; see recently Thiessen 2020; Kazen 2021.
[239] Harrington 2010: 1121; cf. Sanders 1992: 214–230.

nullify the laws on unclean foods. The Markan aside, 'Thus he declared all foods clean', is either a parenthetical remark for Gentile readers[240] or a statement to the effect that 'Jesus declared all *kosher* food clean *and not requiring handwashing*'; the latter point is proved by the Matthean gloss, 'to eat with unwashed hands does not defile' (Matt. 15:20).[241] Accordingly, Jesus does not treat laws about unclean food and purity with indifference[242] so much as subordinate ritual purity to moral imperatives and engage in a halakhic debate with the Pharisees as to how impurities 'work'. This makes sense considering the three following things:

1 If annulling the food laws (i.e. Lev. 11; Deut. 14) was the intended purpose of Jesus' words, it would be an anomaly in the Jesus tradition.[243] It would also seem that Mark has not failed to notice the incongruity of having Jesus attack the Pharisees for nullifying the Torah in favour of their tradition, only to have Jesus in the next breath nullify the Torah in reference to food regulations (i.e. laws of *kashrut*). Further, if the historical Jesus had spoken so clearly on the issue of abrogating the food laws, then why was food such a disputed topic in the early church and why didn't its leaders simply refer back to sayings of Jesus to settle the matter?[244] The answer has to be: because Jesus never said such a thing.[245]

---

240 Cf. similar Jewish Christian perspectives in Rom. 14:14; Acts 10:15; John 13:10. Logan Williams (2024) offers an intriguing proposal that Mark 7:19c is not a parenthetical remark but is part of Jesus' speech, to the effect that 'ritually defiled food cannot defile humans through ingestion because humans purify all foods from ritual impurity through digestion' (371). My primary reason for doubting this is that Matthew's Gospel does not include these words. If it were the case that this was Jesus' own comment, why does Matthew omit the clause from his version of the story, given Matthew's propensity to rejudaize Markan tradition? Also, how does Williams' proposal relate to the contrasts of heart versus stomach and the 'not what goes in but what comes out defiles a person' remark that Jesus makes? Finally, this requires viewing defaecation and excrement as not causing ritual impurity, which appears to have been an ambivalent matter in Jewish sources (noted by Williams [2024: 385 n. 70]).
241 Cf. Crossley 2004: 192–193; 2009: 8; Bockmuehl 2008; Thiessen 2020: 187–195; Strahan 2023.
242 Contra e.g. Witherington 1990: 64; Dunn 2003: 788–789; Hengel and Schwemer 2019 [2007]: 413–414.
243 Jeremias 1971: 210–211; more recently, Strahan 2023: 266–267.
244 See Gal. 2:11–14; 1 Cor. 8:1–13; Rom. 14:23, 15–17; Rev. 2:14, 20.
245 Harvey 1982: 39; Sanders 1985: 246, 249–250, 266; Wright 1996: 380–382; Holmén 2001: 243.

2 A better way to understand Jesus' words in Mark 7:15 is in a comparative sense whereby the point is 'not only ... but also ...'[246] Understood this way, what matters urgently is not so much ritual purity (what one consumes) as moral purity (what one does).[247] The point is that ritual impurity does not harm someone as much as moral impurity can. It is not that ritual purity is bad or silly, but that some commands take precedence over others.[248] That precedence is driven by one's own taxonomy within Torah, in terms of solving debates about *halakhah* and holiness, and by the urgency of the demands of the kingdom.

3 In the light of the immediate context of Mark 7:1–23, Jesus contests the 'traditions of the elders' concerning handwashing. The topic of debate is not whether one can eat unclean food, but whether the washing of hands is necessary to protect oneself against kosher food that has been ritually defiled by hands that may have contracted impurity from somewhere else.[249] Jesus offers two lines of response. First, as something of an aside, he points out that the Pharisaic tradition allows someone to refrain from providing financial support for parents on the grounds that certain monies or goods that could be used to support them have been or will be dedicated to the temple; in which case, the tradition of the Pharisees circumvents the Torah's call to care for one's parents, rather than enabling obedience to the Torah's precepts. In effect, Pharisaic *halakhah* does not enable but instead circumvents scriptural commands. Second, Jesus adds that the taking of food into the body, even if it is food eaten with unclean/unwashed hands, is nothing compared to immoral discharges from the body, which are indicative of an unclean heart. Jesus contests the Pharisaic 'tradition' that one must eat clean food with washed/clean hands, that is, in a state of ritual purity, as it was

---

246 See e.g. Meyer 1979: 149; Sanders 1985: 260; Theissen and Merz 1998 [1996]: 230; Bockmuehl 2000: 10; Holmén 2001: 241; Kazen 2002: 66; Thiessen 2020: 192; Strahan 2023: 278.
247 Cf. Klawans (2000: 149): 'Thus what Mark 7 and Matthew 15 attribute to Jesus is the idea that attention to moral purity is more important than attention to ritual purity.'
248 See similar perspectives in Ps. Phocylides 228; Philo, *Spec. Leg.* 3.208–209; 1QS 3.2–12; *Ass. Mos.* 7.7–9. Note too how repentance is also accompanied by some ritual, e.g. *Life of Adam and Eve* 6–7; *T. Levi* 6.3; Mark 1:4, Matt. 3:6, Luke 3:3.
249 Williams 2024: 375.

not scriptural or even expedient. Kosher food is clean and does not require clean hands: the worst contaminant is unclean hearts which excrete immoral behaviour.[250] For Jesus, then, impurity does not penetrate the body; rather, it springs out of the body. Jesus offers his own instruction on how impurities work (through bodily expulsion rather than ingestion) and what constitutes the real threat posed by impurities, namely behaviour that exudes from the heart.[251]

The probability of this interpretation is underscored by the observation that Jesus was not treading new ground here, since the priority of morality over the rituals of the temple cultus was well known in Judaism. Hence, God's word through the prophet Hosea: 'I desire mercy, not sacrifice' (Hos. 6:6 NIV; cf. Mic. 6:6–8), and the description of the Jews in *Aristeas* where it is reported that the Jews 'honour God *not only* with gifts and sacrifices, *but also* with a purity of heart' (*Arist.* 234, emphasis added), which assumes that piety and cultus are better than cultus alone. For the Qumranites, other Jews are so steeped in wickedness that '[c]eremonies of atonement cannot restore [their] innocence, neither cultic waters [their] purity. [They] cannot be sanctified by baptism in oceans and rivers, nor purified by mere ritual bathing' (1QS 3.4–5). Even one of Jesus' scribal interlocutors agreed that love for God and love for neighbour is 'much more important than all whole burnt offerings and sacrifices' (Mark 12:33). Jesus affirms too the necessity of temple offerings[252] but prioritizes reconciliation in personal relationships.[253] Similarly, in an agraphon, Jesus is rebuffed by the Pharisees for not purifying himself

---

250 Crossley (2012: 96) has a good summary: 'He did not wash his hands or immerse himself before ordinary meals. This meant Jesus rejected the relevance of the view that impurity passed from hands to food to eater via the crucial liquid and so in turn rejected the view that the insides could be made unclean . . . But none of this is in contradiction with any biblical law.' Williams (2024: 379–380) demurs, on the grounds that 'Jesus specifically claims that, even if an object [clean food] has contracted ritual impurity, it cannot defile humans. He does not claim that foods before they go into the body cannot contract impurity in the first place.' Instead, on his 'interpretation of Mark 7.18b–19, food that *has been ritually contaminated* is not able to defile a person because each person, through the operations of their digestive system, purifies any food entering the body from ritual defilement. To put it simply, ritually defiled food cannot defile humans through ingestion because humans purify all foods from ritual impurity through digestion' (emphasis added).
251 Largely following Thiessen 2020: 187–195.
252 Mark 1:44.
253 Matt. 5:23–24.

before entering the temple,²⁵⁴ and he responds by pointing out the futility of washing the outer skin with water that dogs and pigs lie in when one is inwardly defiled by badness of every kind.²⁵⁵ The same theme of right behaviour over cultic purity is memorialized powerfully in the parable of the good Samaritan where showing compassion is more important than avoiding contamination ahead of entering the temple.²⁵⁶ In Jesus' teaching, temple cultus and cultic purity were subordinated to morality and relationships.²⁵⁷ Not because Jesus wanted to replace purity with compassion,²⁵⁸ or because he was 'casual in regard to purity ritual',²⁵⁹ but because he participated in extant debates over holiness, *halakhah* and the coming age. Hence Kazen's point that 'Jesus was part of a moral trajectory which placed relative importance on ethics ... [and] which did not allow purity rules to intervene with social networks, table fellowship and community, [since] his eschatological outlook made impurity subordinate to the kingdom'.²⁶⁰

The Torah's ethical regulations enabled Israel to emulate Yahweh's character, while the Torah's purity regulations enabled Israel to remain separate from the nations.²⁶¹ The Torah sets out categories of 'clean' and 'unclean' for food, items susceptible to impurity such as animal skins or

---

254 Cf. Lev. 15:31; John 11:55; Acts 24:18.

255 P. Oxy. 840 is probably a tradition that marries Mark 7:14–15 with a Johannine belief in the supersession of Jewish purification practices (John 2:1–11) and in Jesus' living water (John 7:38). Cf. Mark 7:14–15; Matt. 23:27–28; John 4:10–11; 7:38.

256 Luke 10:30–37.

257 Klawans (2000: 21–42, 158–162) has argued that moral purity and ritual purity were two parallel systems in Judaism. That partly makes sense given the fact that (1) to be ritually impure was not a sinful state, just part of life, as various bodily functions rendered one impure; and (2) the solution to ritual impurities was ritual washings (e.g. Lev. 15:1–5). However, the fact that some ritual impurities required sin offerings suggests that ritual and moral impurities could converge (Sklar 2005: 149). Further, in a cross-cultural context, the distinction between ritual and moral is somewhat arbitrary (Kazen 2011: 20–31). Plus, the relationship between ritual and moral impurity in Qumran is notoriously complex (see e.g. Ginsburskaya 2009). Thiessen (2020: 15) argues that ritual purity only becomes moral impurity if a person in an impure state does something like coming into contact with the holy (temple, vessels, sacrifices, priests) without first engaging in rituals for purification. Also, 'ritual impurity and moral impurity (sin) are two different categories, although they overlap at times' (87).

258 Contra Borg (1998 [1984]: 15): 'Against the politics of holiness, Jesus not only protested, but advocated an alternative core value for shaping Israel's life – a politics of compassion.' Instead, see Klausner 1925: 366–367; Fredriksen 2005; Thiessen 2020: 4–5, 11.

259 Dunn 2003: 789.

260 Kazen 2002: 347.

261 Lev. 19:2; 20:24–25.

earthenware, and impure bodily states due to a rash or emission. Indeed, within the rhythm of life, where most people were unclean most of the time – due to touching animals, experiencing bodily discharges and finding themselves in predicaments such as having to bury a deceased relative – there was a specified process for becoming clean again.[262] While Jesus does not speak against those categories or processes, he nonetheless does make an internal prioritization within the Torah, as did other Jews, so that Torah's prescriptions and interpretations give greater weight to what expresses itself in justice, mercy and faithfulness.[263] That is similar to the approach of Rabbi Simon ben Gamaliel, for whom Torah study was about justice, truth and peace.[264] Internalization of the law, a true circumcision of the heart, was lauded by Jews.[265] Ritual was meant to be an expression of piety, not a substitute for it![266] Jesus rhetorically rehearses this same elevation of morality over ritual purity in his woe against the Pharisees, who 'clean the outside of the cup and . . . plate, but inside they are full of greed and self-indulgence'.[267]

According to Jesus, the Torah's categories of clean and unclean as they applied to food were not abrogated; neither were the temple's requirements for cultic purity to be ignored; but purity was *more* a matter of heart and behaviour *than* a state to be preserved for its own sake. All of life was lived before God in holiness, and cultic purity where required must be respected. But holiness was more than cultic purity, and holiness was just as much a contagion as impurity.[268] In fact, as Matthew Thiessen puts it, Jesus himself appears as a contagion:

> By inserting a new, mobile, and powerfully contagious force of holiness into the world in the person of Jesus, Israel's God has

---

262 See Sanders 1992: 214–230; Thiessen 2020: 15. Tarja Philip puts it this way: 'Impurities are taken as part of human nature and life, and in themselves are not negative; they become negative only in relation to the holy' (cited from Thiessen 2020: 71 n. 5).
263 Matt. 23:23/Luke 11:42.
264 *m. Abot* 1.18.
265 Deut. 10:16; 30:6; Jer. 4:4; 9:26; Philo, *Spec. Leg.* 1.6; Rom. 2:29; *Od. Sol.* 1.1; cf. *Barn.* 9.1, 5; 10.12.
266 Sanders 1992: 230.
267 Matt. 23:25–26/Luke 11:39–40; *Gos. Thom.* 89.
268 See Berger 1988; Theissen and Merz 1998 [1996]: 229; Blomberg 2005; Tiwald 2012: 406; Thiessen 2020: 7, 20; Schröter 2014 [2012]: 115.

signaled the very coming of the kingdom – a kingdom of holiness and life that through the mission of Jesus overwhelms the forces and sources of impurity and death, be they pneumatic, ritual, or moral.[269]

Sixth, there are pericopae where Jesus appears to be more rigorous than the Torah in the requirements he lays upon followers. When it came to the topic of divorce, ever a live issue, Jesus point blank repeals the Mosaic provision for a man to divorce his wife. The reason he gives is that divorce is not how it was in the beginning with the result that, now, whoever divorces and marries another commits adultery.[270] The logic here is something along the lines of an *Urzeit-Endzeit* argument. The arrival of the kingdom in the 'end time' (*Endzeit*) will mean a restoration of human affairs to resemble the 'original time' (*Urzeit*). But – and here's the kicker – Jesus calls on disciples to disregard the Mosaic divorce concession, which was given because of sin, and to begin living *as if* the future kingdom is already here; that is, to see themselves as modelling in the here and now the manner of life, including in marriage, that the kingdom of God will embody.[271] In addition, there was one occasion when Jesus called a follower, and the man pleaded, 'Lord, first let me go and bury my father', to which Jesus retorted, 'Let the dead bury their own dead; but as for you, go and proclaim the kingdom of God' (Luke 9:59–60). The words might seem harsh, and attempts to ameliorate them by saying that the son was waiting for his father to die are simply beside the point. Jesus called people to leave behind any 'house or brothers or sisters or mother or father or children or fields' to follow him and to proclaim the kingdom (Mark 10:29–31). It is not Mosaic regulation but kingdom mission that is absolute.[272] All other relationships and commitments were relativized to this overarching imperative to join him in announcing the kingdom of God.[273]

---

269 Thiessen 2020: 179.
270 Mark 10:2–12.
271 Harvey 1990: 190–210; Vermes 2004: 55; Allison 2005b: 185–191; Schnelle 2009 [2007]: 143; Tiwald 2012: 403; Hengel and Schwemer 2019 [2007]: 473.
272 See Sanders 1985: 267; Schrage 1988: 67; Vermes 2004: 104; Schröter 2014 [2012]: 151–152; Hengel and Schwemer 2019 [2007]: 441.
273 Meier (1991–2016: 4:658) puts it well: '[I]n Jesus' view of things, the halakic life he demands

The teaching of Jesus

Thus, crucial for Jesus' view of Torah are the following points.

1 Whatever actions the Torah requires, these are subordinated to the demands of the kingdom, both in its enactment and in its proclamation. One does not wait for a father to die, so that you can bury him, before proclaiming the kingdom, any more than one might insist on the principle of rest when Gentile marauders are invading a Galilean town on the sabbath.
2 Where Torah commands are rescinded or intensified, it is not because of a fault in Torah but because the imperatives of the kingdom require something more rigorous or more relaxed in a certain area of life (e.g. divorce, retaliation, sabbath), something that leads people into God's original or eschatological design.
3 Jesus does not terminate Torah but transforms it so that covenant faithfulness is adjusted to the currency of the new moral economy created by the coming age (e.g. compassion prioritized over cultus; kingdom prioritized over kinship; love prioritized over law – all of which can be found within Jewish tradition).[274]
4 Jesus considers loyalty to himself to be the marker of belonging to the kingdom, rather than loyalty to types of Torah obedience, whether espoused by scribal schemas or Pharisaic aphorisms.[275]

---

of his disciples is one that already is made possible by and responds to the power of God's rule, present in Jesus' preaching and actions. Thus, Jesus' legal commands express the proper eschatological implementation of God's will as expressed in Torah – an eschatological implementation that is meant not just for a short, *sui generis* interval but for the whole future of Israel as God's people, restored in the end time.'

274 One may call this 'messianic Torah' if one likes; either way, one must do business with the affirmative pronouncement about the Torah in Matt. 5:17–21 and Jesus' affirmation of the Decalogue in Mark 10:19. Cf. Meyer (1979: 141, 151), who calls this 'Torah for a graced Israel', which was 'Torah transformed by reference to the new and public revelation set before Israel in Jesus' proclamation of the reign of God and his apodictic teaching of the new imperatives which flowed from it'.

275 God's kingship and God's commandments are linked everywhere in Judaism, particularly in the Prophets and the Psalms, as they are combined in rabbinic literature (*m. Ber.* 2.2). Yet the conflict between divine kingdom and divine commands is what had to be worked out in an eschatological *halakhah*; or, simply put, people had to work out how to be faithful in an age of revolution and revelation.

Prophetic warnings

Closely connected to the prophetic vocation is the task of warning of judgment and the accompanying call for repentance. Jesus, as a prophet, spoke much about judgment and repentance, for individuals as for the entire Jewish nation. Indeed, the entire prophetic tradition, from Amos to Zechariah, contains dire warnings of judgment if the Israelites engage in idolatry, trust in foreign military alliances, neglect the temple cultus, deprive the poor and powerless of justice, and naively assume that their elect status excuses them from divine recompense. Judgment of some variety, from calamity to exile, was the threat, while repentance was the way to escape it. Jesus stood in this tradition, quite deeply in fact, and Reiser estimates that more than a quarter of the Jesus tradition is concerned with the theme of judgment.[276] That makes sense, because the subject of judgment constitutes one of the continuities between John the Baptist, Jesus and the early church[277] and shows their deep roots in the Jewish prophetic tradition.[278]

On the one hand, in terms of individuals, repentance was a feature of Jewish piety. The devout life was one of constant contrition for personal sins, given that repentance was necessary to avoid divine judgment and to regain divine favour.[279] We should not fear imputing to Jews the notion of the introspective conscience of the West, as Krister Stendahl said, because our Jewish sources, from the penitential psalms to the *Thanksgiving Hymns* (1QH), constantly show us that Jews feared their sins as an offence to God and saw repentance as the appropriate way to rescind divine judgment. In this environment, Jesus espoused a penitential piety in his warnings that people must repent/change/turn in order to enter the 'kingdom' and avoid 'hell'.[280] Even amputating limbs that cause sin in this life is better than having an able body in perdition.[281] The fear of the Lord and the Lord's judgment in hell should drive one

---

276 Reiser 1997 [1990]: 304.
277 See Allison 2003; 2010a: 548–555, 204–220.
278 See esp. Stettler 2011.
279 Cf. e.g. Pss 7:12; 51:1–19; Job 42:6; Pr. Man. 7–8, 13; *Jos. Asen.* 16.7.
280 Matt. 18:3.
281 Mark 9:43–48.

towards righteousness.[282] Jesus declared that he had come to call 'sinners' to repentance and that God rejoices over their return as a shepherd rejoices over finding a lost sheep.[283] All things considered, it was even better to be a contrite tax-collector than a self-assured Pharisee.[284] The story of Zacchaeus the tax-collector is one such episode where a person's repentance and restitution effectively return him to covenant standing.[285] Jesus amplified scriptural and eschatological themes by calling people to repentance for their sins.

On the other hand, in terms of Israel as a whole, repentance was the way for the nation to escape the judgment that was falling upon it. In particular, exile was the most severe of all judgments, and repentance was the way to avoid it or to bring it to an end. Deuteronomy makes this clear:

> When all these things have happened to you, the blessings and the curses that I have set before you, if you call them to mind among all the nations where the LORD your God has driven you and *return to the LORD your God*, and you and your children obey him with all your heart and with all your soul, just as I am commanding you today, *then the LORD your God will return you from your captivity and have compassion on you, gathering you again from all the peoples among whom the LORD your God has scattered you*. Even if you are exiled to the ends of the world, from there the LORD your God will gather you, and from there he will take you back.
> (Deut. 30:1–4, emphasis added; cf. Lev. 26:40–45)

Solomon's prayer narrated in 1 Kings and 2 Chronicles makes this very same point about exile, and repentance as bringing about the end of exile (see Table 6.1). This repentance is more than contrition for personal sins; it is 'eschatological repentance': what Israel must do if the curses of exile and its lingering effects are to end.[286] The prophets repeatedly called the

---

282 Matt. 10:28/Luke 12:4–5.
283 Mark 2:17; Matt. 18:12–14; Luke 15:7, 10.
284 Luke 18:9–14.
285 Luke 19:1–10.
286 Wright 1996: 248.

Table 6.1 Themes of exile and repentance in the prayer of Solomon

1 Kgs 8:44–51	2 Chr. 6:36–39
If your people go out to battle against their enemy, by whatever way you shall send them, and they pray to the LORD toward the city that you have chosen and the house that I have built for your name, then hear in heaven their prayer and their plea and maintain their cause. If they sin against you – for there is no one who does not sin – and you are angry with them and give them to an enemy, so that they are carried away captive to the land of the enemy, far off or near, then if they come to their senses in the land to which *they have been taken captive and repent* and plead with you in the land of their captors, saying, 'We have sinned, and have done wrong; we have acted wickedly,' *if they repent with all their heart and soul in the land of their enemies who took them captive and pray to you toward their land that you gave to their ancestors, the city that you have chosen, and the house that I have built for your name*, then hear in heaven your dwelling place their prayer and their plea, maintain their cause, and forgive your people who have sinned against you and all their transgressions that they have committed against you, and grant them compassion in the sight of their captors, so that they may have compassion on them (for they are your people and heritage that you brought out of Egypt, from the midst of the iron smelter).	If they sin against you – for there is no one who does not sin – and you are angry with them and give them to an enemy, *so that they are carried away captive to a land far off or near, then if they come to their senses in the land to which they have been taken captive and repent and plead with you in the land of their captivity*, saying, 'We have sinned and have done wrong; we have acted wickedly,' *if they repent with all their heart and soul in the land of their captivity, to which they were taken captive, and pray toward their land that you gave to their ancestors, the city that you have chosen, and the house that I have built for your name*, then hear from heaven your dwelling place their prayer and their pleas, maintain their cause, and forgive your people who have sinned against you.

nation to turn to God so that God would bring it back from exile and end its continued cycle of slavery to foreign powers. In the great prayers of Daniel 9, Ezra 9 and Nehemiah 9, we find a common pattern consisting of praise for God's electing purposes, recognition of Israel's stubborn heart and disobedient behaviour, lament for divine judgment, cries from slaves suffering under pagan powers (like Israel in Egypt!), and an appeal to God for deliverance based on his divine mercy, righteousness and glory. The prophet Jeremiah epitomized this message with the invitation for the exiles to 'return' to him so that they would be brought back to the land:

> Thus says the LORD, the God of Israel: Like these good figs, so I will regard as good the exiles from Judah whom I have sent away from this place to the land of the Chaldeans. I will set my eyes upon them for good, and I will bring them back to this land. I will build them up and not tear them down; I will plant them and not pluck them up. I will give them a heart to know that I am the LORD, and they will be my people, and I will be their God, for they will return to me with their whole heart.
> (Jer. 24:5–7)

In Baruch there is the hope that

> in the land of their exile they will have a change of heart and know that I am the Lord their God. I will give them a heart that obeys and ears that hear; they will praise me in the land of their exile, and will remember my name and turn from their stubbornness and their wicked deeds; for they will remember the ways of their ancestors, who sinned before the Lord. I will bring them again into the land that I swore to give to their ancestors . . .
> (2 Bar. 2.30–34)

Returning to God means a return to the land!

John the Baptist preached a message of judgment and repentance in the Judean wilderness along the River Jordan. He saw himself as the prophetic voice in Isaiah 40 as he was literally out in the wilderness proclaiming the coming of the Lord, who was soon to visit his people to cleanse and purify them for the kingdom.[287] Individuals needed to be baptized as a ritual to mark their preparedness for this eschatological cleansing and to provide fruit demonstrative of true repentance. Claiming Abrahamic heritage was no surety for escaping judgment; only contrition and compassion mattered.[288] John, like the prophets before him, was calling the people to 'return to the Lord'.[289] Here we should see a close analogy with Qumran. The sectarians identified themselves as the priestly 'captives of Israel' and 'the diggers of the well', the vanguard of the end-of-exile people who have entered into 'the covenant of conversion'.[290] For them, 'restoration is not an event that had already taken place in the Persian period, but rather a part of the eschatological future being played out already in their own day'.[291] John was similarly urging the populace to take the initiative and join the repentant remnant who would be cleansed before the cataclysmic upheaval that would transpire at God's visitation; in this way, they would participate in a new exodus and experience the definitive end of exile.[292]

It is in this context that Jesus proclaimed that the good news of the kingdom required the people to 'believe' and 'repent'.[293] He had taken up the message of John about preparing the people for the coming judgment ahead of Israel's restoration.[294] Jesus also sent out his disciples to call the various villages and towns to 'repent'.[295] This was at one level a normal mark of Jewish piety; sins needed to be repented of and even expiated. But, as we've seen, 'repentance' is also what the nation had to do if the full effects of the exile were to end and if the exodus and its eschatological blessings were to be manifest. This is a way of saying that what

---

287 Mark 1:4–8.
288 Matt. 3:1–12/Luke 3:1–18; cf. Josephus, *Ant.* 18.116–119; Acts 13:24.
289 Cf. e.g. Deut. 4:30; 30:2, 10; Pss 78:34; 85:8; Isa. 19:22; 31:6; 55:7; Jer. 3:10–14; 4:1; 24:7; Ezek. 18:30; Hos. 3:5; 6:1; 7:10; 14:2; Joel 2:12–13; Amos 4:6–11; Zech. 1:3; Mal. 3:7.
290 CD 4.2; 6.4–5; 19.16.
291 Schiffman 2010: 290.
292 On Jesus and a continuing 'exile' of Israel, see Wright 1992: 268–279; 1996; 2014: 139–163; Evans 1997a; 1999; Pitre 2005; esp. surveys of debates in Perrin 2013a; Bird 2015; Scott 2017; and critiques of this view by Bryan (2002: 14–19) and Dunn (2003: 401–404, 473–477).
293 Mark 1:15.
294 Cf. Reiser 1997 [1990]: 312–316; Allison 2010a: 204–220.
295 Mark 6:12.

The teaching of Jesus

Israel needed to do was to show covenant loyalty (belief) and repentance (eschatological turning) before God.[296]

The summons to national repentance is where pious contrition, prophetic urgency and political summons all intersect. Israel, like a rebellious son squandering his inheritance on debauched living in a foreign land, could *now* return to God, who was like a father anxiously looking towards the horizon for the wayward son(s) to return home.[297] Those who turned from sin, who turned to Jesus and embraced his kingdom vision, would be among those 'coming from the east and the west' who would one day recline with Abraham and the patriarchs at the eschatological banquet.[298] This eschatological repentance is what would characterize or mark out God's people on the day when Israel's God visited them, vindicated them, vanquished their enemies and brought victory for them: in short, the day when Yahweh became king.[299]

But those who did not heed the warning, or accept the message, who were unrepentant and disbelieving, would not only be left in 'exile' but could also expect an even worse judgment. One particular pericope shows Jesus referencing recent instances of sacrilegious brutality and natural disasters to warn that without repentance even worse calamities are on the horizon:

> At that very time there were some present who told him about the Galileans whose blood Pilate had mingled with their sacrifices. He asked them, 'Do you think that because these Galileans suffered in this way they were worse sinners than all other Galileans? No, I tell you, but unless you repent you will all perish as they did. Or those eighteen who were killed when the tower of Siloam fell on them – do you think that they were worse offenders than all the other

---

[296] Wright (1996: 250–251) understands Mark 1:15 in the light of Josephus, *Life* 110, where Josephus called leaders within the Galilean rebellion to repent of their plot to kill him and to trust him in his strategy. I think that the general idea is correct, but I'm less inclined to see repentance in Jesus' message as purely a matter of abandoning revolutionary zeal. I'm persuaded that this eschatological repentance is more a matter of abandoning all other agendas and allegiances apart from devotion to Yahweh's kingship.

[297] Luke 15:18–20.

[298] See Matt. 8:11–12/Luke 13:28–29.

[299] Wright 1996: 251.

people living in Jerusalem? No, I tell you, but unless you repent you will all perish just as they did.'
(Luke 13:1–5)

Jesus uttered woe oracles against Galilean towns that spurned his message and provocatively implied that pagan cities would respond better, and as a result a fate worse than that of Sodom and Gomorrah would fall upon these towns:

Then he began to reproach the cities in which most of his deeds of power had been done because they did not repent. 'Woe to you, Chorazin! Woe to you, Bethsaida! For if the deeds of power done in you had been done in Tyre and Sidon, they would have repented long ago in sackcloth and ashes. But I tell you, on the day of judgment it will be more tolerable for Tyre and Sidon than for you. And you, Capernaum,

> will you be exalted to heaven?
> No, you will be brought down to Hades.

For if the deeds of power done in you had been done in Sodom, it would have remained until this day. But I tell you that on the day of judgment it will be more tolerable for the land of Sodom than for you.'
(Matt. 11:20–24; cf. Luke 10:13–15; Isa. 14:13–15; *Ass. Mos.* 10.9)

Jesus goes on to declare that pagan figures from Israel's sacred history, such as the Queen of the South who sought out Solomon, and the Ninevehites who repented at Jonah's message, will rise at the resurrection and condemn 'this generation' for its recalcitrance.[300] 'This generation' will be 'charged with the blood of all the prophets shed since the foundation of the world, from the blood of Abel to the blood of Zechariah' since they reject the messenger and the message.[301] There will be a separation of

---

300 Matt. 12:41–42/Luke 11:31–32.
301 Luke 11:50–51/Matt. 35–36.

the righteous from the wicked by the angels.[302] The manifestation of the kingdom will lead to a reordering of power where the first are last and the last are first, the humble will be exalted while the proud are thrown down, and those who lose their life for the kingdom will find it.[303] Many will be sent into an 'outer darkness'[304] or 'outside' where there is 'weeping and gnashing of teeth'.[305] The alternative to participating in the 'kingdom' was 'hell',[306] a terrible place of post-mortem punishment.[307]

'No Jewish prophet before or after Jesus', says McKnight, 'ever gave more attention to eternal consequences than he did.'[308] Among Jesus' oracles and warnings about judgment, those pertaining to the destruction of the temple are particularly intense,[309] as are those that mention a final 'day of judgment' and 'last day'.[310] These two events are not the same; more likely, for Jesus, the destruction of the temple itself marks out the beginning of the final judgment.[311] Combining sayings about future judgment with sayings about the 'coming of the Son of Man' raises the question as to whether Jesus expected the world to end in the imminent future.[312] The view that Jesus expected an imminent and sudden apocalyptic dénouement was programmatic for Albert Schweitzer, who took Jesus' words, 'When they persecute you in one town, flee to the next; for truly I tell you, you will not have gone through all the towns of Israel before the Son of Man comes',[313] to indicate that Jesus announced the soon-to-be end of the world ... and then realized at the end of his life that he had been wrong.[314] Warnings that 'this generation will not pass away

---

302 Matt. 13:47–48; 25:31–46.
303 Mark 8:35–36; 10:31; Matt. 20:16; Luke 13:30; 14:11; 17:23; 18:14; *Gos. Thom.* 4.
304 Matt. 22:13; 25:30.
305 Matt. 8:12; 13:42, 49–50; 22:13; 24:51; 25:30.
306 Mark 9:43–45; Matt. 10:28/Luke 12:5; Matt. 5:22; 23:15, 33.
307 Cf. *1 Enoch* 90.24; *2 Bar.* 85.13; *Sib. Or.* 4.186.
308 McKnight 1999: 139.
309 Mark 13; Matt. 23:37–39/Luke 19:41–44.
310 Matt. 10:15; 11:22, 24; 12:36; Luke 10:14; John 5:27; 12:48.
311 McKnight 1999: 148. One should note that in Revelation and *1 Enoch* there is a series of judgments that take place in the last days.
312 Mark 8:38 – 9:1; 13:26; Luke 12:8–9, 35–40; 17:20–37; Matt. 13:41; 24:37–44; 25:31–33; *Gos. Thom.* 61.
313 Matt. 10:23.
314 Schweitzer 1945 [1906]: 335, 360–361.

until all these things have taken place',[315] promises of soon experiencing 'the age to come'[316] and of God's intention to 'quickly grant justice' to his prayerful chosen ones,[317] and other logia such as 'The heavens and earth will be rolled up in your presence',[318] suggest an intense expectation of an imminent 'end' of some kind. I've already touched on Jesus' view of the kingdom; however, not everyone is convinced by inaugurated eschatology – whereby the kingdom of God is both partially present and ultimately future, or 'now' and 'not yet'. As such, one might well want to read the debate between N. T. Wright and Dale Allison on this score – whether apocalyptic language is merely sociopolitical events dressed up in cosmic imagery (Wright) or whether this language is real and refers to a cataclysmic and supernatural event (Allison).[319]

I tend to think that Jesus preached urgency without a timetable. Jesus was no cartographer of apocalyptic catastrophe, but he employed imagery and symbols soaked in urgency, warning and promise. He described the kingdom's advent as something that happens by a progressive advance[320] until sudden signs point to its climax.[321] The reason one must be watchful[322] is because the date is indeterminable,[323] and delay is part of the anticipation.[324] Imminent eschatology has always had a footnote, a 'but first' followed by an 'and then'.[325] The qualification is not indefinite postponement; rather, God reveals the kingdom in his time, and God's will cannot be cajoled. Jewish tradition frequently moves from the cry 'How long, O Lord?' to a periodization of history with Beast no. 1 and

---

315 Mark 13:30.
316 Mark 10:30.
317 Luke 18:7–8.
318 *Gos. Thom.* 111.
319 See Wright 1996: 202–209; Allison 1998; 1999; 2001; 2005a; 2010a: 31–220; cf. Adams 2007. Allison (1998: 154–157) doesn't think that Jesus was anticipating the 'end of the world' so much as a 'revolutionary change' within the world. See too for discussion of this language, Meyer 1979: 242–249; Bockmuehl 1994: 98–102; McKnight 1999: 138–139; Witherington 1999: 261–265, 291; Horsley 2012: 34–64.
320 Cf. e.g. Mark 4:3–8, 26–32.
321 Luke 17:22–37.
322 Mark 13:9, 23, 33–37; Matt. 24:42–44/Luke 12:39–40; Matt. 25:13; cf. 1 Thess. 5:1–7; Rev. 16:15.
323 Luke 17:20–24.
324 Matt. 24:45–51/Luke 12:42–46; Luke 19:11.
325 Mark 2:19; 8:38; 9:11; 10:34–35; 12:9; 13:10; Luke 17:25; 21:9; 2 Thess. 2:3. See esp. Holmén 1996.

Week no. 1, and reiterates a promise of a coming 'Day' combined with declarations of its suddenness, all the while reinterpreting and reapplying prior prophetic imagery to the present time. In *Jubilees* 23, the shift from Maccabean revolt to the eschatological epoch of deliverance is one of growth and evolution. Otherwise, in *1 Enoch* 91 – 93 there is a periodization of history and several judgments before any dénouement; in *Pesher Habbakuk* (1QpHab), however, deliverance is determined by the interpretation of the Teacher of Righteousness even while it is deferred until God destroys the *kittim* (i.e. Romans). I aver that Jesus, just like other Jews of his day, was prepared to countenance the end as something of an ongoing process and warned that the ultimate restoration of God's reign was imminent as it was also inevitable and indeterminable.[326] A mixture of ever-readiness and patient endurance while waiting for the consummation is a paradoxical part of the prophetic and apocalyptic tradition in which Jesus participated. Statements about 'this generation' are indeed literal, and much of the language points ahead to the temple's destruction, which took place in AD 70, but Jesus envisaged a future beyond that: the resurrection, the final judgment, a kingdom and eternal life.

Jesus as messianic teacher

As a teacher, Jesus rehearsed scriptural imagery, traded in metaphors freighted with theo-political referents, uttered biting one-liners and spoke poignant poetry. He was a storyteller, moral philosopher, sage, rabbi and prophet. He told shocking and subversive stories about what the kingdom would look like, how it would come and who it was for.

Jesus' moral vision meant recasting personal and national priorities in the light of God's covenant justice. In the kingdom, compassion was the new currency, which buttressed the dangers of possessions and stressed the need to give alms. He taught that the Torah was God-given, even if certain aspects were internally prioritized and retooled in the light of the kingdom. Above all, Israel needed to repent if the full effects of the exile were to end and if people were to avoid a coming 'day' of judgment.

---

326 Mark 13:32; Matt. 24:43; Luke 12:35–40; 1 Thess. 5:2.

It should be remembered, importantly, that the diverse pedagogical forms and frames were subordinate to one overarching theme: God, God's kingdom, God coming as king and Israel's restoration. Jesus' message, his 'gospel of the kingdom', was doubly an invitation and a warning, and it would affect people differently, depending on whether they were among the 'sinners', the official or unofficial leaders of Judea, the rich, the poor, the oppressors or the oppressed.

Individuals throughout the entirety of Judean society, from the high priest to Herod, from the fisherman to the woman weaving baskets, were supposed to decide if they were for, against or simply indifferent to Jesus. As Jesus himself said: 'Whoever is not with me is against me, and whoever does not gather with me scatters.'[327] But what did his contemporaries – the Galilean villagers, merchants running between Sepphoris and Tyre, the local priests, Herodian officials and members of the Sanhedrin – make of Jesus and his teaching?

---

327 Luke 11:23.

7
Jesus and his contemporaries

Jesus as others saw him

In popular imagination Jesus was a man of the people, like a cross between a Marxist revolutionary and a popular local pastor, the peasant's peasant. A man who stood up to the religious establishment, who denounced the bourgeois Herodians, and who opposed the Roman colonial powers with its institutions of slavery and taxation. He was perhaps a product of religious influences from various places, such as Qumran, Hellenized Galilean cities, Egypt or even India. Jesus was everyone's favourite evangelist, community organizer, guru and human rights activist – maybe all of these. He was up in the faces of the legalistic Pharisees and the liberal Sadducees. What is more, the people loved him, his message, his ministry and what he was telling them about the kingdom. Such portraits of Jesus have one flaw: they are totally incorrect.

Jesus attracted huge crowds of people who wanted to see and hear him. He had many supporters of all classes, and grateful supplicants for his healing and exorcism ministry in a network of villages. But he also got driven out of various towns, including his own home town, was threatened with stoning, and perhaps even had the odd pitchfork waved in his face. He avoided the Galilean cities of Sepphoris and Tiberias, probably because he knew that he would not be encountering sympathetic audiences.

Imagine yourself as a first-century villager somewhere in the rustic hills of Galilee. When Jesus and his entourage arrive in your village, you are naturally curious as to whether the rumours about him – the good and the bad – are true. A crowd of people gather; you join them; Jesus speaks to everyone about God as king; he lays his hands on a boy with a fever and prays for him; he argues with two local priests about the sabbath; he requests some food for his journey to the next town; he urges some of the men to abandon their families and follow him immediately. Then, just before he leaves, he threatens God's judgment upon the village and makes grandiose claims for himself, laced with messianic rhetoric. This language irks you because you know that messiahs lead revolts, and revolts entail chaos, carnage, death, displacement and famine. The trauma of Judas the Galilean's revolt some twenty-five years earlier, which resulted in the deaths of your parents and the razing of your home, is etched into your mind like a scar. When somebody yells at Jesus, 'Go preach to your own village, you *mamzer*, you son of a motherless pig!' you nod in agreement. Others harangue the angry man, telling him to 'shush' because they are mesmerized by Jesus' teachings and astounded that the fever has left the boy. Note: Jesus was a 'popular' prophet, but he wasn't necessarily popular with all of the people all of the time!

We know that Jesus had bitter debates with the Pharisees. But what if the Pharisees were not the paragons of external religiosity and hypocrisy that the Christian tradition has made them out to be? What if the Pharisees were a popular religious movement concerned with trying to hasten Israel's liberation by calling all Judeans to covenant righteousness, to purity of hand and heart, to the attainment of hope through holiness? What if Christian views of the Pharisees are somewhat skewed because the Pharisees and Christians were the two surviving sects post-AD 70 who competed to define the hope, praxis, belief and boundaries of Judaism in several communities? I would not deny that Jesus caught beef with the Pharisees, but the evangelists' depictions of them are narrated in the light of post-AD 70 internecine rivalry between Jewish Christians and Pharisees. So, what if I told you that Jesus was somewhat aligned with the Pharisees? After all, he believed in the resurrection and in a wider 'canon', including the Prophets. He was visited by Pharisees, invited to dinner by Pharisees, and many Pharisees later joined the early church. Maybe all of Jesus' polemical tirades with the Pharisees were really insider debates within the broad Pharisaic movement. Sociology tells us that people tend to reserve the sharpest blades and deepest cuts for the insiders who are the closest to them and make them feel the most betrayed.

Jesus the quasi-Pharisee who was disliked by rural Galilean villagers might be an unthinkable prospect. My point is that understanding the historical Jesus means understanding him in relation to his many contemporaries: the Galilean villagers, residents of Jerusalem, the priestly leaders and political rulers of his time. Who did they think he was? We might call this a Christology from the side! The historical Jesus makes sense when situated among friends, supporters, critics and enemies. This enables us to imagine how others saw Jesus so that we too might better understand him.[1]

Jesus among the people

Jesus was from the rural or 'peasant' class of Galilean society, perhaps included among the day labourers who worked in Galilean cities, with a standard of living ranging from subsistence to secure, depending on the specific situation. Nonetheless, Jesus' message and deeds drew people from all tiers of society, including some from the elite level. According to Johannine tradition, Jesus was buried by Joseph of Arimathea, a respected member of the Jerusalem Sanhedrin who was 'waiting expectantly for the kingdom of God',[2] along with Nicodemus, a leading Pharisee.[3] He also received financial patronage from 'Joanna, the wife of Herod's steward Chuza',[4] which is quite startling if you think about it. Jesus was thus supported and revered by individuals among the highest levels of Galilean and Judean society. Added to that, he attracted 'chief tax-collectors' to his movement[5] among the various other toll-keepers and tax-farmers.[6] He commanded the loyalty of merchants, such as Mary Magdalene and Susanna,[7] while the fishermen Simon Peter and the Zebedee brothers abandoned their family enterprise to follow him,[8] and even a Judean priest with connections to the high priest known to us as the 'beloved disciple' was among his followers.[9] Many were supplicants

---

1 See Evans 2001a; McKnight and Modica 2008; Hurtado and Keith 2011.
2 Mark 15:43.
3 John 19:38–40.
4 Luke 8:3.
5 See Luke 19:2.
6 Mark 2:15–16; Matt. 11:19/Luke 7:34; Luke 15:1.
7 Luke 8:2–3.
8 Mark 1:16–18.
9 John 18:15.

for healing; others believed his message about God's coming kingdom and wished to enter its domain.

Jesus' message predominantly found traction among those who were religiously and socially marginalized, the disinherited and disempowered, those of low status and on a subsistence living. In particular, his kingdom message found fertile soil among malnourished malcontents and those who looked for a champion against the sinister forces that seemed to hem them in from all sides. 'Eschatology does not flourish in a politically and socially secure world,' said Geza Vermes, because '[u]ncertainty, danger, and continuous political and social unrest generate the eschatological atmosphere and the consequent eschatological outlook'.[10] The substance of much of Jesus' teaching and actions is prophetic protest against systems of exploitation. This is not to romanticize Jesus as a proletarian saviour; nonetheless, he repeatedly aimed his message at the 'poor'.[11]

According to Jesus, the poor are blessed because the kingdom belongs to them;[12] the poor should receive charity in the form of alms and debt relief.[13] Several of Jesus' parables pertain to the poor receiving a reversal of status and respite from their suffering over and against the wealthy who have either neglected them or exploited them.[14] The poor are the economically destitute, but they are also those of lowly status, including those deemed impure, illegitimate, disabled and infirm. The kingdom, for the poor, means a reversal of status and an abundance of material provisions: no more shame, no more hunger, no more death. The poor can be paradoxically happy because they have a promise of misery transformed by mercy, and for them, tilling the earth will be replaced by inheriting the earth. Jesus, just like the Baptist,[15] rehearsed the prophetic tradition that the people of Israel must do justice and show mercy to the poor as part of their preparation for God's redemption.[16]

Jesus also aimed his ministry at 'sinners'. Naturally, this term can

---

10 Vermes 2005: 68.
11 Cf. esp. Luke 4:18; Matt. 11:5/Luke 7:22; Luke 14:13.
12 Matt. 5:3/Luke 6:20/*Gos. Thom.* 54.
13 Mark 10:21; Matt. 6:12/Luke 11:4; Matt. 6:2–4; Luke 11:41; 12:33; 14:14.
14 Luke 14:12–14, 16–24; 16:19–31; cf. *1 Enoch* 103.1–15; *T. Jud.* 24.5; *Sib. Or.* 3.350–355.
15 Mark 1:3–5; Matt. 3:1–6/Luke 3:1–14.
16 Isa. 56:1; 58:6–10; Amos 5:14–15; Mal. 3:1–12. Cf. Hays 2013: 803.

refer to the lawless and immoral.[17] Yet 'sinners' can also designate: (1) Hellenizing Jews who had effectively abandoned Judaism;[18] (2) Jews who did not hold to the distinctive interpretations, calendars and rituals of a particular Jewish sect;[19] (3) the opponents of the pious and devout;[20] (4) Gentiles as the quintessential sinners;[21] and (5) the rich and powerful who exploited the poor and needy.[22]

The identity of the *sinners* that Jesus addressed in his ministry has been disputed in modern scholarship. Joachim Jeremias argued that *sinner* was a specific term in Jesus' day for people who engaged in despised trades and for the general 'people of the land' (i.e. the *amme-ha-aretz*). These persons were thought to be uneducated, ignorant, and lax concerning the Torah. This bucolic impiety was a stumbling block to their salvation in the eyes of the Pharisees.[23] The problem with Jeremias's proposal is that he assumed a formalistic Judaism based on a theology of merit. He also caricatured the dominant perspective to claim that the people of the land were mostly irreligious, and he was too dependent on later rabbinic sources for his reconstruction. It is better to say that, while all *sinners* could be 'people of the land', not all 'people of the land' were therefore *sinners*.[24] Most likely, in the context of Jesus' ministry, 'sinner' designated a person who was known to commit unlawful conduct: those deemed to be offenders by virtue of the corruption of riches (e.g. tax-collectors [Mark 2:13–17]) or those who offended due to their lifestyle and licentiousness (e.g. prostitutes [Luke 7:36–50]).[25] Jesus was concerned to extend God's covenant love to those who had made themselves outsiders by their behaviour. 'The summoning of sinners', argued Meyer, 'showed that all Israel had been invited.'[26]

---

17 Cf. e.g. Ps. 1:1.
18 1 Macc. 1:34; 2:44, 48.
19 Cf. e.g. Enochic Judaism (*1 Enoch* 82.4–7); Qumran community (1QpHab 5.1–12; 1QS 5.7–11; 1QH 7.12); non-Pharisaic Jews (*Ass. Mos.* 7.3, 9–10); Pharisees (*Pss Sol.* 2.34; 17.5–8, 23, 36; John 9:16, 24); priestly/Essenic Judaism (*Jub.* 16.4).
20 Sir. 13:17; 33:14; *Pss Sol.* 17.5–8, 23; Jude 15.
21 Cf. e.g. Gal. 2:15; 1 Macc. 2:58.
22 Sir. 13:24; 27:1; Mark 14:41.
23 Jeremias 1971: 109–112.
24 Wright 1996: 265.
25 See Bird 2013c.
26 Meyer 1979: 166.

One of the most characteristic features of Jesus' prophetic practice was to break bread with people who were deemed immoral, or sinners; specifically, tax-collectors and prostitutes.[27] This resulted in his reputation among critics for being 'a glutton and a drunkard'.[28] To the Pharisees, who were a kind of halakhic luncheon club with political hopes, exclusively dining with people with similar purity scruples, Jesus' behaviour was as outrageous as it was perplexing. Jesus was 'banqueting with the bad',[29] as it were, rendering himself susceptible to moral impurities.[30] This was not necessarily an affront to purity regulations, but Jesus was at the very least breaking 'invisible, unwritten, social rules', which provoked confusion and consternation.[31] There were manifold warnings in Scripture against consorting with bad company![32] The Pharisees considered sinners to be Torah-lax, morally toxic and sometimes treasonous, yet Jesus ate with them as friends. And most perplexing of all – God seemed to approve of it; hence, the wisdom that Jesus had been given and the wondrous deeds that Jesus was performing. Jesus' 'reclining' with sinners was provocative because it was like serving the figurative hors d'oeuvre of the kingdom feast and foreshadowing exactly who would be vindicated in the renewed Israel that he was creating around himself.[33] According to Jesus, those in his culinary company, however alienated or alien, will be among those people who 'will come from east and west, from north and south, and will eat in the kingdom of God'. They are the ones who will join him in the end of exile, at Israel's restoration, whereas for those who look down on them with scorn, only misery awaits: 'There will be weeping and gnashing of teeth when you see Abraham and Isaac and Jacob and all the prophets in the kingdom of God, and you yourselves thrown out.'[34]

A similar sentiment is expressed in a saying such as: 'Truly I tell you, the tax collectors and the prostitutes are going into the kingdom of God

---

27 Mark 2:15–17; Matt. 21:31–32; Luke 15:1–3; P. Oxy. 1224.1; Justin, *1 Apol.* 15.8.
28 Matt. 11:19/Luke 7:34.
29 See Witherington 1990: 73–81; Crossan 1991: 341–344.
30 Jesus was 'accompanying *lepra* and eating with them', according to P. Egert. 2.
31 Wassen 2016: 157.
32 Pss 1:1–6; 26:5; Job 34:8; Sir. 12:13–14; 19:22; 28:9; 41:5.
33 Cf. Wright (1996: 149): 'Like many of his actions, this table-fellowship became seen as a further way in which the kingdom was actually being inaugurated.'
34 Luke 13:28–29/Matt. 8:11–12.

ahead of you.'[35] If Jesus' company was not scandalous enough, he was daring to suggest that sinners might enter the kingdom ahead of the Pharisees and even instead of them. What is more, the three parables about lost-ness in Luke 15 are not timeless tales of divine grace but are instead delivered as a specific defence of Jesus' dining practices with sinners. The Pharisees should be like rejoicing fathers, when in fact they are grumbling like a jaded elder son over the restoration of his delinquent brother.[36] Jesus maintained that the kingdom's advent would not mean the vindication of the self-appointed boundary-keepers of Israel's covenantal life and their criteria for sharing in the kingdom; instead, the kingdom would mean the rescue and restoration of those at the periphery of Israel's socio-religious life. If the so-called righteous could not handle this, then they, rather than the sinners, would be the ones finding themselves outside the kingdom. The reason why 'sinners' are included in the kingdom is not because of a principle that grace trumps law; more likely, as the exilic prophets declared, it is because God is the shepherd-king who gathers together all the lost sheep of the house of Israel, those scattered by exile, and embraces them.[37] For in the kingdom of God, in the new exodus, God's will is sacred, but his mercy is scandalous.

For some of the populace, though, Jesus' message was not welcome, as it appeared he was kicking a hornet's nest, providing false hope, showing brazen disregard for religious scruples, crossing cherished boundaries or messing with powers beyond his ken. Even his own family were worried about his attempt to court fame, which came with the risk of collective shame.[38] There were various types of rejection of Jesus' message as iterated in the parable of the sower.[39] Various leaders tried to discredit his ministry,[40] challenging his *halakhah*,[41] repudiating his healing work on the sabbath[42] and demanding proof of his authority.[43] The response

---

35 Matt. 21:31.
36 Luke 15:1–32.
37 Isa. 40:11; Jer. 31:10–11; Ezek. 34:15–16.
38 Mark 3:21, 31–35; John 7:3–5.
39 Mark 4:1–20; *Gos. Thom.* 9.
40 Mark 3:22–23.
41 Mark 7:1–5.
42 Luke 16:13–14.
43 Mark 8:11–12.

of Jesus' home village of Nazareth to him was, in effect, 'Physician, heal thyself.'[44] Jesus was berated there, and also met a mixture of apathy or antagonism in the towns of Capernaum, Chorazin and Bethsaida, places which he in turn rejected, pronouncing woe oracles of judgment against them.[45]

For others, Jesus excited feelings of hope, joy, praise and expectation. He attracted several large crowds of people, who often tried to follow him, which was always dangerous as it immediately caused alarm among the authorities.[46] Some people heard Jesus' message and responded with admiration, as did one woman who said, 'Blessed is the womb that bore you and the breasts that nursed you!'[47] Others saw what he did and exclaimed, 'A great prophet has risen among us!' and 'God has looked favourably on his people!'[48] Jesus was lauded and God was praised because of his mighty deeds.[49] Jesus could even – with his approval or not – be hailed as the 'Son of David'.[50] The positive perception about Jesus among the people, whether part of the retainer or of the peasant classes, was that he was a prophet, wearing the mantle of Elijah, continuing the ministry of John the Baptist, perhaps even *the* Prophet whom Moses had promised.[51] Many despaired at Jesus' death precisely because they 'had hoped that he was the one to redeem Israel'.[52]

Jesus among rivals

Among the various sects, parties and philosophies of Galilee and Judea, we must give specific attention to groups explicitly mentioned in the Gospels (i.e. Pharisees, Sadducees, scribes, Herodians) as well as groups not mentioned in the Gospels (i.e. Essenes, Qumranites, zealous Jews).

---

44 Luke 4:23 KJV.
45 Mark 6:1–6; Matt. 11:21–24/Luke 10:13–16.
46 Cf. e.g. Matt. 4:25.
47 Luke 11:27.
48 Luke 7:16.
49 Mark 2:12; Matt. 15:30–31; Luke 4:15; 5:25–26; 18:43.
50 Mark 10:47–48; 11:9–10.
51 Mark 6:15; 8:28; Matt. 21:11; John 6:15; 7:40; 9:17; Acts 7:37.
52 Luke 24:21.

Pharisees

As difficult and debated as the quest for the historical Jesus is, no less difficult and debated is the quest for the historical Pharisees. In Christian imagination, a Pharisee is the epitome of hypocrisy and external ritual legalism, yet we must see beyond that stereotype if we are to engage in a concerted appraisal of this group and its relationship to Jesus.[53] As I said above, we must remember that the post-70 period saw a concerted struggle between Jewish Christians and Jewish Pharisees in Jewish communities in Judea, Galilee, the Trans-Jordan, Syria and Asia Minor, and the Gospels all reflect that internecine rivalry. Mark focuses on the Pharisees as Jesus' obtuse and recalcitrant Galilean opponents. Matthew regards them as the chief antagonists against the authority of Jesus, men full of hypocrisy and hubris. Luke depicts them as a somewhat benign, sympathetic opposition to Jesus, yet endlessly perplexed by him. John sees the Pharisees as a microcosm of the darkness of the 'world' which makes them spiritually blind. Even so, I would deny that Jesus-versus-the-Pharisees in the Gospels is a purely anachronistic projection of the post-70 intra-Jewish debates onto the lifetime of Jesus.[54] Be that as it may, the pericopae of Jesus debating with the Pharisees in the Gospels

---

[53] Horsley (2022: 37) notes: 'The greatest source of distortion of the Pharisees as historical figures and defamation of their character has been the Christian reading of the Gospels.' Yinger (2022: ix) laments how sermons depict the Pharisees as 'legalists trying to earn their way to heaven, loading burdens on others, hypocrites who taught others but didn't obey themselves'. Deines (2013) regards the Pharisees as 'Good Guys with Bad Press'. There has been a rightful rehabilitation of the Pharisees of late (see Neusner and Chilton 2007; Sievers and Levine 2021; Yinger 2022), a move away from the caricature of them as exemplars of legalistic religion. However, one must consider too the warning of Dahl (1974: 57) whereby liberal Jews and Christians 'draw an ideal picture of Pharisaism strikingly reminiscent of the liberal picture of Jesus' so that even 'in [Pharisaic] Judaism could be found faith in God as loving Father'.

[54] In the Gospels, the Pharisees and scribes have an obvious literary function as the agents of the Jerusalem authorities and are a foil for controversy in the various pronouncement stories. Even so, as Richard Horsley notes, 'they would have no credibility in either function unless they did, historically, on occasion at least, appear outside of their focus of operations in Jerusalem' (Horsley 1995: 150–152). The presence of Pharisees in Galilee is confirmed by Josephus, who was irritated by a Pharisaic group that tried to undermine him when he was sent to fortify Galilee in the face of the Roman invasion (Josephus, *Life* 196–197). While much of Gospel scholarship has treated the historicity of the conflict stories with a big dose of scepticism, this is unfounded; we don't see Jesus debating the issues that the church was wrestling with: those related to circumcision, collections, food offered to idols, and apostolic authority, which were hot-button issues in Paul's epistles. See Wright 1996: 373–383; Holmén 2001: 88–332; Wilk 2008: 107; Keener 2009: 225–227; and esp. Keith 2014: 129–151 and the scholarship cited there on the case for their general authenticity.

are undoubtedly narrated in the light of post-70 intra-Jewish conflicts.[55] Josephus too is a key source of information about this group, though he remains in many respects tendentious, and scholars debate whether he's trying to exonerate or excoriate the Pharisees. The other major source for the Pharisees is rabbinic literature, which of course post-dates the pre-70 period by some centuries and needs to be carefully sifted. Beyond a few oblique and polemical mentions of the Pharisees in the Qumran scrolls, Paul's biographical sections about his Pharisaic past combined with Luke's epitome of it in Acts, and other tacit references in documents such as the *Psalms of Solomon* and the *Testament of Moses*, we have very little to go on to reconstruct who the Pharisees were and what they were about.[56]

To give an attempted sketch of the Pharisees,[57] their Greek name *Pharisaioi*, as Josephus and Paul call them, is probably based on the underlying Semitic term *perushim* meaning 'separate ones'. Perhaps they were inspired by Leviticus 20:26, 'You shall be holy to me, for I the LORD am holy, and I have separated you from the other peoples to be mine', so that they were inspired to adopt separation by a quest for holiness. There might even be a tacit jibe against them in a Qumran sectarian letter where the teacher boasts that his group have 'separated from the people and from all its impurities' as if to say that they have out-separated the so-called Separate Ones.[58] The question we must ask is: who did the Pharisees think they were separating from and why? From Hellenizing Jews in cahoots with the Seleucid kingdom? From the 'people of the land' who were allegedly lax in Torah observance or refused to prioritize ritual discipline? From other groups who did not share their agendas

---

55 This is apparent in how Matthew and Luke Pharaicize Jesus' disputes with Judean leaders. For instance, whereas Mark describes how the scribes accused Jesus of blasphemy for forgiving the sins of a paralytic man, Luke retells the story so that the scribes and Pharisees accuse him of blasphemy (Mark 2:7; Luke 5:17); and whereas Mark says that the scribes alleged that Jesus cast out demons by the power of Beelzebul, Matthew attributes this accusation to the Pharisees (Mark 3:6; Matt. 12:24).

56 On the Pharisees and sources, see Green 2007; Horsley 2022: 21–44.

57 See in brief Cohick 2013; more fully Wright 1992: 181–203; 1996: 369–383; 2014: 80–90, 179–195. Consideration should be given to the now famous debate between Sanders (1990; 1992) and Neusner (1973; 1993; 2007) with adjudication by Deines and Hengel (1995) and Deines (2001). Important work to note is Neusner and Chilton 2007; Sievers and Levine 2021. Recent volumes include Horsley 2022; Yinger 2022.

58 4QMMT C 7–8.

and interpretations? From the ordinary grind of life so that they could dedicate themselves entirely to the practice of piety and purity? Paul considered himself 'set apart for the gospel of God',[59] and nobody considers him puritanical for doing so.[60]

Although the origins of the Pharisees are obscure, their lineage may go back to groups known from the Maccabean and early Hasmonean periods. Their roots lay varyingly among the *hasidim* ('pious ones'), who fought for the Torah-faithful life against Seleucid attempts to forcibly Hellenize Judea,[61] and various *grammateis* ('scribes'), who were also part of the anti-Hellenistic coalition and looked ahead to a restoration of the temple cult.[62] The Pharisees were perhaps also known as the *sophistai* ('sages'), who were venerable teachers,[63] and the *haberim* ('associates'), who constituted a dining club for teachers with a commitment to tithing and like-minded food-purity scruples.[64] In the post-Seleucid era (i.e. after 164 BC), Judean social, political and religious life was filled with competing perspectives on how to reinstitute the temple cultus and calendar, return to priestly procedures, and reinstate customs connected to food, family and the rhythms of the pious life. The Pharisees emerged in this period as a diverse yet dominating group whose fortunes ebbed and flowed from 164 BC to AD 70.

In the early Hasmonean period, John Hyrcanus I (reigned 134–104 BC) had an ambivalent relationship with the Pharisees. According to Josephus, the Pharisees were purportedly very popular with the masses, and could turn the tide for or against rulers, so Hyrcanus I expectantly became a 'disciple of theirs' and was in turn 'beloved by them'.[65] But his combination of civic leadership and priesthood into one office led a certain Pharisee named Eleazar, a man of ill temper and given to 'sedition' (*stasis*), to denounce Hyrcanus I at a feast as an illegitimate half-Jew since his mother had been a captive and allegedly raped by Syrian soldiers

---

[59] Rom. 1:1.
[60] See Saldarini 1988: 220–225; Baumgarten 1983; Deines 2001: 491–494; Morrison 2021: 10–11.
[61] 1 Macc. 2:42; 2 Macc. 14:6.
[62] 2 Macc. 6:18; 1 Macc. 7:12–13.
[63] Josephus, *Ant.* 17.152, 155; cf. Dan. 12:3.
[64] *m. Dem.* 2.2–3; 6.6, 9, 12; *m. Toh.* 7.4; *m. Hag.* 2.7.
[65] Josephus, *Ant.* 13.288–296.

(many Pharisees were annoyed with Eleazar for, shall we say, biting the hand)![66] Hyrcanus I was obviously insulted and incensed. With some prompting from a Sadducean sympathizer named Jonathan, he thereafter turned on the Pharisees by nullifying their laws, and punished those who observed them (which itself is evidence for the pervasiveness and popularity of Pharisaic legal tradition). In doing so, his popularity with the people soured. Reading between the lines, one gets the impression here that the Pharisees were a group to be courted as much as managed, and while some Pharisees were happy to use their religious capital in exchange for access to royal power, others were not willing to give the Hasmoneans carte blanche and wanted a more pious, pure and perhaps pliable leader. They differed among themselves as to whether it was best to work within the regime or pull the whole thing down and establish a hierocratic order in its place.

We hear little about the Pharisees during the reigns of Aristobulus I (104–103 BC) and Alexander Jannaeus (103–76 BC). There is a strong likelihood that the Pharisees joined a popular uprising against Jannaeus and were brutally suppressed.[67] However, the Pharisees experienced something of a political restoration some thirty years later after Jannaeus died and his wife, Alexandra, took over. Following Jannaeus's deathbed advice, Alexandra sought the intervention of the Pharisees and offered them a share in power if they would incline the people towards her rule (the assumption being that the Pharisees had the ears, hearts and minds of the populace). In the event, she reigned for close to a decade (76–67 BC). Josephus describes her as religiously devout and politically competent, but comments that although Alexandra held the title of a ruler it was the Pharisees who held all the power, for 'while she governed others, the Pharisees governed her'.[68] Alexandra's reign represents something of a political high point for the Pharisees in terms of their influence during the Hasmonean period. It gave them the chance to preserve, as they thought best, their national way of life against the external threat of

---

66 The same accusation was made against Alexander Jannaeus (Josephus, *Ant.* 13.372). Stemberger (1995 [1991], 108–109) thinks that the story of resistance to Hasmonean priesthood fits more naturally with Jannaeus than it does with Hyrcanus I.

67 Josephus, *Ant.* 13.288, 372–383.

68 Josephus, *Ant.* 13.409; *War* 1.112.

pagan power and the internal threat of assimilation to Hellenism.[69] The Pharisees used their new power to settle some old scores against those who had crucified some 800 of their number under Jannaeus, to the point where a delegation of leading men asked Alexandra to place them in a kind of protective custody in her fortresses in order to keep them safe from the Pharisees.[70] Alexandra made her son Hyrcanus II high priest and planned for him to succeed her. But her other son, Aristobulus II, worrying about the Pharisees taking over entirely, seized various fortresses and began gathering an army. During this time, Alexandra died, and a civil war erupted between Hyrcanus II and Aristobulus II, which was only resolved with a power-sharing agreement.[71] The concord was broken by the machinations of a certain Idumean named Herod Antipater, who urged Hyrcanus II to ally himself with King Aretas of Arabia in order to expel Aristobulus II. The second round of hostilities ended when the Roman general Pompey, while finishing off the Mithridatic wars, laid siege to and then occupied Jerusalem. Pompey annexed Judea, deposed Aristobulus II and reinstated Hyrcanus II as high priest with Herod Antipater as the real power behind the throne.[72] It was probably during this time that the Pharisees fled Jerusalem and were expunged from official political power.[73]

During the Herodian period, the Pharisees appear in Josephus's account as given to political meddling.[74] The Roman civil war between Caesar and the Senate gave Aristobulus II's son Antigonus II the opportunity to seize power in Judea in 40 BC with the support of the Parthians. Antipater's son Herod led a Roman army, which laid siege to Jerusalem. At this perilous time, two Pharisees, Pollion and Samaias, urged the populace to accept Herod as leader and allow him to enter the city.[75] They were not inclined towards Herod's character or aptitude for ruling; Herod was simply the lesser of two evils. Pollion had earlier warned Hyrcanus

---

69 Josephus, *Ant.* 13.398–410; *War* 1.107–112; *b. Taan.* 23a.
70 Josephus, *Ant.* 14.410–417; *War* 1.113–114.
71 Josephus, *Ant.* 13.423–432; 14.6–7; *War* 1.117–122.
72 Josephus, *Ant.* 14.73–77; *War* 1.153–157.
73 *Pss Sol.* 17.4–6, 16–19.
74 Mason 2007: 10.
75 Josephus, *Ant.* 15.3.

II that if Herod went unpunished for his extrajudicial murders he would one day return to punish them.[76] Later, once Herod was appointed by the Roman senate as 'King of the Judeans', Pollion and Samaias, together with the other Pharisees, refused to take the oath of loyalty to Herod but avoided punishment due to Herod's respect for Pollion.[77] The same thing happened later (or is replayed by Josephus) when 6,000 Pharisees refused to take the oath of loyalty to Herod and Caesar.[78] The fine imposed on the Pharisees was paid by Herod's sister-in-law because they supported her husband Pheroras over his brother Herod.[79] Herod in turn executed leading Pharisees, even some among his own family and household.[80] Finally, in 4 BC towards the end of Herod's reign, two Pharisees, Judas and Matthias, urged their disciples to cut down the image of an eagle at the front of the temple as it was an affront to their religion.[81] The subsequent relationship between the Pharisees and the high priests was layered and complex, but in many cases it appears as if the Pharisees functioned as advisors or lobbyists, though sometimes acting as a 'loyal opposition'.[82]

We can conclude the following about the Pharisees in the first century AD according to our sources:

1 The Pharisees were a Jewish 'sect',[83] in contrast with the Sadducees and Essenes,[84] and were described by Josephus as a philosophical school reminiscent of the Stoics.[85] A key point of distinction between the Pharisees and Sadducees was that the Pharisees believed in the resurrection of the dead.[86]

---

76 Josephus, *Ant.* 14.172–176; 15.4.
77 Josephus, *Ant.* 15.370.
78 Josephus, *Ant.* 17.42.
79 Josephus, *Ant.* 17.43; *War* 1.571.
80 Josephus, *Ant.* 17.44–45.
81 Josephus, *Ant.* 17.149–167; *War* 1.648–655; 2.5–6.
82 Cf. Horsley 2022: 8: 'The Pharisees [were] serving as advisers of the high priestly rulers, but in certain circumstances [were also] resisting.' Horsley himself emphasizes the role of the Pharisees as 'retainers' or middle-management officials of the Jerusalem temple state, which has a grain of truth but should not be pressed too far as if they were a PR company or department for the Jerusalem leadership.
83 Acts 15:5; 26:5; Josephus, *Ant.* 13.171; 17.41; 18.11; *War* 1.110; 2.119; *Life* 10, 191.
84 Acts 23:6–8; *Ant.* 13.171, 298; 18.11; *War* 2.119; *Life* 10; Acts 23:6–10; *m. Yad.* 4.6–7.
85 Josephus, *Ant.* 13.171–173; 18.11–15; *War* 2.162–163; *Life* 12.
86 Josephus, *Ant.* 18.14; *War* 2.163; Acts 23:6–10; *m. Sanh.* 10.1.

2 The Pharisees' purpose was to please God, and they considered themselves especially favoured by God.[87]
3 The Pharisees had a reputation for precision or exactness in Torah observance,[88] especially in relation to worship, prayers, sacrifices,[89] fasting,[90] tithing, vows[91] and purity,[92] and also, according to rabbinic traditions, in agricultural taboos, sabbath observance and the keeping of festivals.[93] To be a Pharisee, argues Deines, was to have a particular relationship to the Torah, hence Paul's remark in Philippian 3:5 that he had once been, 'according to the Torah, a Pharisee' (MFB trans.). This is because the nation's standing with God and its future was bound up with faithful Torah observance.[94] It was this mixture of Torah study and cultivation of tradition that was the true mark of being a Pharisee, not belief in resurrection, the acceptance of a wider canon, or alignment with a particular rabbi.[95]
4 The Pharisaic *halakhah* was known as the 'traditions of the fathers',[96] which included things 'not written in the Laws of Moses'.[97] This tradition was tethered to Torah to form an indissoluble unity. Thus, Torah, interpretation and application were fused together by the Pharisees into one single socio-religious authority.[98]
5 The Pharisees had a continuous and comprehensive influence on the populace, pertaining to Torah instruction and temple cultus,

---

87 Josephus, *Ant.* 17.41; cf. Luke 16:14–15; 18:10–14.
88 Acts 22:3; Josephus, *Ant.* 17.41; 18.12; *War* 1.110, 648; 2.162; *Life* 191.
89 Josephus, *Ant.* 18.15.
90 Mark 2:18–22; Matt. 6:16–18.
91 Luke 11:42; Matt. 23:16–23; *m. Abot* 1.17.
92 Mark 7:3–5; Matt. 23/Luke 11:39–40.
93 Neusner 1971: 244; 1973: 83.
94 Deines 2001: 492–493.
95 Deines 2001: 493–494.
96 See Gal. 1:14; Mark 7:3, 5; Josephus, *Ant.* 13.296–297, 408; 17.41; *Life* 191; Philo, *Spec. Leg.* 4.149–150; *m. Abot* 1.1; *m. Sanh.* 11.3–4.
97 Josephus, *Ant.* 13.297.
98 Sanders' (1990: 90–137) denial that the Pharisees had an oral Torah is based on a very narrow definition of oral Torah. Such a doctrine seems to be already well known BC in *Jubilees*. Neusner (2007: 396) is correct that the 'Pharisees, like pretty much every other group, had some further law or tradition, and that additional material could have been formulated and transmitted orally, in memory'. That is not to say that it was identical to the doctrine of the two Torahs extant in rabbinic writings.

in both Judea and Galilee,[99] and constituted the informal leaders of Judaism.[100] From Hyrcanus II to Herod the Great, the Pharisees were the default setting for the socio-religious observance of Judea and Galilee. The presence of stone vessels, *miqvaot* (ritual baths), measuring cups made of chalk stone and ossuaries throughout Galilee and Judea does not, as once thought, necessarily indicate widespread acceptance of Pharisaic perspectives about ritual purity and the afterlife, yet there is every chance that the use of such vessels took place according to Pharisaic *halakhah*.[101] The *Halakhic Letter* (4QMMT) critiques what appear to be mainstream halakhic judgments about purity which, according to rabbinic tradition, are attributed to the Pharisees.[102] The Pharisees took measures to transmit their teachings and traditions to others,[103] even to those abroad.[104] This is why Paul treats Pharisaic Judaism as, in effect, normative Judaism, because Pharisaism was regarded by the majority as the legitimate interpretation of God's purposes for the nation, even if everyone did not always adhere to every point of Pharisaic interpretation.[105]

6 According to some of their critics, the Pharisees' reputation for liberality made them in the eyes of the Qumranites the 'expounders of smooth things'[106] or the 'simple minded of Ephraim'.[107] For others, the Pharisees had a fixation on personal purity to the exclusion of anyone else, even as they amassed wealth.[108] Jesus similarly appears to have criticized the Pharisees for their *halakhah*, their tendency to

---

99 On Pharisaic influence in Galilee, see Saldarini (1988: 292–297), who sees them as 'a minor and probably relatively new social force, struggling to influence people toward their way of life' (295).
100 Josephus, *Ant.* 13.288, 298; 17.41; 18.15; Mark 7:3.
101 Reed 2000: 49–51, 125–131; Strange 2007 (with helpful diagrams); and qualifications noted by Meyers (2021).
102 Cf. 4QMMT B 55–58 and *m. Yad.* 4.7 about pouring liquids from one container to another.
103 Josephus, *Ant.* 13.297–298; cf. *m. Abot* 1.12.
104 Josephus, *Ant.* 20.43–47; Matt. 23:15.
105 Gal. 1:13–14; Phil. 3:5–6; Acts 26:5.
106 CD-A I 18–19; 4Q222 2 I 21; 1QH 2.15, 32; based on Isa. 30:10.
107 4QpNah 3–4.iii.5.
108 *T. Mos.* 7.5–10.

prioritize purity over morality, their confidence in God's favour, and their love of riches.

7. The Pharisees were collegial and friendly to one another,[109] which coheres with rabbinic traditions about the *haberim* (associates) who formed *haburot* (associations) and confirms the Lukan meal scenes involving Pharisees.[110] The Pharisees' separation from others was partly about purity, but it was primarily about marking themselves out as a renewal group within Judean society.[111] They were 'a separate movement *within* the nation *for* the nation, whose legitimacy was indeed *accepted* by large parts of the people, even though its requirements were not *observed* to an equal extent'.[112]

8. Many of the Pharisees, but by no means all, were associated with a Jewish tradition of zealous religious violence (towards fellow Jews) and revolutionary violence (against Judean collaborators and Roman rulers). That is not to say that the Pharisees were completely and unequivocally the pro-revolution and anti-Roman party. Every sect has its factions within factions. There were some who resisted calls to violence, who wanted to work with the powers and were disposed to moderation. Many Pharisees, remember, were annoyed by Eleazar's attack on Hyrcanus I. Two leading Judean teachers of the first century BC had different dispositions in these matters; Hillel did not share the anti-Gentile vehemence of Shammai. Rabbi Gamaliel in the 40s AD was remembered for his patience and peacefulness. Josephus tells us that two Pharisees, Gorison ben Joseph and Simon ben Gamaliel II, rejected the zealots' atrocities and their appointment of an illegitimate high priest during the Judean rebellion.[113] Then, after AD 70, Rabbi Johanan ben Zakkai argued that the true response to tyranny was not instigating tumults but Torah study. Nonetheless, the existence of zealous Pharisees, such as Shammai, Saddok, Saul of Tarsus, and, in a similar vein, Rabbi Akiva during the Bar Kochba revolt of AD 132–5, makes it hard to resist the conclusion that the

---

109 Josephus, *War* 2.166.
110 Luke 7:36–39; 11:37–38.
111 Saldarini 1988: 281–282; Deines 2001: 450.
112 Deines 2001: 501 (emphasis original).
113 Josephus, *War* 4.159–160.

Pharisees had deep connections with revolutionary movements from the time of the Hasmoneans through to the time of Hadrian. This is indicated by several incidents and episodes:

(a) The Pharisees were given to 'sedition' against Judean rulers,[114] opposed kings in general and sometimes pursued open warfare.[115] The proof of this is that the Pharisees were probably part of an uprising against Alexander Jannaeus,[116] given that 800 of their number were crucified during his reign,[117] an act for which the Qumran scrolls call him 'the lion of wrath'.[118] The Pharisees were a constant source of irritation to Herod the Great for their refusal to take loyalty oaths to himself and Caesar,[119] as well as for the 'golden eagle' affair (see above).[120] Even though the Pharisees had a mutually beneficial relationship with Alexandra and Hyrcanus II in the first century BC and enjoyed a positive relationship with Agrippa II in the first century AD, many of the Pharisees were theocratic and even messianic in their eschatology.[121] The Pharisees were an 'occasional aggravation to the elite' and used their popular support to stir up the masses against certain authorities.[122]

(b) At the turn of the eras, the Pharisaic teacher Shammai, often juxtaposed with Hillel, was known for his more rigorous *halakhah*, anti-Gentile sentiment and perhaps even a fanatical hatred of the Romans.

(c) After Herod the Great's son Archelaus was deposed in AD 6, the subsequent rebellion led by Judas the Galilean included in its leadership a zealous Pharisee named Saddok.[123]

---

114 Josephus, *Ant.* 13.291.
115 Josephus, *Ant.* 17.41.
116 Josephus, *War* 1.88.
117 Josephus, *Ant.* 13.380; 17.42.
118 4Q169 3–4 I 5.
119 Josephus, *Ant.* 15.370.
120 Josephus, *Ant.* 17.149–167; *War* 1.648–655.
121 Cf. *Pss Sol.* 17 – 18.
122 Mason 2007: 37. That said, I think Mason overcooks Josephus's anti-Pharisaic disposition; while Josephus sees the Pharisees as a cause of unrest, he also portrays them as voices for moderation and peace.
123 Josephus, *Ant.* 18.4, 9; *War* 2.118.

(d) The violent persecutions carried out by the Pharisee Saul of Tarsus against members of a messianic sect in the early 30s AD indicates that the tradition of violent zeal, lifted from Phinehas and the Maccabeans, was still very much in effect.[124] That coheres remarkably well with Philo's comment about numberless zealots among the Judeans who were all too willing to shed the blood of their own compatriots, without mercy, for infringing their national laws.[125]

(e) The Sicarii, knife-wielding fanatics active in the 50s AD, who killed Roman collaborators, had 'pure hands but more evil thoughts', says Josephus, and the mention of pure hands perhaps refers to Pharisaic concern with handwashing.[126]

(f) Many Pharisees shared with the 'Fourth Philosophy' (Josephus's term for zealot-minded Jews) and the Sicarii an intense belief that 'God [was] their only sovereign'.[127]

(g) Many Pharisees in Jerusalem opposed a rebellion against Rome.[128] Be that as it may, many Pharisees played a key part in the Judean rebellion of AD 66–70. One of the rebellion's leaders, John of Gischala, had a close association with a leading Pharisee named Simon ben Gamaliel.[129]

In terms of the aims of the Pharisees at the beginnings of the first century AD, Jacob Neusner argued that the Pharisees abandoned Judean politics for the pursuit of grassroots piety and cultivating associations concerned with food purity, whereby food was to be consumed in a state of priest-like purity.[130] In contrast, Sanders considers the Pharisees to be a relatively small association centred in Jerusalem, pursuing objectives and agendas related to purity, but also transcending it, even leading some

---

124 Gal. 1:14; Phil. 3:6; Acts 22:3.
125 Philo, *Spec. Leg.* 2.253.
126 Wright 1992: 182, based on Josephus, *Ant.* 20.185–197; *War* 2.258–259; Tacitus, *Ann.* 12.54.
127 Josephus, *Ant.* 18.23; *War* 7.410.
128 Josephus, *War* 2.411–418.
129 Josephus, *War* 4.159; *Life* 189–198.
130 Neusner 1973; others, e.g. Stemberger (1995 [1991]: 118), think that the Pharisees remained politically interested.

to revolution.[131] I am inclined to agree with Wright, who believes that the Pharisees had ambitions far beyond preserving and pontificating about ritual purity, since they remained politically invested in Israel's renewal, a prospect which, for some within their ranks, meant embracing violent revolution against Rome if necessary.[132] This was an ambition we could sum up with a number of pithy slogans: 'To defeat the beasts let's become a kingdom of priests'; 'No Torah without Pharisaic *halakhah*'; 'Fasting, food and fellowship are symbols of a faithful Jew'; 'Ritual purity means spiritual security'; 'Revolution begins in the *miqvaot*'; 'Keep the zeal real'; 'Terror for the Torah-breakers!' Forgive the obvious hyperbole, but we have here a mixture of precision in *halakhah* and pursuit of holiness to the point of zealous violence, all tied to hopes for Israel's renewal and redemption from Gentile domination. As Kent Yinger notes: 'Their concern for scrupulous law observance arose not from the question, "How do we save our souls?" but from the question, "How do we preserve our people?"'[133] On that matter, the Pharisees had a purpose and, varyingly, a plan!

Why, then, the focus on ritual purity? It was undoubtedly part of the Pharisees' reform agenda, since reformist groups typically seek to define themselves as a closed and boundary-defined subgroup as they seek to influence and bring about change in wider society in order to form a super-ordinate group, in this case, a purified Israel.[134] The problem is figuring out how the Pharisaic reform agenda relates to their specific instructions about purity and contamination. For instance, according to the Mishnah, priests should eat their tithed rations, even though it is unconsecrated food, only after washing their hands, that is, in a state of ritual purity.[135] Note too that Mark explains in a parenthetical remark in Mark 7:3–4 that the Pharisees took exception to Jesus' disciples eating food with unclean/unwashed hands (*koinos/aniptos*) because 'the Pharisees, and all the Jews, do not eat unless they thoroughly wash their hands, thus observing the

---

131 Sanders 1992: 383–404.
132 Wright 1992: 186–187; 2014: 80–90; cf. Theissen and Merz (1998 [1996]: 228–229), who believe that the Pharisees did not migrate 'from politics to piety' so much as 'alter their strategy', and were 'always both a religious and political factor at the same time'.
133 Yinger 2022: 55.
134 Saldarini 1988: 286.
135 *m. Meg.* 2.5.

tradition of the elders'. The problem with the Mishnaic regulations and Mark's commentary is that the only handwashing regulations explicitly set out in the Torah pertain to priests washing their hands before offering sacrifices in the temple.[136] Why extend this ritual of cultic purity to priests eating tithed food outside the temple, and why extend it even to the laity? Why eat unconsecrated food (i.e. food that has nothing to do with the cultus) as if one were a priest and as if the food consumed had been used in the temple cultus? One might retort that cultic purity is simply good for its own sake.[137] Or was the concern with keeping priestly standards of purity designed to turn all of Israel into 'a kingdom of priests' as per Exodus 19:6; in other words, a democratization of the priesthood?[138] The rationale for this kingdom-of-priests approach is easy to grasp. If the Hellenistic subjugation of Judea, as exemplified by Antiochus IV, was chiefly expressed by an attack on the Jerusalem temple, it made sense then to guard the purity of the temple by having all the people take up the cause of its holiness as epitomized by the priests.[139] Alternatively, and more likely, the Pharisees' objective was holiness, and priestly holiness was the highest standard of holiness to be obtained, which is why the Pharisees adopted some priestly practices such as eating common food in a state of ritual purity, as per Mark 7:3–5.[140] The Pharisees fashioned a

---

136 Exod. 30:18–21; 40:30–32. Note that handwashing was a part of ritual in religion outside the Israelite cultus going back as far as Hesiod: 'Do not pour a libation of bright-colored wine to Zeus after dawn, with unwashed hands. Nor should you do so to any other immortal. Otherwise, they will not heed your prayers but will spit them back' (*Works and Days*, 724–726).

137 Sanders 1990: 235 (more broadly 131–252 for the whole argument).

138 Neusner (1973: 83; cf. 1993: 262–273; 2007) wrote: 'The Pharisees held that even outside of the Temple, in one's own home, the laws of ritual purity were to be followed in the only circumstance in which they might apply, namely, at the table. Therefore, one must eat secular food (ordinary, everyday meals) in a state of ritual purity as if one were a Temple priest.' Sanders (1990: 192, 234–235; cf. 1992: 438–439) admitted a few 'minor symbolic gestures' towards priestly purity, but otherwise dismissed the idea of translating priestly purity to the laity as impossible to do in practice. Schwartz (1992) notes that Exod. 19:6 with its 'kingdom of priests' did not appear to influence the Pharisees in their view. The idea did, however, influence modern Jewish scholars, internally, with respect to identifying the Pharisees as innovators in their tradition, then externally, in Jewish apologetics towards Christians.

139 Deines 2001: 496.

140 This appears to be a line of argument attributed to Rabbi Gamaliel, a senior contemporary of Paul, according to *Tanna Debe Eliyahu* 16: '(The law of) hand-washing is derived from Moses, Aaron and his sons . . . But what is written of Israel? "And you shall make yourselves holy and be holy" (Lev. 11:44; 20:7). On this basis Rabban Gamaliel used to say: Holiness was not given to the priests alone, but, rather, to priests, Levites and all Israel, as it says, "Say to all the children of Israel, You shall be holy" (Lev. 19:1—2)', cited from Schwartz 1992: 64.

graded extension of purity regulations, not simply applying the priestly specifications to the Jews living in *Eretz* Israel.[141] According to de Lacey, 'there is no hint here of usurping or replacing priests, but there is a clear model of establishing a scale of purities, and moving as far towards the priests on that scale as possible'.[142]

In the minds of the Pharisees they were not a niche interest group; rather, they were propagating and practising what they believed to simply be the Judean way of life as God required it, as the Torah taught it and as they understood it. What stood in the way of that was, of course, the contamination of foreign domination, which had to be addressed one way or another, beginning with themselves. Only once they had dealt with the pollution of the self, the village and the land would God cleanse them from the contamination of foreign powers. They had an objective and wanted to see the whole nation get on board with it. Wright puts it well:

> The Pharisaic agenda remained, at this point, what it had always been: to purify Israel by summoning her to return to the true ancestral traditions; to restore Israel to her independent theocratic status; and to be, as a pressure-group, in the vanguard of such movements by the study and practice of Torah.[143]

Why the torrid debates with Jesus? That requires some serious qualification and trying to think it through from the perspective of the Pharisees and then from Jesus.

To begin with, Jesus was closer to the Pharisees than to any other Jewish sect, and he drew many admirers and adherents from the Pharisees.[144]

---

141 Hengel and Schwemer 2019 [2007]: 148.
142 de Lacey 1992: 370. Neusner (2007: 402) would agree: 'Pharisees are not classified as priests, that is, as persons who eat priestly rations or heave offering. But they are persons who are placed within the hierarchy of cultic cleanness in eating food. The food that they eat is not food that is reserved for priests, so it can only be food that is not reserved for priests, which is to say, secular or unconsecrated food. That passage on the face of it therefore sustains the view that Pharisees are persons who eat unconsecrated food in a state of cultic cleanness, or, more accurately, within the hierarchy of states of cultic cleanness that the Mishnah's paragraphs' framer proposes to spell out.'
143 Wright 1992: 189.
144 See Falk 1985; Berger 1988: 261; Maccoby 2004; Schröter 2021.

Jesus and the Pharisees were both very much concerned with the matter of how to advance the kingdom of God, which meant they were natural interlocutors.[145] Some Pharisees, just like Jesus, sought baptism from John the Baptist,[146] while others rebuffed it.[147] Many Pharisees were impressed by Jesus' teaching and his power to heal.[148] They invited him to dinner, which was more than polite hospitality; it meant insider status.[149] On one occasion they warned him about Herod Antipas's pursuit of him.[150] A Pharisee apparently helped to bury Jesus.[151] Many Pharisees joined the early church, bringing with them their erstwhile Pharisaic baggage about Gentiles and insistence on the circumcision of proselytes.[152] In the early days of the Jerusalem church, when Peter and John were before the Sanhedrin, a leading Pharisee named Gamaliel cautioned against punishing them, and instead urged a wait-and-see approach.[153] Later, when James the brother of Jesus was executed in AD 62 at the behest of the high priest Ananus, during an interregnum of Roman governors, one Jerusalem faction complained to Agrippa II about the injustice. This group Josephus describes as 'considered the fairest-minded, and ... strict concerning the law', which is a very probable description of the Pharisees.[154]

Yet, from the Pharisees' point of view, Jesus was something of a potential ally turned bitter adversary. His authority was charismatic rather than halakhic, his mantle was messianic rather than Mosaic, and he operated independently of the temple and other interpretative communities. Jesus and the Pharisees had similar aims for Israel's restoration, but they differed very much over what that would look like and how to achieve it. Pharisees were in effect saying to Jesus: God appears

---

145 Mark 15:43; Luke 17:20.
146 Matt. 3:7.
147 Luke 7:30.
148 John 3:1–4; Luke 5:17.
149 Luke 7:36; 11:37; 14:1.
150 Luke 13:31.
151 John 19:39–40.
152 Acts 15:5.
153 Acts 5:34–40.
154 Josephus, *Ant.* 20.200–201.

to be with you, but if so, then *why* do you eat with 'sinners',[155] *why* don't you fast as we do (Mark 2:18), *why* don't you wash your hands as we do (Mark 7:1–5; Luke 11:38), *why* are you so lenient about the sabbath (Mark 2:24; John 9:16), *why* are you so strict on divorce (Mark 10:2) and *what* is the sign of your authority (Mark 8:11–12)? In the mind of many Pharisees, Jesus appeared to be a holy man, but his refusal to adopt their package of Torah/tradition meant he was a rogue and a rival. Whatever points of convergence there were between Jesus and the Pharisees, they were overshadowed by an immense chasm evidenced by Jesus' practice of open meal-fellowship with sinners, which scandalized the Pharisees.[156] Jesus acted as if holiness were a contagion, not a diminishing commodity to be preserved.[157] Not only that, but his disregard for and denunciation of their traditions was a brutal rebuff to the Pharisees' centre of gravity. In the end, Jesus did not support the Pharisaic project of cultivating holiness by separation as the preferred path to national redemption.

From the perspective of Jesus, the Pharisees were missing the forest for the trees. If the kingdom was in their midst, then much of what they were saying and doing was irrelevant; it was like arguing about phylacteries while crowds were pulling down statues of Caesar and fortifying the walls of the city.[158] Many Pharisees had forgotten how Scripture itself prioritizes righteousness over ritual, and love over law.[159] Some had used their position to amass wealth and seek status.[160] Their *halakhah* was supposed to help with *keeping* Torah, not circumventing it;[161] it had become a cumbersome burden,[162] and their teaching did not match their own example.[163] Their yearning for purity and escape from pollution had

---

155 Mark 2:15–17; Matt. 21:31–32; Luke 15:1–3; P. Oxy. 1224.1; Justin, *1 Apol.* 15.8.
156 Vermes (2003: 11) puts it well: '[T]he conflict between Jesus of Galilee and the Pharisees of his time would, in normal circumstances, merely have resembled the in-fighting of factions belonging to the same religious body, like that between the Karaites and Rabbanites in the Middle Ages, or between the orthodox and progressive branches of Judaism in modern times.' Vermes goes on to add that sociopolitical factors and eschatological visions heightened the conflict between Jesus and his contemporaries.
157 Berger 1988: 240; Blomberg 2005; Stettler 2004: 164.
158 Luke 17:20–21.
159 Matt. 9:13; 12:7; Luke 11:42; P. Oxy. 840.23–45.
160 Mark 12:38–40; Matt. 23:5–12; Luke 16:14–15.
161 Mark 7:8–13; Matt. 23:16–22.
162 Matt. 23:4.
163 Matt. 7:5/Luke 6:41–42; Matt. 23:3.

turned them into, ironically, bad yeast that had spread through all of Israel.[164] They had succumbed to the temptation of making piety a public performance rather than a true habit of holiness.[165] Their claim to divine favour manifested itself as a claim for social status over others, which was a recipe for hubris, a constant 'justifying' of the self and condemnation of others.[166] Such an attitude was manifested in the presumption of favouritism by the elder son in Jesus' parable of the lost son.[167] The Pharisees emphasized their divine favour and legal prowess.[168] Against this, Jesus declared that the line between insiders and outsiders had been redrawn, so that while the Pharisees and sinners were indeed on opposite sides, it was kingdom allegiance that made someone an insider, and the Pharisees were on the wrong side of that line! I know that many scholars will declare that this material is a post-AD 70 Christianized stereotype of the Pharisees, a rhetorical attack without substance, as inaccurate as it is anachronistic. Yet Rabbi Hillel had purportedly warned of similar things in the decades prior to Jesus: 'Do not separate yourself from the community, do not trust in yourself until the day of your death, do not judge your fellow man until you have reached his place' (*m. Abot* 2.4). For some Pharisees, Jesus' message was something, in whole or in part, that they knew they needed to hear, while for others it was an insult to their honour and a threat to their hegemony as the didactic elite.[169] Which is why many were willing to negotiate with the Sadducees, priests and Herodians to see the pernicious prophet from Galilee dealt with most severely.[170]

The difference between Jesus and the Pharisees was not over 'What must I do to be saved?' Nor was it about whether Judaism is a 'relationship' as opposed to a 'religion'. Nor was Jesus attacking the patriarchy and purity of the Pharisees with a view to supplanting it with his own brand

---

164 Mark 8:15; Luke 12:1.
165 Matt. 6:1–5, 16, 18; 23:5, 28.
166 Luke 16:14–15; 18:10–14.
167 Luke 15:25–32.
168 Josephus, *Ant.* 17.41.
169 Luke 11:45, 53–54. Cf. Keener 2009: 231–232.
170 Mark 3:6. Note: the chief priest and Pharisees were natural rivals, but they could come together to deal with certain crises, as they did at the beginning of the Judean rebellion against Rome, according to Josephus (*War* 2.411).

of egalitarianism and inclusivist village ethics. The real issues were: *who* speaks for God and *what* is the programme for Israel's restoration?[171] Jesus competes with the Pharisees for the allegiance of the Galileans and Judeans as to how to love God and how to be faithful to him in the light of the kingdom's coming; a kingdom that comes specifically through his mighty deeds, healings and exorcisms, and even through his own suffering, death and vindication. Jesus placed himself at the centre of God's purposes, precisely where the Pharisees thought Torah and the pursuit of priest-like holiness should be! That was the source of the conflict and why some Pharisees were even willing to cooperate with Herodians and high priests to have Jesus disposed of. He was not only a rival; he was also potentially leading the nation astray as either a false prophet, a rabble-rousing crowd-drawer or a messianic pretender.

Sadducees

The Sadducees were the priestly aristocratic 'sect' who, through the temple and chief priesthood,[172] were the official leaders of Judea and Jerusalem during the time of Jesus and the apostles.[173] The Sadducees are probably named after Zadok, a high priest during the time of David, and they likely emerged in the early Hasmonean period as a priestly reform group as part of the anti-Hellenistic coalition. They were the leading priestly coalition after the departure of the moderate Hellenistic Oniads to Egypt and the fanatically conservative 'Teacher of Righteousness' to Qumran. They evidently were able to live with Hyrcanus I making himself ethnarch, high priest and king of Judea, but their rise to influence at the Hasmonean court was not immediate. During the reign of Hyrcanus I, the Sadducees seemingly ousted the Pharisees as the resident cultic–religious advisors to the Hasmoneans and retained that position of influence all the way through the Herodian period to the time of the Judean rebellion.[174] Thereafter, the Sadducees were the Dr Moriarty to the Pharisees' Sherlock Holmes. The two sects may have made common

---

171 Sanders 1985: 281; cf. Yinger 2022: 76–79, 86–88.
172 Of course, not all priests were Sadducees – some were Pharisees; and not all Sadducees were aristocrats – some were ordinary peasants.
173 Cf. Acts 5:17. In brief, see Sanders 1992: 332–340; Wright 1992: 210–213; Stemberger 1995 [1991]: 119; Strauss 2013.
174 Josephus, *Ant.* 13.293–294.

cause on occasion, and the Sadducees probably felt pressured to adopt Pharisaic views of the temple cultus due to the Pharisees' overwhelming popularity with the people. But for the most part the two groups were at loggerheads, something the Gospels and Acts constantly point out,[175] and rabbinic literature frequently polemicizes against the Sadducees.[176]

The Sadducees were popular with the ruling/landowning class, not so much with the general populace.[177] They were known to be 'savage' or 'cruel' (*hōmos*) in the application of discipline to other Judeans[178] and fiercely competitive among themselves.[179] In other words, they curried favour with the powerful, they wielded power over others with little thought of restraint, and they vied for power among themselves.

Josephus describes the Sadducees as conservative in theology, recognizing only the Torah as a sacred textual authority and rejecting the 'traditions' of the Pharisees, traditions that were generally liberalizing of the Torah's obligations when there was legal ambiguity.[180] Josephus also describes them as libertarian concerning anthropology with their belief in free will, although that might be a philosophizing of their belief that the best men end up in the highest positions to undergird the status quo.[181] The Sadducees denied the resurrection of the dead, so that body and soul die together.[182] This denial might be a bit more than 'I can't find "resurrection" in my Torah concordance, and that stuff about those sleeping in the dust rising to everlasting life in Daniel's ravings ain't kosher with us.' Resurrection was both a metaphor for Israel's political restoration (Ezek. 37) and God's reward to faithful Jews who resisted the idolatry and arrogance of self-deified despots (2 Macc. 7). Resurrection was the theology of revolution; it meant a political upheaval, a renewed Israel with new leaders and a reward for those martyred by the powers that be. The Sadducees therefore rejected resurrection as much for its political ramifications as for its textual basis. Luke's picture of the

---

175 Cf. esp. Acts 23:1–10.
176 Cf. e.g. *m. Sanh.* 10.1.
177 Josephus, *Ant.* 13.298; 18.17.
178 Josephus, *Ant.* 20.199.
179 Josephus, *War* 2.166.
180 Josephus, *Ant.* 13.297.
181 Josephus, *Ant.* 13.173; *War* 2.164–165.
182 Josephus, *Ant.* 18.16; *War* 2.165; Mark 12:18; Acts 23:8; *m. Sanh.* 10.1.

Sadducees as jealously guarding the peace and their position of power by persecuting the church would seem to ring true.[183] It was, after all, the high priest Ananus, presumably a Sadducee, who had James the brother of Jesus executed in AD 62 just before the outbreak of the Judean rebellion against Rome.[184]

The impression the evangelists create is that for the high-priestly faction of Sadducees, Jesus was a rural prophetic agitator, exciting the populace with messianic dreams that could easily become nightmares, and a threat to their own position of power and authority. The synoptic account of Jesus' trial,[185] and John's claims about Caiaphas's belief in the divine necessity of Jesus' death, raise a host of historical questions,[186] but we may admit that they reflect something of the actual rationale for the priestly class to seek Jesus' execution: Jesus had a reputation for exciting hopes of Israel's restoration/liberation, and he was in Jerusalem at a very dangerous time, Passover, when the city's population swelled with hundreds of thousands of pilgrims[187] who had come to celebrate God's deliverance of the Hebrews from a pagan power, during which time he performed a dramatic and incendiary action in the temple; in addition, Jesus seems, when pressed, to have obliquely affirmed belief in his messianic destiny. In their minds, they were snuffing out a potential spark that could burn Jerusalem and all of Judea to the ground.

For Jesus, the Sadducees were like wicked tenants who were not giving the lord of the vineyard his due: they had persecuted his envoys and were now going to dishonour and murder his very own son.[188] On their watch, the temple had become like a cave to which bandits flee,[189] since the chief priests stole the tithes meant for the priests who served in the temple[190] and inflated the price for a pair of doves which the poor

---

[183] Acts 4:1–6; 5:17–18.
[184] Josephus, *Ant.* 20.200.
[185] Mark 14:55–65/Matt. 26:57–68/Luke 22:66–71.
[186] John 11:49–53.
[187] Sanders (1992: 125–128) estimates that between 300,000 and 400,000 pilgrims occupied the city for the Passover.
[188] Mark 12:1–12; *Gos. Thom.* 65.
[189] Mark 11:15–17; cf. Bauckham 1988: 84; Bryan 2002: 218.
[190] Josephus, *Ant.* 20.206.

purchased for their sacrifices.[191] The Sadducees were to be swept aside as the kingdom took root around them, and their tenure in the places of power would one day be overturned in the revolution of all things.

Scribes

The scribes are another group that appear in the Synoptic Gospels as part of the opposition to Jesus, often in the company of the Pharisees and chief priests. However, their precise role and relationship to the other sects in Jewish society is a matter of dispute.

While the term 'scribe' (Aram. *sapar*; Gk *grammateus*) could generally designate a government official of some kind,[192] in the Judean post-exilic context scribes were specifically known as priests skilled as interpreters and teachers of Torah. We should think of figures such as Ezra, who was a priest and 'a scribe skilled in the law of Moses'.[193] Or else, we should identify scribes as administrators of the temple, as they were during the Persian period.[194] Josephus says that Antiochus III exempted the 'priests and scribes of the temple' from taxation in return for Judean support against the Ptolemies.[195] Ben Sirach was not himself a priest, though clearly a supporter of the Oniad priesthood,[196] and he connected the priesthood with a certain teaching authority that was potentially exercised through the scribes.[197] The priest–scribe interrelationship also appears in *Testament of Levi* 8.17 where Levi's descendants are said to include 'priests, judges, and scribes'. In the scribes we have, to use a modern analogy, a cross between the local 'notary public' and a 'biblical exegete'.

The Judean scribes resemble the literate retainer class of Mesopotamia and Egypt. In Judea, the scribes were 'intellectual retainers of the rulers', providing religio-legal expertise to the chief priests, functioning in a role somewhere between that of religious professor and professional

---

191 *m. Ker.* 1.7.
192 Ezra 4:8–9.
193 Ezra 7:6; cf. Neh. 8:1–4.
194 Neh. 13:7–13.
195 Josephus, *Ant.* 14.142.
196 Sir. 50:1–22.
197 Sir. 45:17, 50; so too Josephus, *Apion* 2.187.

administrator, and learned in wisdom traditions, sacred history, prophecy, astronomical knowledge and royal hymnody.[198] Concerning this functionary role, we might think of the Matthean infancy narrative where the Eastern magi visit Herod the Great with news of the Messiah's imminent birth, and Herod calls the 'chief priests and scribes of the people' to identify precisely where the Messiah is supposed to be born.[199] This conclusion is confirmed by Josephus in his mention of Eleazar the 'scribe of the ruler of the temple' whom the Sicarii took hostage as ransom for the release of their comrades;[200] Aristeus too is named as a 'scribe of the Sanhedrin' who was slaughtered with several other priests;[201] and Josephus notes how, during one Passover prior to the Judean rebellion, a bright light that shone around the altar of the temple was interpreted by certain 'sacred scribes' as a portent of the tragic events that were soon to happen.[202] Scribes were part of the priestly retainer class, known for their literacy and expertise in Jewish law.

Even as the scribes were embedded in the echelons of the Jerusalem priestly elites, caught up in their factionalism and their negotiations with foreign imperial authorities, they were nonetheless still guardians of the 'Judean cultural repertoire'.[203] Thus, it was during the crisis of the second century BC that the scribes became prominent as part of a coalition with the *hasidim* and other conservative priests against a party of radical pro-Seleucid Hellenizers.[204] It was a group of *hasidim* and scribes who also consented to the high priesthood of Alcimus as a compromise between the Hellenizers and the Maccabean rebels.[205] During this time, and thereafter too, scribal circles probably composed some of the protest literature that formed part of the book of Daniel, the compilations of *1 Enoch* and perhaps even the sectarian *Jubilees*.[206]

---

198 Horsley 2007: 10.
199 Matt. 2:1–6.
200 Josephus, *Ant.* 20.208.
201 Josephus, *War* 5.532.
202 Josephus, *War* 6.290-291.
203 Horsley 2007: 10.
204 Cf. the story of scribal martyr Eleazar in 2 Macc. 6:18–31.
205 1 Macc. 7:12–15.
206 See the designation of Enoch as a scribe in 4Q203; 4Q530; *1 Enoch* 12.4; 15.1; *Jub.* 4.17–26; cf. Horsley 2007: 12–13.

The evangelists ordinarily associate the scribes with the Jerusalem priestly leadership and the elders,[207] but they were not exclusively a Jerusalemite bureaucracy. Some scribes were associated with the Pharisees, literally scribes belonging to the Pharisees.[208] Josephus mentions 'village scribes',[209] which confirms the picture of the Gospels where scribes are present in Galilean and Judean villages.[210] The scribes appear to act as chief consultants and clerks to rulers, and as a kind of paralegal or privatdozent out in the villages.

The root of the conflict between Jesus and the scribes is over Jesus' status as a Torah-teacher.[211] Since Jesus was neither a priest nor part of the scribal elite, but a rural Galilean artisan, his status as a Torah-teacher or 'textbroker'[212] was a matter of debate among recognized authorities. This debate is unexpected given that Ben Sirach explicitly claims that manual labourers cannot be learned about the Torah,[213] and the Pharisees reportedly dismissed the opinions of the crowds.[214] Not every Jewish teacher shared such a classist perspective: Rabbi Gamaliel was remembered as saying, 'Excellent is the study of the Torah when combined with a worldly occupation, for toil in them both keeps sin out of one's mind' (*m. Abot* 2.2). But, as Chris Keith points out, Jesus' teaching in synagogues – combined with his healings, exorcisms and miracles – prompted diverse responses about whether he was able to occupy a position of teaching authority. Whereas Jesus was accepted in some places as a Torah-teacher,[215] elsewhere his authority in this role was challenged on the grounds that he had 'never been taught' by the scribal authorities[216] and he was merely an artisan or craftsman.[217] The objection being that Jesus does not possess scribal literacy and therefore

---

207 Mark 3:22; 8:31; 10:33; 11:18, 27; 14:1, 43, 53; 15:31; Matt. 2:4; Acts 4:5; 6:12.
208 Mark 2:16; 7:1, 5; Matt. 5:20; 23:2, 13–30; Acts 23:9.
209 Josephus, *War* 1.479.
210 Mark 2:6, 16; 9:14.
211 Here I am closely following the measured and erudite arguments of Keith 2014.
212 Snyder 2000: 222.
213 Sir. 38:24 – 39:1.
214 John 7:49.
215 Luke 4:16–17.
216 John 7:15.
217 Mark 6:3.

cannot exercise scribal authority.[218] The pagan author Celsus would later ridicule Christians on this very point, deriding them for following the teachings of a mere carpenter.[219]

Jesus taught in many places, such as villages, the countryside, lakeshores and in people's houses, but he also had a 'custom' of teaching in synagogues.[220] It was here, on the scribes' home-turf we might say, that scribes questioned his 'authority', that is, his credentials and the content of his instruction.[221] What is more, Jesus' teaching style often led to excited fervour among his listeners, resulting in a contrast between his prophetic/messianic authority, which combined Torah with mighty deeds, and the scribal mode of textual authority.[222] Jesus' teaching possessed an arresting 'authority' in terms of claim, conviction, act and artistry. In addition, it was unmediated, because no priest, rabbi or scribe vouched for his credentials. Jesus was a holy itinerant claiming God as his Father and to have received unction from the Spirit of God.[223] Jesus' response to the criticism of the scribes was to defeat them on their own chosen terrain: Torah. Hence his common retort 'Have you never read . . .?'[224] or his challenge as to whether they know the Scriptures.[225] Jesus can also aggressively contest scribal interpretation of key texts such as Psalm 110[226] and unleash a tirade against the scribes because their Torah talk does not match their hypocritical walk.[227] So, just as with the Pharisees, debates over Torah serve as the 'gravitational center of these controversies as the scribal elite attempt to assess Jesus's action and authority for doing them, and thus his identity, in light of the sacred

---

218 Keith 2014: 43.
219 Origen, *C. Cels.* 6.34.
220 Luke 4:16.
221 Mark 2:1–10.
222 Mark 1:22; Matt. 7:29.
223 Moule (1977: 8) referred to Jesus' 'sheer originality'. Bornkamm (1960 [1956]: 58–60) speaks of Jesus' 'directness', 'astounding sovereignty' and 'patent immediacy'. Vermes (2004: 36) connects it to the 'masterfulness of his message'.
224 Mark 2:25; 12:26; Matt. 21:16, 42.
225 Mark 12:24; John 3:10; 5:39–47; 7:19.
226 Mark 12:35.
227 Matt. 23:5–12.

texts.'[228] In which case, as Keith argues, debates over Torah and authority were two sides of the same coin.

Now, not every encounter between Jesus and the scribes was negative. Jesus can commend one scribe for being 'not far from the kingdom of God',[229] and even tell people to respect their office as those who occupy 'Moses' seat' and to 'do whatever they teach you and follow it'.[230] Yet Jesus' appearance in synagogues as a Torah-teacher met with a divided response, with the most negative reaction emanating from those very scribes who saw Jesus claiming their authority for his controversial practices.

Herodians

Mark mentions in two places a group known as the 'Herodians'.[231] In the first instance, in Galilee, the Pharisees go out to conspire with the Herodians on how to destroy Jesus for publicly shaming them.[232] In the second instance, in Jerusalem, a group of Pharisees and Herodians try to trap Jesus with a catch-22 question about taxes and Caesar,[233] presumably with a view to mounting an accusation of sedition against him.[234] The Pharisees and Herodians were not natural allies, but their cooperation is based on the need of these unofficial grassroots leaders to seek the support of the official ruling class in order to deal with a mutual pest and rival.

The Herodians were presumably partisans of the Herodian dynasty.[235] Herod the Great had gradually exterminated the Hasmonean dynasty and eliminated leading Judean families. In the vacuum, he promoted Idumean relatives, Diaspora Jews, enemies of his opponents, and Gentiles to prominent positions within his kingdom. Josephus says that during a civil war, a group of Galileans loyal to the Parthian-installed ruler

---

228 Keith 2014: 112.
229 Mark 12:34.
230 Matt. 23:2–3.
231 For a good overview of the Herodian dynasty see Bond 2013b; more recent studies of note are Jensen 2010 [2006] and Marshak 2015.
232 Mark 3:6.
233 Mark 12:13/Matt. 22:16.
234 Luke 23:2.
235 BDAG 440.

Antigonus drowned some of Herod's supporters in a lake.[236] Also, the Greek *Hērōdianoi* would have its Latin equivalent as *Herodiani*, which parallels the factional terms *Caesariani* and *Pompeiani* as respective partisans of Caesar and Pompey. There was an association of *Augustiani* for freedmen who offered cultic devotion to Augustus and engaged in acts of public benefaction, but this is unlikely to be an analogue for the Herodians as their partisans were clients rather than cultic devotees. During the life of Jesus, the Herodian dynasty was represented by Herod's three surviving sons: Archelaus (Judea), Antipas (Galilee and Perea) and Philip (Iturea, Panias, Gaulanitis, Bananea and Trachonitis). Among the Herodians of the 20s AD were probably the 'magnates and tribunes and the first men of Galilee' who were invited to Antipas's birthday party.[237] An interesting observation is that Susanna, the wife of Herod's steward Chuza, was a supporter of Jesus – perhaps indicative of a pro-Jesus deep state within the highest echelons of Antipas's political apparatus![238]

Herodian opposition to Jesus was identical to that against John the Baptist. Jesus and John were prophetic ulcers, potentially stirring up unrest and attracting menacing crowds, and they both needed to be monitored and/or destroyed. True, only John had specifically attacked Antipas for his marriage to his sister-in-law Herodias,[239] but Antipas was concerned that Jesus was John 2.0 and would foment similar discontent with a seemingly mysterious aura of divine power.[240] This is precisely why Antipas had his agents pursue Jesus; and Jesus, when tipped off about their pursuit, remained recalcitrant, promising to continue his ministry despite the malevolent machinations of that Herodian 'fox'.[241] Jesus said that John was not a 'reed shaken by the wind' – an oblique allusion to Antipas, who minted coins with reeds on them – so that John, unlike Antipas, was not a spineless shill for the Roman Empire.[242] Otherwise, for Jesus, Antipas was part of the exploitive elite class, with its

---

236 Josephus, *Ant.* 14.450; cf. *War* 1.319.
237 Mark 6:21 (MFB trans.).
238 Luke 8:3.
239 Mark 6:17–20.
240 Mark 6:14–16.
241 Luke 13:31–32.
242 Matt. 11:7/Luke 7:24.

kyriarchy and tyranny, the very antithesis of the servant leadership and covenant righteousness that God calls leaders to exercise.[243]

Essenes

The Essenes were a Jewish sect not mentioned in the Gospels, but they are known from other literature, principally the writings of Philo, Pliny and Josephus.[244] The most likely scenario is that the Essenes were a sect found in several urban centres, quite possibly a splinter group from the Zadokite priesthood, with practices related to celibacy, common property, poverty, pacifism, purity and piety. It was once thought that the Qumranite sectarians were Essenes, but that position is no longer the majority view, even if the Qumranites overlapped with the Essenes in terms of beliefs, practices, and criticism of the Jerusalem priestly leadership (as exemplified in the documents CD and 1QS). There is no evidence for interaction between Jesus and the Essenes, probably because Jesus mostly avoided urban centres.[245]

Qumranites

The Jews who once lived at Qumran, in the Judean wilderness proximate to the caves by the Dead Sea where several jars of scriptural and sectarian texts were found, have excited the imagination of historians, archaeologists and conspiracy theorists.[246]

I think nearly every biblical scholar has come across a stranger, introduced themselves and their vocation, and had the stranger reply: 'But didn't the Dead Sea Scrolls disprove all of that stuff?' At that point, one must decide whether to (1) smile politely, avoid eye contact and slowly walk away; or (b) get into a lengthy and potentially futile argument to the effect that the Dead Sea Scrolls do not prove, much less disprove, anything about Jesus and the church, other than perhaps the sectarian context of Second Temple Judaism.

---

243 Mark 10:42.
244 Philo, *Quod Omn.* 75–91; *Hypoth.* 11.1–18; Josephus, *War* 2.119–161, 566–568; *Ant.* 18.18–22; *Life* 9–12; Pliny the Elder, *Nat. Hist.* 5.15.73.
245 Cf. Collins 1992: 2:622–625; Peters 2013.
246 See Schiffman 2020 for a good introduction to the previous and current study of the Qumran scrolls; Stacey and Doudna 2013 on analysis of the archaeological evidence; and Frey 2022 on the NT and the scrolls.

Most likely, the Qumranites were a priestly protest movement, with some Essenic tendencies, either Sadducean or Sadducean-adjacent, standing in opposition to the Pharisees, and especially to their *halakhah*, with perhaps some connection to 'Enochic Judaism', that is, to the Jewish scribes who composed parts of *1 Enoch*.[247] The Qumranites looked back to their founder, the 'Teacher of Righteousness', who led the group into the wilderness to escape a corrupted temple leadership and a contaminated practice of the Judean way of life.

The Dead Sea Scrolls and the archaeological remains at Qumran are relevant for several aspects of the study of ancient Judaism, the historical Jesus and early Christianity. The scrolls:

- are more than background to Christianity; they are a significant library of ancient literature in their own right, with a distinctive history and reception, and comprise one of our best sources for understanding Second Temple Judaism;
- show an intense interest in purity, which is confirmed by the presence of *miqvaot* (ritual baths);
- exhibit emphatic concern for Torah interpretation and *halakhah* in a way that parallels Christian interpretative strategies and foreshadows rabbinic practices;
- provide insights into the development of the Aramaic and Hebrew languages;
- constitute our best source for the pre-Masoretic Hebrew Bible and its various recensions;
- demonstrate that the Hebrew canon was far from closed, as the Qumran sectarians treasured as sacred certain texts not found in the Hebrew Bible;
- demonstrate that canonical, apocryphal and pseudepigraphical texts were not distinct corpora in antiquity;
- aid us in understanding the significance of a type of writing known as 'rewritten Scripture/Bible' as an exercise in interpretation;
- provide insights into sectarian debates over Torah and temple among Judeans;

---

247 Cf. Jackson 2004 on theories about Enochic Judaism.

- illuminate types of ancient mysticism, magic and messianism among Second Temple Jews;
- attest to the widespread influence of Hellenism even among isolated, sectarian and anti-Gentile Judean communities.

Several scholars have suggested that John the Baptist was perhaps a one-time member of the Qumranites.[248] A connection between the Baptist and the Qumranites is plausible to some degree.[249] There is an obvious geographical proximity, as John's ministry at the River Jordan took place in an area that was at most a day or two's walk from the Qumran settlement. Furthermore, a comparison of John as he is depicted in the Gospels with material drawn from the Qumran scrolls shows a number of striking similarities. John and the Qumranites practised a form of ritual baptism; they separated themselves from ordinary Palestinian life;[250] they practised their religious devotion independently of the institutions of Judaism such as the temple; they pronounced judgment against their contemporaries for moral laxity; they looked ahead to God's imminent and dramatic intervention in Israelite history to effect deliverance; they possessed an apocalyptic world view with messianic themes about coming deliverers; and they saw in Isaiah 40:3 the task of their calling as preparing the way for the Lord out in the wilderness.[251]

However, several key differences would seem to differentiate John the Baptist from the Qumran sectarians. John's ministry was public, whereas the Qumranites were largely secluded. John's ministry was prophetic, while the Qumranites were largely priestly. John interacted with persons who would have been regarded as morally and ceremonially impure (e.g. ritually unclean Jews, non-Jews, prostitutes, tax-collectors). The baptism of John was for eschatological preparation, while baptism at Qumran was part of initiation into the community and part of a daily regime of

---

248 Cf. recently Marcus 2018: 28–33.
249 What follows summarizes Bird 2011: 72.
250 Cf. 4QMMT C 7–8: '[And you know that] we have segregated ourselves from the multitude of the peop[le and] from mingling in these affairs, and from associating wi[th them] in these things.'
251 Cf. Mark 1:2–4 and 1QS 8.14–16.

ritual purity. The 'stronger one' spoken of by John was a dispenser of the Spirit, whereas the messianic figures attested in the Qumran writings are Davidic and priestly. John looks for the deliverance of all Israel, while the Qumranites anticipate that only a remnant of their own group will be saved.

'Jesus and the Qumranites' is a titillating topic but one that is mostly disappointing. True, Jesus shared with the sectarians several things: (1) a messianic exegesis of the Hebrew Bible that associated the Messiah with the Isaianic signs of restoration;[252] (2) an apocalyptic outlook that framed the Judean people as caught up in a contest between the sons of light and the evil one;[253] and (3) a concern with halakhic questions related to the sabbath, purity and Torah interpretation. In addition, (4) Jesus' self-conception as the Son of God[254] and application of Psalm 110:1 to himself[255] has parity with messianic expectations of the *Aramaic Apocalypse*[256] and the Self-Exaltation Hymn;[257] and (5) Jesus shared with the Qumranites a negative assessment of the temple leadership and how it operated the temple.[258]

Yet it is the differences that stand out. Jesus was itinerant rather than 'monastic' or 'static', prophetic rather than priestly, charismatic rather than scribal, unconcerned with debates over the calendar, not interested in establishing a tradition of midrashic minutiae or pedantry about pesher. Jesus negotiated the interface of morality and purity in a different way from the Qumranites, as evidenced by the parable of the good Samaritan. Jesus drew the line between insiders and outsiders in relation to himself, whereas the Qumranites associated their sect, its teacher, its tradition and its partition from the people as the path to covenantal righteousness. Jesus was closer to the Pharisees than the Qumranites because he believed in mixing with ordinary people, as did the later rabbis, who said: 'Do not separate from the ways of the community.'[259]

---

252 4Q521 2.1–20; Luke 7:22–23/Matt. 11:4–6.
253 1QM; Mark 3:23–26; 4:15; 8:33; Luke 10:18.
254 Mark 12:6–7; Matt. 11:27/Luke10:22.
255 Mark 12:35–37; 14:62.
256 4Q246.
257 4Q419c.
258 1QpHab; 4QpPsª; Mark 11:15–17.
259 4QMMT 92; *m. Abot* 2.4.

Zealous Judeans

There was not a 'zealot party' of Judeans that comprised a stable, coherent and continuous revolutionary movement in the first century (i.e. no 'Judean People's Front' of *Monty Python* fame). Older generations of scholarship seemed to have imagined a club of Judean Jacobins who, in good Marxist fashion, were determined to throw off the yoke of their Roman capitalist masters and pursue an agrarian revolution for Judean peasants for which Judaism was merely the grammar of the mythology in which that revolution was couched. Although banditry with an anti-Gentile slant was frequently engaged in by the desperate and destitute, the actual rebellion of AD 66–70 was driven more by disgruntled priestly elites than by an agrarian proletariat. Imagining ubiquitous revolutionary energy across Galilee and Judea made it easy to imagine that Jesus himself was a revolutionary, one who attempted a coup d'état in the temple, failed to achieve that, and was subsequently rounded up and crucified as any bandit or guerrilla fighter would be. H. S. Reimarus first spouted this view in his famous *Fragments*, published posthumously in 1778 by G. E. Lessing, who believed that such views at least needed to be aired. As it goes, the Jesus-the-Zealot view, much like Jesus mythicism, pops up about every fifty years with the same poorly constructed arguments and gets knocked down by the same compelling counter-objections.[260]

Judea was vital to the Romans, not because of any economic bounty, but because it was a strategic land bridge between Asia Minor and Egypt. In addition, Judea constituted the southern flank of Syria and was a buffer between Syria and the provinces in the Trans-Jordan and Arabia. The Romans did not occupy Judea the way the Allies occupied Germany after the Second World War. The Romans preferred to rule through client rulers such as the Herodians and high priests. The primary military force in the east was the legate of Syria, stationed in Antioch, to whom a procurator over Judea was accountable. The procurator had only a small force garrisoned on the coast in Caesarea, and it only occupied Jerusalem

---

260 On the 'zealot Jesus', see Brandon 1967; Reimarus 1971 [1778]; Aslan 2013; Bermejo-Rubio 2014; Martin 2014. For critical responses, Bammel and Moule 1984; Theissen 1987: 146; Witherington 1990: 81–118; Meier 1991–2016: 2.565–569; Bird 2006b.

during major festivals when the city swelled with large crowds, as this was the time when 'sedition [was] most apt to break out'.[261]

The Judean rebellions of AD 66–70 and 132–35 did not occur in a vacuum. They were caused by long-term grievances and accented by recent repressive and rapacious policies of emperors and governors. The primary causes of unrest were: (1) taxation that became increasingly burdensome, especially under Nero; (2) Roman partisanship towards Samaritans and Syro-Phoenicians and against Jews; (3) the collaboration of political and priestly elites with Roman authorities; (4) the brutality of Roman legions when required to put down spasmodic outbreaks of violence; (5) Roman disrespect for Jewish religious scruples; and (6) a series of Roman governors who were incompetent, incendiary and insatiably greedy.

We cannot assume, despite what Josephus says, that Judas the Galilean's revolt and the 'Fourth Philosophy' that allegedly followed him were one and the same as the 'zealot' party of the AD 66–70 revolt.[262] Be that as it may, the climate and context of Galilee and Judea had long stewed with anti-Roman sentiment.[263] In addition, there was a continuing problem of banditry.[264] Upon Herod the Great's death, the bandit chief Judas ben Hezekiah led a serious uprising in Galilee, but this was brutally crushed in 4 BC by the legions of the Syrian legate Varus, who crucified over 2,000 rebels.[265] Several royal pretenders also rose up during the interregnum at the death of Herod.[266] Ten years later, in AD 6, when Herod's son Archelaus was dismissed, Jewish territories reverted to direct Roman rule, and Judas the Galilean launched his revolt in Galilee, which was also brutally repressed.[267]

Over the next few decades there was an array of prophetic protest movements that excited hopes for Israel's liberation, led by several figures

---

261 Josephus, *War* 1.88.
262 With Goodman 1993: 108 and Wright 1992: 176–181.
263 Josephus portrays Titus as telling the last enclave of rebels that the Jewish nation has been rebelling against Rome since the time of Pompey (*War* 6.329).
264 Herod the Great made his name tackling banditry in Judea; see Josephus, *Ant.* 14.158–160, 420–430. But the problem persisted long after Herod's death; see Josephus, *War* 2.266–271, 433; *Ant.* 17.285; 20.5, 97–99, 102, 172–177; Acts 5:36–37.
265 Josephus, *Ant.* 17.271–272, 286–298; *War* 2.55–56, 66–79.
266 Josephus, *Ant.* 17.273–284; *War* 2.57–98.
267 Josephus, *War* 2.118, 433; *Ant.* 18.23–25; Acts 5:37.

known from the NT, including John the Baptist and Jesus of Nazareth, as well as others.[268] Caligula's plan to erect a pagan statue in the Jerusalem temple in AD 40 would have incited rebellion if it had not been thwarted by his death.[269] Festivals in Jerusalem were notoriously susceptible to riots.[270] Archelaus killed many demonstrators during one particular Passover,[271] and a major outbreak of violence took place under Camanus (AD 48–52) during Passover when over 20,000 pilgrims and locals died in the melee.[272] The rise of the Sicarii, dagger-wielding fanatics, in the 50s–60s led to assassinations of imperial officials and Jewish collaborators.[273] And, of course, a factional and fragmented rebellion began in 66 when a clique of high priests, in response to the governor's excessive violence, refused to offer the twice-daily offerings from the emperor in the temple.[274] All of this gives the impression of a complex social, religious and political environment that often ignited into bursts of hostility. Tacitus's claim that 'under Tiberius all was quiet' in Judea is relative to what was happening elsewhere in the empire.[275] There may not have been problems with the Parthian frontier, nor a uniform revolutionary movement and endless rebellions in Judea, but the historical milieu suggests that there was much kindling created for when the fires of rebellion were eventually lit.[276] As a result, says Sanders, 'insurrection was never very far from the surface'.[277]

The inclination towards rebellion was certainly stoked by exploitative economics and pernicious procurators, but one should not sideline the religious inspiration for rebellion. There was a tradition of 'zeal' to the point of sacred violence for Israel's holiness against Hellenism and 'paganism' which can be traced from the Maccabees to the fall of

---

268 Josephus, *Ant.* 20.188; *War* 2.258–265; Acts 21:38.
269 Philo, *Leg. Gai.*; Josephus, *Ant.* 18.302–308; *War* 2.203.
270 Josephus, *War* 1.88.
271 Josephus, *Ant.* 17.213–218; *War* 2.5–13.
272 Josephus, *Ant.* 20.105–117; *War* 2.224–231.
273 Josephus, *Ant.* 20.185–187; *War* 2.254; Tacitus, *Ann.* 12.54.
274 Josephus, *War* 2.409–410.
275 Tacitus, *Hist.* 5.9, on which see Barnett 1975; Hengel 1989 [1961]: 337.
276 For a convenient summary see Wright 1992: 170–181; Heard and Evans 2000. See more fully on Judea and rebellion, Rhoads 1976; Goodman 1993; 2007: 379–413, and interdisciplinary studies assembled in Popović 2011.
277 Sanders 1992: 36.

Masada.[278] As mentioned previously, in Herod's final days some zealous Jews pulled down an ornamental eagle which Herod had placed over the temple gate.[279] During the following Passover, Herod's son Archelaus had to put down a rebellion by 'revolutionary scribes'.[280] At the dismissal of Archelaus, Judas the Galilean and his Pharisaic ally Saddok rallied people using the monotheistic monarchic mantra of 'No king but God'.[281] Josephus makes a cryptic remark as to how many were incited to rebellion by an 'ambiguous oracle', which refers to some messianic or apocalyptic prophecy in the Hebrew Bible.[282] Dovetailing with that observation, Josephus noted repeatedly how prophet imposters, deceivers and bandits incited the people to war.[283] Many prophetic figures, among them John the Baptist, Jesus, and others, were exemplars of what we have called 'restoration eschatology' with its cluster of hopes about Israel's deliverance and the climactic fulfilment of the prophetic vision for Israel's liberation. In addition, when a zealot faction took over the temple during the rebellion, the first thing they did was to burn the records of debt that were deposited in the temple.[284] Thus, the religious, political and economic facets of the uprising were thoroughly interwoven.

On the one hand, is not impossible to imagine Jesus as a zealous Jew. Consider the following.[285] Jesus was from Galilee and grew up in the same region where Judas the Galilean had launched his rebellion, not long after his birth. Jesus' upbringing would have been shaped by the grievances of those who had suffered imperial violence when Roman legions put down the rebellion. His message of the 'kingdom of God', again, resonates with Judas the Galilean's message of 'No king but God'. Jesus warned his followers that they must be willing to 'take up their own

---

278 Jdth 9:4; Josephus, *Ant.* 18.4; Acts 21:20; 22:3; Gal. 1:14; Phil. 3:6; going back of course to the Maccabean rebellion (1 Macc. 2), which itself rehearses the sacred violence of Phinehas (Num. 25:11-13; Sir. 45:23).
279 Josephus, *Ant.* 17.149-166; *War* 1.648-655.
280 Josephus, *Ant.* 17.206-219; *War* 2.1-13.
281 Josephus, *Ant.* 18.23; *War* 2.118; 7.410.
282 Josephus, *War* 6.312-315; cf. Tacitus, *Hist.* 5.13; Suetonius, *Vesp.* 4.
283 Josephus, *Ant.* 20.160, 172; *War* 2.264-265.
284 Josephus, *War* 2.427.
285 See the list of Bermejo-Rubio 2014: 9-14, though I think every point he raises is overstated or easily answered.

cross',[286] which is significant because crucifixion was the punishment for slaves, bandits and enemies of the state. Plus, contempt for one's own life – the preference for death over slavery – is precisely what characterized zealous Jews.[287] In addition, if Jesus did think of himself in messianic categories, there is ample evidence that an anointed leader would engage in a holy war against Israel's enemies, either in a military action (e.g. *Pss Sol.* 17 – 18) or as part of a coalition with angelic legions (e.g. 1QM). Jesus' protest in the temple was at the very least deliberately disruptive, perhaps even seditious if it was intended to start a riot or revolution at the precise moment when the city was swelling with Jewish pilgrims celebrating God's victory over pagan powers.[288] Among Jesus' followers was one known explicitly as 'Simon the Zealot'.[289] Jesus' followers were apparently armed with swords, not gospel tracts and flowers, when Jesus was arrested.[290] Jesus was crucified among bandits (Gk *lestēs*) on the charge of being a messianic pretender who had aspirations of being 'king of the Jews'.[291] Maybe Reimarus and his heirs are right!

Despite all that, we can be practically certain that Jesus himself was not a zealous Jew who believed that he was a militaristic messiah who was about to launch a holy war that would eject the Romans and their Herodian and priestly clients from Judea and Galilee.[292]

Jesus and his disciples may have carried swords at Passover, yet many pilgrims would possess them for self-defence while travelling, or at least have ritual knives to be used during the Passover celebration itself.[293]

---

286 Mark 8:34; Luke 9:23; Matt. 10:38; 16:24; *Gos. Thom.* 55.
287 See e.g. Josephus, *War* 1.310–313; 3.321, 440, 475; 7.334.
288 According to Martin (2014: 9), Jesus' action in the temple 'may even have been an attempt to catalyze that destruction and instigate an angelic, armed overthrow of the rulership of the high priests and their Roman protections'.
289 See Luke 6:15; Acts 1:13.
290 Mark 14:47.
291 Mark 15:26–27.
292 Cf. Theissen (1987: 146) and his fictive narration of people discussing the Jesus movement and Judean 'zealots': 'I learned from them that Simon the Zealot had been one of their number but was now regarded as a traitor because he had attached himself to Jesus. This Jesus is felt by the Zealots to be a threat: he argues for non-violence. He rejects Zealot methods. If he gains any more supporters among them and in the population it would be a serious blow to the resistance movement.' NB: I doubt there was an official Zealot party that organized formal resistance to Roman rule in Judea and Galilee. Hengel and Schwemer (2019 [2007]: 579) comment: 'The "zealot Jesus," who has wandered like a ghost through scholarship time and again since Reimarus, is a false path.'
293 A point made by Fredriksen (2015), *pace* Martin 2014.

Also, quite importantly, Jesus and his followers did not launch an armed insurrection in the temple precincts itself. Jesus caused a commotion, not a series of assassinations. Furthermore, he rejected being made king by force,[294] establishing the kingdom by means of angelic armies,[295] and regarding the kingdom as something to be seized or plundered by violent revolution.[296] Jesus' parables arguably critique alternative ways of conceiving of the kingdom, depicting it as a theocentric event which grows through words rather than warfare, and yet infests territories like a pugnacious weed.[297] Jesus warned too that living by the sword meant dying by the sword, that is, falling into a never-ending spiral of violence.[298] He taught love of enemies and non-retaliation as principles for behaviour for his followers.[299] Jesus' critique of the temple may have included, among such things as economic exploitation, criticizing its role in fostering a Judean 'nationalism' that would propel the nation into a futile war with Rome. A view which is more than plausible, as demonstrated by Sean Freyne's comment that during 'the whole procuratorial period the temple repeatedly became the flashpoint of Jewish nationalist aspirations'.[300] The temple had become, perhaps to Jesus, a talisman of Israelite triumph over the nations rather than a 'house of prayer for all nations'.

Paula Fredriksen also makes a key observation: 'But these latter theories [of Jesus the Zealot] collide head-on with a second incontrovertible fact we have from the earliest movement: Though Jesus was executed as a political insurrectionist, his followers were not.'[301] Fredriksen asks a good question: if Jesus was intending to launch an uprising, then why were his disciples not rounded up after his death? It could be because the Romans, as pragmatists, believed they had destroyed the ringleader of a Galilean insurgency that had infiltrated Jerusalem, and that had resolved the

---

294 John 6.15.
295 Matt. 26:53.
296 Matt. 11:12/Luke 16:16.
297 Mark 4:1–32.
298 Matt. 26:52.
299 Matt. 5:43–44/Luke 6:27, 35.
300 Freyne 1988: 179.
301 Fredriksen 1999: 9.

matter;[302] but the Romans were more thorough than blasé when it came to dealing with threats to the civil power. Maybe it was because Pilate thought Jesus was simply a raving lunatic rather than a revolutionary, and his followers were deluded rather than dangerous?[303] Such a view seems more realistic, but Pilate would surely know that there's no worse revolutionary than the raving religious fanatical kind. That is precisely the reputation that zealous Jews had before, during and after Pilate's day. More likely, the Jewish high priests had a prior agreement with Pilate to dispatch any troublemakers swiftly and brutally, irrespective of whether the discord was political, apocalyptic or militaristic.[304]

If Jesus' followers had even had a whiff of violence or insurrection about them, the priestly leadership would have rounded them up before, during or after the festival. The fact that the followers of Jesus were able to set up a 'church' in Jerusalem which enjoyed increasing popularity, according to Luke, is proof of the very point. The eventual pogroms against the Jerusalem Jesus movement were not motivated by a desire to put down a revolutionary cabal, but by intersectarian rivalry. Also, as far as we know, the Jerusalem church did not participate in the Judean rebellions of AD 66–70 or 132–5. According to tradition, the members of the Jerusalem church fled to Pella on the eve of the first Judean revolt, and Simon bar Kochba persecuted Judean messiah-followers during the second revolt because of their veneration of a rival messianic figure.[305]

I don't think we have to choose between Jesus being executed for challenging the socio-religious capital of the Jerusalem priesthood and Jesus being perceived as a threat to the civil order. Jesus was accused before Pilate of doing the wrong thing (causing a commotion) in the wrong place (the temple) at the wrong time (at Passover).[306] Pilate did not care whether Jesus was an armed *lestēs* (bandit) or an irritating *sophos* (teacher); the Jerusalem priests told Pilate that Jesus was a dangerous man, and Pilate would be wise to execute him.

---

302 Martin 2014: 18.
303 Meggitt 2007.
304 Largely following Bond 2011: 232.
305 Eusebius, *Hist. Eccl.* 3.5.3; Justin, *1 Apol.* 31.5–6.
306 Vermes 1993: x.

In the end, we have no reason to conclude that Jesus and his followers were revolutionaries; if anything, Jesus was more inclined to critique the zealous wing of Judean sociopolitical belief and practice.

Jesus among family and disciples

One of the problems with focusing on Jesus as one of the 'great men of history' is that we forget the importance and influence of the people around him: parents, siblings, family members, friends, disciples and supporters. It takes a village to raise a prophet, it takes a school to create a rabbi, and it takes the apocalyptic devotion of disciples to make a messiah.

First, concerning Jesus' family, Jesus was most likely born into an agrarian–artisan household (as mentioned above), as he was known as the son of the stonemason or carpenter.[307] Only Luke and John relate him specifically to Joseph as his putative son.[308] While Joseph has a prominent role in the infancy narratives, which are a unique mix of midrash and tradition about the holy family, he plays no significant role in Jesus' life, which lends itself to the thesis that Joseph died before Jesus began his public ministry. The parent who is more prominent is Mary.[309] Mary also had some standing or role in the early Jerusalem church.[310] Jesus even came to be known as the 'son of Mary'.[311]

In terms of Jesus' life, the portrait of his mother is mixed. In Johannine tradition, Mary is proud of the prodigiously prophetic son and stays with him even up to his crucifixion.[312] Yet the synoptic tradition depicts Mary and her other offspring as trying to apprehend Jesus for fear that he had gone out of his mind.[313] Mary may have been trying to protect Jesus by sending his kin to save him from the consequences of messing with powers and authorities beyond his ken.[314] On the one hand, Jesus

---

307 Mark 6:3/Matt. 13:55.
308 Luke 4:22; John 1:45; 6:42.
309 See summary in Hood 2008.
310 Acts 1:14.
311 Mark 6:3/Matt. 13:55.
312 John 2:1–12; 19:25.
313 Mark 3:21, 31–32.
314 There is the possibility that, from Johannine tradition, Mary and his brothers were

taught about the necessity of honouring one's parents[315] as per the commandments,[316] and Jesus' family did have a prominent role in the early church. But on the other hand, Jesus' emphasis upon the 'heavenly Father',[317] and his warning that '[p]rophets are not without honour, except in their home town and among their own kin *and in their own house*',[318] urged the necessity of leaving behind family and obligations.[319] Jesus' highlighting of the bond of fictive kinship among disciples[320] makes one wonder if his relationship with his biological family was more ambivalent. As Bauckham puts it:

> What we should probably conclude is that there were serious tensions between Jesus and his relatives at some point or points during the period of his ministry, to which Jesus himself may have contributed by his insistence that service of the kingdom and relationships within the new community of his followers took precedence over natural family ties.[321]

Among Jesus' brothers we know of several who are named: James, Joseph, Jude and Simon.[322] These brothers became prominent in the early church, most notably James, who was known as 'the Lord's brother' and eventually as 'James the Just'. James would later become a witness to the resurrection, a leading elder of the Jerusalem church and a mediator between different factions, and would even write a letter to the Jewish Christian Diaspora congregations,[323] but he was eventually martyred in AD 62.[324] Some of 'the Lord's brothers', in tradition known as the

---

supportive of Jesus and his band of disciples (John 2:12) but later became ambivalent. John depicts Jesus' brothers as like the crowds who need to see signs, 'for not even his brothers believed in him' (John 7:3–6).

315 Mark 7:10; 10:19.
316 Exod. 20:12; Deut. 5:16.
317 Cf. e.g. Matt. 5:48.
318 Mark 6:4 (emphasis added); cf. Luke 4:24; John 4:44; *Gos. Thom.* 31; P. Oxy. 1.32–33.
319 Luke 9:57–62.
320 Mark 3:34; 10:29–30; *Gos. Thom.* 99.
321 Bauckham 2011: 108–109.
322 Mark 3:31; 6:3; Matt. 13:55.
323 1 Cor. 15:7; Acts 15; 21; Gal. 1:19; 2:9, 12; Jas 1:1; Jude 1; *Gos. Thom.* 12.
324 Josephus, *Ant.* 20.200.

desposynoi, meaning 'belonging to the master', became itinerant missionaries[325] who travelled around Judean villages proclaiming Jesus.[326] What is remarkable is that the Jesus movement, despite its explicit royal and messianic spirit, did not adopt a kind of succession from Jesus to his brother as the new 'anointed one'. There was no comparable dynastic bequeathing of Jesus' mantle to his brothers as there was for the Maccabeans, Hasmoneans and Herodians. The situation was not even akin to the loose anti-Roman dynasty of Judas the Galilean. Dovetailing with these observations is the tradition, or perhaps legend, that the grandsons of Jude were summoned before Emperor Domitian in the 90s. Standing before him, they allegedly assuaged the fears of the emperor, denying the charge of possessing any rebellious aspirations by declaring that their kingdom was spiritual and heavenly and posed no threat to him and his dominion.[327] At the very least, the Jesus movement was not a militaristic messianic faction that passed the baton of revolution from brother to brother or from father to son.

We cannot ignore the theological debate as to whether Jesus' brothers and sisters were biological siblings (as stated by Helvidian), cousins (Jerome) or children from a previous marriage on the part of Joseph (Epiphanius). Of course, we also do not have the time to canvass the topic in full. What constrains some interpreters is belief in Mary's perpetual virginity, a view that became widely accepted in the fourth-century church, developed into a doctrine cherished by Roman Catholics and was held by not a few of the magisterial Reformers. Complicating matters, as Bruce Chilton observes, is that more than one scenario might be true: Joseph had children by a previous marriage, and Joseph and Mary had multiple children together.[328] My instinct is to follow the early church – Hegesippus, Irenaeus and Tertullian – and to affirm that Jesus' brother and sisters were blood siblings.[329] Dogmatic theologians will have to appropriate that point in whatever manner they wish. In any case, we can say little about Jesus' brothers and sisters because we know very

---

325 1 Cor. 9:5.
326 Eusebius, *Hist. Eccl.* 1.7.14.
327 Eusebius, *Hist. Eccl.* 3.19–20.
328 Chilton 2004; cf. Bauckham 1994.
329 Pesch (1976–77: 1:322–325) offers a succinct and helpful summary.

little. As Meier puts it: 'If the quest for the "historical Jesus" is difficult, the quest for the "historical relatives of Jesus" is nigh impossible.'[330]

Second, Jesus had three particularly close disciples – an inner circle – in Simon, John and James (in Aramaic, Shimon, Yohanan and Yaakov). These three disciples were particularly close to Jesus as confidants and perhaps advisors.[331] All of them had nicknames: Simon was the 'rock',[332] while James and John were the 'sons of thunder'.[333] They are hardly one-dimensional characters. Simon Peter is one who oscillated from messianic confession[334] to tragic denial[335] to restoration.[336] John guarded Jesus' prophetic turf from alleged imitators;[337] the two brothers were given to prejudice against Samaritans;[338] and they coveted prized positions in the reordering of power that they believed Jesus would usher in.[339] The trio became predominant leaders in the early church, and according to tradition all three experienced martyrdom.

Third, there were also 'the twelve' disciples. They are not a post-Easter invention, as an older generation of scholars suggested, but were intended to be a living and walking symbol of a restored Israelite tribal confederacy in the coming revolution of things.[340] There was some diversity and even confusion about their precise names in the lists among the Synoptic Gospels (perhaps due to the men having Aramaic and Greek names or nicknames – or perhaps some dropped off the list and others were added).[341] Their role was to be prophetic plenipotentiaries of the coming eschatological order that Jesus was inaugurating, as they would periodically be sent out to preach and heal in the various villages of Galilee, Samaria and Judea.[342] They were also recipients of his

---

330 Meier 1991–2016: 1:319.
331 Mark 5:37; 9:2; 14:33.
332 Matt. 16:18.
333 Mark 3:17.
334 Mark 8:29.
335 Cf. esp. the Lukan version in Luke 22:54–62.
336 Mark 16:7 ('tell his disciples and Peter'); John 21:15–19.
337 Mark 9:38.
338 Luke 9:51–56.
339 Mark 10:25–40.
340 Matt. 19:28/Luke 22:30.
341 Mark 3:16–19; Matt. 10:2–4; Luke 6:13–16.
342 Mark 3:13–14; Mark 6:6–13; Matt. 10:5–6; 15:24.

private teaching about his parables, plans, purpose and person.[343] The twelve were neither a cabinet for a new government nor a cabal set on rebellion, but rather a mix between Jesus' devoted pupils and imitators, and promoters of his kingdom message for Israel.

Fourth, the twelve were drawn from a wider circle of followers and admirers (as were the seventy or seventy-two sent out on their own short-term prophetic mission to the villages and towns of Israel in Luke 10:1-18). Jesus appears to have had two streams of disciples: the itinerants who were called to abandon all things and follow him immediately,[344] and those who remained *in situ* and supported him from their homes (see e.g. the families in Capernaum [Mark 1:29-31; 2:1; 6:10] and Bethany [Mark 11:11; 14:3; John 12:1]).[345] Among this wider circle were the sisters Mary and Martha from Bethany.[346] There were also prominent women from the higher echelons of Galilean society, including Mary Magdalene, Joanna the wife of Chuza (Herod's steward) and a certain Joanna.[347] Mary Magdalene has attracted notoriety and excited speculation, both in ancient tradition and in pop culture, largely because she was wrongly conflated with the 'sinful woman' who anointed Jesus' feet.[348] She was a supplicant for exorcism and a member of Jesus' wider circle, even figuring prominently in the resurrection narratives. Interestingly, her name 'Magdalene' could designate the village of Magdala, derived from the Hebrew word *migdal* for 'tower', located on the western shore of the Sea of Galilee, as Mary's home town. Then again, given that nicknames were common among Jesus' followers,[349] maybe 'Magdalene' means something like 'Tower', bestowed on her for her towering faith, industry and support. A speculative but not unreasonable proposal.

The above discussion is a natural segue to a brief examination of my fifth point: Jesus and women.[350] Here we must resist the temptation to

---

343 Mark 4:10; 8:27 - 9:1; 9:35; 10:32; 11:11; 14:17; John 6:66-68.
344 Mark 1:16-20; 2:14; 10:28-30; Luke 9:57-62.
345 On which see Theissen 1978; 1987; Theissen and Merz 1998 [1996]: 223.
346 Luke 10:38-42; John 11:1-14.
347 Luke 8:1-3.
348 Luke 7:36-50.
349 Cf. Mark 3:17; Matt. 16:17.
350 I think the go-to studies remain Witherington 1984 and Bauckham 2002. It is impossible to

make Jesus out to be an egalitarian hero bursting with gloriously anachronistic views of gender equality – views that fit neatly in the twenty-first century yet are patently absurd, like a picture of Julius Caesar holding a smartphone. It is true that every ethical and political cause wants to have nature, young people and Jesus on their side, so it's normal to want to believe that Jesus was way ahead of his time on gender equality or was at least the one nice guy in a maelstrom of misogynistic malevolence. The reality is that Jesus was a man in a man's world, surrounded by male disciples, and spoke of the kingdom of God, not the queendom or queerdom of God. In the broad sway of the Jesus tradition, Jesus could address women, such as his own mother, with frustrated dismissal,[351] cast flippant aspersions on a Syro-Phoenician woman,[352] and give flustered Martha a few words of guidance which some ancient and modern feminists might consider needlessly condescending.[353] Yet Jesus also defended the right of one particular woman, whom he called a 'daughter of Abraham', to be healed even on the sabbath;[354] he defended a sinful woman for her provocative incursion into a dinner amid Pharisaic sneers of impropriety;[355] and he defended from his disciples' own sense of austerity a woman who had spared no expense in her devotion to him.[356] Then, in later imagination, Jesus defended a woman caught in adultery[357] and dismissed Peter's complaint that Mary Magdalene was unworthy of eternal life.[358]

The positive picture is filled out when we consider how women appear in Jesus' ministry as positive examples from Scripture, for example the Queen of the South[359] and the widow from Zarephath.[360] His parables refer to the domestic chores of women in the fields, grinding at the

---

ignore the groundbreaking work of Schüssler Fiorenza 1995 [1983], but be sure to consult the response by Ng (2002). Two notable recent works are McGrath 2021 and Lee 2021.
351 John 2:4.
352 Mark 7:27.
353 Luke 10:41–42.
354 Luke 13:16.
355 Luke 7:40–50.
356 Mark 14:6.
357 John 7:53 – 8:11.
358 *Gos. Thom.* 114.
359 Matt. 12:42/Luke 11:31.
360 Luke 4:26.

mill[361] or turning yeast,[362] to the joy of a woman who finds a lost coin,[363] a persistent widow demanding justice[364] and women in childbirth.[365] He could banter with women among the crowds.[366] Many women were supplicants of Jesus for healing or exorcisms.[367] Jesus uttered an oracle of warning to the women of Jerusalem,[368] grieved over pregnant women during a time of siege warfare,[369] and gave a teaching on divorce that was intended to prevent the destitution of women.[370] He also inspired and received the devotion of women: he was anointed for his burial by an anonymous woman,[371] many women accompanied him in his execution,[372] and a group of female followers observed his burial and performed its rites.[373] Plus, many women joined the church and participated in its mission and ministries.[374] It is a historical judgment, not a theological one, that Jesus expressed concern for women and that women in turn were devoted to him, during his life, at his death, as witnesses to his resurrection and as leading members of the nascent church.

Jesus, just like other men, had to negotiate the gender roles of his society, between the urban and the agrarian; between traditional, normative men and disruptive women; between the patriarchal and the inclusive proclivities forged at the intersection of gender performance and gender-based grievances. Jesus was not a fourth-wave feminist; that much is true. It is equally true that Jesus was born of a woman and had sisters; he knew women, he met women, he healed women, he taught women, he defended women, he told stories about women, and he perhaps even had a special concern for the vulnerability of women

---

361 Matt. 24:40–41/Luke 17:34–35.
362 Matt. 13:33.
363 Luke 15:8–10.
364 Luke 18:1–8.
365 John 16:20–22.
366 Luke 11:27–28; *Gos. Thom.* 79.
367 Mark 5:25–34; 7:24–30; Luke 7:11–17, 36–50; 13:10–17.
368 Luke 23:27–28.
369 Mark 13:17.
370 Mark 10:1–12; Matt. 5:31–32; 19:1–12.
371 Mark 14:3–9.
372 Mark 15:40–41.
373 Mark 15:47 – 16:8.
374 Cf. e.g. Rom. 16:1–7 as a dense list of female followers of Jesus.

and women in vulnerable places. Luke is the evangelist with a particular concern for women of lowly status, widows and, in particular, prostitutes; while Luke might have projected his views onto Jesus, it is no less likely that Jesus was the inspiration for Luke's own liberationist inclinations.

Jesus and Gentiles[375]

What is truly extraordinary about early Christianity is that Jesus of Nazareth was a Jew, his disciples were all Jews, he performed his ministry principally in Galilee and Judea, even after Easter the Jerusalem church remained thoroughly Jewish in its membership, piety and practices, and looked very much like a messianic sect within common Judaism. And yet the first followers of 'the Way' would soon launch a mission to bring Gentiles to faith in Jesus, initially in Syrian Antioch, then as far away as Rome within thirty years of Jesus' death. Later, post-70, the movement would transform itself into the Gentile religion called 'Christianity', whose adherents worshipped Jesus as the Son of God and the second person of the Holy Trinity. How did we get from a Jewish messiah to Jesus the object of Gentile cultic devotion? Or, in other words, how do we get from (1) Jesus instructing his disciples in their own preaching mission: 'Do not take a road leading to gentiles, and do not enter a Samaritan town, but go rather to the lost sheep of the house of Israel',[376] to (2) the risen Jesus instructing the disciples to undertake a worldwide mission to all nations: 'Go therefore and make disciples of all nations, baptizing them in the name of the Father and of the Son and of the Holy Spirit and teaching them to obey everything that I have commanded you'?[377]

To this conundrum, several solutions are proffered. Perhaps the early church retrojected its missionary ethos onto Jesus so that the Gentile

---

375 This is the topic I wrote my doctoral thesis on (Bird 2006a, summarized in Bird 2005; 2006d; 2008a; 2010a; 2010b; 2012). I was led to the topic after reading Wright 1996: 308–10, which intrigued me as to how Jesus, a prophet of Jewish restoration eschatology, could launch a movement that took to the Gentile mission very quickly and (eventually) became a Gentile religion. I read and wrote so much about Jesus and Gentiles between 2002 and 2013 that for a time I considered converting to Judaism and joining a kibbutz in Israel so I would never have to utter the wretched word 'Gentile' ever again. Pivoting to Pauline studies brought no relief as it was, 'Oi vey, again, always with the Gentiles.'
376 Matt. 10:5–6; cf. 15:24.
377 Matt. 28:19–20.

mission, an innovation of the Hellenistic and Pauline churches, was read back onto Jesus. Or else, Jesus was a cosmopolitan Jew able to bring the universalistic impulse of Israelite theism to bear over and against the particularism and ritualism of his Jewish contemporaries. Alternatively, Jesus was focused on Israel yet maintained a strong belief that the Gentiles would be saved by God at the final assize.[378]

The answer to this problem is Jewish restoration eschatology. When Israel's exile ended, when the new exodus happened, when Israel was finally and fully restored from its dire state of domination by foreign powers, when the nation's sins were forgiven, when the covenant was renewed, when a new temple was built, when the Messiah came, the sequel was the inclusion of the nations in Israel's blessings and prosperity, to the point where the whole world would be remade as a new creation. In other words, Jesus was part of a tradition of scriptural hopes whereby a transformed Israel would transform the world.[379] This was a view rooted in Israel's prophetic tradition:

> In days to come
>   the mountain of the LORD's house
> shall be established as the highest of the mountains
>   and shall be raised above the hills;
> all the nations shall stream to it.
>   Many peoples shall come and say,
> 'Come, let us go up to the mountain of the LORD,
>   to the house of the God of Jacob,
> that he may teach us his ways
>   and that we may walk in his paths.'
> For out of Zion shall go forth instruction
>   and the word of the LORD from Jerusalem.
> He shall judge between the nations
>   and shall arbitrate for many peoples;
> they shall beat their swords into ploughshares
>   and their spears into pruning hooks;

---

378 See survey in Bird 2005.
379 Manson 1964: 6–7, 22–23.

nation shall not lift up sword against nation;
   neither shall they learn war any more.
(Isa. 2:2–4)

I am the Lord; I have called you in righteousness;
   I have taken you by the hand and kept you;
I have given you as a covenant to the people,
   a light to the nations,
   to open the eyes that are blind,
to bring out the prisoners from the dungeon,
   from the prison those who sit in darkness.
(Isa. 42:6–7)

It is too light a thing that you should be my servant
   to raise up the tribes of Jacob
   and to restore the survivors of Israel;
I will give you as a light to the nations,
   that my salvation may reach to the end of the earth.
(Isa. 49:6)

Thus says the Lord of hosts: Peoples shall yet come, the inhabitants of many cities; the inhabitants of one city shall go to another, saying, 'Come, let us go to entreat the favour of the Lord and to seek the Lord of hosts; I myself am going.' Many peoples and strong nations shall come to seek the Lord of hosts in Jerusalem and to entreat the favour of the Lord. Thus says the Lord of hosts: In those days ten men from nations of every language shall take hold of a Jew, grasping his garment and saying, 'Let us go with you, for we have heard that God is with you.'
(Zech. 8:20–23)

In days to come
   the mountain of the Lord's temple
shall be established as the highest of the mountains
   and shall be raised up above the hills.
Peoples shall stream to it,

and many nations shall come and say:
'Come, let us go up to the mountain of the Lord,
    to the house of the God of Jacob,
that he may teach us his ways
    and that we may walk in his paths.'
For out of Zion shall go forth instruction,
    and the word of the Lord from Jerusalem.
(Mic. 4:1–2)

Further examples could be cited from biblical, post-biblical and rabbinic traditions to the effect that Israel was meant to be Yahweh's treasured possession, a 'kingdom of priests'[380] and a 'light to the nations'.[381] To give a specific instance, for Philo, the vocation of Israel is to be a priest for the salvation of the entire inhabited world:

> Among the other nations the priests are accustomed to offer prayers and sacrifices for their kinsmen and friends and fellow-countrymen only, but the high priest of the Jews makes prayers and gives thanks not only on behalf of the whole human race but also for the parts of nature, earth, water, air, fire. For he holds the world to be, as in very truth it is, his country, and in its behalf he is wont to propitiate the Ruler with supplication and intercession, beseeching Him to make His creature a partaker of His own kindly and merciful nature.[382]

> The reason of this is that the Jewish nation is to the whole inhabited world what the priest is to the State.[383]

A philosophical reading of the Torah led Philo to the conclusion that Israel was a priestly nation called to the intercession of, and very salvation of, the world. Something picked up by the Christian author of the *Epistle to Diognetus*: 'In a word, what the soul is to the body, Christians are to

---

[380] Exod. 19:6.
[381] Isa. 42:6; 49:6.
[382] Philo, *Spec. Leg.* 1.97.
[383] Philo, *Spec. Leg.* 2.163.

the world.'³⁸⁴ The early church's missionary ethos was picked up, though sometimes with supersessionist rhetoric, to the effect that Christians were the salve for the world's diseases, the medicine for its ailments, priests for its wayward soul, and prophets with a word from God to the world.

I want to suggest that between Philo and *Diognetus* are Jesus, the early church, the Hellenists, Paul, Clement of Rome, Ignatius of Antioch, and countless others, who, beginning with Jesus' mission to Israel, saw implicit in Israel's renewed covenant the beginnings of a new creation of which the Gentiles would partake. Among the nations, believers in Jesus would become recipients of divine mercy and were grafted into God's people. Points which Paul explicitly argues as part of the climax of Romans, using a mélange of scriptural texts densely packed together:

> For I tell you that Christ has become a servant of the circumcised on behalf of the truth of God in order that he might confirm the promises given to the ancestors and that the gentiles might glorify God for his mercy.
> As it is written,
>
> > 'Therefore I will confess you among the gentiles
> > and sing praises to your name' [2 Sam. 22:50; Ps. 18:49];
>
> and again he says,
>
> > 'Rejoice, O gentiles, with his people' [Deut. 32:43];
>
> and again,
>
> > 'Praise the Lord, all you gentiles,
> > and let all the peoples praise him' [Ps. 117:1];
>
> and again Isaiah says,
>
> > 'The root of Jesse shall come,

---

384 *Ep. Diogn.* 6.1.

> the one who rises to rule the gentiles;
> in him the gentiles shall hope' [Isa. 11:10].
> (Rom. 15:8–12)

Accordingly, the Christian mission to the nations, and its concomitant debates about the basis for Gentile inclusion in the church, would be entirely inexplicable without the Israelite scriptural tradition of Yahweh as God of the nations with a chosen people who possess in their covenant something of a vocation towards creation. Similarly, the idea of a Torah-free gospel to the Gentiles would be incomprehensible without the earnest, though spasmodic, interest in proselytism in Diaspora communities.[385] When eschatology was added to the mix, it meant that the sequel to a rescued Israel was the reconciliation of the nations and the healing of the whole of creation. A narrative that proved important not only for the primitive church but also for the apostles and, I would argue, for the historical Jesus.[386]

Gentiles did not figure prominently in the message and ministry of Jesus because his mission was focused on Israel and on Israel alone. Note: this was not a polite offer of salvation to the Jews before salvation history would be unfurled in all of its multi-ethnic glory. Nor was it a mere formality until the real mission, that to the Gentiles, got under way with Paul and his co-workers. None of that will do; Jesus was a prophet of Jewish restoration eschatology who was myopically and messianically focused on Israel's rescue, redemption and renewal. Even so, there is ample material in the Jesus tradition that attests to Jesus' implicit perspective about the place of the Gentiles in the kingdom of God as a sequel to a restored Israel. In accordance with Israel's Scriptures, Jesus appeared to have taught that Gentiles would experience salvation through their incorporation into the restored Israel. What is more, it is in Jesus' understanding of Israel's role vis-à-vis the world that one finds the germinal roots of the Christian Gentile mission. In the Gospels, there are

---

385 Cf. Bird 2010a, esp. 149–156.
386 Argued in substantive fashion in Bird 2006a. Against Vermes (2004: 376–380), who cannot see how anything Jesus said or did laid the groundwork for the later mission to the Gentiles. This fails to wrestle with a crucial aspect of Jewish restoration eschatology.

several complexes that demonstrate Jesus' convictions about the Gentiles and their relationship to the kingdom of God.

First, there are negative remarks about Gentiles as 'pigs' and 'dogs', idolatrous babblers, unclean sinners and self-aggrandizing tyrants.[387] Material which, by itself, is good proof that a Gentile mission has not been projected back onto Jesus; otherwise, such stereotypical denunciations of Gentile behaviour would have been excised.

Second, Jesus was remembered for making jarring juxtapositions between (in)famous Gentiles of Israel's antiquity and the present faithlessness of Israel. In one logion, the Queen of the South and the men of Nineveh will 'rise up' and condemn 'this generation' for requesting a sign from Jesus.[388] Jesus conceived of Gentiles, at least hypothetically, participating in a future kingdom over and against the members of his current Jewish audience who have not responded positively to his message. The memory of Jesus' woe oracles against Chorazin, Bethsaida and Capernaum provocatively proposed that the notorious Gentile cities of Sodom, Gomorrah, Tyre and Sidon would fare better in the final judgment than his recalcitrant audience.[389] In response to the rejection of his Nazareth sermon,[390] Jesus launched into a tirade against the residents of his home town and reminded them of the ministries of Elijah to the widow of Zarephath, and of Elisha to Naaman the Syrian.[391] The function of the stories is to point out that Israel's rejection of a divinely sent prophet can often lead to blessings and healings for Gentiles. That is not to say that these Gentiles somehow replace Jews, but, all things being equal, a grateful Gentile might find themselves more welcomed in the kingdom than a fellow Jew who kicked dirt in the face of a Jewish prophet.

Third, Jesus seems to have explicitly tied the salvation of the Gentiles to Israel's eschatological restoration. One particular logion, found in different contexts in Luke and Matthew, declares that 'many will come from east and west and will take their places at the banquet with

---

387 Mark 7:27; 10:41–45; Matt. 6:7; 7:6; 18:17; Luke 12:30–31/Matt. 6:32–33.
388 Luke 11:29–32/Matt. 12:38–42.
389 Luke 10:12/Matt. 10:15 and Luke 10:13–15/Matt. 11:20–24.
390 Luke 4:16–21.
391 Luke 4:25–27; cf. 1 Kgs 17:1–24; 2 Kgs 5:1–14.

Abraham, Isaac and Jacob in the kingdom of heaven'.[392] The statement on its own may be saying no more than is found in biblical and post-biblical Jewish literature: espousing a hope for the return of the Diaspora to the Jewish homeland.[393] That may be true; however, the motifs of Israel's regathering and the eschatological pilgrimage of the Gentiles are often combined where the Gentiles converge on Jerusalem on the coat tails of the regathered Israel, or else the return of the exiles is contingent upon the repentance and conversion of the Gentiles.[394] The presence of Abraham at this eschatological banquet may also suggest that an audience beyond the Jews is intended, since Abraham was regarded as the link between Israel and the Gentiles.[395] In addition, the logion coheres with the widely attested theme in the Jesus tradition of eschatological reversal. It seems strange to regard Jews of the Diaspora as an unexpected group that is vindicated in the future age, as there was no cause for doubt as to whether Jews of the Diaspora would participate in the renewal and rescue of Israel. The logion has teeth and bites precisely because it is a threat to Jesus' Jewish audience about exclusion from the kingdom, but at another level it is a description of what is already happening in his ministry. In the call of the twelve disciples, in Jesus' proclamation to the poor, and in his healing and exorcism of the afflicted, the kingdom is coming and restoration is beckoning, and therefore many are already coming from near and far and experiencing the saving power of the kingdom. Presumably, then, Gentile inclusion in 'salvation', the fulfilling of the divine promise to make Abraham the father of many nations, is merely another means by which Jesus shames his interlocutors about their obtuseness and recalcitrance. Although Matthew's placement of the logion inside the narrative of Jesus' encounter with the Roman centurion may be redactional, it remains in accordance with the intertextual echoes of the saying that anticipate the regathering of Jews to their homeland and the eschatological pilgrimage of the Gentiles as an accompaniment.

---

392 Matt. 8:11–12/Luke 13:28–30. Cf. Bird 2006a; 2006d.
393 Ps. 107:2–3; Isa. 43:5–6; Zech. 8:7–8; Bar. 4:36–37; 5:5; *1 Enoch* 57.1; *Pss Sol.* 11.1–3.
394 Jer. 3:17–18; Isa. 66:20–21; Zech. 8:7–8, 20–23; *T. Benj.* 9.2; *1 Enoch* 90.33; *Pss Sol.* 17.26, 31; Tob. 13:5, 11; 14:5–7.
395 Gen. 15 – 21; Rom. 4:1–25; Gal. 3:6–29; Josephus, *Ant.* 1.161–167; *T. Benj.* 10.5–6; *b. Hag.* 3a; *Gen. Rab.* 14:6.

Fourth, there are several reported encounters between Jesus and Gentiles: the demoniac in the Decapolis,[396] the deaf and mute man,[397] the Syro-Phoenician/Canaanite woman in Tyre,[398] a centurion in Capernaum[399] and certain Greeks who request to meet Jesus.[400] Although these narratives are often regarded as retrospective projections of the mission theology of the early church onto Jesus, this seems unlikely because: (1) Jesus never seeks out Gentiles, and the Gentile characters usually take the initiative in finding him; (2) none of the Gentiles whom Jesus meets becomes a disciple; (3) in most cases, the healed person remained at a distance from Jesus; (4) several of the stories contain features that were potentially embarrassing, such as Jesus' stern reply to the Syro-Phoenician woman,[401] Jesus' initial reluctance to go to the house of the Roman centurion,[402] and Jesus' refusal to grant the request of the Greeks to meet him;[403] and (5) none of these narratives deals with the question of circumcision, law observance for Gentiles, or disputes over Jew–Gentile fellowship. This confirms the words of Schnabel that 'this nexus between Jesus and mission among the Gentiles cannot simply be ascribed to the aetiological interests of the Gospel writers'.[404] Jesus' movements into Gentile territory were for respite rather than for 'mission'. In these locations, Jesus encountered Gentiles and had (mostly) positive interactions with them, often treating them as supplicants of healing. While these encounters with non-Jews inside or outside Jewish territory are exceptional and ad hoc, they demonstrate that the saving power of the kingdom can already be extended to Gentiles and presage the place of Gentiles as joining a restored Israel in the eschatological dénouement.

---

396 Mark 5:1–20.
397 Mark 7:31–37.
398 Mark 7:24–30; Matt. 15:21–28.
399 Luke 7:1–10/Matt. 8:5–13.
400 John 12:20–23.
401 Mark 7:27.
402 Matt. 8:7.
403 John 12:20–23.
404 Schnabel 1994: 47.

Jesus between anonymity and charisma

To most Galileans and Judeans, Jesus, the son of Joseph and Mary, was entirely unremarkable. He did not walk around surrounded by a fog of incense. People who came upon him did not suddenly startle and stare as if mesmerized by the aura of his divine genius. He was a peasant, an ordinary artisan, etching out a living in the remote hillsides of Galilee like many people in the hundreds of hamlets that littered the countryside. Jesus could carry a pile of bricks through Sepphoris or walk through a village market with anonymity and blend seamlessly into the scenery. A cursory look at the index of Josephus's works shows that there were many men named Jesus (Yeshua) in the first century. Indeed, if someone had asked Josephus which of all the 'Jesuses' mentioned in his work were the most interesting and most influential, Jesus of Nazareth might not even have made the top five.

Be that as it may, Jesus was a significant and influential figure, at least for a short time. During the years AD 27–30 (approximately), Jesus burst out of the shadow of John the Baptist, preaching with a sense of unmediated divine authority, declaring the nearness of the kingdom of God, and engaging in a mixture of healings and prophetic actions that excited hopes just as much as they invited scorn. He flitted from village to village, zigzagged between Galilee and Judea, crossed the Sea of Galilee, and made forays into the Decapolis, as well as Tyre and Sidon. Along the way, he gathered disciples, gained followers, grew sympathizers, amassed crowds, and spoke in homes and on hillsides. His arresting words and challenging actions courted controversy, cultivated enemies, and brought him to the attention of Pharisees, scribes and the high priest, even warranting the judicial intervention of the Roman prefect Pontius Pilate. Jesus was undoubtedly a charismatic figure who made his mark on the landscape of first-century Galilee and Judea. He may have appeared ordinary, his origins may have been from the margins, but the impact he made on his followers and contemporaries suggests that Jesus of Nazareth was a man of prophetic urgency, fierce compassion, covenantal fidelity, and unswerving commitment to a vision that God was king and becoming king through him. A part that he would play even if it led to his death, because, it seemed to him, his death would be the centrepiece in the kingdom's coming.

8
Jesus' last days in Jerusalem

'Surely no prophet can die outside Jerusalem'

One of the perennial questions about Jesus is whether he went to Jerusalem to work or to die. It is possible to construct an argument to the effect that Jesus – in the light of Johannine chronology – had visited Jerusalem several times for annual festivals and performed his ministry of teaching and preaching there with no intervention from priestly authorities. Therefore, so the theory goes, he could well have intended to do so again in AD 30: another festival, another bout of teaching, another walk back to Galilee. Yet on this visit to Jerusalem, Jesus pressed things too far with the temple episode, during a notoriously incendiary time in Jerusalem when the city was heaving with pilgrims and housing armed soldiers, and he did not expect the high priests to come down on him as they did. Let us not forget that, around the time of Jesus' birth, Roman forces had massacred a group of Jews in the temple precincts on account of provocations bordering on sedition.[1] Jesus was thus crucified by the Romans at the behest of the chief priests during the Passover celebration as the throng of Jewish crowds swelled the city to alarming levels; his death was an expedience to maintain civil order. In other words, Jesus was an agitator who had agitated the wrong people, and they responded in a way that not even he had anticipated.

That is one view, but I am of a different mind. For a start, '[a]ny Jewish preacher had to reckon with Jerusalem', says Helen Bond, 'particularly one who prophesied the restoration of Israel and looked for the establishment of God's kingdom on earth.'[2] I propose, then, that Jesus went

---
1 Josephus, *Ant.* 17.250–270.
2 Bond 2012: 136.

to Jerusalem to die. True, there may have been other visits to Jerusalem if there is a kernel of history in the Johannine tradition.[3] But one gets the impression, created by the tradition supplied by the evangelists, that this visit to Jerusalem was going to be prophetically provocative and eschatologically decisive. It would not be a passing stopover but a definitive confrontation. Jesus would deliberately draw out the chief priests and their imperial backers to move against him. He would do more than exclaim about judgment or expound the nature of the kingdom. Rather, he would embody God's kingly power and enact his messianic vocation, doing both by suffering the full effects of Israel's exile, receiving the penalty for transgression, and undergoing the horror of death, indeed the death of a slave. He would enter into the great ordeal so that the new exodus could happen, so that Israel could be restored, so that a new creation could be born.

Jesus knew full well from recent events of his own day, as well as the prophetic script that he was following, that death, destruction and martyrdom were high probabilities for someone declaring that God's kingdom was burgeoning in Galilee and Judea.[4] To begin with, there are ample Jewish traditions about the righteous man who suffers unjustly and is later vindicated by God.[5] One thinks of the Maccabean martyrdom stories narrating the death of Judean heroes who paid for their faithfulness to the covenant with their lives, matched with the hope of resurrection.[6] Many prophets met a grizzly end, including Isaiah, who, according to tradition, was sawn in half.

The significance of the Suffering Servant of Isaiah 52 – 53 for understanding both Jesus and the early church remains contested in scholarship.[7] Still, the Isaianic Servant Songs draw together the motifs of death, atonement and vindication in a way that was perhaps programmatic

---

[3] Cf. Tucker Ferda (2024: 349): 'It seems that the Synoptics give hints that Jesus had more contacts in and around Jerusalem than their narratives adequately explain, which might suggest that John's Jerusalem-frequenting Jesus was not a creation ex nihilo.'

[4] See previously Bird 2008d and most recently Barber 2024.

[5] Pss 22; 69; 34; 118; Dan. 7, 12; Wis. 2:10–24; 3:1–19; 5:1–23; *T. Mos.* 10.9.

[6] 1 Macc. 2:50; 6:44; 2 Macc. 7:33–38; 1QS 5.6; 8.3–10.

[7] Cf. de Jonge (1998: 33): 'All in all we must conclude that the influence of Isa. 52:13–53:12 on the earliest kerygma can hardly be demonstrated. A fortiori, there is no proof that Jesus himself was profoundly or uniquely influenced by this scriptural passage.' For a contrast, see Witherington 2017.

for Jesus. All the more plausible when we consider that the Aramaic Targum on Isaiah 43:10 refers to 'my servant, the messiah', which entails that the notion of an anointed or messianic servant was extant in Jesus' own time.[8] Jesus could have married together Isaiah's prophecy of a 'ransom' required for the new exodus with his own role as an anointed prophet who had to suffer for many.[9] Added to that, the death of John the Baptist is by far by the most telling precedent for what Jesus thought could happen to him. The Baptist was executed in Herod's dungeons. Jesus was aware that he too, with a similar mission, a similar message, could suffer a similar fate to that of John.

At a climactic point in the Markan Gospel, Jesus says that 'the Son of Man must undergo great suffering and be rejected by the elders, the chief priests, and the scribes and be killed and after three days rise again' (Mark 8:31). The 'passion prediction' is repeated twice more in Mark's Gospel as Jesus nears Jerusalem, and Luke and Matthew follow the Markan pattern.[10] The predictions each have the same basic content: (1) the Son of Man; (2) will be betrayed/suffer/rejected/condemned/killed/handed over; (3) by scribes/chief priests/elders/Gentiles; (4) then after three days; (5) he will rise again. This material, with its quasi-confessional content, allusion to Isaiah 53:11–12, plus wider connections to Mark's messianic secret, Matthew's controversial new David and Luke's rejected prophet, could be regarded as *ex eventu* prophecies put onto the lips of Jesus.[11] Yet such scepticism should be assuaged by the observation that these materials are so widely attested in various sources and types of material across the Jesus tradition that it is difficult to detect a better-established motif in Jesus' instruction.[12]

There is a whole range of sayings containing predictions of suffering and vindication that make sense in the context of Jesus' prophetic work.

---

8 Chilton 1984: 200.

9 A combination of Isa. 43:3–4; 53:10–11; 61:1–3, which would explain texts such as Mark 10:45.

10 First prediction   Mark 8:31   Luke 9:22   Matt. 16:21
      Second prediction   Mark 9:31   Luke 9:44   Matt. 17:22–23
      Third prediction   Mark 10:32–34   Luke 18:31–33   Matt. 20:17–19

11 See e.g. Bultmann 1952–55: 1:29.

12 See list in McKnight 2005: 79–82.

Parables

The parable of the bridegroom describes the sudden disappearance of the bridegroom on a climactic 'day', which is one of either grief or judgment or both.[13] The parable of the wicked tenants narrates how the 'beloved son' of the vineyard-owner is killed and thrown outside the vineyard by the murderous tenants, which is combined with a citation from Psalm 118:22 about the rejected stone that becomes a cornerstone.[14] In terms of parabolic speech, there is an enigmatic logion that 'the poor you will have always . . . but you will not always have me', which implies Jesus' premature death.[15] In addition, Jesus predicted that the temple of his body would be torn down and raised within three days.[16]

Metaphors of suffering

Jesus appears to have employed several metaphors to describe the dark fate that awaited him. He spoke of undergoing a *baptism*, which has connotations of being plunged into the watery deluge of judgment.[17] Jesus mentioned his destiny to drink from a *cup* in relation to his forthcoming death.[18] In the prophetic tradition, a cup could signify either Israel[19] or the nations[20] drinking the 'dregs of God's wrath'.[21] There is also the image of the approaching climactic *hour*, which is bound up with Jesus' suffering as a date with messianic destiny[22] and becomes increasingly salient in the Fourth Gospel.[23]

---

13 Mark 2:18–20; *Gos. Thom.* 47.
14 Mark 12:1–12; *Gos. Thom.* 65–66.
15 See Mark 14:7; Matt. 26:11; John 12:8.
16 Mark 14:58; 15:29; Matt. 26:61; John 2:19; *Gos. Thom.* 71; Acts 6:14.
17 Mark 10:38–39; Luke 12:50; cf. Gen. 6 – 7; Exod. 14:16–31; Job 9:31; Pss 32:6; 42:7–8; 69:1–2, 14–15; 124:4–5; 144:7; Isa. 8:7–8; 43:2; Jon. 2:5.
18 Mark 10:38–39; 14:36; John 18:11.
19 Isa. 51:17–23.
20 Jer. 25:15–29.
21 See Pss 11:6; 75:7–8; Ezek. 23:31–34; Hab. 2:16; Zech. 12:2; Rev. 14:10; 16:19; 1QpHab 11.14–15; *Pss Sol.* 8.14; *Mart. Isa.* 5.13.
22 Mark 14:35, 41; Matt. 26:39, 45; Luke 22:53.
23 John 2:4; 7:30; 8:20; 12:23; 13:1; 16:4, 21, 25, 32; 17:1.

'Rejected prophet' sayings

Jesus appeared acutely aware of the prospect that he could experience a violent demise just like the prophets of Israel's sacred history. That would place him in a line of executed prophets from Zechariah ben Joiada[24] to John the Baptist.[25] Jesus may have reckoned with the likelihood of being stoned as a false prophet.[26] Jerusalem is described as the city that 'kills the prophets',[27] and Jesus appears to have seen himself as destined, by divine necessity, to die there.[28] He assumed that he would be 'counted among the lawless'[29] and be the shepherd struck down to protect his flock.[30] The cryptic saying about the 'sign of Jonah' implies that the death and deliverance of a prophet has the effect of confirming that prophet's message.[31] All in all, one did not need to be a prophet to know that a prophet who gathered crowds, spoke about God's coming kingdom, challenged popular and official leaders, and uttered provocative riddles about a reversal of things, could soon find himself dead.

Atonement traditions

In a couple of key places in the Gospels, Jesus indicated not only that he would die, but also that his death would have an atoning, redemptive or saving function.

The famous ransom logion depicts Jesus as saying that he will give his life as a 'ransom' (*lytron*) for many.[32] But questions emerge as to the background of this saying and the precise nature of the ransom/purchase. One could locate the logion in the context of royal discourse about the king who gives his life to save others, ranging from Leonidas of Sparta (of *300* fame) to Marcus Otho (from the year of the four emperors in AD 69), both of whom gave their lives while leading their men into battle for

---

24 Luke 11:47–51/Matt. 23:29–36.
25 Mark 11:27–33.
26 Luke 13:34/Matt. 23:37; John 8:59; 10:31–36; 11:8.
27 Luke 13:33–35/Matt. 23:37–39.
28 Luke 13:33.
29 Luke 22:37.
30 Mark 14:27.
31 Luke 11:29–30/Matt. 12:39–40; 16:4.
32 Mark 10:45/Matt. 20:28.

a greater good.³³ That makes fine sense, since the context of the saying pertains to rulers, lords and tyrants who dominate others, but more may be at play here. The 'ransom' could also be cultic and refer to something offered to a deity to expiate some sin or offence.³⁴ There could well be echoes of Isaiah 53:10 where the Servant is crushed and the Lord makes the Servant's life a 'guilt offering' (MFB trans.; Heb. *asam*) that presages the end of Judea's exile and the launch of the new exodus.³⁵ While others detect allusions to the narratives of Daniel about the anointed one who is cut off,³⁶ when it comes to Mark 10:45, the traction with Isaianic language works because of the dense distribution of language relating to ransom/rescue/renewal throughout Isaiah 40 – 55.³⁷ Isaiah had an obvious impact on Jesus as part of his 'gospel' and prophetic mission.³⁸ Jesus drew on a 'nexus of interrelated motifs, themes, and texts' drawn from Isaiah.³⁹ He declares his intention to make the Isaianic 'ransom' a reality by offering his life as a sacrificial offering for Israel.

There is the final meal that Jesus had with his followers where he spelled out how his death would have a redemptive function. That Jesus spent a final quasi-Passover meal with his disciples prior to his execution is well attested,⁴⁰ and at this meal Jesus probably intimated to them his coming death, its divinely ordained and scriptural character, and its sacrificial meaning, and spoke of the prospect of participating in the eschatological feast in the kingdom of God in the future.

Johannine tradition

The Gospel of John has its own set of passion predictions which merge the Johannine Jesus' death with his exaltation and glorification. The

---

33 Thiessen 2016.
34 Collins 1997.
35 Cf. e.g. Wright 1996: 590–591; Watts 1998.
36 Dan. 9:25; cf. e.g. Hooker 1967: 142–143; McKnight 2005: 239, 338; Pitre 2005: 399–404; Lee and Brueske 2023: 92–116.
37 Cf. Isa. 43:1; 52:3, 9; along with Jer. 31:11; Mic. 4:10; Zech. 10:8.
38 Isa. 52:7 = Mark 1:15 (gospel) and Isa. 61:1 = Luke 4:18–21 (anointed prophet). Note too how John 12:38 draws on Isa. 53:1, and Matt. 8:17 from Isa. 53:4. Yes, this might be the redactional work of the evangelists, but they are rehearsing a tradition they have inherited, not created *ex nihilo*.
39 Witherington 2006: 402.
40 1 Cor. 11:23–26; Mark 14:17–31; Luke 22:13–38; Matt. 26:20–30.

fourth evangelist speaks of the 'lifting up' of the Son of Man[41] as well as his 'glory',[42] which are allusions to Jesus' death. These sayings represent traditional material being interpreted through a grid of incarnational Christology that attributes both soteriological and doxological significance to Jesus' execution.

'And rise'

Jesus appears to have 'scripted' hopes for his individual future with an assortment of texts including Isaiah 52 – 53, Psalm 118, 1 Kings 19, Zechariah 14 and Daniel 7 – 12, all of which allude to suffering and vindication.[43] The passion predictions include the proposition or promise that the Son of Man will be 'killed' and 'after three days rise again',[44] combined also with the enigmatic statement that Jesus would rebuild the temple 'in three days'[45] and the logion of the 'sign of Jonah' where it is implied that the Son of Man is spewed up from the earth just as Jonah was spewed up from the belly of the whale.[46] While it is possible that the idea of resurrection after 'three days' was borrowed from Hosea 6:2 in early Christian reflection on the passion story, this is unlikely for two reasons: (1) Hosea 6:2 is not directly cited anywhere in the NT, even though it is remarkably fitting for the Easter events; and (2) 'the third day' is most likely idiomatic for 'a short while' as in John 16:16–19. What is more, the resurrection predictions are predictions for an individual resurrection ahead of the general resurrection. Such an expectation is at once dissimilar to Jewish hopes, which located resurrection as a corporate event set to transpire at the eschaton.[47] For Jesus to speak of his own resurrection after his death, yet ahead of the general resurrection, was certainly innovative, odd and liable to misunderstanding, which explains why it stuck out like a sore thumb in the transmission of the saying.

---

41 John 3:14; 8:28; 12:32, 34.
42 John 12:23; 13:31; 17:5; 21:19.
43 Cf. Wright 1996: 584–591; McKnight 2005: 190–205, 238.
44 Mark 8:31; 9:31; 10:34; 14:21. Curiously, Casey (2010: 381–382) believes that only Mark 8:31 and 14:21 are authentic passion predictions in the Son of Man sayings.
45 Mark 14:58; 15:29; John 2:19.
46 Matt. 12:40.
47 Cf. e.g. Dan. 12:2; 2 Macc. 7:11, 14, 23; John 5:28–29; 11:24; 1 Cor. 15:51–52.

A necessary confrontation

Jesus' anticipation of his death and martyrdom in Jerusalem, and his subsequent resurrection and eschatological vindication, pervades the entire Jesus tradition and can hardly be doubted. After the death of the Baptist, Jesus knew he *could* face the exact same dark fate as his teacher, but it soon became apparent that, as part of his messianic vocation, *he had to die* in Jerusalem. Thus, when Jesus set his face to go to Jerusalem, he was heading there for an epic confrontation with the city of Jerusalem, its leaders, its temple and the powers who stood behind it. If Jesus predicted his death, there is no reason why he did not already interpret it – as part of his kingdom mission, no less.[48] His death would either move the wheel of history towards the kingdom or function as a shield against its coming wrath. He would go to Jerusalem, and he would die there, not by accident of fate or miscalculation, but by the determined plan and purpose of God, as the prophets had foretold. Jesus would drink the cup of wrath and undergo a baptism of fiery judgment as the hour of travail fell upon him. What is more, in Jewish eschatological hopes the onset of the period of tribulation was the prerequisite to the final restoration of Israel. Thus, by connecting his death to a time of tribulation, Jesus was intimating that his death would have a positive effect for the Jewish nation. As the Messiah, Jesus had to play the part of Isaiah's Servant, the righteous man who suffers, the shepherd who is struck down; he had to suffer as an atonement for sins and enter the eschatological ordeal of the last days. He would give his life to 'ransom captive Israel' as the hymn says[49] – ransom the nation from sin by enduring the suffering of exilic curses and the contamination of covenant transgression, and bearing the weight of the eschatological woes.[50] Beyond that, he anticipated his deliverance from death, his enthronement with the Almighty and his vindication as the divine Son. He would be raised by the power of God's goodness and the goodness of God's power. Crucifixion was a covenant curse, while resurrection, like Ezekiel's valley of dry bones, was always a symbol of Israel's restoration from death. Jesus, in his own person, would

---

48 Synthesizing Barrett 1967: 37–38 and Becker 1998: 341.
49 'O Come, O Come, Immanuel', tr. J. M. Neale (1851).
50 Schweitzer 1945 [1906]: 389; Jeremias 1971: 284–285; Meyer 1979: 209, 216; Wright 1996: 609; McKnight 1999: 116; Dunn 2003: 817; Pitre 2005.

experience death both *for* Israel and *as* Israel in order to *rescue* and *renew* Israel. As Scot McKnight puts it:

> Jesus, from the time of John's death, thought about his possible death. And what he seems to have thought about was that he would die prematurely, that it was part of God's plan, that he was like other martyrs and prophets and figures in the Tanakh, and, most especially, that his death would occur at the onset of the Final Ordeal. The connection Jesus makes in the passion predictions to the Son of man is similar: as the Son of man experienced (what can only be called) eschatological tribulation, so Jesus himself, as one like that Son of man, will also suffer the Final Ordeal. And, like that Son of man, Jesus will also be vindicated.[51]

Triumphal entry

According to E. P. Sanders, the 'triumphal entry' of Jesus into Jerusalem is 'one of the most puzzling [passages] in the Gospels'.[52] All four accounts, though they differ in some details, agree that Jesus entered Jerusalem (1) on a donkey, as Zechariah had claimed that Israel's king one day would,[53] and (2) acclaimed with flourish and fanfare by a crowd celebrating the coming of David's kingdom with phrases from Psalm 118:26. Matthew and John emphasize the royal and messianic dimensions even more acutely by having Jesus lauded as the 'Son of David' and the 'King of Israel'.[54] Given that Jesus was crucified for claiming to be 'King of the Jews [or: Israel]',[55] then, as Sanders observes, 'the entry and the execution fit each other precisely'.[56]

The problem is that if Jesus did deliberately stage such a piece of messianic street theatre, precisely when the priestly leadership and Roman garrison were on edge, how would he possibly have been able

---

51 McKnight 2005: 238.
52 Sanders 1985: 306.
53 Zech. 9:9.
54 Matt. 21:9; John 12:13.
55 Mark 15:26; John 19:19.
56 Sanders 1985: 306.

to get away with it? Surely the authorities would have acted against such a blatant piece of incendiary theo-political live-action role-playing! The Lukan version has the Pharisees making this very complaint; Jesus should get his disciples to shut up, or someone, innocent bystanders even, could be arrested, clubbed or killed.[57] Matthew notes that the action did put the city into turmoil, with crowds hearing rumours and discussing reports about 'the prophet Jesus from Nazareth in Galilee'.[58] So why wasn't Jesus arrested on the spot before he could perform his action in the temple and have a last meal with his disciples?[59]

The answer is fairly obvious:

1 The security forces were not ubiquitous. The Roman soldiers garrisoned in Jerusalem during the festival were housed in the Antonian fortress and focused on the security of the temple precincts[60] which was normally the locus of incidents.[61] If a Roman auxiliary, whether Syrian or Samaritan, Arab or Alexandrian, saw Jesus entering Jerusalem with his followers, with joyous pilgrims around him, he might not have even understood what they were saying (unless he spoke Aramaic) or what they were celebrating.
2 Thousands of bodies were in motion across the city – at its gates and in the temple precincts, shops and streets – and not all of them could be surveilled or seized for looking at a Roman officer with a menacing glare. Even if the Romans knew who they were after, trying to find a Galilean man with a beard named 'Yeshua' wearing a white tunic singing about the kingdom of David is not much different from trying to find a bald guy with a beard called 'Steve' at a meeting of the BBQ Lovers of America at a convention centre in Nashville.

---

57 Luke 19:39.
58 Matt. 21:10-11.
59 Sanders 1985: 306. Fredriksen (1999: 242) thinks the event was 'quite modest with Jesus making a relatively unobtrusive entrance, performing this symbolic act (riding the donkey) only for insiders'. Kinman (2010: 412–415) also thinks the entry was low-key. Witherington (1990: 104–105) suggests: 'it can be argued that Jesus is simply being accompanied by various pilgrims who are singing the pilgrim songs, one of which is based on Ps. 118:26ff.' Keener (2009: 261) supposes that it happened 'relatively quickly' and was limited to Galilean pilgrims. I'm more inclined to split the difference and say that the event was not a messianic Mardi Gras; it raised eyebrows but was not enough for someone to raise the alarm.
60 Josephus, *War* 5.243–245.
61 Cf. e.g. Josephus, *War* 2.223–227; *Ant.* 20.106–112.

Remember, the priests had to find a snitch from within Jesus' circle to identify him!
3 After the triumphal entry, Jesus immediately visited the temple; he did not assault the Antonian fortress. He was acting like an enthusiastic pilgrim, not a bandit. Jesus' entry, for all its royal rhetoric and prophetic ambience, did not lead to a riot or an uprising. When the authorities did hear, some hours later, about the moderate commotion at Jesus' entrance to the city, they probably thought: 'Let's be alert, but not alarmed.' Wise advice as anyone who has dealt with volatile crowds will tell you. Letting the mob blow off some steam, yell their mantras, fly their flags, sing their songs, and snigger at the authorities, was often better than sending in a skull-clubbing squad of soldiers who would probably precipitate a bigger and more deadly backlash. Much better to keep the swords sheathed until you really, really had to use them.

Jesus' entry, whether a grand gesture or a provocative performance among a group of pilgrims, is very probably historical.[62] We've already answered the question of how could he get away with it. But I would add, too, that I do not think the episode was invented on the back of Zechariah 9:9 and then projected into the life of Jesus to make him appear more kingly. Jesus rode into Jerusalem on a donkey quite deliberately with Zechariah 9:9 in mind.[63] The strange thing is that Zechariah 9:9 was marginal in most messianic expectations, yet the book of Zechariah did appear to have provided a prophetic script for how Jesus understood or planned his final week.[64]

The 'triumphal entry' is striking because it shows that Jesus' message was indeed about the kingdom. Not only that, but Jesus saw himself as its king, the primary actor of the coming royal reordering of power, a bespoke agent at its centre and climax.[65] The event was not only royal

---

[62] See Kinman 2010; Sanders (1985: 307; 1993: 253–254) treats it as more 'probable' than not.
[63] Alternatively, Vermes (1973: 145) thinks that Jesus rode a donkey because he found it 'more convenient than walking'.
[64] Cf. Bruce 1961; Moo 1983: 173–224; Wright 1996: 586–587, 599–600; Evans 1998b; Ham 2005.
[65] Cf. Sanders 1993: 238–248.

but also messianic. Scholars who attempt to play down the messianic element or attribute it to the interpretative gloss of the evangelists are simply missing the point.[66] Messianism is royal discourse played in an eschatological key. Jesus' regal performance cannot be abstracted from the hope that God, in his kingly power, through his anointed king, would restore Israel to an even greater glory. Moreover, if we add that the triumphal entry was preceded by the 'anointing' of Jesus by Mary of Bethany (following Johannine rather than Markan chronology),[67] note that the pilgrims were singing Hallel psalms which celebrated God's kingship (e.g. Ps. 118), and observe Jesus' recent oracle of lament and woe over Jerusalem because it did not recognize its 'time of . . . visitation',[68] then we are compelled to regard the entrance as the return of the 'anointed' king in whom God's power and presence visits the people.[69]

Jesus and the Jerusalem temple

Pliny the Elder said that Jerusalem was 'the most famous city of the East'[70] in no small part because of the Herodian temple, which dazzled observers with its size and the scale of its opulence and grandeur.[71] The temple was one of the 'pillars' of ancient Judaism and even venerated in the Jewish Diaspora.[72] A saying attributed to Simon the Righteous declares: 'By three things is the world sustained: by the Law, by the [Temple] service, and by deeds of loving-kindness' (*m. Abot* 1.2). Judea was a temple state operated by a hierocratic elite under the auspices of Roman power in the east centred on the legate of Syria. The Jerusalem

---

66 Cf. e.g. Sanders 1985: 235, 306; 1993: 254; Kinman 2010. Cadoux (1941: 59) called the entry 'quasi-messianic'. Better is Wright (1996: 491): 'The so-called "triumphal entry" was . . . clearly messianic. The meaning is somewhat laboured by the evangelists, particularly Matthew, but is not for that reason to be denied to the original incident.' Bockmuehl (1994: 91) too: 'Jesus clearly appears to accept the Messianic acclamation of his followers, to the consternation of the religious leadership.' A view expounded further in Bird 2009: 123–126.
67 Contrast John 12:1–8 with Mark 14:3–9.
68 Luke 19:44.
69 Cf. Wright and Bird 2019: 240; Wenham 2021: 198–199.
70 Pliny the Elder, *Nat. Hist.* 5.15.70.
71 See Josephus, *War* 5.222–223; *Ant.* 15.381, 388; Philo, *Spec. Leg.* 1.71–72. Cf. descriptions in Sanders 1992: 55–70; Goodman 2005: 459–460.
72 Cf. Sanders 1992: 51–76; Dunn 2003: 287–288.

temple was the place where God had placed his name, its cultus ensured the divine presence and favour, and it was the centre of social, political and economic life in Judea. It was simultaneously the acme of power for priestly collaborators and the symbol of resistance to Roman rule for zealous Judeans.

Accordingly, the temple was also at the centre of conflict between sectarian groups in Judea and determined the nation's posture towards local, regional and imperial Roman authorities. Jesus appears to have had a point of contention against the temple and its priestly curators as part of his kingdom message. Accordingly, researchers of the historical Jesus should repeat this mantra three times a day: 'Hear, O Academy, the historical Jesus had no problem with Jews and Judaism; he had a problem with the priestly leaders of the temple.' As Gerd Theissen noted: 'Criticism of the temple is criticism of the temple aristocracy.'[73]

Jesus did not debate his fellow Jews on the subject of grace versus religion, purity versus compassion, universalism versus particularism, spirituality versus ritual, and so on. Yes, Jesus did somewhat redefine the symbols of Israel's ancestral religion around God's kingdom and himself as God's anointed king. Yes, Jesus did engage in visceral debate with other Jewish groups such as the Pharisees over *halakhah* and future hopes. Yes, Jesus did court controversy over how to observe the sabbath and which scriptural laws took precedence over others. Yes, Jesus did try to form a community around himself, symbolic of a restored Israel, that would in time become the nucleus of the Christian church. But Jesus' principal point of contention was with the Jerusalem temple and its leadership, implicit in the parable of the good Samaritan and explicit in the parable of the wicked tenants. Besides that, Jesus, like others, resented the arrogance and avarice of the priestly class, the direction they were taking Israel, and their hostility towards his own kingdom project.[74] Wright is

---

73 Theissen 1987: 144.

74 This is why there is some wisdom in Sanders beginning his volume *Jesus and Judaism* (1985) with 'Jesus and the Temple'. See also Wright (1996: 405), who thinks that '[o]ne of the chief gains of the last twenty years of Jesus-research is that the question of Jesus and the Temple is back where it belongs, at the centre of the agenda. Apart from one or two dissenting voices, almost all scholars now writing in the field agree on two basic points: Jesus performed a dramatic action in the Temple, and this action was one of the main reasons for his execution.'

correct that 'when Jesus came to Jerusalem the place was not, so to speak, big enough for both him and the Temple together'.[75]

The problem is that Jesus also appears to have acted positively towards the temple in many respects. It is his assumption of the temple's validity and acceptance of its services that makes Jesus' demonstration in the temple and the prophecy of its destruction a truly jarring juxtaposition. We should dispense with the myth of Galilean indifference to the temple due either to the temple's distance or to its leadership's allegedly oppressive role in Galilean society.[76] Galileans, like other Jews, probably made one or more pilgrimages to Jerusalem for the festivals as Torah required.[77] Mary and Joseph presented Jesus in the temple as their firstborn son.[78] It is likely that Jesus and his family paid the half-shekel temple tax for every male child and rendered offerings in the temple as the law stipulated. Jesus probably purified himself before entering the temple, as the Passover had to be consumed in a state of ritual purity (e.g. avoiding corpse impurity).[79] In the course of his career, Jesus probably spent considerable time teaching in the temple precincts[80] and visited the temple for the festivals of Passover,[81] Tabernacles[82] and Dedication.[83] Jesus sent people cleansed of *lepra* to offer sacrifices in the temple,[84] affirmed the payment of the temple tax,[85] commended a widow's offering in the temple treasury,[86] uttered a saying about offering a gift at the temple's altar,[87] recognized the holiness of the temple and its sacrifices,[88] and acknowledged the temple as God's dwelling place.[89] 'Thus Jesus, as

---

75 Wright 1996: 436.
76 Contra e.g. Crossan 1991: 360.
77 Deut. 16:16–17; Exod. 23:14.
78 Luke 2:22.
79 John 11:55–57; Num. 9:6. On Jesus purifying himself for the temple and festivals, see Sanders 1993: 250–252; Fredriksen 1999: 205–206; Kazen 2002: 248–250, 255.
80 Mark 11:27 – 13:2; 14:49; Luke 21:37–38; John 7:14, 28; 8:20, 59; 10:22–23; 18:20.
81 Mark 11:11; John 2:14.
82 John 7:10, 14.
83 John 10:11.
84 Mark 1:40–45; Luke 17:12–19.
85 Matt. 17:24–27.
86 Mark 12:41–44.
87 Matt. 5:23–24.
88 Matt. 23:16–21.
89 Matt. 5:25; 23:21.

a devout adherent of Torah', says James Charlesworth, 'could well have loved Jerusalem and Zion, worshiped in the Temple, chanted with the Levites, sacrificed under the tutelage of the High Priest, even admired the Temple cult.'[90] Jan W. van Henten is similar: 'For Jesus the Temple was the self-evident cultic centre of Judaism and a special place to experience the relationship with God.'[91]

Later, the Jerusalem church continued to assemble regularly in the temple precincts and porticoes[92] even as they came into sporadic conflict with the temple authorities.[93] The Lukan Paul participated in rites of purification and sacrifice for four colleagues in the temple,[94] and Paul claimed that he had previously prayed in the temple and there received a vision with a message from Jesus.[95] As Eyal Regev infers: 'A Jew who believes in Jesus may nevertheless feel the need to visit the Temple and offer sacrifices to fulfill other aspects of cultic worship.'[96] Christian authors could spiritualize the temple and apply it to the church,[97] but that did not amount to a denunciation of the Jerusalem edifice.

Regev points out that Jesus and his followers related to the temple in four ways: by (1) participating in its worship, celebrations and sacrifices; (2) applying symbols from the temple and its cult to themselves; (3) criticizing abuses by the chief priests; and (4) rejecting the temple made with human hands for one given by God in the future.[98] Jesus in no way renounced the idea of a temple and its sacrifices; his criticisms are that of a cultic participant even if they draw on the tradition of prophetic critique of the temple establishment.

---

90 Charlesworth 2014: 154–155. Cf. Meier (1991–2016: 3:500): 'Even if we do not think that all of these narratives and sayings are authentic – the sayings in John are especially problematic – we still have widespread multiple attestation of both sources and forms for Jesus's acceptance of the Jerusalem temple of his day.'
91 van Henten 2015: 1.
92 Acts 2:47; 5:12, 42.
93 Acts 4:1–3; 5:19–21, 25–26; Josephus, *Ant.* 20.200.
94 Acts 21:24–26.
95 Acts 22:17–18.
96 Regev 2019: 5.
97 1 Cor. 3:16; 6:19; Eph. 2:20–22; 1 Pet. 2:4–9. See Klawans 2002 on how sacrificial metaphors applied to non-sacrificial acts are a way of saying, 'This too is a divine service.'
98 Regev 2019: 16.

We come, then, to the tricky topic of Jesus and the temple as one of the most significant topics in the domain of historical Jesus studies. This requires, first up, looking at contemporary Jewish critiques of the temple. Thereafter, attention needs to be given to Jesus' own prophetic action in the temple, as well as his prophecy against the temple, both of which, when understood correctly, will enable us to integrate Jesus as kingdom-proclaimer with his contention against the temple establishment.

Jewish critiques of the temple

The Samaritans obviously repudiated the Jerusalem temple in favour of their altar on Mount Gerizim. During the Persian period, an alternative Jewish temple was built at Elephantine in Egypt, and during the Hellenistic period the Diaspora Jews erected another makeshift temple at Leontopolis, also in Egypt. When the Hasmonean ruler Atistobulus combined the office of king and priest into one powerful position ca. 102 BC, it met with much consternation and condemnation. Criticism of the Jerusalem temple's operation and its operators was a feature of Judean life from the time of the priest Ezra under Cyrus all the way until its destruction in AD 70. Alan Segal notes that: 'Virtually everyone but the Sadducees had a critique of the Temple, including the Pharisees and the Dead Sea Scrolls sectarians.'[99] Lee Levine comments:

> the Temple was not only revered as Judaism's single most holy site by an ever-growing population in Judea, but was also accorded much attention and debate among the new established sects, each of which in its own way enhanced the centrality of Jerusalem's sacred site. No sect denied the sanctity of this site, although many were critical of the ways in which the Temple was being managed.[100]

Why was that the case? It helps if we remember that Jerusalem was basically a temple with a city built around it. The Jerusalem temple was not a 'religious' monument the way we would think of the Kaaba in Mecca or Westminster Abbey in London. The Jerusalem temple was

---

99 Segal 2002: 138.
100 Levine 2010: 1282.

a cross between the White House, the Statue of Liberty, Stonehenge, Fort Knox, the Mall of America and Notre Dame Cathedral. It was the political, social, economic and religious epicentre of Judaism and Judea. For the Jews it was *axis mundi*, and the level of pilgrimage to it by Jews from the Roman west and Parthian east was unparalleled. People were bound to exhibit displeasure with *something* associated with the temple, for example its relationship to taxation, tithes, commerce, debt, liturgies, sacrifices, calendars, appointment of high priests, treatment of priests, adornments, and more.

In the Hebrew Bible, the Isaianic oracles accuse the priests of drunkenness and question the moral fitness of those who perform sacrifices.[101] Jeremiah was brazen in his criticism of the temple, including the greed and impiety of the prophets and priests,[102] the moral duplicity of the masses, and the misplaced sense of security of the priests, meaning that the temple had been reduced to a 'hideout for bandits'.[103] In Lamentations, the disaster that befell the nation was due in part to the 'iniquities of her priests'.[104] Hosea prophesied against certain priests for faithlessness and ignorance of the Torah,[105] as well as for acting like bandits.[106] Zephaniah denounced the wickedness of Jerusalem with its priests who defiled sacred things and violated the Torah.[107] Malachi chided the priests for offering blemished sacrifices and for corrupting the covenant.[108]

In Second Temple literature, the *Testament of Moses* decries the apostasy of Hellenizing priests of the Seleucid era who 'pollute the house of their worship with the customs of the nations' and Hasmonean priest-kings who 'perform great impiety in the Holy of Holies'.[109] The *Psalms of Solomon* deride the priests for adultery, for pilfering the temple treasury, and for defiling the sacrifices by their intercourse with menstruating

---

101 Isa. 28:7; 66:3.
102 Jer. 6:13; 23:11–12.
103 Jer. 7:11 ISV.
104 Lam. 4:13.
105 Hos. 4:4–10.
106 Hos. 6:9.
107 Zeph. 3:4.
108 Mal. 1:6–14; 2:8.
109 *T. Mos.* 5.3; 6.1.

women, rendering the offerings profane.[110] The Qumran texts are replete with various cultic and social critiques of the Jerusalem priests and high priest for adultery, greed and defiling the temple.[111] In the Qumran pesher on Habakkuk 2:17, the verse allegedly refers to the 'Wicked Priest' who 'performed repulsive acts and defiled the Sanctuary of God'.[112] Similarly, the pesher on Nahum 2:14 decries the priests who have accumulated wealth through the violence of their gangs.[113] A Qumran sectarian letter complains that some priests defile the holy seed with their fornications.[114] According to the *Testament of Levi*, the priests plunder the Lord's offerings and eat them with whores, and so deride sacred things.[115] Furthermore, between 37 BC and AD 70, all but two of twenty-eight priests came from power-hungry and non-Zadokite families who often purchased their office.[116] In sum, neither the Hasmonean nor Herodian priests covered themselves in glory and fiscal modesty, but were often regarded as exploitative, perverse and guilty of contaminating the Jerusalem cultus.

Jesus' protest in the temple

Jesus, like many other Jews before him, around him and after him, stood in a line of those who had a critique of the temple and its priestly establishment.[117] He engaged in a dramatic and provocative demonstration during that fateful week of Passover, an action which many consider his

---

110 *Pss Sol.* 8.9–14; cf. CD–A 5.6–7; Lev. 15:19–24.
111 CD–A 4.17–18.
112 1QpHab 12.8–9.
113 4QpNah III–IV 1.10.
114 4QMMT C 4.9–11.
115 *T. Levi* 14.1 – 15.1.
116 Bockmuehl 1994: 69.
117 Bultmann (1952–55: 1:17) claimed that Jesus was simply indifferent to the temple, debates about its leaders, and how they operated the cultus: 'Polemic against the temple cult is completely absent from the words of Jesus' and that the closest Jesus came to an attack of the temple was his denunciation of 'legalistic ritualism' in Mark 7:6–8 and Luke 11:39. That is believable for a Lutheran theologian who has never set foot in Jerusalem and who knows nothing of cultures with ritual slaying of animals for religious festivals, but not persuasive for the rest of us. Such a view has filtered through even to Vermes (2003: 309–310), who reports: 'The historical Jesus displayed no particular interest in the temple.' My quibble with Vermes has always been that his Jewish Jesus had a bit too much existential rather than ritual interest (i.e. it was a Bultmannian Jesus in the light of the Dead Sea Scrolls and Josephus).

'greatest public deed'[118] and the 'key to understanding the man and his mission'.[119] The Markan and Johannine accounts read:

> Then they came to Jerusalem. And he entered the temple and began driving out those who were selling and those who were buying in the temple, and he threw over the tables of the money-changers and the seats of those who sold doves, and he would not permit anyone to carry anything through the temple. He was teaching and saying, 'Is it not written, "My house shall be called a house of prayer for all the nations"? [Isa. 56:7] But you have made it a "cave of bandits"' [Jer. 7:11].
> (Mark 11:15-17, MFB trans.)

> The Passover of the Jews was near, and Jesus went up to Jerusalem. In the temple he found people selling cattle, sheep, and doves and the money changers seated at their tables. Making a whip of cords, he drove all of them out of the temple, with the sheep and the cattle. He also poured out the coins of the money changers and overturned their tables. He told those who were selling the doves, 'Take these things out of here! Stop making my Father's house a marketplace!' [Zech. 14:21]. His disciples remembered that it was written, 'Zeal for your house will consume me' [Ps. 69:9].
> (John 2:13-17)[120]

Jesus' action most likely transpired in the outer court, known in modern parlance as the 'court of the Gentiles', or else began in the adjacent southern plaza and made its way up to the royal porticoes where the money-changers were probably set up, before spilling into the outer court. There are good arguments for the historicity of the action and the accompanying saying.[121] Above all, it was this provocative action and

---

118 Klausner 1925: 312.
119 Luff 2019: 195.
120 Despite the consensus of the patristic and medieval tradition (Metzdorf 2003: 42-127), I think it most unlikely that Jesus cleansed the temple twice, once at the beginning of his career and again at the very end. See discussion in Blomberg 2001: 87-91.
121 Meyer 1979: 168-170; Meier 1991-2016: 2:893; Ådna 2000: 300-333; 2010; Bryan 2002: 206-208; Wedderburn 2006: 6-8; Snodgrass 2010.

prophetic aphorism that explains why the priestly authorities sought Jesus' demise. In any case, plausibility is enhanced when we remember that what Jesus attempted was not an occupation of the temple, much less an insurrection.[122] What happened was probably a short sharp dramatic gesture, lasting only a few minutes, with Jesus making a ruckus as he moved along with his disciples behind him, annoying some and scandalizing others.[123] Of course, Jesus' action was not necessarily a show-stealing event like someone jumping onto the stage during a Taylor Swift concert. There were thousands of pilgrims, locals and officials crowded into the temple precincts, making a cacophony of noise which might have drowned out Jesus' actions and any yelling.[124] Plus, the porticoes were often filled with teachers spouting controversial views, and the outer court was a forum for public debate and the voicing of grievances. Nevertheless, Jesus' words possessed theocratic rhetoric, his actions conveyed indomitable purpose, and the two together were pregnant with messianic authority. Some priests and pilgrims did notice the commotion, including the officials who reported his incendiary antics to the high priests,[125] who did after that conspire against him.[126]

The real question is: what was Jesus doing and why was he doing it? This is where the consensus breaks down. The event is something of a 'puzzle'[127] because the 'incident is inherently ambiguous, almost a conundrum, as is evidenced by the divergent explanations of its intent'.[128]

This episode is sometimes, and erroneously to my mind, referred to as the 'cleansing' of the temple. On this view, Jesus allegedly cleansed the

---

122 Contra Brandon 1967: 331–341 ('an abortive coup' [340]).
123 Cf. too Borg 1998 [1984]: 171–172; Sanders 1985: 69–70; Witherington 1990: 110–115; Wardle 2010: 172; Perrin 2010: 83; Hengel and Schwemer 2019 [2007]: 592 ('a small tumult followed by a battle of words').
124 Fredriksen 1999: 231–232.
125 According to *m. Mid.* 1.1, Levites and priests were stationed at various positions around the temple during festivals.
126 I have to acknowledge the complaint of Snodgrass (2010: 447) that people cannot have it both ways. You cannot affirm that (1) the event was small scale, and (2) it was the reason for Jesus' arrest by the chief priests. But I'm unsure whether this is quite the problem. I would reply that enough people, pilgrims and priests, saw and heard Jesus' action to be excited/concerned about it. Plus, the triumphal entry, combined with Jesus' controversial teachings that week, led to a series of incidents that compelled the chief priests to have Jesus arrested and executed.
127 Wedderburn 2006.
128 Snodgrass 2010: 431; so too Wright 1996: 405; Perrin 2010: 81.

temple of commerce the same way that Judas Maccabeus cleansed it of Hellenistic religion.[129] According to many scholars and preachers, Jesus protested against what he saw as the mixing of religion and business in the outer court, evident in the purchasing of animals for sacrifice and the exchange of money suitable for usage in the temple.[130] That impression is a reasonable inference from John 2:16 and its allusion to Zechariah 14:21 about the lack of traders in the new temple. The same view appears in the *Gospel of Thomas* where Jesus declares, 'Businessmen and merchants will not enter the places of my father' (*Gos. Thom.* 64).[131] The modern equivalent would be some zealous Christian kicking in the windows of the gift shop at St Paul's Cathedral in Melbourne because the vergers and shop assistants have turned the cathedral into a 'den of thieves' by selling cringy kitsch religious merchandise.[132] The problem is that it can be retorted that the temple market was not a con job but a genuine convenience for pilgrims. No one would want to bring a lamb all the way from Galilee or even from Gaza; better to buy one on location, at the temple, approved for sacrifice, even if prices were steep. Not only that, but it could also be said that the high priests were merely benefiting from an economic system that benefited everyone in the city, including its market traders, artisans, bakers, butchers and visitors.[133]

A better variation is to see Jesus' action as protesting at the hierocratic elite who, as Roman clients of Judea, enriched themselves by exploiting lower-tier priests and the poor.[134] The chief priests had a monopoly via the temple tax and the pilgrim economy. The influx of funds into the upper echelons of Jerusalem society, dominated by four priestly families, created an oligarchy where credit and capital were located in a small group of elites who charged crippling interest on loans and foreclosed on

---

129 Josephus, *Ant.* 12.316–322.
130 Cf. e.g. Betz 1997: 461–462; Snodgrass 2010: 462, 469.
131 Crossan (1991: 356) thinks that the Thomasine version is the most primitive version of the saying.
132 If that is you, please don't – some of my students work in the gift shop!
133 Cf. Sanders 1985: 62–65; 1992: 87; Fredriksen 1999: 207–209; Goodman 1999; Ådna 2000: 335–342; 2010: 4:2655.
134 Bauckham 1988; Evans 1995: 267–280, 319–344; 1997b; Tan 1997: 185–187; Perrin 2010: 95–97; Cohen 2016: 270–271. Charlesworth (2014: 164–165) thinks that Jesus protested against the presence of Tyrian coins which had the image of the pagan god Melkart on them and were used to pay the temple tax.

properties whenever possible, resulting in more land concentrated in the hands of fewer and fewer people.[135] The Qumranites read Habakkuk as a critique of the Hasmonean priesthood's self-enrichment.[136] Elsewhere in the scrolls it was the greed and avarice of the Jerusalem priests that was the subject of complaint and invective polemics.[137] Josephus recounts how, during the reign of several high priests, servants were sent to the threshing floors of the temple to steal the tithes due to the lower-tier priests.[138] Josephus says the priests had a 'hardness' (*anaideia*) and were even prone to 'violence' (*biazō*) towards those who would not hand over the tithes.[139] The picture develops more fully if the money-changers in Jesus' day were themselves Levites, priests or agents of the chief priests.[140] Later, during the Judean rebellion, many of the rebels burned the records of debt in the temple, an action which associated the temple with the economic grievances of the masses.[141]

I think there is something correct about this position. The chief priests did enrich themselves in their office, a complaint that resonates from the days of Hosea, the Hasmoneans and the Herods. The priests did monopolize all trade associated with the cultus: they set premium prices for sacrificial animals, charged a levy for entering the temple and often stole the tithes intended for lower priests. Even so, we must be wary of Robin-Hood-izing Jesus. It is nauseating, white liberal middle-class, pseudo-Marxist drivel to propound that Jesus was the temple's 'functional opponent, alternative and substitute' because he was set on mounting a pro-peasant proletarian 'egalitarian challenge' to the temple's socio-economic hierarchy.[142] In addition, we have to observe that Jesus' words are not restricted to or even typical of prophetic rhetoric about priestly greed and avarice. In Jeremiah 7:11, the Hebrew term *paris* refers to someone who is rapacious, a robber or brigand, while the Greek word *lestēs* is closer to 'bandit' or 'terrorist' than 'thief'.

---

135 Goodman 1982; 1993: 56–59.
136 1QpHab 9.5; 12.10.
137 4QpNah III–IV 1.10; CD-A 4.17; 6.14–17.
138 Josephus, *Ant.* 20.179–181, 206–207.
139 Josephus, *Ant.* 20.181, 206.
140 Bauckham 1988: 75.
141 Josephus, *War* 2.427.
142 Contra Crossan 1991: 355.

Another interpretation, one I formerly adhered to, was that Jesus critiqued the temple for its exclusion of Gentiles and support for Judean militancy.[143] While the temple was for Israel's worship of Yahweh, there was a sense, from the beginning, that the temple was intended to attract the worship of the nations,[144] that foreigners were able to offer sacrifices in the temple[145] and that the eschatological temple would see foreigners throng to Jerusalem with the returning exiles to worship Yahweh there.[146] At the same time, the cultic holiness of the temple meant that the unclean and uncircumcised, including Gentiles, were eventually excluded from entering its precincts.[147] In fact, the *soreg*, the wall that marked the boundary between the outer court and the inner court of the temple, contained a warning that any foreigners who transgressed the boundary would be put to death: 'Let no foreigner enter within the partition and barrier surrounding the temple; whosoever is caught shall be responsible for his subsequent death.'[148] It was perhaps the fear of another desecration by a Gentile ruler like Antiochus IV,[149] and halakhic debates about the nature of Gentile impurity vis-à-vis the temple cultus,[150] that had led to the erection of this barrier. Alternatively, the wall was perhaps a compromise position, allowing Gentiles access to the temple precincts but putting a limit on their proximity to the Holy of Holies.[151] In addition, the catalyst that sparked the Judean rebellion of AD 66 was the refusal of the priests to offer any more sacrifices on behalf of the Roman emperor Nero.[152] The citizens of Sepphoris were asked to join the rebellion against Rome on the grounds that the 'temple that

---

143 Bird 2006a: 134–161, following Wright 1996: 417–421 and Borg 1998 [1984]: 185–186.
144 1 Kgs 8:41 – 41.4.
145 Num. 14:15–16.
146 Cf. e.g. Isa. 2:2–4; 56:6–8; Mic. 4:1–4; Zech. 8:20–23.
147 Cf. e.g. Ezek. 44:7–9; 4Q174 1.3–4.
148 *CIJ* 2: § 1400; cf. Josephus, *War* 5.193–194; 6.124–128; *Ant.* 12.145; 15.417; *Apion* 2.103; Philo, *Leg. Gai.* 212; Acts 21.28–29; Eph. 2.14; *m. Kel.* 1.8; *m. Mid.* 2.3.
149 Cf. the emphasis on cleansing the sanctuary that had been profaned by foreigners and the fear of the sanctuary's destruction and transformation into a pagan shrine in 2 Macc. 10 – 15.
150 Precisely what the Qumranites wanted according to their sectarian letter 4QMMT frags. 3–7, 1.5–19.
151 Cf. Bryan (2002: 176), who supposes that the erection of the dividing wall was an act of 'liberalization whereby Gentiles were permitted a degree of access which they had been previously denied'.
152 Josephus, *War* 2.409–410, 14.

is common to us all was in danger of falling into the enemy's hands'.[153] Freyne's survey of riots and rebellions indicates how during 'the whole procuratorial period the temple repeatedly became the flashpoint of Jewish nationalist aspirations'.[154]

One can imagine, then, that Jesus was protesting against the exclusion of Gentiles from the worship of the one God of creation and covenant, the Father of Abraham and Moses, the God who dwelt in a house of worship for Israel and for all foreigners who called upon his name. Moreover, the opposite of a temple that was a cave of Judean terrorists wrongly trusting in the supposed invincibility of Zion was a house of prayer for all nations.[155] As Caird wrote: 'Instead of being the centre of a world religion, the Temple had become the symbol of nationalism and division'.[156] Barrett paraphrased Jesus' words as: 'God intended this place for international prayer; you have made it a nationalistic stronghold'.[157]

I regard that view now as deficient because it always runs the risk of sounding like the mission theology of the Gentile churches projected onto Jesus and perhaps plays off Jewish particularism against Christian universalism. That said, I take it as granted that Jesus believed that a transformed Israel would transform the nations and that the eschatological temple would have Gentiles thronging to it. We do better to see Jesus pronouncing a judgment against the temple establishment's fiscal and moral corruption (Jer. 7:11) and also looking ahead to what the new temple would be in contrast (Isa. 56:7).[158] Michael Barber sums up what was probably Jesus' position: 'Isaiah foretold an eschatological temple, but this one is not it. It shall be destroyed like the one of Jeremiah's day.'[159]

What I take as the most likely meaning of the temple demonstration is that Jesus' action, by temporarily disturbing the temple cultus, was foreshadowing the temple's destruction.[160] Jesus drove out those buying and selling animals, turned over the tables of money-changers, and

---

153 Josephus, *Life* 348; cf. *War* 2.330.
154 Freyne 1988: 179, teased out further in Bird 2006a: 141–143.
155 Juxtaposing Jer. 7:11 and Isa. 56:7.
156 Caird 1950–51: 260.
157 Barrett 1978: 16.
158 Cf. discussion in Perrin 2010: 83–88 and Barber 2023: 98–101.
159 Barber 2023: 101.
160 Sanders 1985: 69–71; Wright 1996: 334, 424; Theissen and Merz 1998 [1996]: 432–433;

stopped people from carrying animals for sacrifices or vessels of incense and salt, all of which made it impossible for anyone to offer sacrifices, at least for the duration of his protest.[161] He was foreshadowing what would happen when the temple was destroyed, the cultus would cease, and sacrifices would be ended. Sanders remains correct:

> Jesus predicted (or threatened) the destruction of the temple and carried out an action symbolic of its destruction by demonstrating against the performance of the sacrifices. He did not wish to purify the temple, either of dishonest trading or of trading in contrast to 'pure' worship. Nor was he opposed to the temple sacrifices which God commanded to Israel. He intended, rather, to indicate that the end was at hand and that the temple would be destroyed, so that the new and perfect temple might arise.[162]

Where I depart from Sanders is that Jesus believed in not only the coming destruction of the temple but also its deserved destruction, the judgment of God falling upon it.

At this point, we must be cautious. Jesus did not attack the notion of sacrifices, as if it were external religion, contaminated with icky blood and strange rituals.[163] The temple cultus with its sacrifices was commanded by God, and it intersected with election, holiness, reconciliation and the divine presence. Some later Christians did, however, move in this direction. In the *Gospel of the Ebionites*, Jesus utters a saying: 'I have come to destroy the sacrifices. And if you do not stop making sacrifice, God's wrath will not stop afflicting you' (*Gos. Eb.* 7). Such words might make a great justification for a non-cultic species of messianic Judaism post-AD 70 or 135, but they don't fit a man who commanded a person with a skin affliction to 'bring the offering that Moses commanded for your cleansing'.[164] Jesus taught that love and mercy were better than sacrifices,

---

Holmén 2001: 323–329; Meier 1991–2016: 3:501; Crossan and Reed 2001: 262; Dunn 2003: 637.

161 Cf. Josephus, *Apion* 2.106, 109.
162 Sanders 1985: 75.
163 This is the concern of Sanders (1985: 67); Fredriksen (1999: 209); Ehrman (1999: 172); and Barber (2023: 76).
164 Mark 1:44.

not a replacement for sacrifices.[165] Even more tendentious is the critique of the Jerusalem cultus in the *Epistle to Diognetus* (c. AD 150–200) which alleges that the worship of the Jews is erroneous because they treat the sacrifices as things that God needs and insult divine aseity.[166]

According to Luke,[167] the Jerusalem crowd heard rumours that Stephen had said Jesus would destroy the temple (truth) and change the Mosaic law (misunderstood claims), but there is no sense in which the Hellenistic Christians declared in Jesus' name that sacrifices were obsolete or offensive to God. The apostle Paul applied cultic language to Jesus' death[168] and also in a metaphorical way to Messiah-believers as living or bloodless sacrifices.[169] Thus, Paul did not reject cultic ideas per se; on the contrary, he saw his own career as the priestly service of proclaiming the gospel.[170] Even the epistle to the Hebrews says that Jesus is a better sacrifice than those of the past, not that the old sacrifices were bad, externalized rituals.[171] For the author of Hebrews, the temple was not the antithesis of true religion but rather the anticipation of something better that was coming. But did Jesus think that the new temple would have sacrifices, or that his own sacrificial death would eclipse it in that regard? Jesus said nothing for or against such propositions, even if the later church was vocal on this topic.[172]

Jesus could have symbolized the destruction of the temple because he believed that God's kingly power would be manifested in a new eschatological temple which was still to come. In other words, the temple's

---

165 Mark 12:33; Matt. 9:13; 12:7. Contra Joseph (2016: 90), who thinks Jesus' demonstration in the temple was meant to demonstrate that God did not require animal sacrifice.
166 *Ep. Diogn.* 3.1–5.
167 Acts 6:14.
168 Rom. 3:25–26.
169 Rom. 12:2.
170 Rom. 15:15–16.
171 Heb. 9:26–28.
172 More enthusiastic on this implication is Schnabel (2018: 161–162), who writes: '[Jesus] performed a symbolic action that prophetically enacted the destruction of the temple in preparation for the building of the new, messianic temple in which gentiles also would worship Israel's God, and which prophetically pointed forward to the cessation of the sacrifices in view of Jesus's coming death.' Similar is Ådna (2010: 4:2670), who comments: 'The old atonement cult must be brought to an end because it is inappropriate in the eschatological era, about to be ushered in, in which it will be replaced by the eternal worship of the redeemed from all the nations.' This might be an inference from Jesus' actions and sayings, one the early church would prosecute in various ways, but it was not the main point.

destruction looked forward towards its restoration. A consistent element of Jewish hopes for the future was for a new temple. Ezekiel's vision of restoration included a renewed temple and priesthood, which was to be a common staple of post-exilic Jewish hopes.[173] There was also a royal-messianic dimension to the temple's rebuilding, as it was a Davidide who was destined to build God's temple:[174] Cyrus the 'anointed one' had passed a decree to rebuild the temple,[175] and Herod the Great refurbished the temple precisely because he wanted to proclaim his royal credentials as Israel's king. Thus, if Jesus declared himself to be the one who would raise up the temple, he was making a de facto messianic claim.[176] Perhaps we have here the locus of Jesus' complaint. The rebuilding of the temple under Cyrus, its cleansing by Judas Maccabee and its refurbishment by Herod had not realized the great promises associated with the new temple. There was no return of the dispersed Jews to Judea, no pilgrimage of the Gentiles to Zion, no amazing agricultural fecundity, no aspiration to covenant justice; and no new Davidic leader had arrived on the scene. The temple was not a 'house of prayer for all people' but more like a house run by blind sentinels who were as lethargic as sleeping dogs, gluttonous with greed and given to sitting around in a drunken stupor.[177]

If we take the temple action and temple saying together, then, what did Jesus find wrong with the Jerusalem temple? I surmise that for Jesus, the problem with the Jerusalem temple *materially* was that its leaders were acting like brigands, mercilessly mercantile; they were rapacious and brutal, overbearing, devious and divisive, clinging to power over piety; and the temple was a talisman of a misplaced confidence in Judea's national invincibility.[178] The problem with the Jerusalem temple *ultimately* was that it was not the eschatological temple.[179] It had become a monument to Herod, not the embodiment of Israel's hopes

---

173 Ezek. 40 – 44. Cf. Tob. 13:16–17; 1QS 8.5–7, 8–10; 9.6; 4Q171 3.10–11; 4Q174 1.6–7; 11Q19 29; *4 Ezra* 10.19–54; *2 Bar.* 4.1–6; 68.5–6; *1 Enoch* 53.5–7; 71.3–13; 90.28–29; *Sib. Or.* 3.290–294; 5.420–33. See discussion in Sanders 1985: 77–86; Ådna 2000: 25–89.
174 2 Sam. 7:13.
175 Isa. 44:28; 45:1.
176 John 2:19.
177 Isa. 56:6–12.
178 Cf. Bryan (2002: 217), who thinks that Jesus criticized the entire operation of the temple, not just one aspect of it.
179 Cf. Tan 1997: 219.

and Yahweh's holiness. The waters of the Dead Sea were not flowing into it; the Gentiles were not arriving at its steps with gifts and offerings; the priestly vestments were not delivered to the high priest by an angel but by the Roman procurator. This was a temple made with 'human hands', whereas one made 'without human hands' had been promised and this was not it![180] The kingdom could not be present or manifested if there was not a new eschatological temple.[181] The manifold problems with commerce, corruption, calendar, cultus, cooking points and priestly curators meant that this building was not the temple of Isaiah 56, Ezekiel 40 - 44 or Zechariah 14. The issue was more than 'Who speaks for the temple?' It was also 'What does it mean to be the temple?' and 'What will the future temple look like in the restoration of Israel?'[182]

Jesus' prophecy against the temple

It was at one particular festival, before the Judean rebellion, that the peasant-cum-prophet Jesus stood in front of the temple and cried out, 'A voice from the east, a voice from the west, a voice from the four winds; a voice against Jerusalem and the sanctuary, a voice against the bridegroom and the bride, a voice against all the people.' The leading citizens of Jerusalem were disturbed by these words and had Jesus arrested and beaten, but he still continued his prophetic tirades against the city and its temple. When brought before the governor, Jesus was 'flayed to the bone with scourges', yet he did not ask for mercy nor even shed a tear, but instead kept bursting forth with baneful words against Jerusalem. When questioned by the governor, he would not answer, so the governor set him free as a lunatic. Jesus continued his dirge of woe and warning for several more years, in and around Jerusalem, repeating his laments for the city, showing no signs of giving up. He did so, right up until the

---

180 Cf. Acts 7:48; 17:24; Heb. 9:24.
181 On viewing Jesus' temple action in view of his kingdom message and hopes, Ådna (2010: 4:2668) is correct: 'These sayings and the act in the temple must be seen against the background of Jesus' proclamation of the imminent kingdom of God and his messianic mission related to the realisation of the kingdom.' Cf. too Snodgrass 2010: 473–474. Christopher Blumhofer (2020: 82–83) is close to the mark: 'Jesus indicts those in the temple *not* for their immorality, financial exploitation of worshipers, or exclusion of Gentiles; rather, he indicts them for the incongruity of the temple's operations vis-à-vis the eschatological moment in which Israel lives' (emphasis added). I would change his 'not' to 'not so much'.
182 Riffing off Perrin 2010: 112.

siege of Jerusalem, when he was seen wandering about the city's walls, screaming in a piercing voice, 'Woe once more to the city and to the people and to the temple!' Then he added a last word: 'and woe to me also', and with that a projectile fired from a ballista struck and killed him on the spot.[183]

The description here is not about Jesus of Nazareth, but one Jesus ben Ananias, a peasant who took his prophetic message of woe and warning to Jerusalem in the early 60s AD until he was killed in the very calamity that he warned his compatriots about. The parallels with Jesus' own warning against the temple are remarkable, as are the similarities in the later fate of the two men, including the Sanhedrin's opposition to them, the punishment of scourging, and the climax in a trial before the Roman governor. Both figures were agrarian prophets named Yeshua who prophesied against the temple and the city, and received scorn, derision and violence for their efforts.

Of course, both Jesuses stood in a line of prophets who predicted the temple's destruction.[184] Jeremiah declared the divine verdict to the Jerusalemites: 'I will make this house like Shiloh [i.e. destroyed], and I will make this city a curse for all the nations of the earth' (Jer. 26:6, 9; cf. 7:14).[185] Similarly, Ezekiel spoke to the Babylonian exiles:

Say to the house of Israel: Thus says the Lord GOD: I will profane my sanctuary, the pride of your power, the delight of your eyes, and your heart's desire, and your sons and your daughters whom you left behind shall fall by the sword.
(Ezek. 24:21)

It was quite possible for God to stand in judgment and bring judgment against the temple that bore the divine name. Similar denunciations and predictions of the temple's destruction were made by several authors of the Hasmonean and Herodian periods.[186] Josephus, writing after

---

183 Josephus, *War* 6.300–309.
184 Cf. Evans 1992; 1995: 367–380.
185 Affirmed even though God will bring judgment on the Babylonians as 'vengeance for his temple' (Jer. 50:28; 51:11).
186 Cf. *T. Levi* 10.3; 14.1 – 15.3; *1 Enoch* 90.28; *Sib. Or.* 3.665.

the temple's destruction by Titus, believed that Judean obstinacy and Rome's ordained sovereignty meant that God had sentenced the temple to the flames.[187] Such sentiments frightened many Jews who feared the cessation of sacrifices and the profanation of the holy place by invading hordes.[188] These statements about the temple's destruction/desecration are remarkable because they are not about the mere end of a 'religious' institution, but the collapse of a civilization, the ruin of Israel's purpose, vocation and destiny. As Meyer commented: 'To evoke, even conditionally, the destruction of "this temple" was to touch not just stone and gold and not only the general well-being but history and hope, national identity, self-understanding and pride.'[189]

Jesus, it seems, also declared the imminence of the temple's destruction for the reasons explained above, but the frequency and contents of those predictions are worth noting. Jesus engaged in a prophetic and weeping lament over Jerusalem, longing to protect it from judgment like a hen protecting its chicks from a barnyard fire, even though its 'house' was abandoned or destined to be made desolate.[190] The city would be laid to siege because it would not make for peace or recognize the time of Yahweh's visitation in the coming of the messianic son.[191] The temple mount – the entire edifice of the Jerusalem priestly establishment – could be thrown into the sea.[192] The admiration of the temple's furnishings by the disciples was met with Jesus' cold retort that '[n]ot one stone will be left here upon another; all will be thrown down'[193] when a foreign army invaded, laid Jerusalem to siege, desecrated the temple and brought it all crashing down. The judgment of Jerusalem is, for Mark and Luke, the first instalment of the final judgment, and for Matthew a beta-test of Jesus' return as judge. There is also the strange saying attributed to Jesus that he would destroy the temple and build another,[194] but it is difficult to say whether this is a deliberate misattribution to Jesus, a garbled

---

187 Josephus, *War* 6.250.
188 Cf. Dan. 8.11–12; 9:26–27; 11:31; 12:11; 1 Macc. 1:45–46, 54; Mark 13:14; Matt. 24.15–16.
189 Meyer 1979: 183.
190 Luke 13:34–35/Matt. 23:37–39.
191 Luke 19:41–44.
192 Mark 11:23.
193 Mark 13:2.
194 Mark 14:58/Matt. 26:61.

account of something he said or a later invention of the early church attributed to Jesus.

A new temple?

To recap the preceding subsections: (1) Jesus shared with many Jews a critical attitude towards the Jerusalem priestly leadership; (2) Jesus' critique was partly that the current temple was corrupted by the greed and guilt of the chief priests; (3) Jesus, as did many Jews before him, uttered prophetic oracles of judgment against the temple establishment; and (4) Jesus, like many of his Jewish contemporaries, believed that there would be a new eschatological temple as part and parcel of prophetic restorationist eschatology. So, then, what was Jesus' relationship to this new temple that would eclipse the old one?

Jesus spoke of himself, and potentially his 'movement', in language and imagery associated with the temple. In a Matthean logion, Jesus disputed Pharisaic *halakhah* on the sabbath by appeal to his own authority as neither scribal nor priestly but based on the fact of his identity: 'I tell you, something greater than the temple is here.'[195] If we combine that with the statement where Jesus identifies himself as the rejected stone which becomes the 'cornerstone'[196] – a citation of Psalm 118:22 and an allusion to Isaiah 28:16 where the 'stone' stands for the Jerusalem temple, cultus and kingdom – then we have evidence that Jesus regarded himself and his followers as symbolic of or perhaps constituting a temple, perhaps even an alternative to the current corrupt Jerusalem temple. That said, we must be cautious. We do not know for sure if we are dealing with a Matthean gloss, and we must concede that Psalm 118:22 was a favourite text in Christological apologetics,[197] which is not the firmest historical ground to build upon.

Yet any pessimism can be assuaged when we remember that hope for a new temple was a foundational part of Jewish restoration eschatology. In addition, we must likewise understand that applying temple language to an in-group fits perfectly into the sectarian claims and counter-claims

---

195 Matt. 12:6.
196 Mark 12:10.
197 Cf. Acts 4:11; 1 Pet. 2:7.

made by other Judean movements that operated in juxtaposition to the temple establishment. In some cases, the righteous remnant could be identified with the coming new temple. The Qumran *Community Rule* implies that the sectarians themselves either supersede the current temple and/or anticipate the future temple: 'The Community council shall be founded on truth, [...] to be an everlasting plantation, a holy house for Israel and the foundation of the holy of holies for Aaron' (1QS 8.5–6). The members of the community themselves constituted a metaphorical temple as the representative fixture for the coming messianic age, in which their purpose was

> to implement truth, justice, judgment, compassionate love and unassuming behaviour of one to another, to preserve faithfulness in the land with firm purpose and repentant spirit in order to atone for sin by doing justice and undergoing trials, and to walk with everyone in the measure of the truth and the regulation of the time. (1QS 8.2–4)[198]

'It seems likely', argued Bertil Gärtner, 'that the [Qumran] community regarded itself as that Servant of the Lord who was to carry out the work of the Lord for the salvation of the "land."'[199] I submit that the *Community Rule* provides a very close analogue for Jesus and the early church, who could employ temple language for themselves even while maintaining a complex and contested relationship with the Jerusalem temple, all the while reworking traditions pertaining to Israel's restoration.[200]

It should be added that belief in the temple's destruction and a forecast of its replacement with a new temple go hand in hand as well. The Enochic *Book of Dreams and Visions* includes an oracle about the

---

198 Cf. 4Q174 1.6–7: 'And he commanded to build for himself a temple of man, to offer him in it, before him, the works of thanksgiving.'

199 Gärtner 1965: 124–125.

200 Paul refers to believers and the church as 'the temple of the living God' (2 Cor. 6:16) and 'God's temple' (1 Cor. 3:16–17; 6:19). Stephen had the saying attributed to him that 'Jesus of Nazareth will destroy this place' (Acts 6:14), even while the early Christians spent time in the temple (Acts 2:46; 3:3; 5:21, 42); in addition, the Lukan Paul had a messianic vision in the temple (Acts 22:17) and even engaged in rites of purification (Acts 21:26). See discussion in Perrin 2010: 46–79.

temple's demolition and replacement with a new temple as part of a vision for the reconstitution of Israel:

> All the pillars and all the columns were pulled out; and the ornaments of that house were packed and taken out together with them and abandoned in a certain place in the south of the land. I went on seeing until the Lord of the sheep brought about a new house, greater and loftier than the first one, and set it up in the first location which had been covered up – all its pillars were new, the columns new; and the ornaments new as well as greater than those of the first, (that is) the old (house) which was gone. All the sheep were within it.
> (*1 Enoch* 90.28–29)

It is passages like these which allow us to make sense of the notoriously strange logion attributed to Jesus in multiple places and with multiple variations about destroying the temple and building a new one:[201]

> We heard him say, 'I will destroy this temple that is made with hands, and in three days I will build another, not made with hands.'
> (Mark 14:58/Matt. 26:61)

> [W]e have heard him say that this Jesus of Nazareth will destroy this place and will change the customs that Moses handed on to us.
> (Acts 6:14)

> Jesus answered them, 'Destroy this temple, and in three days I will raise it up.' The Jews then said, 'This temple has been under

---

201 Cf. Allison (1998: 100): 'When the tradition struggles this much with a saying one is prodded to infer that it goes back to something Jesus said.' Van Henten (2015: 8) objects on the grounds that '[t]here is no evidence in Jewish passages that a messianic or prophetic figure would destroy the Temple at the end of times . . . and the depiction that Jesus would do that, as implied in Mark 14:58 . . . is a radical novelty from the perspective of Jewish traditions'. He is wrong on both counts. First, Dan. 9:26 refers to an anointed ruler (good or bad) who destroys 'the city and sanctuary' and who puts 'an end to sacrifice and offering'. Second, the Hebrew Scriptures are replete with promises of God's judgment on the temple, and while the agents are usually people like Nebuchadnezzar, it is possible that a Judean king could destroy the temple in order to build another one.

construction for forty-six years, and will you raise it up in three days?' But he was speaking of the temple of his body.
(John 2:19–21)

Jesus said, 'I shall destroy this house, and no one will be able to build it.'
(*Gos. Thom.* 71)

The gist of this logion is that Jesus contrasted the terrestrial and human temple with a coming heavenly, God-fashioned new temple that would appear in the future. The Herodian temple was ripe for judgment, with Jesus himself standing in judgment over it, symbolized by his temple action. Jesus thus predicted the temple's destruction, threatened to be the one who opened the doors of eschatological fire against it, and intended to see or be part of its replacement.[202] This shocking statement was enigmatic enough to be open to a Christological reapplication by John to Jesus' own body, reiterated by Stephen in the Jerusalem church, and even found useful for the Thomasine renunciation of Jewish rituals.

Pulling the threads together, Jesus shared in the tradition of prophetic denunciation of the temple; he predicted the temple's destruction, symbolized its destruction by his commotion in the temple precincts, and looked ahead to a new temple that he and his followers either symbolized or were somehow anticipating, even if that meant that they did not have to completely and utterly disavow everything to do with the temple in the meantime. A new temple fits with Jesus' prophetic paradigm of a new exodus, a new Passover, a new covenant, a new family of faith and a new messianic agent of deliverance for Israel. The people of this renewed Israel, formed around Jesus and bound to his way of being God's people, would be the eschatological representatives of the new temple until the earth was returned to its Edenic quality as a living temple of God.[203] Nicholas Perrin is thus on to something with his thesis: 'I wish to argue

---

[202] Cf. Sanders 1985: 71–73; 1993: 261–272; van Henten 2015.
[203] Perrin (2010: 33) writes: 'As ancient Judaism envisaged it, this renewed creation would break into earthly reality through the temple. More exactly, where the new temple stood there was new creation – and vice versa.' Cf. Gärtner 1965: 27–28; Beale and Kim 2021, ch. 6.

that Jesus of Nazareth saw himself and his movement as nothing less than the decisive embodiment of Yahweh's eschatological temple.'[204]

Courting controversy with sayings and stories

Jesus' final week in Jerusalem involved more than prophesying the temple's destruction. It featured encounters with key groups within Judea. In such combative clashes, Jesus uttered several sayings indicative of his prophetic and messianic vocation, rehearsed his negative disposition towards leaders and reiterated his ambitions for Israel. While the Markan chronology is probably artificial, there is nothing implausible about the debates, disputes and discourses that Jesus engaged in, as they are what one might expect for a popular teacher of growing notoriety.

Marriage and resurrection

At one point, some Sadducees asked Jesus about the possibility/absurdity of marriage in the post-resurrection state, giving the example of a woman who had been married to several brothers who each had died successively one after the other. Therefore, they sneer, to which brother would she be married in the age of resurrection, since she had been married to all of them at one time?[205] This question was much like an atheist asking a theologian, 'Can an omnipotent God make a rock so heavy that not even he can lift it?' or an Arminian asking a Calvinist, 'If God has elected some to salvation and some to perdition, then what is the point of evangelism?' The topic of resurrection was a point of serious debate and sectarian distinction between Pharisees and Sadducees, one that Paul exploited when finding himself standing before the Jerusalem Sanhedrin.[206] At the same time, it showcases something of Jesus' own eschatology.

Resurrection was important because, at one level, it was a metaphor for the reconstitution of Israel, seen in Hosea's exhortation for Israel to

---

204 Perrin 2010: 12.
205 Mark 12:18–26.
206 Acts 26:6–10.

repent and rise up from Yahweh's punishment (Hos. 6), Ezekiel's vision of a valley filled with dry bones that are brought back to life from the death and dust of exile (Ezek. 37), and Isaiah's prophecy that Israel's dead shall rise from the pit of death and despair (Isa. 26). Later, resurrection was a hope for the vindication of those who remained faithful to Yahweh and to Torah in times of apostasy and geopolitical upheaval. Daniel wrote that the wise or righteous would rise from the dead to shine like stars in an everlasting life (Dan. 12). A similar confidence was embodied by the Maccabean martyrs who proclaimed their own resurrection in the face of torture and death, trusting that God would undo whatever the idolatrous tyrant did to them (2 Macc. 7).[207]

Jesus replies, first, that the Sadducees have an inadequate view of the post-resurrection state. People in the coming age – Luke calls them 'sons and daughters of the resurrection'[208] – will have a bodily existence. Yet this post-mortem existence is not a continuation of ordinary earthly life, as people will be 'like the angels in heaven' where their bodies are asexual, and there will be no need for procreation and thus no need for marriage. So their objection is moot. Second, Jesus did not appeal to the testimony of the prophets – writings which the Sadducees rejected – but to the witness of the Pentateuch, the summit of the Mosaic tradition which Sadducees recognized. He did that by way of a quotation of Exodus 3:6: 'I am . . . the God of Abraham, the God of Isaac, and the God of Jacob.' It is not a matter of verb tenses, which are not there in the original Hebrew. The point is that when God spoke to Moses, he spoke not as the God who *was* the God of the dead and buried patriarchs, but as the God who was and still is the God of Abraham, Isaac and Jacob. 'The argument is better understood', said Dick France, 'as a reflection on the character of the covenant God whom Moses encountered, a God who through his new name "I AM" is revealed as the living God, the ever-present helper and deliverer of his people.'[209] In other words, the nature of God's covenant love for his people is such that even death cannot break that covenant bond.

---

207 On resurrection in the Hebrew Bible and Jewish literature, see Wright 2003: 85–206.
208 Luke 20:36 (MFB trans.).
209 France 2002: 471.

Jesus thus throws his flag on the Pharisaic side of the debate and affirms a particular political eschatology that envisaged resurrection as a reward for the righteous – moves that anticipate how he envisaged his own death and subsequent vindication.

The greatest commandment

The Jewish legal tradition is premised on the notion that laws frequently come into conflict with one another and the solution requires identifying which laws are weightier than others. A good example is whether one should help an animal who has fallen into a ditch on the sabbath;[210] or the difficulties of assigning inheritance from a father who passed away leaving multiple offspring from deceased wives. The growing body of Jewish tradition from Pharisaic *halakhah*, to oral law, to Mishnah, and to Talmud, was concerned with such things: which laws count the most and what to do in cases where laws bump against one another. It is not surprising that many teachers often stated what they thought was the essence or centre of gravity in the Torah so as to guide moral and legal reasoning in solving such legal disputes.

On one occasion, during Jesus' time in Jerusalem, he was asked by a scribe to state what he thought was the most important commandment.[211] Jesus answered by way of an affirmation of Israel's covenantal command to worship and love the one God,[212] yet added a second commandment: the command to love one's neighbour as oneself.[213] Jesus had spoken similarly before in the 'golden rule' about treating others as one would have them treat oneself.[214] Many Jewish teachers had uttered things along near-identical lines about the pre-eminence of love in the Jewish law,[215] though Jesus was the first as far as we know to combine Deuteronomy 6:4–5 with Leviticus 19:18.[216] The legal logic behind Jesus' words, as Schnabel suggests, is as follows:

---

210 Cf. Luke 13:14–16; 14:1–6.
211 Mark 12:28–31.
212 Deut. 6:4–5.
213 Lev. 19:18.
214 Matt. 7:12/Luke 6:31; cf. *Gos. Thom.* 25.
215 *Jub.* 20.2; *T. Dan.* 5.3; Philo, *Spec. Leg.* 2.63; *b. Shab.* 31a.
216 Cf. Luke 10:25–27 where the combining of Deut. 6:4 and Lev. 19:18 is done by a scribe, creating a legal judgment that Jesus affirms.

The commandment to love God and to love one's neighbor is the reality from which all the other commandments derive and on the basis of which they can be understood. A person who loves God will love God's law, and a person who loves the neighbor will keep the commandments.[217]

The scribe agreed with Jesus, concurring with his judgment that God is one and that Israelites are to love both God and their neighbour, and adding a comment that such a triage of laws is 'more important than all burnt offerings and sacrifices'.[218] Jesus had a more expansive definition of the 'neighbour' one was called to love, extending it to Samaritans, an idea which not all Galileans and Judeans would have been delighted with.[219] In any case, Jesus' midrashic commentary demonstrates two things: first, Jesus could interface positively with scribal tradition; and second, Christianity is at its most Jewish when it confesses God's oneness and the imperative to love one's neighbour: a tradition rehearsed by both Paul and James when it comes to God's oneness,[220] and in the *Didache* and Polycarp in terms of uniting the two commandments.[221]

Paying taxes to Caesar

When tax-collectors claimed that the temple of Amphiaraus was liable to pay taxation because the prophet Amphiaraus had been a man and was not an immortal deity, a senatorial delegation was sent to Boeotia to investigate the matter; if Amphiaraus was in fact a god, he was exempt from taxation on the grounds that the Romans serve the gods – they do not tax them.[222] Alas, the debate about religion and tax-exempt status is as old as the Roman Republic! However, while the pericope in Mark 12:13–17 on the surface looks like a question about paying taxes to Caesar – 'Is it right to pay taxes to Caesar or not?' – the objective is not

---

[217] Schnabel 2018: 183.
[218] Mark 12:32–33.
[219] Luke 10:29–36.
[220] Love of the one God (Rom. 3:30; 1 Cor. 8:4; Gal. 3:20; Jas 2:19) and love of neighbour (Rom. 13:9–10; Gal. 5:14; Jas 2:8).
[221] *Did.* 1.2; Pol. *Phil.* 3.3.
[222] Cicero, *Nat. Deo.* 3.49.

Jesus' last days in Jerusalem

a dispute about taxation and religion; rather, it is a trap.[223] The question is not posed as if the Herodians and Pharisees are genuinely interested in Jesus' thoughts about whether faithful Jews should pay taxes to the emperor – the emperor was going to get his taxes whether freely offered or by coercion. The question is instead an attempt to force Jesus into endorsing either sedition against Rome or acquiescence to Roman power, both of which had dire consequences.[224]

How does the trap work? Josephus reports that during the uprising of Judas the Galilean, zealous Galileans had a motto, 'No king but God', and since paying taxes to Caesar meant recognizing him as king, paying taxes to Caesar was viewed as a mixture of both blasphemy and betrayal of the nation.[225] So when Jesus is asked about paying taxes to Caesar, he's put in a catch-22 situation. If he says, 'Sure, pay them', then Jesus would look as if he has freely submitted to Roman oppression. But if he says, 'No, don't pay taxes', then the Herodians could have Jesus arrested on charges of sedition for forbidding the payment of taxes, which was an offence – precisely the claim they fabricated against Jesus at his trial.[226]

What is interesting is how Jesus splits the horns of the dilemma. Jesus doesn't try to bluff his way through an answer by offering an indecipherable verbiage of pros and cons while affirming nothing.[227] Instead, he requests a coin, a denarius, and asks, 'Whose image and inscription are on it?' Various coins were minted in Judea, always without imperial images, usually with floral designs. It was Pontius Pilate who minted coins depicting pagan cultic utensils in his provocative but veiled attempt to insult Jewish religious scruples.[228] The denarius that Jesus requested was probably a Tiberian tribute penny which had on one side an 'image' of Tiberius's bust with an inscription that read, 'Son of the Divine Augustus', then on the obverse side it said, 'High Priest', accompanied by a depiction of Tiberius's mother Livia posing as the goddess Roma. The rub is that if Caesar is 'divine', and if this is his image, then

---

223 Cf. *Gos. Thom.* 100; P. Egert. 2.
224 This section restates the point of Wright and Bird 2019: 51–53.
225 Josephus, *Ant.* 18.23; *War* 2.118; 7.410.
226 See Luke 23:2.
227 Proof that Jesus was not an Anglican bishop!
228 Kindler 1973: 37–38, 94–103.

it is a violation of the second commandment about making images of deity.[229] Jesus is implying that paying taxes to Caesar is less of a problem than carrying his godless graven money, something the Herodians did as mediators of Roman power. By rendering to Caesar what is Caesar's, Jesus is not saying the same thing that Paul says in Romans 13:6–7 about the rightness of paying taxes and tribute to imperial authorities. Rather, Jesus is telling the Herodians to give the blasphemous emperor back his blasphemous money.[230]

Yet there is perhaps even more going here, a hidden transcript of resistance, a double entendre that throws not only money but also insults back into the face of Caesar. Jesus declares that Caesar should receive the taxes he deserves, because Caesar should get *all* that he deserves. There might even be a not-so-subtle echo of the Maccabean mantra, 'Pay back the Gentiles in full', which meant violent retribution.[231] Thus, far from acquiescing to the view that Jews should pay taxes, or from throwing his lot in with the seditious wing of Judaism, Jesus avoids the trap by turning his interlocutors into impious collaborators and stating his hope that Caesar gets everything he deserves.

By what authority?

One striking thing that people recognized about Jesus was his overwhelming sense of authority, a mixture of charisma, power and popularity.[232] Jesus' authority was not priestly (derived from the temple), nor scribal (derived from study and knowledge of the Torah), nor sectarian (validated by a group consensus among like-minded people such as the Essenes or Pharisees), nor militaristic (established by military prowess earned in battle), but largely prophetic (provocative speech and mighty deeds that earned a popular following) and claims to have been authorized by God and not by any human institution (divine calling and empowerment). Precisely because he operated outside the official avenues

---

229 See Exod. 20:4; Deut. 5:8.
230 Theissen 1987: 126.
231 1 Macc. 2:68.
232 Mark 1:22, 27; 2:10; 3:15; 11:28–33; Jesus amplifies his claims to authority in the Johannine tradition: John 3:35; 5:27; 7:17–18; 10:18; 12:49; 17:2.

of religious authority, he was liable to be called demon-possessed,[233] a magician,[234] a blasphemer,[235] a deceiver,[236] a law-breaker[237] and a royal pretender.[238]

It was during his fateful visit to Jerusalem that leading priests and scribes confronted Jesus on the subject of his authority, that is, his authorization to perform his prophetic and provocative deeds and discourses without the sponsorship of the normal channels of religious authority.[239] Jesus' response – indicative of many rabbis – was to answer with a counter-question: 'John's baptism, was it from heaven or from mere people?' he posed to them. The conundrum was that the Baptist too was someone outside the normal bounds of authority, yet he had been beloved and believed by the people as a prophet who came to an unjust and needlessly gruesome end. If the Jewish religious leaders answer 'From heaven' (i.e. from God), they are confronted with the problem of not following John's teaching. But if they reply that the Baptist was a deceiver, they will earn the ire of the people. The interlocutors chose to retreat, accepting the shame of being bested in the encounter rather than falling into the trap.

What is revealing is that even Jesus' opponents recognize his 'authority', his ability to operate in ways they could not control, that God was somehow with him, even if they failed to understand why. Also, Jesus located his authority in the same tradition as that of the Baptist, popular prophecy, which meant he was at risk of suffering the same fate as John – even more so if Jesus, in distinction to John, was willing to interweave messianic motifs into his ministry.

Is the Messiah a son of David?

Given the messianic resonance of Jesus' triumphal entry and temple action, it is entirely unsurprising that Judean authorities would suspect

---

233 Mark 3:22; Matt. 12:28/Luke 11:20; John 7:20; 8:48–49, 52; 10:20–21.
234 *b. Sanh.* 43a; 107b; Justin, *Dial.* 69.7; *Ps.-Clem. Recogn.* 1.58; *Acts of Pilate* 1–3; Origen, *C. Cels.* 1.71.
235 Mark 2:6; 14:64; John 10:33; *Acts of Pilate* 2–3.
236 Matt. 27:63; Luke 23:2, 5; Justin, *Dial.* 69.7; *b. Sanh.* 43a.
237 Mark 2:24–26; Luke 13:14; 14:1–6; John 5:16–18; *Acts of Pilate* 1; cf. Acts 6:11, 14; 18:13; 20:21; Josephus, *Ant.* 20.200. See Bird 2008b.
238 Mark 15:2–3, 26, 32; Luke 23:2; John 18:37; 19:19–21; cf. Acts 17:7–8.
239 Mark 11:27–33.

his royal ambitions and seek to apprehend him, as in the case of any would-be pretender to the Judean throne. Jesus, seeking to get ahead of the narrative as it were, taunted the scribes by posing a question to the crowds about the lineage of the Messiah. While teaching in the temple, he asked his followers, observers and passersby:

> 'How can the scribes say that the Messiah is the son of David? David himself, by the Holy Spirit, declared,
>
> > "The Lord said to my Lord,
> > 'Sit at my right hand,
> >   until I put your enemies under your feet.'"
>
> 'David himself calls him Lord; so how can he be his son?' And the large crowd was listening to him with delight.
> (Mark 12:35–37)[240]

Bruce Chilton notes: 'The authenticity of our passage seems as open a question as its meaning.'[241] Is this an example of later Christian apologetic exegesis of the OT, in particular of Psalm 110:1, which was the John 3:16 of Christian apologetics and proclamation? Is Mark's Jesus teaching that the Messiah is not from David's line or is it the case that Jesus himself thought in fact that the Messiah is not a Davidide? Paula Fredriksen speaks for many when she writes: 'Mark's Jesus seems to refute as unnecessary the Davidic pedigree of the Messiah. This passage subtly asserts Jesus' messianic status despite his not being David's "son." Mark's Jesus cites David himself to make his case.'[242]

On the question of historicity, I find it unlikely that the early church would invent a saying that left Jesus' Davidic lineage or Davidic status in doubt when it figured so prominently in early tradition.[243] Bock is probably correct:

---

240 See discussion in Bird 2009: 130–132.
241 Chilton 1982: 92.
242 Fredriksen 1999: 141.
243 Cf. Rom. 1:3–4; Matt. 1:1; Acts 15:16; Rev. 5:5; 22:16.

[I]t is far more likely that [the quotation of] Ps 110:1 goes back to a period when the issues surrounding Jesus' identity were surfacing than to roots in a community that was openly confessing him in the midst of dispute [over his messiahship].[244]

On the meaning of the saying, there is no escaping the genuinely enigmatic nature of the utterance. This could be a polite debate among religious leaders about who the Messiah will be. Will he be a Davidide?[245] While it is possible to read this passage as Fredriksen does, as rejecting the view that the Messiah must be a Davidide, that seems unlikely to me. As Schweitzer observed: 'Far from rejecting the Davidic Sonship in this saying, Jesus, on the contrary, presupposes His possession of it.'[246] It is Jesus' messianic actions that lead him to play with the scribes in this ambiguous, albeit suggestive, aphorism. More likely, what we have here is a redefinition of what Davidic sonship means. The point is that although the Messiah might be a Son of David, he is more than an earthly descendant of David.[247] Jesus identifies the coming Davidic Messiah with a tradition of the Messiah's exalted status and priestly role in the coming age of deliverance. The quotation of Psalm 110 underscores both the priestly function of the Messiah (given the reference to the Davidide as 'a priest for ever according to the order of Melchizedek' in 110:4) and the status of the Messiah as throne-sharer or divine vice-regent (given the bestowal of the title 'Lord' and the honorary position described in 'Sit at my right hand' in 110:1). Indeed, both themes, priestly Messiah and exalted Messiah, were current in Second Temple Judaism.[248]

Such a claim, even if obliquely made, was pertinent to a debate with the priestly class over who spoke for God and what type of messiah God would send to Israel. The fact that shortly after saying this Jesus was denounced to Pilate and then crucified as a messianic claimant is further

---

244 Bock 1998: 222.
245 Cf. 'If the Messiah-King comes from among the living, his name will be David. If he comes from among the dead, it will be King David himself' (*y. Ber.* 2.3).
246 Schweitzer 1945 [1906]: 393.
247 Wright 1996: 509–510.
248 See Bird 2022: 318–341.

proof that the issue of Jesus' messianic identity was in the air prior to his death.[249]

Parable of the tenants

The parable of the tenants[250] is the apogee of Jesus' conflict with the priestly elite, who were also the landowning aristocracy and were often resented by peasant or commercial farmers who worked their fields, farms and vineyards and were required to give the absentee landlord up to or over 50 per cent of the harvest. However, in this instance, Jesus reverses the story so that Yahweh is the landowner, Israel or maybe Jerusalem is the vineyard, and the high priests are the tenant farmers who murder the landlord's envoys and even his son, and so deserve the violent reprisal of the landlord. The climactic ending with its quote from Psalm 118:22–23, though often thought to be secondary, is a fitting conclusion because it uses scriptural rhetoric to portray Jesus as the murdered son / rejected stone, and his murder is the reason for divine judgment against the landowning priestly ruling class. Jesus thus takes up scriptural language for Yahweh's vineyard from Isaiah and reapplies the imagery in an antagonistic and adversarial way against the priestly elites. Jesus is willing to challenge members of the priestly ruling class, not out on the banks of the River Jordan, but in the very heart of Jerusalem, and call them out as wicked stewards of the people who dishonour the prophets and even murder the messianic envoy sent to them. Regardless of the reprisal he elicits from them, he chooses to depend on Yahweh for vindication.[251]

The parable of the tenants is typical of rabbinic parables, which focus on the relationship between God and Israel, and characteristic too of Jesus' parables with their polemical and provocative purposes. Further,

---

249 Dunn 2003: 635.
250 Mark 12:1–12/Matt. 21:33–46/Luke 20:9–19/*Gos. Thom.* 65–66. Kloppenborg (2006: 350–353) thinks the Thomasine version more primitive because it lacks the Isaianic allegory and Deuteronomistic allusions found in Mark 12:5, 9, 11 which he regards as secondary. In addition, he claims that the Thomasine version belongs to 'the earliest Jesus movement and perhaps to the discourse of the historical Jesus, where it serves to put into question important values of Jewish Palestine' (352) because it rejects land-based wealth, inheritance, status and retaliatory violence. Mark, by portraying the landowner as the victim with rights of revenge over his tenants, is more conducive to 'a post-Constantinian world, where ownership, inheritance, status and sanctioned violence were part of the normal order of things', is even akin to 'Restorationist Britain or colonial India' and also underwrites 'élite-leaning ideology' (48).
251 Keener 2009: 287.

the reworking of scriptural language is indicative of Jesus' style of teaching; in this case, he reworks Isaiah's song of the vineyard,[252] where the vineyard is either Israel or Jerusalem,[253] which is ripe for judgment because of its injustices and bloodshed. Also, the 'others' to whom the vineyard is given represent, not the church, let alone the Gentiles, but more probably the nucleus of the restored Israel that Jesus is building around himself: his disciples, supporters and wider followers. This discredits the idea that the parable is an allegory invented by the later Gentile church to the effect that God has rejected the Jews for rejecting his divine Son.[254] Importantly, Jesus' usage of Isaiah 5:1–7 resonates closely with the *Targum of Isaiah* which also glosses the Hebrew text to lodge a protest against the temple establishment.[255]

Several things are worth noting:

1 The tenants reject various 'slaves', that is, the prophets, the most recent example being John the Baptist, who alarmed the priests and earned the deadly reprisal of Herod Antipas for his denunciation of Herod's marriage to his sister-in-law.
2 The tenants refuse to provide the appropriate quantity and quality of fruit to the master, which may either indicate an economic squandering or perhaps be a general critique of their poor stewardship as leaders of Israel. The tenants' intent to steal the inheritance of the son indicts them for their rapacity but implies too a usurpation of something that belongs to Yahweh.
3 The master sends, finally and climactically, 'a beloved son', and here it is hard not to hear echoes of 2 Samuel 7:13–16 (a Davidic descendant presented as Yahweh's own son), plus Psalm 2:7 (an anointed king presented as Yahweh's son) and Isaiah 42:1 (a servant in whom Yahweh delights) in the background. The language 'emphasizes the son's unique and intimate relationship to the owner of the

---

252 Isa. 5:1–7.
253 On Israel as a 'vineyard', see Moor 1998.
254 Even the Matthean gloss ('Therefore I tell you, the kingdom of God will be taken away from you and given to a people that produces its fruits' [Matt. 21:43]) need not imply a Gentile church that replaces the Jews, because Matthew's narrative world is very much that of intra-sectarian conflict between Jews and Jewish Christ-followers.
255 Evans 2001b: 226.

vineyard'.²⁵⁶ The parable, if authentic, showcases Jesus' sense not only of standing in line with the prophets, but also of his filial identity as a divine 'son' (Heb. *ben*) and a rejected 'stone' (Heb. *eben*).²⁵⁷ Such words activate a cluster of messianic themes in the light of associations of Davidic kingship with divine sonship²⁵⁸ and the stone that shatters pagan kingdoms.²⁵⁹

4 There is also a passion prediction, as the son is seized, killed and expelled from the vineyard, intimating once more the violent fate that Jesus expects at the behest of the priestly leaders.

Anointing in Bethany

The story of the woman who anoints Jesus in Bethany is found in all four Gospels, albeit in difference shapes.²⁶⁰ According to Mark and Matthew, the woman is anonymous, and the incident happens two days before Passover in the house of Simon the Leper, while in John, the anointer is Mary, the sister of Lazarus, and it happens six days before Passover. Then, for Luke, the episode takes place much earlier in Galilee and is performed by a woman known for her sexual impropriety in the house of a Pharisee named Simon. The sober fact is that the tradition here has become mangled, misremembered or perhaps maladjusted by some of the evangelists. Even so, Kathleen Corley argues for the authenticity of the kernel of this story on the grounds that: (1) it coheres with the tradition of Jesus' eating and drinking with 'tax collectors and sinners';²⁶¹ (2) Jesus' approval of the woman's actions is consistent with his sympathetic attitude towards women and outcasts found elsewhere in the tradition; and (3) the very presence of a woman at the meal could suggest impropriety or sexual innuendo, which custodians of the tradition would be unlikely to invent.²⁶² I would add that there is no reason for the primitive church to invent the story. Jesus does not have to be 'anointed' in order

---

256 de Jonge 1998: 118–119.
257 Cf. Wright 1996: 497–501; Evans 2001b: 228–229.
258 See 2 Sam. 7:13–16; Pss 2:7; 89:27–28; 4Q246 1.9 – 2.1.
259 Cf. Isa. 8:13–15; 28:16; Ps. 118:22–23; Dan. 2:34–35, 45.
260 Mark 14:3–9; Matt. 26:6–13; Luke 7:36–50; John 12:1–8; Ignatius, *Eph.* 17.2.
261 Mark 2:15–16; Matt. 11:19/Luke 7:34; Luke 15:1.
262 Corley 2003. Vermes (2003: 300–301) thinks Luke's account the most original.

to be *the* anointed one. In Jewish expectations, messianic claimants who appear on the scene do not have to be anointed; they simply appear as anointed persons.[263]

Most likely, Jesus was anointed by a woman in Bethany, probably an anonymous person, in an act intended to be prophetic, even if it was slightly provocative.[264] Her furtive faith in Jesus' messianic identity, as well as the exuberant display of devotion to him evident in her use of ridiculously expensive perfume, perhaps triggered Judas to betray Jesus to the authorities. Her action led to scolding words against her; words which Jesus denounced. Overall, the episode proves to be part of a consistent picture of a messianic mélange that makes up Jesus' final week. We have Jesus' dramatic entry into Jerusalem, his demonstration in the temple, his prophecy against the temple, and questions about a messiah, sources of authority, and taxes. Then Jesus tells a jarring parable about certain vineyard-owners who slay the master's 'son', and now he's informally 'anointed'. All of this presents a consistent pattern of symbolic messianic actions and intentions that confirmed to his followers his messianic status.

Final (Passover) meal

That Jesus had a final meal with his disciples before his crucifixion is accepted commonly enough. As to *when* it happened, *what* Jesus said and *what* it meant, well, that's where the consensus breaks down.

The date of the last supper

On chronology, Mark, Matthew and Luke make explicit that the final meal Jesus had with the twelve disciples and a wider body of followers was a Passover meal, after the Passover lambs were sacrificed, on 14 Nisan, AD 30.[265] In support of a Passover setting for the meal, we can

---

263 Becker 1998: 192.
264 Schüssler Fiorenza 2003: 240–242.
265 Mark 14:12; Matt. 26:17; Luke 22:8. On the Passover as it was conducted, see Josephus, *War* 6.423; Philo, *Spec. Leg.* 2.145–175; McKnight 2005: 244–248. In favour of synoptic chronology so that the last supper was eaten during Passover, see Jeremias 1966 [1960]: 41–62; Sanders 1993: 285–286; Keener 2009: 297–299, 372–374; Casey 2010: 429–437; Marshall 2010: 541–551; Hengel and Schwemer 2019 [2007]: 587–589; Pitre 2015: 372–373

note that the meal was eaten in Jerusalem,[266] at night,[267] as Jewish tradition stipulated. In addition, the conduct of the meal, including reclining at the table, drinking wine, eating bread and singing a hymn, is also indicative of a Passover celebration. Paul's liturgical representation of the Lord's Supper with a recitation of words and a blessing has points of contact with the Jewish Passover liturgy.[268]

In contrast, John narrates how the meal took place before the Passover, so that Jesus himself died on the afternoon of 14 Nisan.[269] In support of this chronology, no lamb is mentioned in the synoptic or Johannine account. Also, gathering the Sanhedrin during the Passover celebration would be like assembling the US Supreme Court on Christmas night.[270] Jewish sources (albeit late) claim that Jesus died on the eve of Passover.[271] If so, then what John describes was a communal meal, not a Passover celebration. A common meal perhaps analogous to the meals among the Yahad at Qumran, which also had bread and wine as a foretaste of the messianic banquet;[272] or like the banquets of the Therapeutae, which included a reading of Scripture, a homily and singing.[273] In addition, however convenient it would have been for John's Christology and atonement theology to have Jesus die on the eve of Passover, he never actually makes any point of it; perhaps the congruity did not even occur to him.[274] Many scholars support the Johannine chronology.[275]

(who thinks the Passover was a more elastic time than commentators realize). Bond (2013a: 471) makes a good point that the 14/15 Nisan debate might be moot in the memory of Jesus' death: 'To talk of a death "at Passover" in the first century, just as now, did not necessarily mean that a person had died on Nisan 15, any more than for a Christian to talk of the death of a loved one "at Christmas" means that he or she died on 25 December.' Bornkamm (1960 [1956]: 160) was prepared to 'to accept any date shortly before the beginning of the festival'.

266 The Passover had to be eaten in Jerusalem: Deut. 16:2; *m. Pesah.* 7.9.
267 The Passover had to be eaten at night: Exod. 12:8; *Jub.* 49.12; *m. Zeb.* 5.8.
268 1 Cor. 5:6; 10:16–17; 11:23–26.
269 John 18:28; cf. 19:14, 31, 42. Also, *Gos. Pet.* 5.
270 Levine 2006b: 208; Meier 1991–2016: 1:396.
271 *b. Sanh.* 43a: 'It was taught: On the day before the Passover they hanged Jesus.' Cited from Van Voorst 2000: 114.
272 1QSa 2.17–23.
273 Philo, *Vit. Cont.* 69–87.
274 Pitre 2015: 325.
275 Cf. e.g. Meier 1991–2016: 1:395–401; Becker 1998: 340; Theissen and Merz 1998 [1996]: 426–427; Fredriksen 1999: 223; Blomberg 2001: 246–258; Klawans 2001; Dunn 2003: 772–773; Vermes 2003: 307; McKnight 2005: 272; Schnabel 2018: 144–147, 202–205.

The standard solution is to follow the synoptic chronology and to suggest that John has tinkered with the tradition to make a theological point, namely, Jesus is the Lamb of God who takes away the sin of the world, as proved by the occurrence of his death at the exact moment when the Passover lambs were being sacrificed.[276] Of course, it is not so simple. For it is possible that either Mark or Paul have 'paschalized' the tradition about Jesus' final meal with his disciples and that John is restoring the meal to its proper chronology.[277] Alternatively, there is the persistent minority view that Jesus adhered to a calendrical reckoning that departed from that of the temple establishment, which explains the disparity.[278] Another possibility, one I think more likely, is that Jesus held a Passover meal prematurely, deliberately so, because he knew he would not live long enough to see Passover.[279] I find it interesting that the Lukan version of the meal, which many regard as feasibly the most 'original' version of the sayings, implies that Jesus was longing to eat the Passover but would not make it that far.

The words of institution

As for the 'words of institution' for the Lord's Supper or Eucharist, these are among the most memorable and most important according to the Christian tradition (see Table 8.1).[280] Poignant as these words are, according to Barry Smith '[t]he words of institution have never been a strong candidate for authenticity'.[281] I am more sanguine because we

---

[276] Cf. 'Here is the Lamb of God who takes away the sin of the world!' (John 1:28) and 'For our paschal lamb, Christ, has been sacrificed' (1 Cor. 5:7). See similar language in Justin, *Dial.* 40; Melito of Sardis, *Paschal Homily*. For the Johannine final meal as theologically driven, see Sanders 1993: 286; Gnilka 1997 [1993]: 280; Keener 2009: 373.

[277] Cf. Bornkamm 1960 [1956]: 161–162; Klawans 2001; Evans 2001b: 370–372; Vermes 2003: 307; McKnight 2005: 271–272. Perrin (2013b: 492) notes that 'Mark's historical interest in the event does not mean that his presentation remained untouched by his consciousness of contemporary eucharistic practice'. I'm unconvinced that early (Jewish) Christians associated Christ's death with Passover in order to compel (Jewish) Christians not to celebrate Passover on the grounds that Jesus 'is' the Passover lamb. That might fly with Ignatius of Antioch, but the Quartodecimans continued the tradition of celebrating Easter on the date of the Jewish Passover using the lunar calendar.

[278] Cf. Humphreys 2011.

[279] Meier 1991–2016: 1:399; Bockmuehl 1994: 92–93; Wright 1996: 555–556; McKnight 2005: 272–273; Pitre 2005: 441–442; Marshall 2010: 551.

[280] Cf. Theissen and Merz 1998 [1996]: 414–423 for a synopsis and commentary; also Gräbe 2006: 68–70.

[281] B. Smith 2008: 68.

Table 8.1 The words of institution in the New Testament

1 Cor. 11:23-26
For I received from the Lord what I also handed on to you, that the Lord Jesus on the night when he was betrayed took a loaf of bread, and when he had given thanks, he broke it and said, 'This is my body that is for you. Do this in remembrance of me.' In the same way he took the cup also, after supper, saying, 'This cup is the new covenant in my blood. Do this, as often as you drink it, in remembrance of me.' For as often as you eat this bread and drink the cup, you proclaim the Lord's death until he comes.

Luke 22:14-20
When the hour came, he took his place at the table, and the apostles with him. He said to them, 'I have eagerly desired to eat this Passover with you before I suffer, for I tell you, I will not eat it until it is fulfilled in the kingdom of God.' Then he took a cup, and after giving thanks he said, 'Take this and divide it among yourselves, for I tell you that from now on I will not drink of the fruit of the vine until the kingdom of God comes.' Then he took a loaf of bread, and when he had given thanks he broke it and gave it to them, saying, 'This is my body, which is given for you. Do this in remembrance of me.' And he did the same with the cup after supper, saying, 'This cup that is poured out for you is the new covenant in my blood.'

Mark 14:22-25
While they were eating, he took a loaf of bread, and after blessing it he broke it, gave it to them, and said, 'Take; this is my body.' Then he took a cup, and after giving thanks he gave it to them, and all of them drank from it. He said to them, 'This is my blood of the covenant, which is poured out for many. Truly I tell you, I will never again drink of the fruit of the vine until that day when I drink it new in the kingdom of God.'

Matthew 26:26-29
While they were eating, Jesus took a loaf of bread, and after blessing it he broke it, gave it to the disciples, and said, 'Take, eat; this is my body.' Then he took a cup, and after giving thanks he gave it to them, saying, 'Drink from it, all of you, for this is my blood of the covenant, which is poured out for many for the forgiveness of sins. I tell you, I will never again drink of this fruit of the vine until that day when I drink it new with you in my Father's kingdom.'

Key scriptural intertexts

Exod. 24:8 – 'Moses took the blood and dashed it on the people, and said, "Here is the blood of the covenant that the Lord has made with you in accordance with all these words."'

Isa. 53:11-12 – 'The righteous one, my servant, shall make many righteous, and he shall bear their iniquities. Therefore I will allot him a portion with the great, and he shall divide the spoil with the strong, because he poured out himself to death and was numbered with the transgressors, yet he bore the sin of many and made intercession for the transgressors.'

Zech. 9:11 – 'As for you also, because of the blood of my covenant with you, I will set your prisoners free from the waterless pit.'

have early Pauline attestation of the tradition about Jesus' final meal with his followers, and further evidence is attested in Syro-Palestinian Christianity in the *Didache*.[282] I am unpersuaded that Christians took up Hellenistic mystery cult meals and applied them to Jesus when the meal is saturated with Jewish traditions and imagery pertaining to Passover. In contrast, Hellenistic association meals with their patron deity were not sacramental; nor did they communicate mystical elements of the deity.[283] Instead, as Klawans puts it, 'the antiquity and multiple attestation of the Last Supper tradition can hardly be questioned'.[284]

Paul and Luke are clearly congruent, perhaps because Luke knew Paul or knew Paul's epistles (or both), and they agree that Jesus identified his death as inaugurating a 'new' covenant. Luke's version has a sequence of cup–bread–cup, which sets it apart, as well as a gloss where Jesus says that 'from now' he will not drink the fruit of the vine until the kingdom comes. Otherwise, Matthew correlates closely with Mark.

There is one curious textual issue we must broach and that is the Western non-interpolation in Luke 22:19b-20. The problem is Codex Bezae (D), a fifth-century majuscule diglot, which is normally longer in its readings, especially in Luke and Acts. Here, however, D has a shorter reading which omits verses 19b-20 ('This is my body . . . poured out for you'). The question remains why that is so, and what that means for the original Lukan wording. The strong external support for the longer reading of verses 17-20 (including P^{75}, the earliest copy of Luke) is seemingly countered by the tendency of critics to normally prefer the shorter reading and the observation that the passage 19b-20 employs non-Lukan language and was perhaps lifted out of 1 Corinthians 11:24b-25. What breaks the deadlock is that the shorter reading in D is followed only by a few Old Latin witnesses and is otherwise a minority

---

[282] *Did.* 9.1 - 10.5.

[283] Taylor 1952: 457; Pesch 1976-77: 2:364-377; Hengel 1981 [1980]: 28-32; Keener 2009: 296-297; Marshall 2010: 507-529. Contra Bultmann (1963 [1921]: 265), who said: 'After the work of Eichhorn and Heitmueller I do not need to prove that a cult legend lies behind Mk. 14.22-25.' Even if Paul's version shows signs of Hellenistic cults, which I doubt, Pesch comments: 'The narrative embedded in the Marcan version proves to be consistently older, more original, linguistically and factually, compared to the aetiological cult narrative of Paul's version' (MFB trans.).

[284] Klawans 2002: 3. Cf. Fredriksen 1999: 117-119, 241-242, 252; Sanders 1985: 107; 1993: 263-264.

witness among Western manuscripts.[285] Brad Billings has convincingly argued that the omission was deliberate and served to safeguard a Christian community and its shared meal against misunderstanding from outsiders who may have regarded the verbal pronouncements over the elements of bread and wine in the light of anti-Christian polemics and rumours of cannibalism, consuming human blood and infanticide. Billings thus furnishes a reasonable sociological explanation for a seemingly strange textual phenomenon.[286]

The primary points to be noted are that Jesus, anticipating his arrest and execution, was remembered as interpreting his forthcoming death along several lines and calling for ritualized rehearsal of its meaning:

- Jesus identified the broken loaf of bread with the breaking of his body.
- Jesus' body was to be broken 'for' the disciples.
- Jesus identified the wine with the shedding of his blood.
- The blood shed was the blood of the (new [Luke/Paul]) covenant.
- The blood would be poured out for 'you' (Luke/Paul) or 'many' (Mark/Matt.) for the 'forgiveness of sins' (Matt.).
- The meal was an anticipation of the messianic banquet.
- The ritual of sharing bread and wine should be repeated by his followers as a memorial/remembrance of him.

The meaning of the meal

The real challenge is not so much to determine whether Jesus said these words, but what these words meant. Unfortunately, it is difficult for people in the Christian tradition to disengage their own debates and liturgies of eucharistic theology from discussion of these words in the context of Jewish traditions and practices. As I write this, I can hear in my head Luther saying, '"Is" means "Is"!' Or John Calvin announcing against mere memorialists that 'no presence means no point!' Hard as it is, we must move ourselves out of the seminar room called

---

285 Cf. Metzger and Omanson 2006 [1971]: 147–148.
286 Billings 2006a; 2006b.

'Eucharistic Theologies from Aquinas to Zwingli' and corral ourselves into the seminar room called 'Jewish Restoration Eschatology, Food and Festivals'. We must situate Jesus' words here in relation to his prophetic mantle, messianic matrix, kingdom message and Judean festival traditions. Such a framework will give us a better chance of landing on a historically plausible and preferable hypothesis for what Jesus intended this meal to symbolize and achieve.

To eliminate one proposal, I do not think that Jesus intended this meal to replace the temple cultus.[287] Jesus had criticized the temple for several reasons and warned that it would be destroyed by divine judgment. But there is nothing to suggest that Jesus was instituting a ritual meal for the purpose of replacing the temple, and for three reasons: (1) Jesus most likely arrived in Jerusalem several days before Passover with other pilgrims to purify himself and to participate in the daily worship and rituals, as it is narrated in John's Gospel: 'Now the Passover of the Jews was near, and many went up from the country to Jerusalem before the Passover to purify themselves' (John 11:55);[288] (2) Jesus does not mention here the destruction of the temple, and the meal is to be repeated irrespective of whether the temple is standing or not; and (3) according to the book of Acts,[289] Jesus' followers continued to participate in the temple cultus in some ways, not least in the case of Paul paying for the Nazirite vow for some of his fellow Jewish Christians. The incongruity of participating in both a messianic memorial meal and the Jerusalem cultus, while rendered moot by the events of AD 70, did not appear to have occurred to anybody in the Jerusalem church.

So what was Jesus conveying through the words spoken over the bread and wine? To begin with, I think the elements were intended to be a prophetic sign[290] of Jesus' death, and symbolized its salvific meaning as

---

287 Contra Neusner 1989; Crossan 1991: 357–358; Chilton 1992: 150–154; 1994a: 46–74; 1996: 124; 2000: 250–254; Wright 1996: 557–558; Tan 1997: 218–219; Theissen and Merz 1998 [1996]: 433–436; Holmén 2001: 319–323. Better is Klawans 2002. McKnight (2005: 327–328) wisely puts it: 'That the last supper had implications for temple ritual is within a typical mapping of Israel; that it replaces the temple system draws lines right off the map.'

288 Jesus' view was probably that whereas the temple was corrupted and contemptible, ripe for judgment, it was not redundant.

289 Acts 2:46–47; 3:1; 5:42; 21:27–29. So too Bockmuehl 1994: 75, 201–202 n. 50; Klawans 2002: 9–10; Dunn 2003: 796.

290 Wenham 1995: 14–15; Hooker 1997: 48; Klawans 2002: 7.

providing atonement and inaugurating a new covenant, with a dividend of divine forgiveness. 'Jesus symbolically acted out', says David Wenham, 'what he was about to do on the cross before his gathered disciples. And he did not just act it out before them: he involved them personally, in a terribly vivid way.'[291]

The Passover context is of paramount importance. Whether it took place in the week of Passover or on the eve of Passover, Jesus' final meal deliberately included elements of the Passover ritual and its story of redemption. The Passover was a festival of recollection, celebration, and hope for a new day of salvation. The Passover rehearsed the story of the first exodus, even as it reminded those who partook of the meal that God had promised them a new one, not just 'for them' long ago, but 'for us' here and now. If so, if a new sacrificial lamb was needed, if an expiation had to be made for many, then a new covenant would be brokered, with people prepared to leave in haste to be set free from bondage, and a new song of Moses would be sung.

Jesus appears to have regarded his body as destined to be broken, putting the meal and its commentary in a coherent association with various other 'passion predictions' indicating that Jesus knew he was to suffer a martyr's death or a prophet's fate. The Passover bread, unleavened as it was, was the 'bread of affliction',[292] an affliction, perhaps *the* affliction, that Jesus believed he was destined to enter.

Similarly, Jesus' blood was to be 'poured out', much in the same way that the Suffering Servant's life was 'poured out for many' as one who carried and carried away the transgressions of Israel.[293] Although verbal connections are admittedly thin, this does bring to mind various Jewish sacrificial traditions that are focused on events and persons outside the Jerusalem temple cultus. The Qumran community depicted the community abiding in cultic purity and resolute righteousness in order 'to make atonement for' the sins of 'Israel' in the 'land', for

> the guilt of transgression and the rebellion of sin . . . by working justice and suffering affliction . . . by becoming an acceptable

---

291 Wenham 1995: 14.
292 Deut. 16:3.
293 Isa. 53:11–12.

sacrifice for the land through the flesh of burnt offerings, the fat of sacrificial portions, and prayer, becoming – as it were – justice itself, a sweet savour of righteousness and blameless behaviour, a pleasing free will offering.[294]

Similarly, in Hellenistic Jewish tradition the Maccabean martyrs could make atonement for others: 'Make my blood their purification, and take my life in exchange for theirs.'[295] By way of analogy, Jesus identified his life as an offering, a ransom, perhaps an atonement of some kind. If so, this is arguably the root of the church's later atonement theologies, where Jesus died 'for' his followers, for Israel and for the whole world.[296] Sanders notes that '[t]he Christian interpretation of Jesus' death as atoning was so immediate and so thorough that one could argue that even here Jesus prepared his followers [for the meaning of his death]'.[297] Jesus becomes, then, a redemptive representative whose death 'expiates' (i.e. removes) the iniquities of the people.[298] This is buttressed by the Passover context in which the Passover lamb was sacrificed in remembrance of the first Passover where the lamb had died in the stead of the firstborn sons of Israel.[299] Thus, Jesus saw himself as the eschatological Passover lamb whose death would bring about expiation for eschatological Israel.[300]

Finally, the meal was celebrating the advent of the new covenant achieved by Jesus' death. True, Jeremiah 31:31, with its hope for a new covenant, does not mention blood or sacrifice, but a covenant was 'cut' between parties by the killing of a sacrificial animal, and this blood of the covenant symbolized the agreement between the two parties. The juxtaposition of 'blood' with 'covenant' alludes rather concretely to the sacrificial aspect of the covenant ceremony of Exodus 24.[301] In such a

---

[294] 1QS 5.6; 8.3–10; 9.4–5.
[295] 4 Macc. 6.27–29.
[296] Cf. Hengel 1981 [1980]): 65.
[297] Sanders 1985: 324.
[298] Pesch 1976–77: 2:362; Fredriksen 1999: 117.
[299] Exod. 12:14: 'This day shall be a day of remembrance for you. You shall celebrate it as a festival to the Lord; throughout your generations you shall observe it as a perpetual ordinance.'
[300] B. Smith 2008: 67.
[301] Klawans 2002: 15.

covenant, the blood symbolized that Israel was bound to Yahweh for obedience (Exod. 24:3–8), and it stained the people with the promise that Yahweh would be the deliverer of the people on the basis of the covenant (Zech. 9:11). Jesus, according to Smith, was declaring: 'The red wine in this cup represents the blood that I will shed in my death in order that the new covenant be established.'[302]

Furthermore, kingdom and covenant are correlative concepts; one implies the other:[303] one is admitted into the kingdom of a king by entering into covenant with him. The promise of a new, or perhaps renewed, covenant was very much a theme of the exilic prophets with respect to the advent of Yahweh's reign.[304] This meal Jesus had with his disciples was rehearsing the exodus story by acclaiming that a new exodus was under way, a new lamb was to be slaughtered, the blood of a new covenant would be poured out for many for the forgiveness of sins, and this would be the instrument, through Jesus himself, by which God's kingly power was revealed.[305]

If the problem of the Lord's Supper is *the* problem of the historical Jesus, as Albert Schweitzer famously said, then it is equally true that solving that problem is a key part of the puzzle of who Jesus was and what his aims and intentions were.[306] Jesus was, in his mind, an anointed one; he symbolized his martyrdom by elements of bread and wine, set in the narrative of Passover and hopes for a new exodus and a new covenant where God's kingly power would renew Israel and redeem those who remained faithful to him.

A destiny in death

The arrest and execution of Jesus was not an accident that Jesus failed to foresee. Jesus believed that he was destined to die in Jerusalem; indeed, it was part of his messianic vocation to do so, to take the curse of Israel's

---

302 B. Smith 2008: 67.
303 Cf. Taylor 1952: 456; Gnilka 1997 [1993]: 287; Gräbe 2006: 97–100; Marshall 2010: 563–564; contra McKnight 2005: 341–342.
304 Jer. 31:31–34; Hos. 2:14–23; cf. CD 6.19; 8.21; 22.12.
305 Cf. Wright 1996: 557.
306 Cf. Hengel (1981 [1980]: 72), who said that Jesus' interpretation of his death as an atoning sacrifice in the context of his kingdom proclamation is 'the ultimate mystery of Jesus' career'.

exile upon himself, so that a restoration, a renewal, a resurrection would take place. He entered Jerusalem among pilgrims, as a prophet, but more than a prophet, as a jubilant Son of David, with messiahship and martyrdom tangled together. His action in the temple was not the tantrum of a peasant who felt he had been ripped off by the prices required to purchase a sacrifice. His prophecy against the temple had nothing to do with antipathy towards rituals and sacrifices, but forecast woe upon the self-aggrandizing and self-enriching Judean leaders who had not turned this temple into the house of glory that it was meant to be. Jesus' time in Jerusalem was not spent plotting revolution, but courting controversy over taxes, the temple, commandments and resurrection, and presaging the judgment of the ruling class. His final meal was a festive metaphor for what his death would achieve: atonement, a new covenant, forgiveness and a new exodus. Jesus came to Jerusalem to die for Israel's redemption and the world's renewal. Wright put it elegantly:

> He would turn the other cheek; he would go the second mile; he would take up the cross. He would be the light of the world, the salt of the earth. He would be Israel for the sake of the world. He would be the means of the kingdom's coming, both in that he would embody in himself the renewed Israel and in that he would defeat evil once and for all. But the way in which he would defeat evil would be the way consistent with the deeply subversive nature of his own kingdom-announcement. He would defeat evil by letting it do its worst to him. Jesus' Jewish context supplied him, as we shall see presently, with several spheres of meaning in which such a line of thought, and of action, would make sense, albeit startling sense.[307]

In crucifixion, Jesus believed he would be the Servant stricken for the iniquities of many, a Shepherd struck down to save the flock, the righteous one of the Psalms who falls into the hands of the wicked. His death would be, in fact, the kingdom of God in power.

---

307 Wright 1996: 564-565.

9
The death and resurrection of Jesus

The death of the Messiah

That Jesus was crucified under Pontius Pilate is perhaps the indisputable fact about him.[1] For Bultmann, Jesus' death was the only historical kernel that he needed for his existential theology to have any root in the history of Jesus. The rest of the Gospels, for all it mattered to Bultmann, was kerygma encased in myth waiting for his demythologizing project to translate the fantasy and fiction of the evangelists into something digestible for modern sensibilities. Indeed, from pre-Pauline traditions,[2] to Paul's own preaching,[3] to the canonical Gospels as extended passion narratives, to the later Passion Gospels such as the *Gospel of Peter* and *Acts of Pilate*, to Melito of Sardis's *Paschal Homily*, the cross of Jesus loomed large in the memory, liturgy, proclamation, story, symbols, apologetics, worship and identity of the first Christian generations. Christians of many varieties were devoted to a crucified man despite the disgust of their critics, both Jewish and pagan. Added to that, Jesus' crucifixion was an event attested by non-Christian sources as well.[4]

The consensus of even the most suspicious critics is that Jesus was executed by crucifixion, probably in the year AD 30 on 7 April.[5] Jesus

---

1 Cf. Sanders 1985: 11; 1993: 11; Evans 1998a: 23–24; Barnett 2009: 265; Bock 2010b: 845–847; Webb 2010: 671–691; Hengel and Schwemer 2019 [2007]: 603. Dunn (2003: 775) comments: 'That Jesus was crucified on the direct authority of Pilate himself need not be doubted for a minute.'
2 1 Cor. 11:23–26; 15:3–5; Rom. 4:25; 1 Thess. 4:14; 2 Cor. 5:14–15.
3 Gal. 3:1; 1 Cor. 1:18–2:5; Rom. 3:21–31.
4 Josephus, *Ant.* 18.63; Tacitus, *Ann.* 15.44.
5 Bond (2013a) argues that we cannot be precise beyond a date between AD 29 and 34. Those in favour of the AD 30 date include Meier 1991–2016: 1:402; Sanders 1993: 54, 282–290; Theissen and Merz 1998 [1996]: 160; Dunn 2003: 312.

was executed, at the instruction of the prefect Pontius Pilate,[6] beside two brigands in the most gruesome, grotesque and ghastly manner of execution that the Romans knew of. Jesus died, perhaps as the evangelists narrate, with a great cry of accomplishment (John), in the despair of God-forsakenness (Mark and Matthew), with a committal of his life to his heavenly Father (Luke),[7] or else with a whisper of misery as the final gasp of air was expelled from his lungs, as was the case for so many other Judeans subjected to such a slow and torturous death. Yet the crucible of Jesus would not mark his end but rather the beginning of the story of arguably the most influential person in human history. What we must do now is pursue the precise details around his death and explore what that meant for Jesus' aims and for his mission to restore Israel.[8]

Arrest

After the supper, Jesus and his disciples left the city, probably by one of the gates in the south wall, and walked across the Kidron Valley until they reached Gethsemane at the foot of the Mount of Olives. Jesus often retreated to Bethany in the evenings,[9] but he also had a custom, Luke says, of going to this garden.[10] It was a place of prayer and rest, on this occasion with particular acuteness, as the evangelists depict Jesus experiencing a moment of vexation and agony.[11] Jesus is here at his most prophetic and most human, wrestling with his – as he understood it – appointed destiny, yet with apprehension, despair, even doubt. The Jesus of *Jesus Christ Superstar*'s powerful ballad 'Gethsemane', which

---

6 Although Philo (*Leg. Gai.* 299), Josephus (*War* 2.169) and Tacitus (*Ann.* 15.44) refer to Pilate as a 'procurator', an inscription found in Caesarea Maritima in 1961 describes Pilate explicitly as a *praefectus*.

7 Mark 15:27/Matt. 27:50/Luke 23:46/John 19:30.

8 Crossan (1991: 372 [with Bultmann 1963 [1921]: 280–291; Bornkamm 1960 [1956]: 156–157]) treats much of the passion narratives as the historicization of prophecy, i.e. scriptural texts that provided the inspiration to invent the passion story, such as the lots cast for Jesus' garments (John 19:24 drawn from Ps. 22:18). More likely, the scriptural texts drawn from Pss 22, 31 and 69, were hastily compiled to prove that Jesus' death was according to Scripture. It reminds me of the time a church decided to divide into three congregations rather than fully split and someone then recalled the verse from Eccl. 4:12 that '[a] threefold cord is not quickly broken' to show that it was 'biblical'. For a critique of Crossan, see Evans 1996b; Goodacre 2006; Dunn 2003: 777–781.

9 Mark 11:11–12; 14:3; John 19:29.

10 Luke 22:39.

11 Mark 14:33/Matt. 26:37/Luke 22:44.

depicts Jesus wrestling over whether his sense of messiahship is perhaps a form of madness, whether his death matters, whether he is about to be thrown into the cogs of a divine machine that has no regard for him, is probably closer to the history than the pious imaginations of Jesus as having a brief martyr's moment before steeling himself to embrace his destiny with resolve and exercising his courageous, active obedience. If Jesus' distress was real, then we do better to imagine him wondering if he really is the Son of God or maybe just another raving religious fanatic, and why his heavenly Father requires him, indeed would allow him, to suffer this terrible ordeal that is about to come upon him.

Judas, whose motives and memory continue to fascinate, tipped off the priestly authorities that Jesus would be in the Garden of Gethsemane located at the foot of the Mount of Olives, not far from the temple. Led by Judas, Jesus was ambushed by an arresting squad comprised of temple guards as well as servants and retainers of the chief priests and Jerusalem aristocracy.[12] Jesus was betrayed by an infamous kiss of greeting from Judas, whereupon a group of armed men seized Jesus. While a few of his disciples, such as Peter, apparently scuffled with the arresting party, the majority of his followers fled into the night, as Jesus seems to have predicted. It was from there, under the cover of darkness, that Jesus was taken to the quarters of Caiaphas, the high priest, for questioning and a hearing on whether to hand him over to the Romans.

Josephus recounts that Jesus' death was orchestrated by the 'leading men among us', meaning the ruling priestly elites.[13] The impetus to arrest Jesus was aristocratic anxiety about his prophetic protest in the temple, his apocalyptic announcements about the kingdom which excited the crowds, and insulting tirades wrapped in metaphor and messianic authority against the chief priests.[14] Their fears were perhaps spurred by a belief that Jesus would do something dramatic on the day of the festival. All that, combined with the combustible atmosphere of Passover, when

---

12 The evangelists differ on the make-up of the arresting squad, whether it was a 'crowd' from the chief priests and elders (Mark 14:43/Matt. 26:47), chief priests, temple guards and elders (Luke 22:52), or a 'cohort' of 'servants/retainers' of the chief priests and Pharisees (John 18:3, MFB trans.).

13 Josephus, *Ant.* 18.64.

14 Sanders (1985: 295) is right: 'A man who spoke of a kingdom, spoke against the temple, and had a following was one marked for execution.'

'sedition is most apt to break out',[15] led the priests to send the members of their security apparatus to have Jesus arrested with a view to handing him over to the Roman prefect to be expediently dispensed of, and thus mitigate further risks of an even greater disturbance.

The priestly interest in Jesus' destruction was due to a mixture of sectarian suspicion, a security threat during a major festival, and slights publicly made against them. The priests were accountable to the prefect of Judea[16] and the legate of Syria, who both acted on behalf of the emperor. The high priest's job description had several items: (1) preserve the peace; (2) keep revenues flowing; (3) preserve the peace; (4) promote Rome's economic and geopolitical interests; (5) preserve the peace; (6) support lines of communications between the Mediterranean and Mesopotamia; and did I mention (7) preserve the peace.

There is, then, a ring of truth to the reasoning that the fourth evangelist puts on the lips of Caiaphas for the priests' machinations towards Jesus, namely that it was 'better . . . to have one man die for the people than to have the whole nation destroyed' (John 11:50). The phrase 'for the people' is obviously a double entendre, dripping with Johannine irony, yet it conveys a salient point: the chief priests were pugnaciously pragmatic when it came to maintaining the peace, because their positions of power depended entirely upon it.

Of course, keeping the peace was not easy: there was always a delicate balancing act. Some incidents called for a demonstration of violence suitable enough to subdue any agitators and deter further unrest, but not too much violence to the point where it inspired an uprising or an embassy sent to Rome. Pilate and Caiaphas would eventually learn the lesson together that with angry crowds sometimes you needed less stick and more carrot. Sometime around AD 36, after Pilate's massacre of a group of Samaritans who followed a prophet to Mount Gerizim, a Samaritan delegation complained to Vitellius, the Syrian legate, who sent

---

15 Josephus, *War* 1.88.

16 The Roman prefects kept the high-priestly vestments in the Antonian fortress and handed them over annually, most likely after a bribe was paid to the prefect (see Josephus, *Ant.* 18.90, 95; 20.12).

Pilate to Rome for trial and stripped Caiaphas of his priesthood.[17] On that day, too many died to avert the destruction of the nation.

Trials

The arraignment of Jesus before the Sanhedrin and the trial before Pilate have obvious historical doubts about them.[18] It is not as if we have a transcript of the proceedings as we do for Cicero's prosecution of Verres (70 BC) or for the Scillitan Martyrs in Roman Carthage (AD 180). What is more, the evangelists' kerygmatic ethos and apologetic aims become most acute when assigning blame to the high priests and Jerusalemites while portraying Jesus as an innocent martyr who undergoes an unjust yet divinely determined and atoning death. The hearing in the high priest's house where the Sanhedrin was assembled was not a public affair, and even the trial before Pilate was probably expedited with a view to execution rather than a thorough and transparent judicial enquiry into a capital offence. Some scepticism at the veracity of the trial narratives is understandable.

However, because of the popularity of Jesus, the notoriety of Pilate and the abruptness with which the events transpired, news of the proceedings, rumours, hearsay, and snippets from eyewitnesses would have been circulating almost immediately. In addition, Jesus had sympathizers in the higher echelons of Judean society such as Joseph of Arimathea and 'another disciple' who, John says, gained access to the high priest's courtyard (probably because he was a priest himself!).[19] Such persons were privy to the trial and may have conveyed the gist of the event, narrated the key moments and remembered the definitive statements. The hearing before the Sanhedrin was a closed-door session but involved a large number of people, and many were waiting outside to hear the verdict. Likewise, the trial before Pilate was held before a crowd; it was public, albeit turbulent and loud. Attention should be given to Andrade's point that parallels exist between the Markan version and Josephus's reports of legal proceedings undertaken by the chief priests in

---

17 Josephus, *Ant.* 18.85–89.
18 Cf. Sanders 1985: 298, contrasted with Bock 2003 and Webb 2010. An even-handed account of the issues is canvassed in Theissen and Merz 1998 [1996]: 440–473.
19 Mark 15:43; Luke 23:51; John 18:15; 19:38.

the 50s–60s, which means that Mark's account, the earliest one, probably reflects practices that occurred in Jerusalem during Jesus' lifetime.[20] Critical suspicions about the trial narrative cannot be overwhelmingly refuted, but they can be partly assuaged.

The interrogation, hearing and trial – whatever we call them – were the necessary conditions for any authority to proceed in the crucifixion of Jesus near Passover. Jesus was not found fleeing a city under siege, seized by Roman legionaries and then crucified beside hundreds of others. Jesus was a prophet, a public figure, who had a relatively wide base of support, even as he courted controversy, and instigated opposition among the official and unofficial leaders of Galilee and Judea. His trial also tells us something of his career, aims and intentions, as well as its reception by the Judean and Roman authorities. Theissen and Merz, I think, capture well the significance of Jesus' trial:

> The death of Jesus is the consequence of the tensions between a charismatic coming from the country and an urban elite, between a Jewish renewal movement and alien Roman rule, between someone who proclaimed cosmic change which was also to transform the temple and the representatives of the *status quo*. Religious and political grounds cannot be separated . . . Both groups [Judean and Roman authorities] were his opponents, but they pursued different interests. The Sanhedrin took offence at his prophecy against the temple; his criticism of the temple shattered the legitimacy of their privileges. The Roman prefect must have been mistrustful of the 'kingdom' of which Jesus spoke. He must have seen it as a danger to his power. Therefore Jesus was mocked before the Sanhedrin as a 'prophet' (Mark 14.65) and before the Romans as a 'king' (Mark 15.16–18). However, both groups had the same interest in avoiding unrest. Both worked together in the proceedings against Jesus.[21]

---

20 See Barnett 2024; Andrade 2025.
21 Theissen and Merz 1998 [1996]: 466–467.

Hearing before the Sanhedrin

When brought to the high priest's residence adjacent to the temple, Jesus was initially received by Caiaphas's father-in-law Annas,[22] himself a former high priest (AD 6–15). Annas was the 'éminence grise of Jerusalem politics',[23] a reliable hand to triage what was a volatile situation. His task was to tell Jesus the accusation he was facing, or else to extract information for an accusation against him.

Whatever Annas gathered, Jesus was taken deeper into the rooms of the high priest's residence where Caiaphas waited to preside over a meeting of the Sanhedrin, chief priests and scribal scholars. Jewish law, later codified in the Mishnah, did not permit a capital charge to be heard on the eve of the sabbath or a festival.[24] The gathering was not, then, a formal trial but a hearing about whether to hand Jesus over to the prefect for a capital trial and, if so, to establish the precise charge.[25] Mark is clear that the council was already set on a capital charge and was attempting to gather the appropriate evidence to justify a charge and hand Jesus over to the prefect.[26] That might not have been the intention of everyone on the council, but it was probably the intention of the chief priests.

Witnesses were then found who accused Jesus of threatening to destroy the temple and build another in its place.[27] The charge does have an air of truth to it: Jesus probably had said something to that effect, as we have seen. But the problem remained: what did it mean and was it a crime to look forward to a new eschatological temple? The scribes

---

22 John 18:13–14, 19–24.

23 Schnabel 2018: 232.

24 *m. Sanh.* 4.1, though obviously whether such procedures existed pre-AD 70 is disputed.

25 Bock (2010a: 602) states that 'this gathering was never seen or intended as a formal Jewish capital case but as a kind of preliminary hearing to determine if Jesus was as dangerous as the leadership sensed and whether he could be sent credibly for judgment by Rome', though he believes that 'the Jewish leadership's intended goal for Jesus was to present him to Pilate as Rome's representative who could execute him'. He admits, however, that such a hearing 'would still be a legal procedure, just not the ultimate one' (603). Schnabel (2018: 242) may have a point when he notes: 'It is a moot point whether Jesus' interrogation by the members of the Sanhedrin should be called an interrogation, an examination, or a legal trial – there is no evidence that such matters were defined, classified, and regulated in Roman law for the provinces in the first century AD.' Yet he wants to be particular in the end: 'There is little doubt that the Jewish authorities would have regarded the proceedings against Jesus as a trial.'

26 Mark 14:55.

27 Mark 14:58; 15:29; Matt. 26:61; John 2:19; *Gos. Thom.* 71; Acts 6:14.

could not agree on the offence, and Jesus' response to their litigation of one another's interpretation of his alleged words was silence.[28] It soon become apparent that this line of investigation – what did Jesus say about the temple, what did it mean, why was it a crime? – was not going to secure a convincing capital charge against Jesus that outsiders, such as the prefect, would see as grounds for execution.

Caiaphas accordingly took charge and confronted Jesus with a more direct line of questioning about his identity as a messianic claimant, namely whether he claimed to be 'the Son of the blessed one'.[29] To this Jesus answered with some hesitation in the affirmative, 'I am', but then provocatively announced that 'from now on' (Luke/Matt.) Caiaphas would 'see the Son of Man seated at the right hand of the power and coming with the clouds of heaven' (Mark) – a stunning retort that elicited an instant reaction from the chief priest, declaring it blasphemy.

The charge of blasphemy was not for pronouncing the divine name,[30] since Jesus' composite allusion to Psalm 110:1 and Daniel 7:13 meant that he was paraphrasing a sacred text, even if he failed to replace the divine name with a circumlocution.[31] More likely, the blasphemy was because Jesus claimed, via these two texts, that he was going to be co-enthroned with Yahweh in the tradition of an eschatological Davidic lord and Daniel's son of man. In effect, Jesus lays forth a claim to prerogatives associated with one who shares in the aegis of divine sovereignty, a cultic 'throne-sharer', a familiar position in antiquity but one that Jews forbade for humans.[32] Jesus will be victorious, vindicated, will sit in judgment of his accusers and, *from this moment*, shares in the regency of the Blessed One. For Philo, a man who claimed divine prerogatives had a manifest 'evil of an extraordinary nature' by daring to 'compare himself to the all blessed God'.[33] The Qumranites envisaged David sitting before God

---

28 Mark 14:59.
29 Mark 14:61–65/Matt. 26:63–68/Luke 22:66–71.
30 Contra Gundry 1993: 915–918; with Bock 2010a: 610–613 and Evans 1995: 412–413.
31 *m. Sanh.* 7.5 talks about uttering the divine name *and* cursing it in some form.
32 Cf. discussion in Bird 2022: 318–326; Wright 1996: 624–629; contrasted with Vermes (2003: 12), who believed that turning Jesus into an object of worship, or a god, 'would have filled this Galilean Hasid with stupefaction, anger, and deepest grief'.
33 Philo, *Somn.* 2.130–131.

on Israel's throne, not on God's throne,[34] while Rabbi Akiva got into trouble from his peers by suggesting that the plural 'thrones' in Daniel 7:9 suggested one throne for God and another for David.[35] The theology of the divine throne in many strands of Jewish thought was allergic to anything that sounded like full vice-regency. Further, Allison is right to ask why the first Christians did not associate Jesus' enthronement with his parousia rather than with the sequel to his resurrection. The Enochic Son of Man and the Targumic Son of David receive their throne at the end of time, not in the middle.[36] It appears that, as Allison claims, '[s]oon after Easter, some of his followers envisaged him as enthroned because, already before Easter, they had expected his enthronement'.[37]

Trial before Pontius Pilate

Jesus' trial before Pilate was perhaps unusual but probably not extraordinary as far as Pilate was concerned. The prefect was not running a 24/7 people's court, but emergency requests to act, desist, adjudicate, or hear petitions at short notice were normal. Pilate knew the lie of the land legally and militarily; he also knew the priests and their interests, and how to deal with the web of Judean affairs. What he definitely did not know was that he was about to preside over the greatest legal trial in human history. Nor did he know that in later commentary he would be defamed as a spineless speck of a man, or else turned into an innocent official who was duped by Jewish trickery and later became a penitent Christian. Pilate's name would be routinely recited by adherents of a new global religion in a statement that would mention only three people: Jesus, his mother Mary, and Pilate under whom Jesus 'suffered', as the Apostles' Creed states.[38] Pilate had condemned and executed many Judeans, but none of his decisions would echo down the corridors of history as much as the verdict he rendered that fateful morning.

---

34 4Q504 frag. II 4.6: 'You have established Your covenant with David, making him a princely shepherd over your people, that he sit before you upon the throne of Israel eternally.'
35 *b. Hag.* 14a; *b. Sanh.* 38b.
36 *1 Enoch* 51.3; *Tg. Isa.* on 16:5.
37 Allison 2010a: 249–250, agreeing with Hengel 1995: 217.
38 Cf. 1 Tim. 6:13; Josephus, *Ant.* 18.64; Ignatius, *Magn.* 11; *Trall.* 9.1; *Smyrn.* 1.2; Tacitus, *Ann.* 15.44.

The death and resurrection of Jesus

Caiaphas did not bring to Pilate a charge of blasphemy against Jesus. Confronted with such an accusation, Pilate would probably have responded as Gallio did when the Jews of Corinth accused Paul of promoting divine worship contrary to Jewish custom, which was to refuse to get involved at all.[39] Or else, Pilate might have retorted with Emperor Tiberius's very quotable aphorism, *Deorum injuriae diis curae*, 'Offences against the gods are the gods' concern.'[40] Instead, Caiaphas probably briefed Pilate that Jesus claimed to be the anointed king,[41] plus he was exciting the pilgrims with promises to reveal God's kingdom, forbade paying taxes to Caesar, and had deliberately disturbed the temple cultus and thus offended the local deity.[42] Such allegations the client priestly elite and the Roman governor could not ignore.[43]

Pilate's interrogation of Jesus, even after soliciting Herod Antipas's advice, was perhaps one of perplexity rather than clarity about what to do, as this man was not an obvious brigand in the same class as Barabbas, who was guilty of murder and insurrection.[44] If Jesus was a clear danger, he would have been arrested on sight by temple guards, not engaged in disputation about authority, taxes and resurrection (hence Jesus' incredulity at the high priest's gaggle of rent-a-thugs that fell upon him at his arrest).[45] Pilate probably thought Jesus was *relatively* harmless and intuited that the priestly antagonism towards Jesus was more sectarian than based on security concerns.[46] For Pilate, Jesus was perhaps a zealous religious enthusiast, or even a madman,[47] someone spouting 'ambiguous oracles' of Israel's deliverance.[48] But he was not a *direct* threat, as Jesus had not been found hiding in caves with other brigands, discovered stockpiling weapons on some Galilean estate, intercepted with letters to the Parthian shah detailing plans to seize Antioch,

---

39 Acts 18:12–17.
40 Tacitus, *Ann.* 1.73.
41 Mark 15:2/Matt. 27:11/Luke 23:2/John 18:33.
42 This is where Luke's version (23:3, 5) is either authentic or highly realistic!
43 Rightly too Horsley 2012: 156.
44 Mark 15:6–15.
45 Mark 14.48–58.
46 Cf. Mark 15:10, 'For he realized that it was out of jealousy that the chief priests had handed him over.'
47 Cf. Meggitt 2007.
48 Josephus, *War* 6.312–313.

seen urging pilgrims to storm the Antonian fortress, nor reported for conspiring with Herod Antipas and Caiaphas to launch an insurrection against the Roman garrison. This is precisely why Jesus' followers were not also rounded up shortly afterwards as one would expect for someone leading an uprising.[49]

Some will complain that Pilate's apparent sympathy towards Jesus is pure Christian invention. To be fair, the Gospel-writers go to extreme lengths to make Pilate positively evangelical about Jesus' innocence and declaim the travesty of justice that the chief priests are asking him to commit by executing Jesus. Yet Pilate's inclination was always to find leverage over the chief priests any way he could; the trial of Jesus of Nazareth was just one more opportunity in this tit-for-tat game that they played. We see this in several episodes where Pilate and the high priests squared up against each other (see Table 9.1).

Pilate, given his habit of routinely provoking the priestly leaders, whether inadvertently or deliberately,[50] may well have wanted to release Jesus as payback, as a reminder of who really wielded power in their sacred city, not least during Passover when the stakes were higher. Knowing that, it's quite possible that the priests surreptitiously used the crowd to apply pressure to Pilate. There is perhaps some kernel of truth to (planted) voices in the crowd announcing to Pilate, 'If you release this man, you are no friend of Caesar. Everyone who claims to be a king sets himself against Caesar.'[51] The priests knew what Pilate knew on that topic: these are not words that one wants the Syrian legate in Antioch, the suspicious praetorian prefect Sejanus in Rome[52] or the paranoid emperor Tiberius on his island of Capri to hear! Added to that, Pilate

---

49 Rightly stressed by Fredriksen 1999: 9.

50 Pilate minted a variety of coins (Gosline 2001), usually with a benign image of grain or a wreath on the obverse side, then with a Roman religious symbol such as a *simpulum* (a spoon used in libations) or a *lituus* (a wand used in augury) on the reverse side. The pagan utensils could be viewed either as an innocuous way of propagating Roman images in a Jewish context, or perhaps as provocatively designed to see how much 'pagan' imagery Pilate could get away with (see discussion in Bond 1996). The coins circulated in Jewish and non-Jewish urban centres in Syro-Palestine and were minted for both audiences. To sensitive Jewish tastes, the coins were not as offensive as, say, a Tiberian tribute penny with its image of Tiberius Caesar and identification of him as son of the divine Augustus. Yet, as Webb (2010: 713) observes, the coins had association 'either with the Roman imperial cult or Roman political power'.

51 John 19:12.

52 Philo depicts the praetorian prefect Sejanus as plotting against the Jews in *Leg. Gai.* 159–161,

Table 9.1 Confrontations between Pontius Pilate and the chief priests of Judea

Date	Event
26	Soon after his arrival in Judea, Pilate had tried to bring Roman standards into Jerusalem with busts of the emperor on them, but was forced to back down after a mass protest.[1]
27–29	Pilate confiscated monies from the temple treasury to build an aqueduct and crushed the backlash.[2]
28–29	For reasons now lost to us, Pilate slaughtered Galilean pilgrims while they were offering sacrifices in the temple.[3]
31–32	Pilate overplayed his hand by placing Roman votive shields, albeit without images, in the Antonian fortress, which Philo says annoyed Tiberius as much as it did the Jerusalemites.[4]

1 Josephus, *Ant.* 18.55–59; *War* 2.169–174.
2 Josephus, *Ant.* 18.60–62; *War* 2.175–177.
3 Luke 13:1.
4 Philo, *Leg. Gai.* 299–306.

was always quick to draw the sword, as it was better to be tried by Caesar for hot-headedness than for dereliction of duty.[53] Pilate, despite possible misgivings or disinterest in the details, consented to the priests' request; he did so either because he took seriously the veiled threat to cast aspersions on his loyalty to the emperor, or perhaps simply due to the banal brutality of imperial administration. It was as if Pilate rolled his eyes and blurted out, 'So be it. Death it is. Scourge him, then take him away and crucify him, just like the others! What's next? Another slave found sleeping with his mistress? A shortage of figs in the market? Another Nabatean merchant claims he was ripped off by Antipas's nephew? The Dead Sea losing its saltiness? And where in Hades is my breakfast?'[54]

---

but it's impossible to say whether this is correct, or whether Philo is joining the *damnatio memoriae* of Sejanus after his execution for treason in AD 31.
53 Philo, *Leg. Gai.* 302; Josephus, *War* 2.175–177; *Ant.* 18.60–62; Luke 13:1–5.
54 Cf. similarly Webb (2010: 757), who believes that Pilate did not actually think Jesus was planning to lead Judea into independence from Rome; rather, as a realist, Pilate saw Jesus as a popular figure who was a potential threat to the civic peace and a potential cause of unrest.

Pilate, armed with the power of *imperium* and *ius gladii*,[55] granted the chief priest's request to execute Jesus, a commoner (*humilior*) and provincial (*peregrinus*), not merely because of the not-so-subtle threat to dob him in to the Syrian legate for letting a would-be king off the hook, but because Jesus was, despite his apparent innocuousness, genuinely capable of inspiring a direct threat. In the words of Nathanael Andrade, Jesus had 'a real potential to stimulate outbreaks of crowd violence that could get innocent pilgrims hurt or killed'.[56] Jesus had, after all, proclaimed God's coming kingdom, gathered large crowds, excited pilgrims with messianic rhetoric and offended the sanctity of the temple, and at Passover no less. Jesus might be innocent, but he was no less incendiary. It was thus prudence and expedience rather than jurisprudence which necessitated the execution of Jesus. Indeed, such was standard operating procedure for dealing with any prophetic mass movement, no matter how heavenly or benign their intentions had been.[57] Pilate handed Jesus over to be crucified, probably on the charge of *seditio* ('sedition'), to make a point, and to communicate it in the clearest and cruellest way possible.[58]

Pilate's mocking of Jesus as the so-called king and having him scourged are true to his form. Pilate had Jesus lashed so cruelly that the bones on his ribs, shoulder blades and spine were exposed by the laceration of his flesh, precisely as Albinus would do to Jesus ben Ananias some decades later.[59] When it came to law and order, the medium was the message.[60] Pilate determined that if Jesus was a messiah, whether by name or public acclaim, the Jerusalemites and the many pilgrims present in the city for

---

55 Tacitus (*Ann.* 12.60) observes that 'the emperor was heard to remark that judgments given by his procurators [and prefects we should imagine] ought to have as much validity as if the ruling had come from himself'. Josephus (*War* 2.117) says that the first prefect after Archelaus's dismissal, Coponius (AD 6–9), was given full powers, including 'the infliction of capital punishment'. This gives credence to John's account that the Jewish complaint to Pilate was: 'We are not permitted to put anyone to death' (John 18:31).

56 Andrade 2025.

57 Cf. Josephus, *Ant.* 20.97–98, 168–170; *War* 2.259–262; Acts 5:36; 21:38.

58 Cf. Andrade 2025.

59 Josephus, *War* 6.303–304. Cf. discussion of the parallels in Evans 1995: 359–361.

60 During several uprisings, various figures had not claimed to be the Messiah but certainly had attempted to claim royal authority and titles, including Judas ben Hezekiah (Josephus, *Ant.* 17.271–272; *War* 2.56), Simon (*Ant.* 17.272–274; *War* 2.57) and Athronges (*Ant.* 17.278–281; *War* 2.60–62). See discussion in Bird 2009: 47–51.

the festival would wake up that morning to find their so-called 'king' nailed to a cross.

Crucifixion

There is a late-second-century bloodstone, very small, only 2 cm x 3 cm (¾ in. x 1 in.), which is engraved with a depiction of Jesus on a T-shaped cross, with his body portrayed as naked and contorted, and his legs awkwardly nailed to opposite sides of the cross.[61] The stone was perhaps part of an amulet thought to possess healing properties or hold redemptive significance for its wearer. It is one of the earliest depictions of Jesus' execution and is far away from the sanitized and saintly depictions of Jesus crucified with a loincloth conveniently covering his genitals, in a painful yet sublime pose, somehow ready to receive the worship of the world.

We do better to imagine crucifixion as a grotesque symbol of the human capacity for cruelty, a method of execution developed by the Carthaginians and enthusiastically adopted by the Romans. Crucifixion was designed to make death an excruciating and drawn-out affair, a feat of horror, disgrace and writhing agony. To witness a crucifixion was truly haunting. As Wright says, it would leave the observer with

> memories of humans half alive and half dead, lingering on perhaps for days on end, covered in blood and flies, nibbled by rats, pecked at by crows, with weeping but helpless relatives still keeping watch, and with hostile or mocking crowds adding their insults to the terrible injuries.[62]

No wonder Cicero called crucifixion 'this cruellest and vilest penalty'[63] and Josephus the 'most pitiable of deaths'.[64] Crucifixion could be performed in various ways: with or without a crossbeam; a crossbeam placed differently, sometimes with a seat to prolong the death; with feet nailed together or spread apart; or with a stake impaled through the

---

61 Cf. Harley and Spier 2007; Kotansky 2017.
62 Wright 2016: 54.
63 Cicero, *Verr.* 2.5.165; Chapman 2010: 43–46.
64 Josephus, *War* 7.202–203.

anus or genitals.[65] What was common was the public placement of the execution: it was not merely a punishment; it was an instrument of state terror to remind the plebs of what happened to those who messed with political powers.[66] However, the evangelists do not dwell on the hideous horrors; Mark for instance simply writes 'and they crucified him', and the other evangelists write similarly.[67]

The *titulus*[68] hanging on the cross identifying Jesus as 'King of the Jews',[69] in Greek, Aramaic and Latin according to John,[70] is undoubtedly historical.[71] The *titulus* was a deliberate provocation to make a point – an insult to the idea of a Judean king beyond one appointed by Rome.[72] This confirms that a charge of sedition was the reason for Jesus' execution and confirms that Jesus was a messianic claimant, a would-be king.

The precise cause of death in crucifixion probably varied. It could include blood loss, dehydration and shock, as well as respiratory failure leading to asphyxiation, resulting in organ failure and cardiac arrest.[73] Maslen and Mitchell note that:

> There is insufficient evidence to safely state exactly how people did die from crucifixion in Roman times. It is quite likely that different individuals died from different physiological causes, and we would expect that the orientation in which they were crucified would be crucial in this respect.[74]

---

65 Seneca, *Dial.* 6.20.3.
66 Quintilian, *Decl.* 274.13.
67 Mark 15:24–27; cf. Luke 23:23; Matt. 27:35; John 19:18; *Gos. Pet.* 10.
68 The Greek *titlos* means 'inscription' and is a loanword of the Latin *titulus*.
69 Mark 15:26/Matt. 27:37/Luke 22:38/John 19:19/*Gos. Pet.* 11.
70 John 19:20.
71 Cf. Pesch 1976–77: 2:484; Harvey 1982: 13; Wright 1996: 486–489; Becker 1998: 353–354; Theissen and Merz 1998 [1996]: 458–459; Dunn 2003: 628; Bird 2009: 140–142; Webb 2010: 747–749.
72 Cf. Fredriksen 1999: 254; Cohick 2008: 127–131.
73 Cf. Habermas, Kopel and Shaw 2021.
74 Maslen and Mitchell 2006: 188.

Be that as it may, most clinicians believe 'that the combination of physical abuse Jesus experienced before and during the crucifixion contributed to his ultimate demise on the cross'.[75]

Jesus died condemned by the priestly aristocracy, betrayed by a friend, denied by a follower, abandoned by his disciples and crucified by a Roman prefect, just as Jesus had prophesied. Whatever his final words were, a lament from Psalm 22, or a whisper of pain and despair, Jesus of Nazareth breathed his last as a gaggle of soldiers sat around waiting for him to expire. A group of his women followers grieved over his lifeless corpse. For Caiaphas and the priests, it was a Passover disaster averted, with a blasphemous false prophet given his due for challenging God's anointed high priest and for profaning the holy temple with his offensive rantings. For Pilate, it was another dead Jew, one of hundreds executed for banditry, uprisings, sedition or being in the wrong place at the wrong time with the wrong people.

However, for Jesus, this was the climax of his messianic vocation, the cup of wrath he had to drink, the great ordeal that he and only he had to go through, the stripes he had to bear, the token of his love that he had laid down for many, the surety of his triumph in his apparent defeat. Jesus had staked his life on the coming of God as king in and through himself. Yet at the climax of his story, in the throes of his death, we see the *titulus* mocking him as another failed royal pretender. However, this crucifixion, what seemed to many to be a ruin and perhaps even a blight on God's faithfulness, would soon be transformed into a symbol of victory, triumph and love. In the course of a mere week, if not days, Jesus' crucifixion would be hailed as the proof of his kingship, the kingship of the crucified, the kingdom of God in power, and the coming of God as king to redeem his people and to renew the world.

Burial

Mark reports that Jesus was hastily buried by Joseph of Arimathea after he petitioned Pilate for the body, placing him in a nearby tomb among

---

75 Habermas, Kopel and Shaw 2021: 749.

his own family's holdings.⁷⁶ The authenticity of the burial story is established by several facts:

1. Its place in the earliest tradition is attested in Paul – Jesus 'the Messiah died ... and was buried'.⁷⁷
2. The Gospel burial story is primitive, full of Judean ambience as it references Jewish purity concerns and sabbath observance, and lacks signs of legendary embellishment.⁷⁸
3. The Torah stipulated that the corpse of an executed criminal must be taken down before nightfall because such a person is cursed by God and such a curse defiles the land, and such a practice is confirmed by the Qumran scrolls, Philo, Josephus and the Mishnah.⁷⁹ This is precisely why in the Gospel of John and the *Gospel of Peter* Jesus' body is quickly disposed of by burial, with respect to Deuteronomy 21:22–23 and the approaching sabbath and Passover.⁸⁰ To say that Jesus was executed, not by Jews, but by Romans who had no interest in respecting local customs, is simply not true.⁸¹ Romans did respect local customs, often releasing the body of criminals executed for capital crimes.⁸² The reason why the legs of the two brigands executed with Jesus were broken was to hasten their death, so they could be buried before sunset in accordance with Jewish custom.⁸³ Pilate would not have wanted to offend Jewish burial customs during Passover with hundreds of thousands of pilgrims in the vicinity.⁸⁴
4. We have examples from Philo and Josephus of victims of crucifixion being taken down at the behest of family and friends.⁸⁵ There is also material evidence for the burial of victims of crucifixion such as a man named Yehohanan whose bones were discovered in 1968 in

---

76 Mark 15:42–47/Matt. 27:57–61/Luke 23:50–56/John 19:38–42/*Gos. Pet.* 23–24.
77 1 Cor. 15.3–4 (MFB trans.); cf. Rom. 6.4; Col. 2.12.
78 Bultmann 1963 [1921]: 274; Bornkamm 1960 [1956]: 168.
79 Deut. 21:22–23; 11QT^a 64.9–12; Philo, *Spec. Leg.* 3.151–152; Josephus, *Ant.* 4.202, 264–265; *War* 4.317; *m. Sanh.* 6.5–6. See Chapman 2010: 117–149.
80 John 19:31; *Gos. Pet.* 5.
81 Contra Ehrman 2014: 157 and with Evans 2005b: 239–241; 2014: 73–75.
82 Evans 2014: 76–78, citing Josephus, *Apion* 2.73, 211; *War* 2.220.
83 John 19:32–33.
84 Chilton 2000: 270.
85 Philo, *Flacc.* 83–85 (on the eve of a festival!); Josephus, *Life* 420.

a family tomb at Givat ha-Mivtar in north-eastern Jerusalem with a nail still lodged in his heel.[86] In addition, it is also possible that the crucified and decapitated bones of the last Hasmonean king, Mattathias son of Judah (aka Antigonus), have also been excavated, again showing that victims of crucifixion could be buried.[87] This is not necessarily an exception that proves the rule because identifying victims of crucifixion is not altogether easy, especially if they had been tied to a cross rather than nailed. The account of Jesus' crucifixion and burial is beyond merely plausible as it accords with Jewish custom, legal permission and archaeological evidence.[88]

5 That Jesus was interred by Joseph of Arimathea is very *probable* since a Christian fictive account would be unlikely to depict a member of the Jewish Sanhedrin as undertaking this generous and gracious act for Jesus when the evangelists had a tendency to criticize and condemn the Judean leadership en masse for their part in orchestrating Jesus' death.[89]

An alternative to the burial story is that Jesus' body was left on the cross as carrion for scavengers and that any remains of his corpse were thrown in an unmarked grave.[90] Crossan notes:

> In normal circumstances the soldiers guarded the body until death and thereafter it was left for carrion crow, scavenger dog, or wild beasts to finish the brutal job. That non-burial consummated authority's dreadful warning to any observer and every passerby.[91]

If that is what happened, then the burial story was invented by the early church, prior to both Mark and Paul, in order to move Jesus' body from

---

86 Cf. Zias and Charlesworth 1992: 279–280; Chapman 2010: 86–89.
87 Evans 2014: 85–86.
88 Cf. Magness 2006; Cook 2011.
89 Cf. Acts 3:17; 13:26–29. See Allison 2005b: 352–362 on Joseph and the burial story, which is very persuasive.
90 Cf. e.g. Horace (*Ep.* 1.16.48): 'hanging on a cross to feed crows'; Juvenal (*Sat.* 14.77–78): 'The vulture hurries from dead cattle and dogs and crosses to bring some of the carrion to her offspring.' Also Josephus, *Ant.* 17.295; *War* 2.306–307; 5.450.
91 Crossan 1994: 153; cf. Crossan and Reed 2001: 289–290; Ehrman 2014: 157–164.

a criminal's grave to a more respectable tomb conveniently supplied by a Judean aristocrat. Yet a robust challenge to Crossan's argument comes from Bruce Chilton:

> A straightforward reading of the Gospels' portrait of the burial has been challenged by revisionist scholars, who theorize that Jesus died in a mass crucifixion: the body was thrown into a common, shallow trench, to become carrion for vultures and scavenging dogs. This makes for vivid drama but implausible history. Pilate, after all, had been forced in the face of Jewish opposition to withdraw his military shields from public view in the city when he first acceded to power. What likelihood was there, especially after Sejanus' death, that he would get away with flagrantly exposing the corpse of an executed Jew beyond the interval permitted by the Torah, and encouraging its mutilation by scavengers just outside Jerusalem? Revisionism can be productive. But it can also become more intent on explaining away traditional beliefs than on coming to grips with the evidence at hand, and I think this is a case in point.[92]

This goes to show that the hypothesis that Jesus' body *must* have been dumped into a mass grave with violent criminals and insurrectionists is disproved.[93]

Jesus was, then, buried, but what happened after that? Well, what is implied by Paul,[94] and narrated by the evangelists, is that on the Sunday morning after his crucifixion, several of Jesus' female disciples went to the tomb only to discover it empty and his body no longer there.[95] The ending of Mark's Gospel is abrupt and perplexing, with many textual problems abounding, as well as reports of angels, bewildered women and

---

[92] Chilton 2000: 270. Also good on this is Cook 2011.
[93] Charlesworth 1989: 123; Evans 2005b; Hengel and Schwemer 2019 [2007]: 655. Note Crossan and Reed (2001: 292, 298), who regard the Holy Sepulchre in Jerusalem as one of the few holy sites with credibility and who 'stipulate' bracketing out historical debates 'that Jesus was buried beneath what is now called the Church of the Holy Sepulcher'.
[94] In 1 Cor. 15:3-4, Paul says that the Messiah died, was buried and was then raised, which requires an empty tomb. See Hengel 2001; Wright 2003: 321 contra Bultmann 1952-55: 1:48: 'Accounts of the empty tomb, of which Paul still knows nothing, are legend.'
[95] Matt. 28:1-8/Mark 16:1-8/ Luke 24:1-10/John 20:1-2; *Gos. Pet.* 50-56.

The death and resurrection of Jesus

resurrection appearances to contend with also. Be that as it may, several reasons suggest that the tomb was indeed discovered without Jesus' body:

1 The whole tenor in Mark 16:1–8 appears rooted in early Judean tradition given the very Torah-obedient action of the women in waiting for the end of the sabbath; the fact that Jesus is called 'the Nazarene'; the way it reflects the Jewish custom of anointing dead bodies with spices and perfumes; and the presence in the pericopae of several words not found elsewhere in Mark (i.e. *diaginomai* [elapse]; *arōma* [spices]; *apokliō* [roll away]; *sphodra* [exceedingly]; and *tromos* [trembling]).[96]
2 What of Paul's failure to mention the empty tomb and any witnesses to it in 1 Corinthians 15:3–5? True, Paul doesn't explicitly mention an empty tomb, but neither does he mention Pontius Pilate or Jerusalem. His gospel tradition is a formulaic summary; it does not rehearse the entire tradition or recapitulate the memory in every detail.[97]
3 The lack of scriptural echoes and citations shows that the story has not been made up on the back of a cantata of OT proof texts.[98]
4 The primitive Jewish polemic against the resurrection proclamation presupposes that the tomb was empty. The Jewish counter-claim that the disciples stole the body assumes that the tomb was somehow vacated by Jesus' corpse.[99]
5 The empty-tomb story is based on the testimony of female disciples whose legal testimony would have been considered worthless in antiquity; women did not amount to ideal witnesses for someone wanting to vouch for an extraordinary event.[100]

---

96 Cf. Allison 2005b: 328.
97 Allison 2005b: 305–307.
98 Cf. Wright 2003: 599–602.
99 Matt. 28:13; *Gos. Pet.* 30; Tatian, *Diat.* 53.28; Justin, *Dial.* 108.2; Tertullian, *Spect.* 30.
100 Precisely what is stated in Luke 24:22–23, confirmed by Celsus's (*C. Cels.* 2.59) derision of women as fanatical, and confirmed by Josephus who regarded women as legally unreliable (*Ant.* 4.219). Corley (2002: 138) notes that given 'the tenacity of the women's lament traditions, as well as the overall interest in family retrieval of executed family members, we can at least assume that the women, and perhaps even some men, would have tried to watch the crucifixion proceedings, and would have tried to find Jesus' body after he died in spite of the risks that would entail'.

6 The early apostolic preaching in Jerusalem immediately after Jesus' crucifixion would have been highly problematic if the whereabouts of the body were known to the Judean authorities.

There are, of course, several possible objections to the empty tomb. The women went to the wrong tomb; no one knew where the body was; there were no witnesses to the burial of the body; and the resurrection accounts are inconsistent and mythical. Yet an empty tomb, whether Jesus was raised from the dead or not, remains highly probable. The conclusion I come to is the same as that of the Jewish scholar Geza Vermes:

> [I]n the end, when every argument has been considered and weighed, the only conclusion acceptable to the historian must be that the opinions of the orthodox, the liberal sympathizer and the critical agnostic alike – and even perhaps of the disciples themselves – are simply interpretations of the one disconcerting fact: namely that the women who set out to pay their last respects to Jesus found to their consternation, not a body, but an empty tomb.[101]

The resurrection of the Lord

As a fan of musical theatre, I've always enjoyed the musical *Jesus Christ Superstar*. I find it astounding that even in a post-religious world, in places where Jesus is regarded as a myth, where the media is often hostile to the church, the show always plays to packed theatres. Yet the Andrew Lloyd Webber and Tim Rice masterpiece ends with Jesus' crucifixion, Jesus dying in death, defeat and despair – there is no resurrection, no prospect of vindication and no hope of a return. For me, it doesn't feel right, as it is not the whole story, and the same could be said of Mel Gibson's *The Passion of the Christ*. To leave out 'Jesus himself stood among them and said, "Peace be with you"' or 'But God raised him from the dead'[102] is unsatisfactory for a comprehensive telling of the story of Jesus because it's the after-story that kind of explains why the main story

---

101 Vermes 1973: 41.
102 Luke 24:36; Acts 13:30.

The death and resurrection of Jesus

is such a big deal. If Jesus were not proclaimed as 'risen', we might think of Jesus of Nazareth the same way we think of Jesus ben Ananias, as a raving prophet who proclaimed the temple's destruction, and was scourged by the Roman governor, until he was killed by a Roman projectile during the siege of Jerusalem. Or else we might think of Jesus of Nazareth going to his grave with the same grief as another Jesus, Jesus ben Phameis, who died in Leontopolis in the same century as Jesus of Nazareth. His funeral inscription reads:

> Traveller, my name is Jesus, and my father's name is Phameis;
> when descending into Hades I was 60 years of age.
> All of you should weep together for this man, who went
>   at once to the hiding place of ages, to abide there in the dark.
> Will you also bewail me, dear Dositheos, because you are in
>   need of shedding bitter tears upon my tomb?
> When I died I had no offspring, you will be my child instead.
> All of you, therefore, bewail me, Jesus the unhappy man.[103]

But nobody laments Jesus in such terms because Mark's beginning of his Gospel (Mark 1:1), Matthew's book of Jesus' origins (Matt. 1:1), Luke's prologue to his narratival account (Luke 1:1–4), John's testimony to Jesus (John 1:1–18; 20:30–31; 21:24–25), Paul's gospel summaries (Rom. 1:3–4; 1 Cor. 15:3–5; 2. Tim. 2:8) and even the introduction to Thomas's account of the secret sayings of the living Jesus (*Gos. Thom.* 1) tell the story as either climaxing in or at least presuming his resurrection. Indeed, they only tell the story of Jesus as Messiah, Lord and Teacher because of faith in him as risen from the dead. The life of Jesus cannot be told, narrated or understood apart from his afterlife.[104] Jesus' memory did not abide beyond the devotion of his disciples and the worship of the early church. Whether the resurrection is history is one question, but there is no doubt

---

103 Safrai and Stern 1974–76: 2:1043–1044.
104 Cf. too Sanders 1985: 240; Wright 1996: 488; Barnett 2024: 201.

that it is part of the effective history of Jesus. Resurrection faith is the presupposition to the storytelling about Jesus that we find in our primary sources. And this is the problem with our sources: trying to separate fact from faith, scriptural reflection from naked evidence, joyous testimony from disinterested observation, is like trying to separate red and blue in the colour purple. Our historical investigation of Jesus will always be haunted by the shadow of faith in Jesus as one who walked out of the shadow of the tomb.

Perhaps we can reach a middle ground and be content with the claim that *belief* in the resurrection was a historical fact, insofar as Mary Magdalene, Cephas/Peter, James the brother of Jesus, and the apostle Paul most truly and energetically *believed* that God had raised Jesus from the dead.[105] We might concede that proof or confidence that Jesus' resurrection *actually happened* as a historical event is neither established nor refuted, for history does not deal in miracles, whether for Alexander the Great, for Krishna or for Jesus of Nazareth. Accordingly, resurrection must be countenanced not as history but as metaphysics, a theistic presupposition, supra-history and a matter of faith. Resurrection, then, belongs within a web of Christian belief, internally coherent, but with a question mark on its historical veracity as a material event in our space–time universe.[106] That marks a fair and reasonable line of demarcation for a truce between the sceptic and the apologist . . . if it were not for the fact that Christian testimony is that Jesus rose from the dead as an event in history, and everything – grace and glory, hope and hell, apostolic preaching, misery and paradise – rides on it, says Paul.[107] In Christian resurrection discourse, Jesus did not rise into a metaphor, not into the kerygma, not into the church, not into a cause, not into the affections of the Godward heart; nor did he metamorphose into a type of civilization. Plus, the curiosity about what did materially happen to Jesus (are his bones out there somewhere?), and what made people believe that he had been raised from the dead (even being willing to endure persecution and

---

[105] Cf. Schnelle 2020: 85: 'One cannot prove the appearances and the resurrection as a historical fact, but neither can one exclude the possibility. In historical terms, one can only say that followers of Jesus – the itinerant Jewish preacher, Jesus of Nazareth – affirmed that, after his death, he appeared to them alive.'
[106] Watson 1987.
[107] 1 Cor. 15:1–11.

face martyrdom for announcing it), is never going to go away. The truce will never hold; human curiosity and the gravity of faith force the matter upon us. But addressing it is not our task today.[108]

Jesus lived and died – that much we know; but whether Jesus lived, died and lived again – that is always going to haunt historians, sceptics, believers and agnostics. Perhaps that is why the best-attested ending of Mark's Gospel is so abrupt, finishing at 16:8. We have to decide. Did the story of Jesus end with a crucifixion, an empty tomb, and fearful women spouting all sorts of strange stories about an angel and the promise of an appearance: is that how the story ends, or are we supposed to expect more?

---

108 My favourite studies on the resurrection remain Wright 2003 and Licona 2010.

Postscript

The indisputable historical facts about Jesus

If one were to list the essential and most indisputable historical facts about Jesus' life, what would they be? While others might well disagree, I would proffer the following list:

- Jesus was born in the final years of the reign of Herod the Great (37–4 BC).
- Jesus' early life was spent in the small village of Nazareth, in an artisan family, growing up in the aftermath of the Galilean rebellion instigated by 'Judas', and its subsequent brutal pacification by Roman legions in 4 BC.
- Jesus was baptized by John the Baptizer in the River Jordan.
- Jesus soon split from John's movement and called his own followers.
- Jesus' central message was the kingdom of God, influenced by motifs from Daniel and Isaiah, and warning that Israel as a whole must decide how to respond to the coming of God in his kingly power.
- Jesus travelled itinerantly around the villages and hamlets of Galilee, proclaiming a time of judgment and a new exodus.
- Jesus was Torah-observant, even though he engaged in halakhic debates with other Jewish parties, and his eschatology influenced his approach to ethics and his life in community with others.
- Jesus was widely considered a prophet, teacher, miracle-worker and exorcist.
- Jesus obliquely identified himself as Israel's Messiah.
- Jesus believed that it was his destiny in his messianic role to be destroyed by the Romans.
- Jesus may have visited the Jerusalem temple more than once, but he made one dramatic visit to Jerusalem during Passover around AD 30.

- Jesus created a disturbance in the temple which caused alarm among the high priests.
- Jesus prophesied the temple's destruction.
- Jesus held a final meal with his followers where he attributed symbolic meaning to the bread and wine.
- Jesus was arrested by the chief priests at the specific behest of the high priest Caiaphas.
- Jesus was crucified by the Roman prefect Pontius Pilate on a charge of sedition.
- Jesus was buried in a tomb belonging to Joseph of Arimathea, a member of the Sanhedrin, and his tomb was later found empty.
- Jesus' disciples soon afterwards proclaimed that God had raised him from the dead.

That is the bare-bones account of Jesus' life, which of course requires a lot of filling out in terms of detail, such as the meaning of 'messiah' and 'kingdom of God', precisely what this volume has tried to do. That list is the basic gist of Jesus' life as we can reconstruct it. But creating such a list cannot be the end of our search for the man Jesus. Ultimately, these factoids need to be situated in a socio-religious and economic context (first-century Galilee and Judea), an after-effect (origins of the early church) and a particular narrative (Jewish restoration eschatology and apocalyptic world view), and combined with a macro-level analysis of a cross-section of the Jesus traditions (Jesus' kingdom message and announcement of a new exodus).

'Who then is this?'

The reason why there is a thing called Christianity, and a socio-religious organism called the church, and why there have been several phases of the 'Quest' for the historical Jesus, is because many have asked the same question: 'Who then is this?'[1] Or else we are simply attempting to

---

1 Mark 4:41.

answer the same question that Jesus himself posed to his disciples: 'Who do you say that I am?'[2] That indeed is the question!

As I've made clear from the outset, the study of the historical Jesus, at least the reason I'm interested in it and how I am pursuing it, is part of a wider theological project. To ask 'Who is Jesus?' is to say something about Jesus and history, but also to speak about God and contemporary religion. There's no bracketing out the God question or the significance of Jesus for our own age: they are interlocked, no matter how much one might feign disinterest in those other dimensions. However, while mapping Jesus onto first-century Galilee and Judea and unearthing his story is an important part of that project, it's only the beginning, the preliminary phrase. It is a first Christology, not a final account, for a larger task remains to be done. That is because who Jesus is cannot be reduced to who he was and who he claimed to be. The early church proclaimed Jesus as the 'Prince of life' (Acts 3:15 KJV) and 'God from God' (Nicene Creed). For such titles and judgments to be true and meaningful, they do not depend upon Jesus claiming them for himself. Who Jesus is is more than what he said and what he did; it is the primitive memory of him, the proclamation about him, the devotions directed towards him, the liturgies he is celebrated in, the debates he spawned, the inspiration that continues to draw from him, and the unveiling of his future reign and glory.[3]

The Jesus story began with a whisper, a rumour, a daring claim: God is coming, coming as king, in the life, teachings and destiny of Jesus of Nazareth. Jesus himself started the whisper of this revolution, one involving a reordering of power, Israel's regathering, the redemption of the Jews, the defeat of Satan and the renewal of creation. But his teaching, its promises and warnings, could not remain a whisper; it had to be shared, repeated, declared, argued and even shouted afar. Something Jesus told his followers to do:

---

2 Mark 8:29.

3 Cf. Bockmuehl (1994: 169): 'Christian faith in this sense is faith in a Messiah whose identity in fact is not to be found in the past or present alone, but who always also meets us as the One who is to Come.'

Postscript

> What I say to you in the dark, tell in the light, and what you hear whispered, proclaim from the housetops.
> (Matt. 10:27)

> Therefore whatever you have said in the dark will be heard in the light, and what you have whispered behind closed doors will be proclaimed from the housetops.
> (Luke 12:3)

The Jesus movement began with a whisper, an insignificant murmuring in a backwater province of the Roman Empire, yet by the fourth century it had become a deafening roar that transformed an entire civilization. Jesus was crucified by a Roman official, yet when Roman soldiers put the chi-rho symbol onto their shields as Constantine ordered them to, it was clear that the crucified Nazarene had bested the Caesars in his contest against them. And so the Word became an empire.

And now, even in our own day, we hear the echo of a thousand voices of testimony to Jesus reverberate all around us. A cacophony of noise, including the tomes of bishops and the prayers of African slaves, all focused on Jesus; voices that we now attempt to understand amid the rampaging turmoil of our own times, finding in those voices truth, wisdom, beauty, life, love and hope; and somewhere in there too is the original whisper of Jesus himself.

Consequently, the study of the historical Jesus is not an end but only a small part of a bigger picture: to know Jesus and share in the joy of knowing him with others. As such, the study of the historical Jesus has a necessary sequel: Christology, Christology and more Christology! Christology, in its widest sense, means to explore Jesus all the more, from Nazareth to Nicea, in canon and creeds, among Jews and pagans, in medieval manuscripts, in the minds of mystics and monks, in Islamic traditions, in letters written from prison, in film, television and art, between faith and doubt, until history is no more.

Where to next?

It is somewhat of a paradox that just as we cannot study Jesus apart from the memory and testimony of his earliest followers, so too we cannot investigate the early church apart from the history of Jesus and his impact upon it. The early church shaped the story of Jesus, but it too had been shaped by Jesus.

In that case, a study of primitive Christianity as the immediate after-effect of Jesus' own history is the next logical step for such a project – in particular, exploring the continuities and discontinuities between Jesus, the Jerusalem church and the Pauline assemblies in the eastern Mediterranean. Such a task requires much discussion, the starting point of which is probably Alfred Loisy's dictum that Jesus proclaimed the kingdom of God while the church proclaimed Jesus, something that was programmatic for Bultmann's approach to the kerygma and grappling with the theological witness of the NT. But things are more complicated than stating: 'Jesus' "kingdom of God" was soon replaced by Paul's "righteousness of God"', or 'The imminence of the kingdom for Jesus was eventually replaced by "early Catholicism". The organic developments, foreign influences and discursive debates in early Christianity are complex and contested. Even if we regard Easter as a kind of line of demarcation between the Jesus of history and the Christ of faith, treating them as different theatres of reality will not work; the two epochs are organically related because the latter grew from the former. Jörg Frey puts it well:

> Naturally, there is a profound difference between the preaching of the earthly Jesus and the image of Christ in later epochs, and in the final stage of the New Testament's development of its own discourse, seen in the language of the Gospel of John, in which Jesus ultimately proclaims himself, this transformation becomes particularly palpable. But precisely when one seeks to understand the earthly Jesus and early Christianity historically in the context of contemporary Judaism, it becomes apparent how such a development in the tradition could occur and what rationale it follows. The development of early Christian Christology can be understood

as an immense achievement in theological discourse, which is essentially nourished by the traditions of ancient Judaism and is based on a dual foundation: the interpreted experience of Easter and the memory of the work and event of Jesus of Nazareth.[4]

Jesus and the church are, then, umbilically connected; one does not make sense without the other.[5] True, Jesus did not intend to be the 'Founder of Christianity',[6] any more than Wesley set out to establish the Wesleyan Methodist churches outside Anglicanism! But retrospectively, Jesus was, in a sense, the founder of what would *become* Christianity. He called followers and expected them to form a movement, sect or group that would keep his teachings alive. He told them to be alert to the future, until the kingdom came, in many ways similar to the movements launched by John the Baptist and the Teacher of Righteousness at Qumran.[7] But exploring that forces us to ask: how does the history of Jesus the Galilean prophet, soon heralded as the risen and exalted Messiah and Lord, explain why the church began, and why and how it spread, and why it took the shape that it did?

In a wider theological project bent on exploring all things pertaining to Jesus, after the study of the historical Jesus, next comes the task of

---

4 Frey (2016 [2002]: 84): 'Natürlich besteht zwischen der Predigt des Irdischen und dem Christusbild späterer Epochen eine tiefgreifende Differenz, und auf der letzten Stufe der neutestamentlichen Sprachentwicklung, in der Sprache des Johannesevangeliums, in der Jesus letztlich sich selbst verkündigt, wird diese Transformation besonders augenfällig. Aber gerade wenn man den irdischen Jesus und das frühe Christentum historisch im Horizont des zeitgenössischen Judentums zu verstehen versucht, dann wird auch erkennbar, wie es in der Tradition zu einer solchen Entwicklung kommen konnte und welcher *ratio* diese folgt. Die Entwicklung der urchristlichen Christologie lässt sich verstehen als ein immenser theologischer Sprachgewinn, der sich wesentlich aus den Traditionen des antiken Judentums speist und auf einer doppelten Grundlage beruht: Der gedeuteten Ostererfahrung und der Erinnerung an das Wirken und das Geschick Jesu von Nazareth' (MFB trans.).

5 Cf. Bockmuehl (1994: 8): '[I]t can be historically legitimate to see Jesus of Nazareth in organic and causal unity with the faith of the early Church.' Cf. Meyer 1979: 252; Wright 1992: 418-427; Barnett 1997: 34-35.

6 Dodd 1970.

7 Cf. Bird 2006a: 173-177 on Jesus as movement founder. There is a sense in which the 'parting of the ways' between Judaism and Christianity – a contested topic, I know – has some roots even in the life of Jesus. See Bird 2010b and literature cited therein. Bockmuehl (1994: 124) is measured and persuasive: 'In the end, Jesus was not a Christian, but a Jew. Nevertheless, the Judaism of his time was the seedbed out of which grew two movements that ultimately became world religions: Christianity and Rabbinic Judaism. Although not identical, the Christian faith *in* Jesus is organically and inextricably linked to the Jewish faith *of* Jesus' (emphasis original).

wrestling with the story of the beginnings of the early church and how it carried forward the gospel of Jesus the Messiah to the ends of the world that it knew.

More anon!

Bibliography

Adams, Edward (2007), *The Stars Will Fall from Heaven: Cosmic Catastrophe in the New Testament and Its World*, LNTS 347, London: T&T Clark.

Ådna, Jostein (2000), *Jesu Stellung zum Tempel: Die Tempelaktion und das Tempelwort als Ausdruck seiner messianischen Sendung*, WUNT 2.119, Tübingen: Mohr Siebeck.

—— (2010), 'Jesus and the Temple', in T. Holmén and S. E. Porter (eds.), *Handbook for the Study of the Historical Jesus*, 4 vols., Leiden: Brill, 2625-2675.

Allison, Dale C. (1998), *Jesus of Nazareth: Millenarian Prophet*, Minneapolis: Fortress.

—— (1999), 'Jesus and the Victory of Apocalyptic', in Carey C. Newman (ed.), *Jesus and the Restoration of Israel: A Critical Assessment of N. T. Wright's Jesus and the Victory of God*, Downers Grove: InterVarsity Press, 61-82.

—— (2001), 'Assessing Arguments', in Robert J. Miller (ed.), *The Apocalyptic Jesus: A Debate*, Santa Rosa: Polebridge, 99-105.

—— (2003), 'The Continuity between John and Jesus', *JSHJ* 1: 6-27.

—— (2005a), 'The Allusive Jesus', in James D. G. Dunn and Scot McKnight (eds.), *The Historical Jesus in Recent Research*, Winona Lake: Eisenbrauns, 238-248.

—— (2005b), *Resurrecting Jesus: The Earliest Christian Tradition and Its Interpreters*, London: T&T Clark.

—— (2008), 'The Historian's Jesus and the Church', in Beverly Roberts Gaventa and Richard B. Hays (eds.), *Seeking the Identity of Jesus: A Pilgrimage*, Grand Rapids: Eerdmans, 79-95.

—— (2009), *The Historical Christ and the Theological Jesus*, Grand Rapids: Eerdmans.

—— (2010a), *Constructing Jesus: Memory, Imagination, and History*, Grand Rapids: Baker.

—— (2010b), 'How to Marginalize the Traditional Criteria of Authenticity', in T. Holmén and S. E. Porter (eds.), *Handbook for the Study of the Historical Jesus*, 4 vols., Leiden: Brill, 3–30.

—— (2010c), 'Kingdom of God', in John J. Collins and Daniel C. Harlow (eds.), *Eerdmans Dictionary of Early Judaism*, Grand Rapids: Eerdmans, 860–861.

Anderson, Gary A. (2013), *Charity: The Place of the Poor in Biblical Tradition*, New Haven: Yale University Press.

Anderson, Paul N. (2006), *The Fourth Question and the Quest for Jesus: Modern Foundations Reconsidered*, LNTS 321, London: T&T Clark.

—— (2021), 'Jesus in Johannine Perspective: Inviting a Fourth Quest for Jesus', *JSATS* 32: 7–41.

Andrade, Nathanael (2025), *Killing the Messiah: The Trial and Crucifixion of Jesus*, Oxford: Oxford University Press.

Andrejevs, Olegs (2019), 'The Background of the Term "Son of Man" in Light of Recent Research', *ExpT* 130: 477–484.

Aslan, Reza (2013), *Zealot: The Life and Times of Jesus of Nazareth*, Random House.

Aune, David E. (1997), 'Jesus and Cynics in First-Century Palestine: Some Critical Considerations', in J. H. Charlesworth and L. L. Johns (eds.), *Hillel and Jesus: Comparative Studies of Two Major Religious Leaders*, Minneapolis: Fortress, 176–192.

Bammel, Ernst, and C. F. D. Moule (eds.) (1984), *Jesus and the Politics of His Day*, Cambridge: Cambridge University Press.

Barber, Michael (2023), *The Historical Jesus and the Temple: Memory, Methodology and the Gospel of Matthew*, Cambridge: Cambridge University Press.

—— (2024), 'Death and Martyrdom', in James G. Crossley and Chris Keith (eds.), *The Next Quest for the Historical Jesus*, Grand Rapids: Eerdmans, 487–506.

Barclay, John M. G. (1996), *Jews in the Mediterranean Diaspora from Alexander to Trajan (323 BCE - 117 CE)*, Edinburgh: T&T Clark.

Barnett, Paul W. (1975), '"Under Tiberius All Was Quiet"', *NTS* 21: 564–571.

—— (1997), *Jesus and the Logic of History*, NSBT 3, Leicester: Apollos; Downers Grove: InterVarsity Press.

—— (2009), *Finding the Historical Christ*, Grand Rapids: Eerdmans.
—— (2024), *The Trials of Jesus: Evidence, Conclusions, and Aftermath*, Grand Rapids: Eerdmans.
Barrett, C. K. (1967), *Jesus and the Gospel Tradition*, London: SPCK.
—— (1978), 'The House of Prayer and Den of Thieves', in E. Earle Ellis and E. Grässer (eds.), *Jesus und Paulus*, FS Werner George Kümmel, Göttingen: Vandenhoeck & Ruprecht, 13–20.
Bauckham, Richard (1985), 'The Son of Man: "A Man in My Position" or "Someone"?' *JSNT* 23: 23–33.
—— (1988), 'Jesus' Demonstration in the Temple', in Barnabas Lindars (ed.), *Law and Religion: Essays on the Place of the Law in Israel and Early Christianity*, Cambridge: James Clarke & Co., 72–89.
—— (1994), 'The Brothers and Sisters of Jesus: An Epiphanian Response to John P. Meier', *CBQ* 56: 686–700.
—— (2002), *Gospel Women: Studies of the Named Women in the Gospels*, Grand Rapids: Eerdmans.
—— (2011), 'The Family of Jesus', in Chris Keith and Larry W. Hurtado (eds.), *Jesus among Friends and Enemies: A Historical Literary Introduction to Jesus in the Gospels*, Grand Rapids: Baker, 103–124.
—— (2017), *Jesus and the Eyewitnesses: The Gospels as Eyewitness Testimony*, 2nd edn, Grand Rapids: Eerdmans.
Baumgarten, A. I. (1983), 'The Name of the Pharisees', *JBL* 102: 411–428.
Beale, G. K. (2011), *A New Testament Biblical Theology: The Unfolding of the Old Testament in the New*, Grand Rapids: Baker.
Beale, G. K., and Mitchell Kim (2021), *God Dwells among Us: A Biblical Theology of the Temple*, Downers Grove: InterVarsity Press.
Becker, J. (1998), *Jesus of Nazareth*, tr. J. E. Crouch, New York: De Gruyter.
Berger, Klaus (1988), 'Jesus als Pharisäer und frühe Christen als Pharisäer', *NTS* 30: 231–262.
—— (1994), *Theologiegeschichte des Urchristentums: Theologie des Neuen Testaments*, Tübingen: Francke.
Bermejo-Rubio, Fernando (2014), 'Jesus and the Anti-Roman Resistance: A Reassessment of the Arguments', *JSHJ* 12: 1–105.
Bernier, Jonathan (2016), *The Quest for the Historical Jesus after the*

Demise of Authenticity: Toward a Critical Realist Philosophy of History in Jesus Studies, London: T&T Clark.

Betz, Hans Dieter (1997), 'Jesus and the Purity of the Temple (Mk 11:15–18): A Comparative Religion Approach', *JBL* 116: 455–472.

Billings, Bradly S. (2006a), 'The Disputed Words in the Lukan Institution Narrative (Luke 22:19b-20): A Sociological Answer to a Textual Problem', *JBL* 125: 507–526.

—— (2006b), *Do This in Remembrance of Me: The Disputed Works in the Lukan Institution Narrative (Luke 22.19b-20): An Historico-Exegetical, Theological and Sociological Analysis*, LNTS 314, London: T&T Clark.

Bird, Michael F. (2004), 'Should Evangelicals Participate in the "Third Quest for the Historical Jesus"?' *Themelios* 29: 4–14.

—— (2005), 'Jesus and the Gentiles since Jeremias: Patterns and Prospects', *CBR* 4: 83–108.

—— (2006a), *Jesus and the Origins of the Gentile Mission*, LNTS 331, LHJS, London: T&T Clark.

—— (2006b), 'Jesus and the Revolutionaries: Did Jesus Call Israel to Repent of Nationalistic Ambitions?' *Colloquium* 38.2: 127–139.

—— (2006c), 'The Peril of Modernizing Jesus and the Crisis of Not Contemporizing the Christ', *EQ* 78.4: 291–312.

—— (2006d), 'Who Comes from the East and the West? Luke 13.28-39/ Matt 8.11-12 and the Historical Jesus', *NTS* 52: 441–457.

—— (2008a), 'Gentiles', in Craig A. Evans (ed.), *Encyclopedia of the Historical Jesus*, New York: Routledge, 213–216.

—— (2008b), 'Jesus the Law-Breaker', in Scot McKnight and Joseph B. Modica (eds.), *Who Do My Opponents Say That I Am? An Investigation of the Accusations against Jesus*, LNTS 327, LHJS, London: T&T Clark, 3–26.

—— (2008c), 'Mary Magdalene', in Craig A. Evans (ed.), *Encyclopedia of the Historical Jesus*, New York: Routledge, 393–394.

—— (2008d), 'Passion Predictions', in Craig A. Evans (ed.), *Encyclopedia of the Historical Jesus*, New York: Routledge, 442–446.

—— (2009), *Are You the One Who Is to Come? The Historical Jesus and the Messianic Question*, Grand Rapids: Baker.

—— (2010a), *Crossing over Sea and Land: Jewish Missionary Activity in the Second Temple Period*, Peabody: Hendrickson.

—— (2010b), 'Jesus and the "Parting of the Ways"', in Stanley E. Porter and Tom Holmén (eds.), *The Handbook of the Study of the Historical Jesus*, 4 vols., Leiden: Brill, 2:1183–1215.

—— (2011), 'John the Baptist', in Chris Keith and Larry W. Hurtado (eds.), *Jesus among Friends and Enemies: A Historical and Literary Introduction to Jesus in the Gospels*, Grand Rapids: Baker, 60–80.

—— (2012), 'The Historical Jesus and the Early Christian Gentile Missions', in Tom Holmén (ed.), *Jesus in Continuum*, WUNT 289, Tübingen: Mohr Siebeck, 63–86.

—— (2013a), 'Christ', in Joel B. Green, Jeannine K. Brown and Nicholas Perrin (eds.), *Dictionary of Jesus and the Gospels*, 2nd edn, Downers Grove: InterVarsity Press, 115–125.

—— (2013b), *Jesus is the Christ: The Messianic Testimony of the Gospels*, Downers Grove: InterVarsity Press.

—— (2013c), 'Sin, Sinner', in Joel B. Green, Jeannine K. Brown and Nicholas Perrin (eds.), *Dictionary of Jesus and the Gospels*, 2nd edn, Downers Grove: InterVarsity Press, 863–869.

—— (2014a), 'Did Jesus Think He Was God?' in Michael F. Bird (ed.), *How God Became Jesus: The Real Origins of Belief in Jesus' Divine Nature*, Grand Rapids: Zondervan, 45–70.

—— (2014b), *The Gospel of the Lord: How the Early Church Wrote the Story of Jesus*, Grand Rapids: Eerdmans.

—— (2015), 'Jesus and the Continuing Exile of Israel in the Writings of N.T. Wright', *JSHJ* 13: 209–231.

—— (2020), *Evangelical Theology: A Biblical and Systematic Introduction*, 2nd edn, Grand Rapids: Zondervan.

—— (2022), *Jesus among the Gods: Early Christology in the Greco-Roman World*, Waco: Baylor University Press.

Blomberg, Craig L. (1999), *Neither Poverty Nor Riches: A Biblical Theology of Possessions*, NSBT 7, Leicester: Apollos; Downers Grove: InterVarsity Press.

—— (2001), *The Historical Reliability of John's Gospel: Issues and Commentary*, Downers Grove: InterVarsity Press.

—— (2005), *Contagious Holiness: Jesus' Meals with Sinners*, NSBT 19, Leicester: Apollos; Downers Grove: InterVarsity Press.

—— (2016), *The Historical Reliability of the Gospels: Countering the*

Challenges to Evangelical Christian Beliefs, Nashville: Broadman & Holman.

—— (2018), *A New Testament Theology*, Waco: Baylor University Press.

—— (2023), *Jesus the Purifier: John's Gospel and the Fourth Quest for the Historical Jesus*, Grand Rapids: Baker.

Blumhofer, Christopher M. (2020), *The Gospel of John and the Future of Israel*, SNTSMS 177, Cambridge: Cambridge University Press.

Bock, Darrell L. (1998), *Blasphemy and Exaltation in Judaism: The Charge against Jesus in Mark 14:53-65*, BSL, Grand Rapids: Baker.

—— (2003), 'Jewish Expression in Mark 14.61-62 and the Authenticity of the Jewish Examination of Jesus', *JSHJ* 1: 147–159.

—— (2010a), 'Blasphemy and the Jewish Examination of Jesus', in Darrell L. Bock and Robert L. Webb (eds.), *Key Events in the Life of the Historical Jesus: A Collaborative Exploration of Context and Coherence*, Grand Rapids: Eerdmans, 589–667.

—— (2010b), 'Key Events in the Life of the Historical Jesus: A Summary', in Darrell L. Bock and Robert L. Webb (eds.), *Key Events in the Life of the Historical Jesus: A Collaborative Exploration of Context and Coherence*, Grand Rapids: Eerdmans, 827–853.

—— (2013), 'Son of Man', in Joel G. Green, Jeannine K. Brown and Nicholas Perrin (eds.), *Dictionary of Jesus and the Gospels*, Downers Grove: InterVarsity Press, 894–900.

Bock, Darrell L., and J. Ed Komoszewski (eds.) (2019), *Jesus, Skepticism and the Problem of History: Criteria and Context in the Study of Christian Origins*, Grand Rapids: Zondervan.

Bockmuehl, Markus (1994), *This Jesus: Martyr, Lord, Messiah*, London: T&T Clark.

—— (2000), *Jewish Law in Gentile Churches: Halakhah and the Beginning of Christian Public Ethics*, Edinburgh: T&T Clark.

—— (2006), *Seeing the Word: Refocusing New Testament Study*, Grand Rapids: Baker.

—— (2008), 'God's Life as a Jew: Remembering the Son of God as Son of David', in Beverly Roberts Gaventa and Richard B. Hays (eds.), *Seeking the Identity of Jesus: A Pilgrimage*, Grand Rapids: Eerdmans, 60–78.

Bond, Helen (1996), 'The Coins of Pontius Pilate: Part of an Attempt to Provoke the People or Integrate Them into the Empire?' *JSJ* 27: 241–262.

—— (2011), 'Political Authorities: The Herods, Caiaphas, and Pontius Pilate', in Chris Keith and Larry W. Hurtado (eds.), *Jesus among Friends and Enemies: A Historical and Literary Introduction to Jesus in the Gospels*, Grand Rapids: Baker, 219–247.

—— (2012), *The Historical Jesus: A Guide for the Perplexed*, London: Bloomsbury.

—— (2013a), 'Dating the Death of Jesus: Memory and the Religious Imagination', *NTS* 59: 461–475.

—— (2013b), 'Herodian Dynasty', in Joel B. Green, Jeannine K. Brown and Nicholas Perrin (eds.), *Dictionary of Jesus and the Gospels*, 2nd edn, Downers Grove: InterVarsity Press, 379–392.

Borg, Marcus J. (1998 [1984]), *Conflict, Holiness and Politics in the Teachings of Jesus*, New York: Edward Mellen.

Boring, M. Eugene (1998), 'The "Third Quest" and the Apostolic Faith', in Jack Dean Kingsbury (ed.), *Gospel Interpretation: Narrative-Critical and Social Scientific Approaches*, Harrisburg: Trinity Press International, 237–252.

Bornkamm, Günther (1960 [1956]), *Jesus of Nazareth*, London: Hodder & Stoughton.

Brandon, S. G. F. (1967), *Jesus and the Zealots*, Manchester: Manchester University Press.

Brown, Colin (2022), *A History of the Quests for the Historical Jesus*, 2 vols., Grand Rapids: Zondervan.

Brown, Raymond E. (1993), *The Birth of the Messiah: A Commentary on the Infancy Narratives in the Gospels of Matthew and Luke*, 2 vols., AYBRL, New York: Doubleday.

Bruce, F. F. (1961), 'The Book of Zechariah and the Passion Narrative', *BJRL* 43: 336–353.

Bruno, Chris (2019), *Paul versus James: What We've Been Missing in the Faith and Works Debate*, Chicago: Moody.

Bryan, Steven M. (2002), *Jesus and Israel's Traditions of Judgement and Restoration*, SNTSMS 117, Cambridge: Cambridge University Press.

Bultmann, Rudolf (1952–55), *Theology of the New Testament*, 2 vols, tr. K. Grobel, London: SCM Press.

—— (1958), *Jesus and the Word*, tr. Louise Pettibone Smith and Erminie Huntress Lantero, New York: Scribner.

—— (1963 [1921]), *History of the Synoptic Tradition*, tr. J. Marsh, 2nd edn, New York: Harper & Row.

—— (1985 [1973]), 'Is Exegesis without Presuppositions Possible?' in K. Mueller-Vollmer (ed.), *The Hermeneutics Reader: Texts of German Tradition from the Enlightenment to the Present*, New York: Continuum, 242–248.

Burridge, Richard A., and Graham Gould (2004), *Jesus Now and Then*, Grand Rapids: Eerdmans.

Butticaz, Simon, and Enrico Norelli (eds.) (2018), *Memory and Memories in Early Christianity: Proceedings of the International Conference Held at the Universities of Geneva and Lausanne (June 2–3, 2016)*, WUNT 398, Tübingen: Mohr Siebeck.

Byrskog, S. (2010), 'The Historicity of Jesus: How Do We Know That Jesus Existed?' in T. Holmén and S. E. Porter (eds.), *Handbook for the Study of the Historical Jesus*, 4 vols., Leiden: Brill, 2183–2212.

—— (2011), 'The Transmission of the Jesus Tradition', in T. Holmén and S. E. Porter (eds.), *Handbook for the Study of the Historical Jesus*, 4 vols., Leiden: Brill, 1465–1494.

Cadbury, Henry J. (1937), *The Peril of Modernizing Jesus*, New York: Macmillan.

Cadoux, Arthur J. (1900), *The Parables of Jesus: Their Art and Use*, London: J. Clarke.

Cadoux, C. J. (1941), *The Historic Mission of Jesus: A Constructive Re-examination of the Eschatological Teaching in the Synoptic Gospels*, London: Lutterworth.

Cahill, Michael (2002), 'Did Jesus Refer to Himself in the Third Person? A Contribution to the Son of Man Debate', *PIBA* 25: 58–68.

Caird, G. B. (1950–51), 'The Mind of Christ: Christ's Attitude to Institutions', *ExpT* 62: 259–262.

—— (1965), *Jesus and the Jewish Nation*, London: Athlone.

Camponovo, Odo (1984), *Königtum, Königsherrschaft und Reich Gottes in den frühjudischen Schriften*, Göttingen: Vandenhoeck & Ruprecht.

Casey, Maurice (1991), *From Jewish Prophet to Gentile God: The Origins and Development of New Testament Christology*, London: James Clark & Co.

—— (2007), *The Solution to the 'Son of Man' Problem*, LNTS 343, London: T&T Clark.

—— (2010), *Jesus of Nazareth: An Independent Historian's Account of His Life and Teaching*, London: T&T Clark.

—— (2014), *Jesus: Evidence and Argument or Mythicist Myths?* London: Bloomsbury.

Chancey, Mark A. (2005), *Greco-Roman Culture and the Galilee of Jesus*, SNTSMS 134, Cambridge: Cambridge University Press.

Chapman, David W. (2010), *Ancient Jewish and Christian Perceptions of Crucifixion*, Grand Rapids: Baker.

Charlesworth, James H. (1989), *Jesus within Judaism: New Light from Exciting Archaeological Discoveries*, London: SPCK.

—— (2014), 'Jesus and the Temple', in J. H. Charlesworth (ed.), *Jesus and the Temple: Textual and Archaeological Explorations*, Minneapolis: Fortress, 145–182.

Chilton, Bruce D. (1978a), 'An Evangelical and Critical Approach to the Sayings of Jesus', *Themelios* 3: 78–85.

—— (1978b), 'Regnum Dei Deus Est', *SJT* 31: 261–270.

—— (1982), 'Jesus *ben David*: Reflections on the *Davidssohnfrage*', *JSNT* 14: 88–112.

—— (1984), *A Galilean Rabbi and His Bible: Jesus' Use of the Interpreted Scripture of His Time*, Wilmington: Michael Glazier.

—— (1987), *God in Strength: Jesus' Announcement of the Kingdom*, Sheffield: JSOT Press.

—— (1992), *The Temple of Jesus: His Sacrificial Program within a Cultural History of Sacrifice*, University Park: Pennsylvania State University Press.

—— (1994a), *A Feast of Meanings: Eucharistic Theologies from Jesus through Johannine Circles*, Leiden: Brill.

—— (1994b), 'The Kingdom of God in Recent Discussion', in Bruce Chilton and Craig A. Evans (eds.), *Studying the Historical Jesus: Evaluations of the State of Current Research*, Leiden: Brill, 255–280.

—— (1996), *Pure Kingdom: Jesus' Vision of God*, Grand Rapids: Eerdmans.

—— (2000), *Rabbi Jesus: An Intimate Biography*. New York: Doubleday.

—— (2004), 'James, Jesus' Brother', in Scot McKnight and Grant R. Osborne (eds.), *The Face of New Testament Studies: A Survey of Recent Research*, Grand Rapids: Baker, 251–262.

Cohen, Akiva (2016), *Matthew and the Mishnah: Redefining Identity and Ethos in the Shadow of the Second Temple's Destruction*, WUNT 2.418, Tübingen: Mohr Siebeck.

Cohick, Lynn (2008), 'Jesus as King of the Jews', in Scot McKnight and Joseph B. Modica (eds.), *Who Do My Opponents Say That I Am? An Investigation of the Accusations against the Historical Jesus*, LNTS 327, LHJS, London: T&T Clark, 111–132.

—— (2013), 'Pharisees', in Joel B. Green, Jeannine K. Brown and Nicholas Perrin (eds.), *Dictionary of Jesus and the Gospels*, 2nd edn, Downers Grove: InterVarsity Press, 673–679.

Collins, Adela Yarbro (1996), 'The Origin of the Designation of Jesus as "Son of Man"', in *Cosmology and Eschatology in Jewish and Christian Apocalypticism*, Leiden: Brill, 139–158.

—— (1997), 'The Signification of Mark 10:45 among Gentile Christians', *HTR* 90: 371–382.

Collins, John J. (1987), 'The Kingdom of God in Apocrypha and Pseudepigrapha', in Wendell Willis (ed.), *The Kingdom of God in 20th-Century Interpretation*, Peabody: Hendrickson, 81–95.

—— (1992), 'Essenes', in D. N. Freedman (ed.), *Anchor Bible Dictionary*, 6 vols., New York: Doubleday, 2:619–626.

Cook, J. G. (2011), 'Crucifixion and Burial', *NTS* 57: 193–213.

Corley, Kathleen E. (2002), *Women and the Historical Jesus: Feminist Myths of Christian Origins*, Santa Rosa: Polebridge.

—— (2003), 'The Anointing of Jesus in the Synoptic Tradition: An Argument for Authenticity', *JSHJ* 1: 61–72.

Court, John M. (2006), 'Burnett Hillman Streeter* (17th November 1874 – 10th September 1937)', *ExpT* 118: 19–25.

Crisp, Oliver D. (2009), 'The "Fittingness" of the Virgin Birth', in *God Incarnate: Explorations in Christology*, London: T&T Clark, 77–102.

Crossan, John Dominic (1991), *The Historical Jesus: The Life of a Mediterranean Jewish Peasant*, San Francisco: HarperCollins.

—— (1994), *Jesus: A Revolutionary Biography*, San Francisco: HarperCollins.

Crossan, John Dominic, and Jonathan L. Reed (2001), *Excavating Jesus: Beneath the Stones, behind the Texts*, San Francisco: HarperSanFrancisco.

Crossley, James G. (2004), *The Date of Mark's Gospel: Insights from the Law in Earliest Christianity*, JSNTSup 266, London: T&T Clark.

—— (2006), *Why Christianity Happened: A Sociohistorical Account of Christian Origins (26–50 CE)*, London: Westminster John Knox.

—— (2009), 'Mark 7.1-23: Revisiting the Question of "All Foods Clean"', in Michael Tait and Peter Oaks (eds.), *Torah in the New Testament: Papers Delivered at the Manchester-Lausanne Seminar of June 2008*, London: T&T Clark, 8–20.

—— (2012), 'From Jesus Observing Food and Purity Laws to Some Christians Not Bothering: A Socio-Historical Explanation', in Tom Holmén (ed.), *Jesus in Continuum*, WUNT 289, Tübingen: Mohr Siebeck, 87–113.

—— (2013), 'A "Very Jewish" Jesus: Perpetuating the Myth of Superiority', *JSHJ* 11: 109–129.

—— (2015), *Jesus and the Chaos of History: Redirecting the Life of the Historical Jesus*, Oxford: Oxford University Press.

—— (2021), 'The Next Quest for the Historical Jesus', *JSHJ* 21: 261–264.

—— (2024), 'Introduction: The New Quest', in James G. Crossley and Chris Keith (eds.), *The Next Quest for the Historical Jesus*, Grand Rapids: Eerdmans, 1–4.

Crossley, James G., and Chris Keith (eds.) (2024), *The Next Quest for the Historical Jesus*, Grand Rapids: Eerdmans.

Crump, David M. (2013), 'Prayer', in Joel B. Green, Jeannine K. Brown and Nicholas Perrin (eds.), *Dictionary of Jesus and the Gospels*, 2nd edn, Downers Grove: InterVarsity Press, 684–692.

Dahl, Nils Alstrup (1974), 'The Problem of the Historical Jesus', in *The Crucified Messiah and Other Essays*, Minneapolis: Augsburg, 48–89.

Dalman, Gustaf (1902 [1898]), *The Words of Jesus: Considered in Light of Post-Biblical Jewish Writings and the Aramaic Language*, Edinburgh: T&T Clark.

Dapaah, Daniel S. (2005), *The Relationship between John the Baptist and Jesus of Nazareth: A Critical Study*, Lanham: University of America Press.

de Jonge, Marinus (1998), *God's Final Envoy: Early Christology and Jesus' Own View of His Mission*, Grand Rapids: Eerdmans.

de Lacey, D. R. (1992), 'In Search of a Pharisee', *TynB* 43: 353–372.

Deines, Roland (2001), 'The Pharisees between "Judaisms" and "Common Judaisms"', in D. A. Carson, M. A. Seifrid and P. T. O'Brien (eds.), *Justification and Variegated Nomism, vol. 1: The Complexities of Second Temple Judaism*, Grand Rapids: Baker, 443–502.

—— Deines, Roland. 'Biblical Views: The Pharisees – Good Guys with Bad Press,' *Biblical Archaeology Review* 39.4 (2013): 22, 57.

Deines, Roland, and Martin Hengel (1995), 'E.P. Sanders' "Common Judaism," Jesus, and the Pharisees: A Review Article', *JTS* 46: 1–70.

—— (2013), 'The Pharisees: Good Guys with Bad Press', *BAR* 39: 22, 57–58.

Dibelius, Martin (1963 [1939]), *Jesus: A Study of the Gospels and an Essay on 'The Motive for Social Action in the New Testament'*, London: SCM Press.

Dodd, C. H. (1953), *According to the Scriptures: The Substructure of New Testament Theology*, London: Nisbet.

—— (1970), *The Founder of Christianity*, New York: Macmillan.

Downs, David J. (2016), *Alms: Charity, Reward and Atonement in Early Christianity*, Waco: Baylor University Press.

Duling, Dennis C. (1992), 'Kingdom of God, Kingdom of Heaven: OT, Early Judaism, and Hellenistic Usage', in D. N. Freedman (ed.), *Anchor Bible Dictionary*, 6 vols., New York: Doubleday, 4:49–56.

Dunn, James D. G. (1989), *Christology in the Making: A New Testament Inquiry into the Origins of the Doctrine of the Incarnation*, 2nd edn, Grand Rapids: Eerdmans.

—— (2003), *Jesus Remembered*, CITM, Grand Rapids: Eerdmans.

—— (2006), *Unity and Diversity in the New Testament: An Inquiry into the Character of Earliest Christianity*, 3rd edn, London: SCM Press.

—— (2011), 'Methodology of Evangelism in the New Testament: Some Preliminary Reflections', in Jon C. Laansma, Grant Osborne and Ray Van Neste (eds.), *New Testament Theology in Light of the Church's Mission: Essays in Honor of I. Howard Marshall*, Eugene: Cascade, 25–40.

Eddy, Paul Rhodes (1996), 'Jesus as Diogenes? Reflections on the Cynic Jesus Thesis', *JBL* 115: 449–469.

Eddy, Paul Rhodes, and Gregory A. Boyd (2008), *The Jesus Legend: A Case for the Historical Reliability of the Synoptic Jesus Tradition*, Grand Rapids: Baker.

Ehrman, Bart E. (1999), *Jesus: Apocalyptic Prophet of the New Millennium*, Oxford: Oxford University Press.

—— (2003), *Lost Christianities: The Battles for Scripture and Faiths We Never Knew*, Oxford: Oxford University Press.

—— (2005), *Misquoting Jesus: The Story behind Who Changed the Bible and Why*, New York: HarperOne.

—— (2009), *Jesus Interrupted: Revealing the Hidden Contradictions in the Bible (and Why We Don't Know about Them)*, New York: HarperOne.

—— (2013), *Did Jesus Exist? The Historical Argument for Jesus of Nazareth*, New York: HarperOne.

—— (2014), *How Jesus Became God: The Exaltation of a Jewish Preacher from Galilee*, New York: HarperOne.

—— (2016), *Jesus before the Gospels: How the Earliest Christians Remembered, Changed, and Invented Their Stories of the Savior*, New York: HarperOne.

Elliott, John H. (2007), 'Jesus the Israelite Was Neither a "Jew" Nor a "Christian": On Correcting a Misleading Nomenclature', *JSHJ* 5: 119–154.

Evans, Craig A. (1992), 'Predictions of the Destruction of the Herodian Temple in the Pseudepigrapha, Qumran Scrolls, and Related Texts', *JSP* 10: 89–147.

—— (1994), 'The Need for the "Historical Jesus": A Response to Jacob Neusner's Review of Crossan and Meier', *BBR* 4: 127–133.

—— (1995), *Jesus and His Contemporaries: Comparative Studies*, Leiden: Brill.

—— (1996a), 'Jesus' Parable of the Tenant Farmers in Light of Lease Agreements in Antiquity', *JSP* 14: 65–83.

—— (1996b), 'The Passion of Jesus: History Remembered or Prophecy Historicized?' *BBR* 6: 159–165.

—— (1997a), 'Aspects of Exile and Restoration in the Proclamation of Jesus and the Gospels', in Bruce Chilton and Craig A. Evans (eds.), *Jesus in Context: Temple, Purity and Restoration*, Leiden: Brill, 263–294.

—— (1997b), 'Jesus' Action in the Temple: Cleansing or Portent of Destruction?' in Bruce Chilton and Craig A. Evans (eds.), *Jesus in Context: Temple, Purity, and Restoration*, Leiden: Brill, 395–439.

—— (1998a), 'Authenticating the Activities of Jesus', in Bruce Chilton and Craig A. Evans (eds.), *Authenticating the Activities of Jesus*, NTTS 28, Leiden: Brill, 3–29.

—— (1998b), 'Jesus and Zechariah's Messianic Hope', in Bruce Chilton and Craig A. Evans (eds.) *Authenticating the Activities of Jesus*, NTTS 28, Leiden: Brill, 373–388.

—— (1999), 'Jesus and the Continuing Exile of Israel', in Carey C. Newman (ed.), *Jesus and the Restoration of Israel: A Critical Assessment of N. T. Wright's Jesus and the Victory of God*, Downers Grove: InterVarsity Press, 77–100.

—— (2001a), *Jesus and His Contemporaries: Comparative Studies*, Leiden: Brill.

—— (2001b), *Mark 8:27 - 16:20*, WBC, Nashville: Thomas Nelson.

—— (2003), 'Defeating Satan and Liberating Israel: Jesus and Daniel's Visions', *JSHJ* 1: 161–170.

—— (2005a), 'Inaugurating the Kingdom of God and Defeating the Kingdom of Satan', *BBR* 15: 49–75.

—— (2005b), 'Jewish Burial Traditions and the Resurrection of Jesus', *JSHJ* 3: 233–248.

—— (2008), 'Nazareth', in Craig A. Evans (ed.), *Encyclopedia of the Historical Jesus*, New York: Routledge, 423–425.

—— (2012), *Jesus and His World: The Archaeological Evidence*, London: SPCK.

—— (2014), 'Getting the Burial Traditions and Evidences Right', in Michael F. Bird (ed.), *How God Became Jesus: The Real Origins of Belief in Jesus' Divine Nature*, Grand Rapids: Zondervan, 71–92.

Eve, Eric (2002), *The Jewish Context of Jesus' Miracles*, JSNTSup 231, Sheffield: Sheffield Academic Press.

Falk, Harvey (1985), *Jesus the Pharisee: A New Look at the Jewishness of Jesus*, New York: Paulist.

Feldmeier, Reinhard, and Hermann Spieckermann (2021), *God Becoming Human: Incarnation in the Christian Bible*, tr. Brian McNeil, Waco: Baylor University Press.

Ferda, Tucker S. (2024), 'Galilee and Jerusalem', in James G. Crossley and Chris Keith (eds.), *The Next Quest for the Historical Jesus*, Grand Rapids: Eerdmans, 343–356.

Fiore, B. (2000), 'Cynicism and Skepticism', in Craig A. Evans and Stanley E. Porter (eds.), *Dictionary of New Testament Background*, Downers Grove: InterVarsity Press, 242–245.

Flusser, David, and R. Steven Notley (2001), *Jesus*, 3rd edn, Jerusalem: Hebrew University Magnes Press.

Foster, Paul (2006), 'Educating Jesus: The Search for a Plausible Context', *JSHJ* 4: 7–33.

France, R. T. (2002), *The Gospel of Mark*, NIGTC, Grand Rapids; Eerdmans.

Fredriksen, Paula (1999), *Jesus of Nazareth, King of the Jews: A Jewish Life and the Emergence of Christianity*, New York: Vintage.

—— (2005), 'Compassion Is to Purity as Fish Is to Bicycle and Other Reflections on Constructions of "Judaism" in Current Work on the Historical Jesus', in John S. Kloppenborg and John W. Marshall (eds.), *Apocalypticism, Anti-Semitism and the Historical Jesus: Subtexts in Criticisms*, JSHJSup 275, London: T&T Clark, 55–67.

—— (2015), 'Arms and the Man: A Response to Dale Martin's "Jesus in Jerusalem: Armed and Not Dangerous"', *JSNT* 37: 312–325.

—— (2019), *When Christians Were Jews: The First Generation*, New Haven: Yale University Press.

Frey, Jörg (2016 [2002]), 'Der historische Jesus und der Christus der Evangelien', in *Von Jesus zur neutestamentlichen Theologie*, WUNT 368, Tübingen: Mohr Siebeck, 29–84.

—— (2019), *Qumran, Early Judaism, and New Testament Interpretation: Kleine Schriften III*, ed. Jacob N. Cerone, WUNT 424, Tübingen: Mohr Siebeck.

—— (2022), *Qumran and Christian Origins*, ed. Jacob Cerone, Waco: Baylor University Press.

Freyne, Sean (1988), *Galilee, Jesus and the Gospels*, Philadelphia: Fortress.

—— (2005), *Jesus, a Jewish Galilean: A New Reading of the Jesus-Story*, London: T&T Clark.

Funk, Robert W., and Roy W. Hoover (1993), *The Five Gospels: The Search for the Authentic Words of Jesus*, New York: Macmillan.

Gamble, Harry (1995), *Books and Readers in the Early Church: A History of Early Christian Texts*, New Haven: Yale University Press.

Gärtner, Bertil (1965), *The Temple and the Community in Qumran and the New Testament*, SNTSMS 1, Cambridge: Cambridge University Press.

Gathercole, Simon (2018), 'The Historical and Human Existence of Jesus in Paul's Letters', *JSHJ* 16: 183–212.

Ginsburskaya, Mila (2009), 'The Idea of Sin-Impurity: The Dead Sea Scrolls in Light of Leviticus', *TynB* 60: 309–311.

Gnilka, Joachim (1997 [1993]), *Jesus of Nazareth: Message and History*, Peabody: Hendrickson.

Goldingay, John (2003), *Old Testament Theology: Israel's Gospel*, Downers Grove: InterVarsity Press.

Goodacre, Mark (2006), 'Scripturalization in Mark's Crucifixion Narrative', in Geert van Oyen and Tom Shepherd (eds.), *The Trial and Death of Jesus: Essays on the Passion in Mark*, Leuven: Peeters, 33–47.

Goodman, Martin (1982), 'The First Jewish Revolt: Social Conflict and the Problem of Debt', *JJS* 33: 417–427.

—— (1993), *The Ruling Class of Judaea: The Origins of the Jewish Revolt against Rome A.D. 66–70*, Cambridge: Cambridge University Press.

—— (1999), 'The Pilgrimage Economy of Jerusalem in the Second Temple Period', in Lee I. Levine (ed.), *Jerusalem; Its Sanctity and Centrality to Judaism, Christianity and Islam*, New York: Continuum, 69–76.

—— (2005), 'The Temple in First Century CE Judaism', in John Day (ed.), *Temple and Worship in Biblical Israel*, London: T&T Clark, 459–468.

—— (2007), *Rome and Jerusalem: The Clash of Ancient Civilizations*, New York: Vintage.

Goppelt, Leonhard (1981–82), *Theology of the New Testament*, 2 vols., Grand Rapids: Eerdmans.

Gosline, Sheldon Lee (2001), *The Coins of Pontius Pilate*, Warren Center: Shangri-La Publications.

Gräbe, Petrus J. (2006), *New Covenant, New Community: The Significance of Biblical and Patristic Covenant Theology for Contemporary Understanding*, Milton Keynes: Paternoster.

Graeig, David (2024), *Resurrection Remembered: A Memory Approach to Jesus' Resurrection in First Corinthians*, London: Routledge.

Green, Joel B. (2013), 'Kingdom of God/Heaven', in Joel B. Green, Jeannine K. Brown and Nicholas Perrin (eds.), *Dictionary of Jesus and the Gospels*, 2nd edn, Downers Grove: InterVarsity Press, 468–481.

Green, William Scott (2007), 'What Do We Really Know about the Pharisees, and How Do We Know it?' in Jacob Neusner and Bruce D. Chilton (eds.), *In Quest of the Historical Pharisees*, Waco: Baylor University Press, 409–423.

Gullotta, Daniel N. (2017), 'On Richard Carrier's Doubts: A Response to Richard Carrier's *On the Historicity of Jesus: Why We Might Have Reason for Doubt*', *JSHJ* 15: 310–346.

Gundry, Robert H. (1993), *Mark: A Commentary on His Apology for the Cross*, Grand Rapids: Baker.

Habermas, Gary, Jonathan Kopel and Benjamin C. Shaw (2021), 'Medical Views on the Death by Crucifixion of Jesus Christ', *Baylor University Medical Center Proceedings* 34: 748–752.

Hahn, Ferdinand (1969), 'The Quest of the Historical Jesus and the Special Character of the Sources Available to Us', in Ferdinand Hahn, Wenzel Lohff and Günther Bornkamm (eds.), *What Can We Know about Jesus?* Edinburgh: Saint Andrew Press, 9–48.

—— (2002), *Theologie des Neuen Testaments*, 2 vols., Tübingen: Mohr Siebeck.

Ham, Clay Alan (2005), *The Coming King and the Rejected Shepherd: Matthew's Reading of Zechariah's Messianic Hope*, NTM, Sheffield: Sheffield Phoenix.

Hare, Douglas A. (1990), *The Son of Man Tradition*, Philadelphia: Fortress.

Harley, Felicity, and Jeffrey Spier (2007), 'The Crucifixion', in Jeffrey Spier (ed.), *Picturing the Bible: The Earliest Christian Art*, New Haven: Yale University Press, 227–232.

Harrington, Hannah K. (2010), 'Purity and Impurity', in John J. Collins and Daniel C. Harlow (eds.), *The Eerdmans Dictionary of Early Judaism*, Grand Rapids: Eerdmans, 1121–1123.

Harvey, A. E. (1982), *Jesus and the Constraints of History*, London: Duckworth.

—— (1990), *Strenuous Commands: The Ethics of Jesus*, London: SCM Press.

Havukainen, Tuomas (2020), *The Quest for the Memory of Jesus: A Viable Path or a Dead End?* Leuven: Peeters.

Hays, Christopher M. (2013), 'Rich and Poor', in Joel B. Green, Jeannine K. Brown and Nicholas Perrin (eds.), *Dictionary of Jesus and the Gospels*, Downers Grove: InterVarsity Press, 800–810.

Hays, Richard B. (2008), 'The Story of God's Son: The Identity of Jesus in the Letters of Paul', in Beverly Roberts Gaventa and Richard B. Hays (eds.), *Seeking the Identity of Jesus: A Pilgrimage*, Grand Rapids: Eerdmans, 180–199.

—— (2014), *Reading Backwards: Figural Christology and the Fourfold Gospel Witness*, Waco: Baylor University Press.

—— (2016), *Echoes of Scripture in the Gospels*, Waco: Baylor University Press.

Heard, W. J., and Craig A. Evans (2000), 'Revolutionary Movements, Jewish', in Craig A. Evans and Stanley E. Porter (eds.), *Dictionary of New Testament Background*, Downers Grove: InterVarsity Press, 936–947.

Henaut, Barry W. (1993), *Oral Tradition and the Gospels: The Problem of Mark 4*, JSNTSup 82, Sheffield: Sheffield Academic Press.

Hengel, Martin (1968), 'Das Gleichnis von den Weingärten Mc 12 1–12 im Lichte der Zenonpapyri und der rabbinischen Gleichnisse', *ZNW* 59: 1–39.

—— (1973 [1971]), *Victory over Violence: Jesus and the Revolutionists*, Philadelphia: Fortress.

—— (1981 [1968]), *The Charismatic Leader and His Followers*, tr. James C. G. Greig, Edinburgh: T&T Clark.

—— (1981 [1980]), *The Atonement: The Origins of the Doctrine in the New Testament*, London: SCM Press.

—— (1989 [1961]), *The Zealots: Investigations into the Jewish Freedom Movement in the Period from Herod I until 70 A.D.*, 2nd edn, Edinburgh: T&T Clark.

—— (1995), *Studies in Early Christology*, London: T&T Clark.

—— (2000), *Judaica et Hellenistica: Kleine Schriften I*, WUNT 90: Tübingen: Mohr Siebeck.

—— (2001), 'Das Begräbnis Jesu bei Paulus und die leibliche Auferstehung aus dem Grabe', in Friedrich Avemarie and Hermann Lichtenberger (eds.), *Auferstehung – Resurrection*, WUNT 135, Tübingen: Mohr Siebeck, 119–183.

—— (2003), *The Son of God: The Origin of Christology and the Development of the Doctrine of the Trinity*, London: SCM Press.

Hengel, Martin, and Anna Maria Schwemer (1991), *Königsherrschaft Gottes und himmlischer Kult im Judentum, Urchristentum und in der hellenistischen Welt*, WUNT 65, Tübingen: Mohr Siebeck.

—— (2019 [2007]), *Jesus and Judaism*, Waco: Baylor University Press.

Himmelfarb, M. (1997), '"A Kingdom of Priests": The Democratization of the Priesthood in the Literature of Second Temple Judaism', *Journal of Jewish Thought and Philosophy* 6: 89–104.

Hofius, Otfried (1993), 'Ist Jesus der Messias? Thesen', *JBT* 8: 103–129.

Holland, Tom (2019), *Dominion: How the Christian Revolution Re-Made the World*, New York: Basic Books.

Hollander, Harm W. (2000), 'The Words of Jesus: From Oral Traditions to Written Record in Paul and Q', *NovT* 42: 340–357.

Holmén, Tom (1996), *Till Jesus Comes: Origins of Christian Apocalyptic Expectation*, Peabody: Hendrickson.

—— (2001), *Jesus and Jewish Covenant Thinking*, BIS 55, Leiden: Brill.

Holtzmann, H. J. (1911), *Lehrbuch der neutestamentlichen Theologie*, 2 vols., 2nd edn, ed. D. A. Jülicher and W. Bauer, Tübingen: Mohr Siebeck.

Hood, Jason (2008), 'Mary, Mother of Jesus', in Craig A. Evans (ed.), *Encyclopedia of the Historical Jesus*, New York: Routledge, 394–395.

Hooker, Morna D. (1967), *The Son of Man in Mark: A Study of the Background of the Term and Its Use in St. Mark's Gospel*, London: SPCK.

—— (1972), 'On Using the Wrong Tool', *Theology* 75: 570–581.

—— (1979), 'Is the Son of Man Problem Really Insoluble?' in E. Best and R. McL. Wilson (eds.), *Text and Interpretation*, FS Matthew Black, Cambridge: Cambridge University Press, 155–168.

—— (1997), *The Signs of a Prophet: The Prophetic Actions of Jesus*, London: SCM Press.

Horsley, Richard (1995), *Galilee: History, Politics, People*, Valley Forge: Trinity Press International.

—— (2003), *Jesus and Empire: The Kingdom of God and the New World Disorder*, Minneapolis: Fortress.

—— (2007), *Scribes, Visionaries, and the Politics of Second Temple Judea*, Louisville: Westminster John Knox.

—— (2012), *The Prophet Jesus and the Renewal of Israel: Moving beyond a Diversionary Debate*, Grand Rapids: Eerdmans.

—— (2014), *Jesus and Magic: Freeing the Gospel Stories from Modern Misconceptions*, Eugene: Cascade.

—— (2022), *The Pharisees and the Temple-State of Judea*, Eugene: Cascade.

Hultgren, Arland J. (1994), *The Rise of Normative Christianity*, Eugene: Wipf & Stock.

Humphreys, Colin J. (2011), *The Mystery of the Last Supper: Reconstructing the Final Days of Jesus*, Cambridge: Cambridge University Press.

Hurtado, Larry (1988), *One God, One Lord: Early Christian Devotion and Ancient Jewish Monotheism*, Philadelphia: Fortress.

—— (2003), *Lord Jesus Christ: Devotion to Jesus in Earliest Christianity*, Grand Rapids: Eerdmans.

—— (2013), 'Interactive Diversity: A Proposed Model of Christian Origins', *JTS* NS: 1–18.

Hurtado, Larry, and Chris L. Keith (eds.) (2011), *Jesus amongst His Friends and Enemies*, Grand Rapids: Baker.

Hvalvik, Reidar (2005), 'All Those Who in Every Place Call on the Name of Our Lord Jesus Christ: The Unity of the Pauline Churches', in Jostein Ådna (ed.), *The Formation of the Early Church*, WUNT 183, Tübingen: Mohr Siebeck, 123–143.

Jackson, David R. (2004), *Enochic Judaism: Three Defining Paradigms*, London: T&T Clark.

Jensen, Morten Hørning (2010 [2006]), *Herod Antipas in Galilee: The Literary and Archaeological Sources on the Reign of Herod Antipas and Its Socio-Economic Impact on Galilee*, WUNT 2.215, Tübingen: Mohr Siebeck.

Jeremias, Joachim (1966 [1960]), *The Eucharistic Words of Jesus*, London: SCM Press.

—— (1971), *New Testament Theology: The Proclamation of Jesus*, New York: Charles Scribner's Sons.

—— (1972 [1954]), *The Parables of Jesus*, 3rd edn, London: SCM Press.

Johnson, Luke Timothy (1996), *The Real Jesus: The Misguided Quest for the Historical Jesus and the Truth of the Traditional Gospels*, New York: HarperCollins.

—— (2018), *Miracles: God's Presence and Power in Creation*, Louisville: Westminster John Knox.

Joseph, Simon J. (2016), 'Jesus and the Temple Incident: A New Proposal', *JSHJ* 14: 71–95.

Kähler, Martin (1988 [1882]), *The So-Called Historical Jesus and the Historic Biblical Christ*, Philadelphia: Fortress.

Käsemann, Ernst (1964a), 'The Canon of the New Testament and the Unity of the Church', in *Essays on New Testament Themes*, tr. W. J. Montague, London: SCM Press, 95–107.

—— (1964b), 'The Problem of the Historical Jesus', in *Essays on New Testament Themes*, tr. W. J. Montague, London: SCM Press, 15–47.

—— (1973), 'The Problem of a New Testament Theology', *NTS* 19: 235–245.

Kazen, Thomas (2002), *Jesus and Purity Halakhah: Was Jesus Indifferent to Impurity?* CONBNT 38, Stockholm: Almquist & Wiksell.

—— (2007), 'The Coming Son of Man Revisited', *JSHJ* 5: 155–174.

—— (2011), *Emotions in Biblical Law: A Cognitive Science Approach*, HBM 36, Sheffield: Sheffield Phoenix.

—— (2021), *Impurity and Purification in Early Judaism and the Jesus Tradition*, Atlanta: SBL Press.

Keck, Leander E. (2000), *Who Is Jesus? History in Perfect Tense*, Columbia: University of South Carolina Press.

Keener, Craig S. (2009), *The Historical Jesus of the Gospels*, Grand Rapids: Eerdmans.

—— (2011), *Miracles: The Credibility of New Testament Accounts*, Grand Rapids: Baker.

—— (2019), *Christobiography: Memory, History, and Reliability of the Gospels*, Grand Rapids: Eerdmans.

Keith, Chris (2011), 'Memory and Authenticity: Jesus Tradition and What Really Happened', *ZNW* 102: 155–177.

—— (2014), *Jesus against the Scribal Elite: The Origins of the Conflict*, Grand Rapids: Baker.

—— (2016), 'The Narratives of the Gospels and the Historical Jesus: Current Debates, Prior Debates, and the Goal of Historical Jesus Research', *JSNT* 38: 426–455.

—— (2024), 'Beyond What Is Written', in James G. Crossley and Chris Keith (eds.), *The Next Quest for the Historical Jesus*, Grand Rapids: Eerdmans, 96–112.

Keith, Chris, and Anthony Le Donne (eds.) (2012), *Jesus, Criteria, and the Demise of Authenticity*, London: T&T Clark.

Kindler, Arie (1973), *Coins of the Land of Israel*, Jerusalem: Keter.

Kinman, Brent (2010), 'Jesus' Royal Entry into Jerusalem', in Darrell L. Bock and Robert L. Webb (eds.), *Key Events in the Life of the Historical Jesus: A Collaborative Exploration of Context and Coherence*, Grand Rapids: Eerdmans, 383–427.

Klausner, Joseph (1925), *Jesus of Nazareth: His Life, Times, and Teaching*, New York: Macmillan.

Klawans, Jonathan (2000), *Impurity and Sin in Ancient Judaism*, Oxford: Oxford University Press.

—— (2001), 'Was Jesus' Last Supper a Seder?' *BRev* 17: 24–33, 47.

—— (2002), 'Interpreting the Last Supper', *NTS* 48: 1–17.

—— (2006), *Purity, Sacrifice and the Temple: Symbolism and Supersessionism in the Study of Ancient Judaism*, Oxford: Oxford University Press.

Kloppenborg, John S. (2006), *The Tenants in the Vineyard: Ideology, Economics, and Agrarian Conflict in Jewish Palestine*, WUNT 195; Tübingen: Mohr Siebeck.

Knight, Jonathan (2004), *Jesus: An Historical and Theological Investigation*, London: T&T Clark.

Koester, Helmut (1991), 'Epilogue: Current Issues in New Testament Scholarship', in Birger A. Pearson (ed.), *The Future of Early Christianity: Essays in Honor of Helmut Koester*, Minneapolis: Fortress, 467–476.

Kotansky, Roy (2017), 'The Magic Crucifixion Gem', *Greek, Roman and Byzantine Studies* 57: 631–659.

Kümmel, Werner Georg (1974 [1972]), *The Theology of the New Testament*, tr. J. Steely, London: SCM Press.

Kvalbein, Hans (1998), 'The Kingdom of God in the Ethics of Jesus', *Communio Viatorum* 60: 197–227.

Ladd (1993 [1974]), *A Theology of the New Testament*, rev. edn, Grand Rapids: Eerdmans.

Lee, Dorothy A. (2021), *The Ministry of Women in the New Testament: Reclaiming Their Vision for Biblical Leadership*, Grand Rapids: Eerdmans.

Lee, John J. R., and Daniel Brueske (2023), *A Ransom for Many: Mark 10:45 as a Key to the Gospel*, Bellingham: Lexham.

Levine, Amy-Jill (2006a), 'Introduction', in Amy-Jill Levine, Dale C. Allison Jr and John Dominic Crossan (eds.), *The Historical Jesus in Context*, Princeton: Princeton University Press, 1–39.

—— (2006b), *The Misunderstood Jew: The Church and the Scandal of the Jewish Jesus*, New York: HarperOne.

Levine, Lee I. (2010), 'Temple, Jerusalem', in John J. Collins and Daniel C. Harlow (eds.), *The Eerdmans Dictionary of Early Judaism*, Grand Rapids: Eerdmans, 1281–1291.

Licona, Michael (2010), *The Resurrection of Jesus: A New Historiographical Approach*, Downers Grove: InterVarsity Press.

Lincoln, Andrew (2013), *Born of a Virgin? Reconceiving Jesus in the Bible, Tradition, and Theology*, Grand Rapids: Eerdmans.

Loader, William (2002 [1997]), *Jesus' Attitude towards the Law: A Study of the Gospel*, Grand Rapids: Eerdmans.

Lohse, Eduard (1974), *Grundriss der neutestamentlichen Theologie*, Stuttgart: Kohlhammer.

Luff, Rosemary M. (2019), *The Impact of Jesus in First-Century Palestine: Textual and Archaeological Evidence for Long-standing Discontent*, Cambridge: Cambridge University Press.

Lukaszewski, Albert L. (2011), 'Issues Concerning the Aramaic behind ὁ υἱὸς τοῦ ἀνθρώπου: A Critical Review of Scholarship', in Larry W. Hurtado and Paul L. Owen (eds.), *'Who Is the Son of Man?' The Latest Scholarship on a Puzzling Expression of the Historical Jesus*, LNTS 390, London: T&T Clark, 1–27.

Maccoby, Hyam (2004), 'Jesus the Pharisee', *JQ* 51: 37–52.

McGrath, James F. (2021), *What Jesus Learned from Women*, Eugene: Cascade.

—— (2024), *John of History and Baptist of Faith: The Quest for the Historical Baptizer*, Grand Rapids: Eerdmans.

McKnight, Scot (1991), *A Light among the Gentiles: Jewish Missionary Activity in the Second Temple Period*, Minneapolis: Fortress.
—— (1999), *A New Vision for Israel: The Teachings of Jesus in National Context*, Grand Rapids: Eerdmans.
—— (2001), 'Jesus and the Twelve', *BBR* 11: 203–231.
—— (2004), *The Jesus Creed: Loving God, Loving Others*, Brewster: Paraclete.
—— (2005), *Jesus and His Death: Historiography, the Historical Jesus, and Atonement Theory*, Waco: Baylor University Press.
—— (2011), *The King Jesus Gospel: The Original Good News Revisited*, Grand Rapids: Zondervan.
—— (2014), *Kingdom Conspiracy: Returning to the Radical Mission of the Local Church*, Grand Rapids: Brazos.
McKnight, Scot, and Joseph B. Modica (eds.) (2008), *Who Do My Opponents Say That I Am? An Investigation of the Accusations against Jesus*, LNTS 327, LHJS, London: T&T Clark.
Magness, Jodi (2006), 'Jesus' Tomb: What Did It Look Like?' in Hershel Shanks (ed.), *Where Christianity Was Born*, Washington: Biblical Archaeology Society, 212–226.
Manson, T. W. (1935), *The Teaching of Jesus: Studies in Its Form and Content*, 2nd edn, Cambridge: Cambridge University Press.
—— (1964), *Only to the House of Israel? Jesus and the Non-Jews*, Philadelphia: Fortress.
Marcus, Joel (1984), 'Mark 4:10–12 and Marcan Epistemology', *JBL* 103: 557–574.
—— (2018), *John the Baptist in History and Theology*, Columbia: University of South Carolina Press.
Marshak, Adam Kolman (2015), *The Many Faces of Herod the Great*, Grand Rapids: Eerdmans.
Marshall, I. Howard (2004), *New Testament Theology: Many Witnesses, One Gospel*, Downers Grove: InterVarsity Press.
—— (2010), 'The Last Supper', in Darrell L. Bock and Robert L. Webb (eds.), *Key Events in the Life of the Historical Jesus: A Collaborative Exploration of Context and Coherence*, Grand Rapids: Eerdmans, 481–588.
Martin, Dale B. (2014), 'Jesus in Jerusalem: Armed and Not Dangerous', *JSNT* 37: 3–24.

Maslen, Matthew W., and Piers D. Mitchell (2006), 'Medical Theories on the Cause of Death in Crucifixion', *Journal of the Royal Society of Medicine* 99: 185–188.

Mason, Steve (2007), 'Josephus's Pharisees: The Narratives', in Jacob Neusner and Bruce D. Chilton (eds.), *In Quest of the Historical Pharisees*, Waco: Baylor University Press, 3–40.

Matera, Frank (1999), *New Testament Christology*, Louisville: Westminster John Knox.

—— (2007), *New Testament Theology: Exploring Diversity in Unity*, Louisville: Westminster John Knox.

Mead, James K. (2007), *Biblical Theology: Issues, Methods, and Themes*, Louisville: Westminster John Knox.

Meggitt, Justin (2007), 'The Madness of King Jesus: Why Was Jesus Put to Death, but His Followers Were Not?' *JSNT* 29: 370–413.

—— (2019), '"More Ingenious Than Learned?" Examining the Quest for the Non-Historical Jesus', *NTS* 65: 443–460.

Meier, John P. (1991–2016), *A Marginal Jew: Rethinking the Historical Jesus*, 5 vols., AYBRL, New Haven: Yale University Press.

Metzdorf, Christina (2003), *Die Tempelaktion Jesu: Patristische und historisch-kritische Exegese im Vergleich*, WUNT 2.168, Tübingen: Mohr Siebeck.

Metzger, Bruce M., and Roger L. Omanson (2006 [1971]), *A Textual Guide to the Greek New Testament*, Stuttgart: Deutsche Bibelgesellschaft.

Meyer, Ben F. (1979), *The Aims of Jesus*, London: SCM Press.

Meyers, Eric M. (2021), 'Purity Concerns and Common Judaism in Light of Archaeology', in Joseph Sievers and Amy-Jill Levine (eds.), *The Pharisees*, Grand Rapids: Eerdmans, 41–54.

Moo, Douglas J. (1983), *The Old Testament in the Gospel Passion Narratives*, Sheffield: Almond Press.

Moor, Johannes C. (1998), 'The Targumic Background of Mark 12:1–12: The Parable of the Wicked Tenants', *JSJ* 29: 63–80.

Morgan, Robert (1987), 'The Historical Jesus and the Theology of the New Testament', in L. D. Hurst and N. T. Wright (eds.), *The Glory of Christ in the New Testament: Studies in Christology in Memory of G.B. Caird*, Oxford: Clarendon, 187–206.

Morrison, Craig E. (2021), 'Interpreting the Name "Pharisee"', in Joseph Sievers and Amy-Jill Levine (eds.), *The Pharisees*, Grand Rapids: Eerdmans, 3–19.

Moule, C. F. D. (1977), *The Origins of Christology*, Cambridge: Cambridge University Press.

Murphy, Catherine M. (2003), *John the Baptist: Prophet of Purity for a New Age*, Collegeville: Liturgical Press.

Myles, Robert (2016), 'The Fetish for a Subversive Jesus', *JSHJ* 14: 52–70.

Neusner, Jacob (1971), *Rabbinic Traditions about the Pharisees before 70, Part III: Conclusions*, Leiden: Brill.

—— (1973), *From Politics to Piety: The Emergence of Pharisaic Judaism*, Englewood Cliffs: Prentice Hall.

—— (1989), 'Money-Changers in the Temple; the Mishnah's Explanation', *NTS* 35: 287–290.

—— (1993), *Judaic Law from Jesus to the Mishnah: A Systematic Reply to Professor E.P. Sanders*, Atlanta: Scholars.

—— (2007), 'The Debate with E.P. Sanders since 1970', in Jacob Neusner and Bruce D. Chilton (eds.), *In Quest of the Historical Pharisees*, Waco: Baylor University Press, 395–405.

Neusner, Jacob, and Bruce D. Chilton (eds.) (2007), *In Quest of the Historical Pharisees*, Waco: Baylor University Press.

Ng, Esther Yue L. (2002), *Reconstructing Christian Origins? The Feminist Theology of Elisabeth Schüssler Fiorenza: An Evaluation*, PTM, Carlisle: Paternoster.

Nickelsburg, George W. E. (2003), *Ancient Judaism and Christian Origins: Diversity, Continuity, and Transformation*, Minneapolis: Fortress.

Novenson, Matthew V. (2012), *Christ among the Messiahs: Christ Language in Paul and Messiah Language in Ancient Judaism*, Oxford: Oxford University Press.

—— (2017), *The Grammar of Messianism: An Ancient Jewish Political Idiom and Its Users*, Oxford: Oxford University Press.

O'Grady, Selina (2013), 'Killing Jesus: A History by Bill O'Reilly and Martin Dugard', *The Guardian*, www.theguardian.com/books/2013/dec/18/killing-jesus-bill-oreilly-review (accessed 28 April 2019).

O'Reilly, Bill, and Martin Dugard (2017), *Killing Jesus: A History*, New York: St. Martin's.

Owen, Paul (2011), 'Problems with Casey's "Solution"', in Larry W. Hurtado and Paul L. Owen (eds.), *'Who Is the Son of Man?' The Latest Scholarship on a Puzzling Expression of the Historical Jesus*, LNTS 390, London: T&T Clark, 28–49.

Owen, Paul, and David Shepherd (2001), 'Speaking up for Qumran, Dalman and the Son of Man: Was *Bar Enasha* a Common Term for "Man" in the Time of Jesus?' *JSNT* 23: 81–122.

Palu, Ma'afu (2012), *Jesus and Time: An Interpretation of Mark 1.15*, LNTS 468, London: T&T Clark.

Park, Wongi (2024), 'Race, Ethnicity, and Whiteness', in James G. Crossley and Chris Keith (eds.), *The Next Quest for the Historical Jesus*, Grand Rapids: Eerdmans, 357–370.

Perrin, Nicholas (2010), *Jesus the Temple*, Grand Rapids: Baker Academic.

—— (2013a), 'Exile', in Joel B. Green and Lee Martin McDonald (eds.), *The World of the New Testament: Cultural, Social, and Historical Contexts*, Grand Rapids: Baker, 25–37.

—— (2013b), 'Last Supper', in Joel B. Green, Jeannine K. Brown and Nicholas Perrin (eds.), *Dictionary of Jesus and the Gospels*, Downers Grove: InterVarsity Press, 492–501.

—— (2019), *The Kingdom of God: A Biblical Theology*, Grand Rapids: Zondervan.

Perrin, Norman (1976), *Jesus and the Language of the Kingdom: Symbol and Metaphor in New Testament Interpretation*, Philadelphia: Fortress.

Pesch, Rudolf (1976–77), *Das Markusevangelium*, 2 vols., HTKNT, Herder: Freiburg.

Peters, D. M. (2013), 'Essenes', in Joel B. Green, Jeannine K. Brown and Nicholas Perrin (eds.), *Dictionary of Jesus and the Gospels*, 2nd edn, Downers Grove: InterVarsity Press, 239–242.

Pitre, Brant (2005), *Jesus, the Tribulation, and the End of Exile: Restoration Eschatology and Origin of the Atonement*, WUNT 2.204, Tübingen: Mohr Siebeck.

—— (2011), *Jesus and the Jewish Roots of the Eucharist: Unlocking the Secrets of the Last Supper*, New York: Doubleday.

—— (2015), *Jesus and the Last Supper*, Grand Rapids: Eerdmans.
Popović, Mladen (2011), *The Jewish Revolt against Rome: Interdisciplinary Perspectives*, Leiden: Brill.
Porter, Stanley E. (2000), *The Criteria for Authenticity in Historical-Jesus Research: Previous Discussion and New Proposal*, JSNTSup 191, Sheffield: Sheffield Academic Press.
Reed, Jonathan L. (2000), *Archaeology and the Galilean Jesus: A Re-examination of the Evidence*, Harrisburg: Trinity Press International.
—— (2006), 'Archaeological Contributions to the Study of Jesus and the Gospels', in Amy-Jill Levine, Dale C. Allison and John Dominic Crossan (eds.), *The Historical Jesus in Context*, Princeton: Princeton University Press, 40–54.
Regev, Eyal (1999), 'Non-Priestly Purity and Its Religious Aspects According to Historical Sources and Archaeological Findings', in M. J. H. M. and J. Schwartz (eds.), *Purity and Holiness: The Heritage of Leviticus*, Leiden: Brill, 223–244.
—— (2000), 'Pure Individualism: The Idea of Non-Priestly Purity in Ancient Judaism', *JSJ* 31: 176–202.
—— (2019), *The Temple in Early Christianity: Experiencing the Sacred*, AYBRL, New Haven: Yale University Press.
Reimarus, H. S. (1971 [1778]), *Fragments*, ed. Charles H. Talbert, tr. Ralph S. Fraser, London: SCM Press.
Reimer, Andy M. (2002), *Miracle and Magic: A Study in the Acts of the Apostles and the Life of Apollonius of Tyana*, Sheffield: Sheffield Academic Press.
Reinhartz, Adele (2024), 'Beyond the Jewish Jesus Debate', in James G. Crossley and Chris Keith (eds.), *The Next Quest for the Historical Jesus*, Grand Rapids: Eerdmans, 49–61.
Reiser, Marius (1997 [1990]), *Jesus and Judgment: The Eschatological Proclamation in Its Jewish Context*, Minneapolis: Fortress.
Rhoads, David M. (1976), *Israel in Revolution, 6–7 C.E.: A Political History Based on the Writings of Josephus*, Philadelphia: Fortress.
Rhodes, Paul Eddy (1996), 'Jesus as Diogenes? Reflections on the Cynic Jesus Thesis', *JBL* 115: 449–469.
Rodríguez, Rafael (2009), 'Authenticating Criteria: The Use and Misuse of a Critical Method', *JSHJ* 7: 152–167.

—— (2010), *Structuring Early Christian Memory: Jesus in Tradition, Performance and Text*, LNTS 407, London: T&T Clark.

Rowlands, Jonathan (2023), *The Metaphysics of Historical Jesus Research: A Prolegomenon to a Future Quest for the Historical Jesus*, London: Routledge.

Sacchi, Paolo (1992), 'Recovering Jesus' Formative Background', in James H. Charlesworth (ed.), *Jesus and the Dead Sea Scrolls: The Controversy Resolved*, New York: Doubleday, 123–139.

Safrai S., and M. Stern (eds.) (1974–76), *The Jewish People in the First Century: Historical Geography, Political History, Social, Cultural and Religious Life and Institutions*, 2 vols., Amsterdam: Van Gorcum.

Saldarini, Anthony J. (1988), *Pharisees, Scribes and Sadducees: A Sociological Approach*, Wilmington: Michael Glazier.

Sanders, E. P. (1985), *Jesus and Judaism*, London: SCM Press.

—— (1990), *Jewish Law from Jesus to the Mishnah: Five Studies*, London: SCM Press.

—— (1992), *Judaism: Practice and Belief 63 BCE - 66 CE*, London: SCM Press.

—— (1993), *The Historical Figure of Jesus*, London: SCM Press.

—— (2016), *Paul: The Apostle's Life, Letters and Thought*, Minneapolis: Fortress.

Schiffman, Lawrence H. (2010), *Qumran and Jerusalem: Studies in the Dead Sea Scrolls and the History of Judaism*, Grand Rapids: Eerdmans.

—— (2020), 'Where Are We in the Study of the Dead Sea Scrolls?' Paper presented at *The Dead Sea Scrolls in Recent Scholarship: A Public Conference*, 17–20 May 2020, New York University, https://as.nyu.edu/hebrewjudaic/about/HJS-Media.html (accessed 30 August 2020).

Schmithals, Walter (1998 [1994]), *The Theology of the First Christians*, tr. O. C. Dean, Louisville: Westminster John Knox.

Schnabel, Eckhard J. (1994), 'Jesus and the Beginnings of the Mission to the Gentiles', in Joel B. Green and Max Turner (eds.), *Jesus of Nazareth, Lord and Christ*, Grand Rapids: Eerdmans, 37–58.

—— (2004), *The Early Christian Mission*, 2 vols., Downers Grove: InterVarsity Press.

—— (2018), *Jesus in Jerusalem: The Last Days*, Grand Rapids: Eerdmans.
—— (2023), *New Testament Theology*, Grand Rapids: Baker.
Schnelle, Udo (2009 [2007]), *Theology of the New Testament*, tr. Eugene Boring, Grand Rapids: Baker.
—— (2020), *The First One Hundred Years of Christianity: An Introduction to Its History, Literature, and Development*, Grand Rapids: Baker.
Schrage, Wolfgang (1988), *The Ethics of the New Testament*, London: Continuum.
Schreiner, Patrick (2016), *The Body of Jesus: A Spatial Analysis of the Kingdom of Heaven in Matthew*, LNTS 555, London: T&T Clark.
Schreiner, Thomas R. (2008), *New Testament Theology: Magnifying God in Christ*, Grand Rapids: Baker.
Schröter, Jens (2013 [2007]), *From Jesus to the New Testament: Early Christian Theology and the Origin of the New Testament Canon*, tr. W. Coppins, Waco: Baylor University Press.
—— (2014 [2012]), *Jesus of Nazareth: Jew from Galilee, Savior of the World*, Waco: Baylor University Press.
—— (2018a), 'Memory and Memories in Early Christianity: The Remembered Jesus as a Test Case', in S. Butticaz and E. Norelli (eds.), *Memory and Memories in Early Christianity: Proceedings of the International Conference Held at the Universities of Geneva and Lausanne (June 2-3, 2016)*, WUNT 398, Tübingen: Mohr Siebeck, 79-96.
—— (2018b), 'Memory, Theories of History, and the Reception of Jesus', *JSHJ* 16: 85-107.
—— (2020), 'The Quest for the Historical Jesus: Current Debates and Prospects', *EC* 11: 283-296.
—— (2021), 'How Close Were Jesus and the Pharisees?' in Joseph Sievers and Amy-Jill Levine (ed.), *The Pharisees*, Grand Rapids: Eerdmans, 220-239.
Schürer, Emil (1973-87), *The History of the Jewish People in the Age of Jesus Christ*, rev. and ed. G. Vermes, F. Millar and M. Black, 3 vols., Edinburgh: T&T Clark.
Schüssler Fiorenza, Elisabeth (1995 [1983]), *In Memory of Her: A Feminist Reconstruction of Christian Origins*, 2nd edn, London: SCM Press.

—— (2003), 'Re-Visioning Christian Origins: *In Memory of Her* Revisited', in K. J. O'Mahoney (ed.), *Christian Origins: Worship, Belief, and Society*, JSNTSup 241, Sheffield: Sheffield Academic Press, 225–250.

Schwartz, Daniel R. (1992), '"Kingdom of Priests" – a Pharisaic Slogan?' in *Studies in the Jewish Background of Christianity*, WUNT 1.60, Tübingen: Mohr Siebeck, 57–80.

Schweitzer, Albert (1945 [1906]), *The Quest of the Historical Jesus*, tr. W. Montgomery, London: Adam & Charles Black.

Scott, Bernard B. (1989), *Hear Then the Parable: A Commentary on the Parables of Jesus*, Minneapolis: Augsburg Fortress.

Scott, James M. (ed.) (2017), *Exile: A Conversation with N. T. Wright*, Downers Grove: InterVarsity Press.

Seeley, David (1997), 'Jesus and the Cynics Revisited', *JBL* 116: 704–712.

Segal, Alan F. (2002), 'The Incarnation: The Jewish Milieu', in Stephen T. Davis, Daniel Kendall and Gerald O'Collins (eds.), *The Incarnation: An Interdisciplinary Symposium on the Incarnation of the Son of God*, Oxford: Oxford University Press, 116–139.

Shepherd, David (2011), 'Re-Solving the Son of Man "Problem" in Aramaic', in Larry W. Hurtado and Paul L. Owen (eds.), *'Who Is the Son of Man?' The Latest Scholarship on a Puzzling Expression of the Historical Jesus*, LNTS 390, London: T&T Clark, 50–60.

Sievers, Joseph, and Amy-Jill Levine (eds.) (2021), *The Pharisees*, Grand Rapids: Eerdmans.

Sklar, Jay (2005), *Impurity, Sacrifice, Atonement: The Priestly Conceptions*, HBM 2, Sheffield: Sheffield Phoenix.

Smith, Barry D. (2008), 'Last Supper, Words of Institution', in Craig A. Evans (ed.), *Encyclopedia of the Historical Jesus*, New York: Routledge, 65–68.

Smith, Mitzi J. (2024), 'Born of a *Doulē*', in James G. Crossley and Chris Keith (eds.), *The Next Quest for the Historical Jesus*, Grand Rapids: Eerdmans, 371–382.

Snodgrass, Klyne (1998), 'Recent Research on the Parable of the Wicked Tenants: An Assessment', *BBR* 8: 187–215.

—— (2008), *Stories with Intent: A Comprehensive Guide to the Parables*, Grand Rapids: Eerdmans.

—— (2010), 'The Temple Incident', in Darrell L. Bock and Robert

L. Webb (eds.), *Key Events in the Life of the Historical Jesus: A Collaborative Exploration of Context and Coherence*, Grand Rapids: Eerdmans, 428–480.

—— (2011 [1983]), *Parable of the Wicked Tenants: An Inquiry into Parable Interpretation*, Eugene: Wipf & Stock.

Snyder, H. Gregory (2000), *Teachers and Texts in the Ancient World: Philosophers, Jews, and Christians*, London: Routledge.

Stacey, David, and Gregory Doudna (2013), *Qumran Revisited: A Reassessment of the Archaeology of the Site and Its Texts*, BAR International Series 2520, Oxford: Archaeopress.

Stark, Rodney (2006), *Cities of God: Christianizing the Urban Empire*, San Francisco: HarperSanFrancisco.

Stauffer, Ethelberg (1955), *New Testament Theology*, tr. J. Marsh, London: SCM Press.

Stemberger, Günter (1995 [1991]), *Jewish Contemporaries of Jesus: Pharisees, Sadducees, Essenes*, Minneapolis: Fortress.

Stettler, Christian (2011), *Das letze Gericht: Studien zur Endgerichtserwartung von den Schriftenpropheten bis Jesus*, WUNT 299, Tübingen: Mohr Siebeck.

Stettler, Hanna (2004), 'Sanctification in the Jesus Tradition', *Biblica* 85: 153–178.

—— (2014), *Heiligung bei Paulus: Ein Beitrag aus biblisch-theologischer Sicht*, WUNT 2.368, Tübingen: Mohr Siebeck.

Strahan, Joshua (2023), 'Did Jesus Nullify the Torah and Declare Nonkosher Foods Clean? Toward a Better Reading of Mark 7:19b', *BBR* 33: 259–280.

Strange, James F. (2007), 'Archaeology and the Pharisees', in Jacob Neusner and Bruce D. Chilton (eds.), *In Quest of the Historical Pharisees*, Waco: Baylor University Press, 237–251.

Strauss, Mark L. (2013), 'Sadducees', in Joel B. Green, Jeannine K. Brown and Nicholas Perrin (eds.), *Dictionary of Jesus and the Gospels*, 2nd edn, Downers Grove: InterVarsity Press, 824–825.

Strecker, Georg (2000 [1996]), *Theology of the New Testament*, tr. M. Eugene Boring, Louisville: Westminster John Knox.

Stuhlmacher, Peter (1995), *How to Do Biblical Theology*, Eugene: Pickwick.

—— (2018 [1999]), *Biblical Theology of the New Testament*, tr. Daniel P. Bailey, Grand Rapids: Eerdmans.

Tan, Kim Huat (1997), *The Zion Traditions and the Aims of Jesus*, SNTSMS 91, Cambridge: Cambridge University Press.

Taylor, Joan E. (1997), *The Immerser: John the Baptist within Second Temple Judaism*, Grand Rapids: Eerdmans.

Taylor, Vincent (1952), *The Gospel According to St. Mark*, London: Macmillan.

Theissen, Gerd (1976), 'Die Tempelweissangung Jesu: Prophetie im Spannungsfeld von Stadt und Land', *TZ* 32: 144–158.

—— (1978), *Sociology of Early Palestinian Christianity*, tr. John Bowden, Philadelphia: Fortress.

—— (1987), *The Shadow of the Galilean*, tr. John Bowden, Philadelphia: Fortress.

Theissen, Gerd, and Anna Merz (1998 [1996]), *The Historical Jesus: A Comprehensive Guide*, tr. John Bowden, Minneapolis: Fortress.

Theissen, Gerd, and Dagmar Winter (2002 [1998]), *The Quest for the Plausible Jesus: The Question of Criteria*, Louisville: Westminster John Knox.

Thielman, Frank (2005), *New Testament Theology: A Canonical and Synthetic Approach*, Grand Rapids: Zondervan.

Thiessen, Matthew (2016), 'The Many for One or One for the Many? Reading Mark 10:45 in the Roman Empire', *HTR* 109: 447–466.

—— (2020), *Jesus and the Forces of Death: The Gospels' Portrayal of Ritual Impurity within First-Century Judaism*, Grand Rapids: Baker.

Thoma, Clemens (1980), *A Christian Theology of Judaism*, New York: Paulist Press.

Tiwald, Markus (2012), 'Jewish-Christian Trajectories in Torah and Temple Theology', in Tom Holmén (ed.), *Jesus in Continuum*, WUNT 289, Tübingen: Mohr Siebeck, 385–409.

Tomson, Peter J. (2001), 'Jesus and His Judaism', in Markus Bockmuehl (ed.), *The Cambridge Companion to Jesus*, Cambridge: Cambridge University Press, 25–40.

Trebilco, Paul (2004), *The Early Christians in Ephesus from Paul to Ignatius*, WUNT 166, Tübingen: Mohr Siebeck.

—— (2006), '"Global" and "Local" in the New Testament and in Early

Christianity', inaugural professorial lecture, University of Otago, 21 September 2006.
Twelftree, Graham (1993), *Jesus the Exorcist: A Contribution to the Study of the Historical Jesus*, Peabody: Hendrickson.
—— (1999), *Jesus the Miracle Worker: A Historical and Theological Study*, Downers Grove: InterVarsity Press.
—— (2017), *The Nature Miracles of Jesus: Problems, Perspectives, and Prospects*, Eugene: Wipf & Stock.
Tyrell, George (1909), *Christianity at the Cross-Roads*, London: Longmans.
van Henten, J. W. (2015), 'Josephus, Fifth Evangelist, and Jesus on the Temple', *HTS* 71: 1–11.
Van Voorst, Robert E. (2000), *Jesus Outside the New Testament: An Introduction to the Ancient Evidence*, Grand Rapids: Eerdmans.
Vermes, Geza (1973), *Jesus the Jew*, London: SCM Press.
—— (1983), *Jesus and the World of Judaism*, London: SCM Press.
—— (1993), *The Religion of Jesus the Jew*, Minneapolis: Fortress.
—— (2003), *Jesus in His Jewish Context*, London: SCM Press.
—— (2004), *The Authentic Gospel of Jesus*, London: Penguin.
—— (2005), *Scrolls, Scriptures and Early Christianity*, London: T&T Clark.
Wardle, Timothy (2010), *The Jerusalem Temple and Early Christian Identity*, Tübingen: Mohr Siebeck.
Wassen, Cecilia (2016), 'Jesus' Table Fellowship with "Toll Collectors and Sinners"', *JSHJ* 14: 137–157.
Watson, Francis B. (1987), '"Historical Evidence" and the Resurrection of Jesus', *Theology* 90: 365–372.
—— (1994), *Text, Church and World: Biblical Interpretation in Theological Perspective*, Edinburgh: T&T Clark.
—— (1997), *Text and Truth: Redefining Biblical Theology*, Grand Rapids: Eerdmans.
—— (2008), '*Veritas Christi*: How to Get from the Jesus of History to the Christ of Faith without Losing One's Way', in Beverly Roberts Gaventa and Richard B. Hays (eds.), *Seeking the Identity of Jesus: A Pilgrimage*, Grand Rapids: Eerdmans, 96–114.
Watts, Rikki E. (1998), 'Jesus' Death, Isaiah 53, and Mark 10:45: A Crux

Revisited', in William H. Bellinger Jr and William F. Farmer (eds.), *Jesus and the Suffering Servant: Isaiah 53 and Christian Origins*, Harrisburg: Trinity Press International, 125–151.

Webb, Robert L. (1991), *John the Baptizer and Prophet: A Socio-Historical Study*, JSNTSup 62; Sheffield: Sheffield University Press.

—— (2010), 'The Roman Examination and Crucifixion of Jesus', in Darrell L. Bock and Robert L. Webb (eds.), *Key Events in the Life of the Historical Jesus: A Collaborative Exploration of Context and Coherence*, Grand Rapids: Eerdmans, 669–773.

Wedderburn, Alexander J. M. (2006), 'Jesus' Action in the Temple: A Key or a Puzzle?' *ZNW* 97: 1–22.

Wenham, David (1989), *The Parables of Jesus: Pictures of a Revolution*, London: Hodder & Stoughton.

—— (1995), 'How Jesus Understood the Last Supper: A Parable in Action', *Themelios* 20: 11–16.

—— (2021), *Jesus in Context: Making Sense of the Historical Figure*, Cambridge: Cambridge University Press.

Wilk, Florian (2008), 'Die synoptischen Evangelien des Neuen Testaments als Quellen für die Geschichte der Pharisäer', in Lutz Doering et al. (eds.), *Judaistik und neutestamentliche Wissenschaft: Standorte, Grenzen, Beziehungen*, Göttingen: Vandenhoeck & Ruprecht, 85–107.

Williams, Logan (2024), 'The Stomach Purifies All Foods: Jesus' Anatomical Argument in Mark 7.18-19', *JSNT* 70: 371–391.

Williams, Peter J. (2011), 'Expressing Definiteness in Aramaic: A Response to Casey's Theory Concerning the Son of Man Sayings', in Larry W. Hurtado and Paul L. Owen (eds.), *'Who Is the Son of Man?' The Latest Scholarship on a Puzzling Expression of the Historical Jesus*, LNTS 390, London: T&T Clark, 61–77.

—— (2018), *Can We Trust the Gospels?* Wheaton: Crossway.

Willitts, Joel (2005), 'Presuppositions and Procedures in the Study of the "Historical Jesus": Or, Why I Decided Not to Be a "Historical Jesus" Scholar', *JSHJ* 3: 61–108.

Winton, Alan P. (1990), *The Proverbs of Jesus: Issues of History and Rhetoric*, JSNTSup 35, Sheffield: JSOT Press.

Witherington, Ben (1984), *Women in the Ministry of Jesus: A Study of*

Jesus' Attitude to Women and Their Roles as Reflected in His Earthly Life, SNTSMS 51, Cambridge: Cambridge University Press.

—— (1990), *The Christology of Jesus*, Minneapolis: Fortress.

—— (1994), *Jesus the Sage: The Pilgrimage of Wisdom*, Minneapolis: Fortress.

—— (1997), *The Jesus Quest: The Third Search for the Jew of Nazareth*, 2nd edn, Downers Grove: InterVarsity Press.

—— (1999), *Jesus the Seer: The Progress of Prophecy*, Peabody: Hendrickson.

—— (2006), 'Isaiah 53:1–12 (Septuagint)', in Amy-Jill Levine, Dale C. Allison and John Dominic Crossan (eds.), *The Historical Jesus in Context*, Princeton: Princeton University Press, 400–404.

—— (2009–10), *The Indelible Image: The Theological and Ethical Thought World of the New Testament*, 2 vols., Downers Grove: InterVarsity Press.

—— (2017), *Isaiah Old and New: Exegesis, Intertextuality, and Hermeneutics*, Minneapolis: Fortress.

Wrede, W. (1971), *The Messianic Secret*, tr. J. C. G. Greig, Cambridge: James Clark & Co.

Wright, Brian J. (2017), *Communal Reading in the Time of Jesus: A Window into Early Christian Reading Practices*, Minneapolis: Fortress.

Wright, N. T. (1992), *The New Testament and the People of God*, COQG 1, London: SPCK.

—— (1996), *Jesus and the Victory of God*, COQG 2, London: SPCK.

—— (1999), *The Challenge of Jesus*, London: SPCK.

—— (2003), *The Resurrection of the Son of God*, COQG 3, London: SPCK.

—— (2007), *Surprised by Hope*, London: SPCK.

—— (2012), *How God Became King*, London: SPCK.

—— (2014), *Paul and the Faithfulness of God*, COQG 4, London: SPCK.

—— (2016), *The Day the Revolution Began: Reconsidering the Meaning of Jesus's Crucifixion*, San Francisco: HarperOne.

Wright, N. T., and Michael F. Bird (2019), *The New Testament in Its World: An Introduction to the History, Literature and Theology of the First Christians*, Grand Rapids: Zondervan; London: SPCK.

Yarbrough, Robert W. (2004), *The Salvation Historical Fallacy? Reassessing the History of New Testament Theology*, Leiden: Deo.

Yinger, Kent L. (2022), *The Pharisees: Their History, Character, and New Testament Portrait*, Eugene: Cascade.

Young, Brad H. (1995), *Jesus the Jewish Theologian*, Peabody: Hendrickson.

—— (2007), *Meet the Rabbis: Rabbinic Thought and the Teachings of Jesus*, Peabody: Hendrickson.

Zias, Joe, and James H. Charlesworth (1992), 'Crucifixion: Archaeology, Jesus, and the Dead Sea Scrolls', in James H. Charlesworth, *Jesus and the Dead Sea Scrolls: The Controversy Resolved*, AYBRL, New York: Doubleday, 273–289.

Index of Scripture references and ancient sources

OLD TESTAMENT

Genesis
28:11-12 *72*

Exodus
3:6 *252*
7 - 19 *26*
12:14 *271*
13:17 *117*
19:5-6 *133*
19:6 *175, 210*
24 *271*
24:3-8 *272*
24:8 *266*

Leviticus
10:10 *136*
11 *137*
11:44 *175*
15:31 *136*
19:1-2 *175*
19:18 *253*
20:7 *175*
20:26 *164*
26:40-45 *145*

Numbers
23:21 *33*

Deuteronomy
6:4-5 *253*
14 *137*
16:3 *270*
18:15 *71*
21:22-23 *290*
30:1-4 *145*
32:43 *211*

Joshua
3 - 4 *26*

2 Samuel
7:11-14 *103*
7:13-16 *261*
12:7 *110*
22:50 *211*

1 Kings
8:44-51 *146*
19 *223*

1 Chronicles
29:11 *32*

2 Chronicles
6:36-39 *146*

Ezra
7:6 *183*
9 *147*

Nehemiah
9 *147*

Psalms
2:7 *87, 261*
8:4 LXX *88*
8:4 *89*
8:4-6 *97*
8:5-6 *90*
18:49 *211*
22 *289*
22:18 *275*
47:2 *37*
47:3 *37*
47:5 *37*
47:9 *37*
69:9 *235*
72:2 *115*
80:8 *117*
110 *15, 98, 186*
110:1 *87, 95, 103, 192,*
  258, 259, 281
110:4 *259*
117:1 *211*
118 *223, 228*
118:22 *247*
118:22-23 *118, 260*
118:26 *225*
119:97 *132*

Proverbs
9:3-5 *75*

Isaiah
2:2-4 *208-209*
5 *116*
5:1-7 *117, 261*
6 *72*
6:9-10 *115*
11:10 *211-212*

Index of Scripture references and ancient sources

14:13–15 *150*
26 *252*
28:7 *233*
28:16 *247*
29:6 *210*
40 *26, 147*
40 – 55 *222*
40:3 *191*
42:1 *261*
42:6 *210*
42:6–7 *209*
43:10 *219*
49:6 *209*
52 – 53 *218, 223*
52:7 *34, 45, 222*
52:7–10 *61*
52:10 *34*
52:13 – 53:12 *218*
53 *98*
53:1 *222*
53:10 *222*
53:11–12 *219, 266, 270*
56 *244*
56:7 *235, 240*
60:5 *53*
61 *102*
61:1 *222*
65:13–14 *53*
66:3 *233*

Jeremiah
6:13 *233*
7:11 *233, 235, 238, 240*
7:14 *245*
11:17 *117*
12:10 *117*
23:11–12 *233*
24:5–7 *147*
26:6 *245*
26:9 *245*
31:31 *271*
50:28 *245*
51:11 *245*

Lamentations
4:13 *233*

Ezekiel
1 *72*
2:1–3 *89*
19:10 *117*
24:21 *245*
34:15–16 *33*
34:23 *33*
36:24–27 *27*
37 *181, 252*
40 – 44 *243–244*

Daniel
2 *72*
2:44 *35*
4 *72*
7 *83*
7 – 12 *72, 223*
7:9 *282*
7:13 *87, 92, 97–98, 103, 281*
7:13–14 *92–95, 98*
7:18 *94*
7:22 *45, 94*
7:27 *94*
9 *147*
9:25 *222*
9:26 *249*
12 *252*

Hosea
4:4–10 *233*
6 *252*
6:2 *223*
6:6 *139*
6:9 *233*

Joel
2:24 *117*

Amos
9:11–12 LXX *65*

Obadiah
21 *34*

Micah
4:1–2 *209–210*
4:6–7 *34*
6:6–8 *139*

Nahum
2:14 *234*

Habakkuk
2:17 *234*

Zephaniah
3:4 *233*
3:14–20 *34–35*

Zechariah
1 – 6 *72*
4:14 *39*
8:20–23 *209*
9 *103*
9:9 *225, 227*
9:11 *266, 272*
9:17 *117*
13:7 *103*
14 *244*
14:9 *34*
14:21 *235, 237*

Malachi
1:6–14 *233*
2:8 *233*
3 *26*
3:1 *35*
4:5–6 *63*

NEW TESTAMENT

Matthew
1:1 *295*
4:11 *73*
4:17 *30*
5–7 *121*
5:11 *93*
5:17–21 *143*
5:45 *84*
6:3-4 *78*
6:9 *84*
8:11 *61*
8:17 *222*
8:20 *88, 91*
8:22 *77*
9:6 *96*
9:6-7 *89*
9:8 *89*
9:36 *71*
10:5-6 *207*
10:23 *151*
10:27 *301*
10:28 *145*
10:32-33 *93*
11:2-6 *102*
11:3 *47, 82*
11:4-6 *47*
11:18-19 *96*
11:20-24 *150*
11:25-27 *74, 86*
11:28-30 *75*
12:6 *247*
12:8 *89*
12:24 *164*
12:27 *79*
12:28 *49*
12:29 *81*
12:31 *96*
12:32 *96*
12:42 *75, 103*
13:11 *87*

13:34-55 *115*
15 *138*
15:20 *137*
15:24 *16*
16:13 *93, 96*
18:3 *144*
19:28-30 *103*
21:11 *21, 68, 69*
21:31 *161*
21:33-46 *116, 260*
21:37 *87*
21:41 *69*
21:43 *261*
23:2-3 *187*
23:8-10 *78*
23:37 *70*
24:36 *86*
26:6-13 *262*
26:17 *263*
26:26-29 *266*
26:45 *96*
26:47 *276*
26:61 *249*
27:37 *103*
27:50 *275*
28:19-20 *207*
53:4 *222*

Mark
1:1 *295*
1:7 *82*
1:10-13 *73*
1:15 *45, 61, 148, 149, 222*
1:44 *102*
2:7 *164*
2:10 *96*
2:10-11 *89*
2:17 *77*
2:18 *178*
2:23-28 *103*
2:24 *178*
2:27-28 *89*

2:28 *88*
3:6 *164*
3:13-16 *102*
3:22-27 *81*
3:27 *74*
4:1-20 *161*
4:11 *87*
4:12 *115*
4:41 *299*
5:9 *79*
6:4 *201*
6:12 *148*
6:14-16 *68*
6:15 *69*
6:34 *71*
7:1-5 *178*
7:1-23 *136-138*
7:3-4 *174*
7:3-5 *175*
7:6-8 *234*
7:15 *136-138*
7:19 *137*
7:36 *102*
8:11-12 *69, 178*
8:22-23 *79*
8:27 *68, 93*
8:28 *69*
8:31 *88, 223*
8:38 *88*
9:2-8 *74*
9:9-12 *63*
9:29 *79*
10:2 *178*
10:19 *143*
10:29-31 *142*
10:30 *152*
10:45 *96, 222*
10:47-48 *87*
10:47-49 *102*
11:1-10 *102, 103*
11:11-18 *103*
11:15-17 *235*

Index of Scripture references and ancient sources

12:1-12 *70, 116, 260*
12:6 *87*
12:7 *87*
12:10 *247*
12:13-17 *254*
12:18-26 *251*
12:28-31 *253*
12:28-34 *120*
12:32-33 *254*
12:33 *139*
12:35-37 *87, 102, 103, 258*
13:26 *88*
13:30 *152*
13:32 *86*
14:3-9 *262*
14:12 *263*
14:21 *223*
14:22-25 *266, 267*
14:27 *103*
14:41 *96*
14:43 *276*
14:55-59 *70*
14:58 *63, 103, 249*
14:61 *69*
14:61-62 *87*
14:62 *88, 97, 103*
14:65 *279*
15:16-18 *279*
15:26 *103*
15:27 *275*
15:43 *157*
16:1-8 *293*
16:8 *297*

Luke
1:1-4 *295*
1:46-55 *64*
1:67-79 *64*
2:25-26 *64*
2:30 *64*
2:32 *64*
2:38 *64*

4:1-13 *73*
4:16-30 *64*
4:18-21 *102, 222*
4:23 *162*
5:17 *164*
5:24 *89, 96*
6 *121*
6:5 *89*
6:22 *93, 96*
6:35 *84*
7:16 *70, 162*
7:19 *82*
7:20 *47*
7:22-23 *47*
7:33-34 *96*
7:36-50 *262*
7:37-39 *70*
8:3 *157*
8:10 *87*
9:58 *88, 91*
9:59-60 *142*
9:60 *77*
10:13-15 *150*
10:18 *73*
10:21-22 *86*
10:21-24 *74*
10:25-27 *253*
10:29-36 *254*
10:37 *109*
11:2 *81*
11:19 *79*
11:20 *49*
11:23 *154*
11:27 *162*
11:31 *103*
11:38 *178*
11:39 *234*
11:49-51 *70*
11:50-51 *150*
12:3 *301*
12:4-5 *145*
12:8-9 *93, 94, 95*

12:10 *96*
13:1-5 *149-150*
13:29 *61*
13:31 *102*
13:32 *94*
13:33 *70*
13:34 *70*
15:1-32 *161*
17:20-21 *49*
18:7-8 *152*
18:9-14 *109*
19:9-10 *96*
20:9-19 *116, 260*
20:13 *87*
20:36 *252*
22:8 *263*
22:14-20 *266*
22:17-20 *267*
22:28-30 *103*
22:52 *276*
23:38 *103*
23:46 *275*
24:19 *68, 71*
24:21 *64*
24:22-23 *293*

John
1:1-18 *295*
1:27 *82*
1:28 *265*
1:45 *21*
1:51 *89*
2:12 *201*
2:13-17 *235*
2:16 *237*
2:17 *103*
2:18 *69*
2:19-21 *249-250*
3:13 *89*
3:14 *89*
5:20 *85*
5:27 *89*

6:14 *68*
6:15 *69, 104*
6:27 *89*
6:30 *69*
7:3–6 *201*
8:28 *89*
8:38 *85*
8:58 *16*
9:16 *178*
10:36 *84*
11:2 *84*
11:41–42 *86*
11:50 *277*
11:55 *269*
12:1–8 *262*
12:23 *89*
12:38 *222*
13:31 *89*
13:34–35 *120*
15:12–13 *120*
15:15 *86*
16:16–19 *223*
18:3 *276*
18:28 *264*
18:31 *286*
18:36 *41*
19:19 *103*
19:24 *275*
19:30 *275*
19:31 *290*
20:30–31 *295*
21:24–25 *295*

Acts
1:6 *65*
1:6–8 *30*
2:22 *71, 79*
3:15 *300*
3:19–21 *65*
3:23 *71*
6:14 *249*
7:37 *71*
7:56 *88*
8:12 *50, 66*
9:10–11 *73*
10:9–16 *73*
13:32–33 *66*
15:13–18 *65*
16:9–10 *73*
17:28–29 *84*
18:9–10 *73*
19:13–17 *79*
24:5 *21*
26:6–8 *65–66*
26:12–23 *73*
28:23 *66*
28:31 *50, 66*

Romans
1:1 *165*
1:3–4 *295*
3:31 *132*
7:12 *132*
15:8–12 *211–212*

1 Corinthians
5:7 *265*
9:21 *134*
11:23–26 *266*
11:24–25 *267*
13 *6*
15:3–4 *292*
15:3–5 *293, 295*
15:24–26 *50*

2 Corinthians
12:1–7 *73*

Galatians
6:2 *134*

Ephesians
2:10 *134*
4:1 *134*
4:17 *134*
5:2 *134*
5:5 *50*
5:8 *134*
5:15 *134*

Philippians
3:5 *169*

Colossians
1:13 *50*

2 Timothy
2:8 *295*

Hebrews
2:6 *88*

Revelation
1:1–2 *73*
1:13 *88*
2 – 3 *18*
11:15 *50*
12:10 *50*
14:14 *88*

DEUTEROCANONICAL WORKS

Sirach
4:10 *84*
24:19–22 *75*
29:11 *129*
48:10 *63*
51:23 *75*
51:26 *75*

2 Maccabees
7 *181, 252*
10 – 15 *239*

Index of Scripture references and ancient sources

OLD TESTAMENT PSEUDEPIGRAPHA

Assumption of Moses
10.9 *150*

2 Baruch
2.30–34 *147*
51.1–6 *116*

3 Baruch
11.2 *38*

1 Enoch *134, 190, 238, 252, 271*
22.1–7 *39*
37 – 71 *95*
46.1–8 *40–41*
48.1–10 *40–41*
49.1–4 *75*
51.3 *75*
52.4 *40–41*
62 – 63 *40–41*
69.29 *40–41*
89 *116*
90.28–29 *249*
91—93 *153*
91.8–11
93.7 *39*

2 Enoch *72*

4 Ezra *72*

Jubilees *134*
16.18 *39*
23 *153*
50.9 *39*

Letter of Aristeas
234 *139*

4 Maccabees
6.27–29 *271*

Psalms of Solomon *233*
8.9–14 *234*
17 – 18 *197*
17.3 *40*
17.7 *40*
17.32 *40*
17.46 *40*

Sibylline Oracles
3 *72*
3.45–49 *36*

Testament of Dan
5.10 *46*
5.10–17 *36–37*

Testament of Levi
8.17 *183*
14.1 – 15.1 *234*

Testament of Moses
5.3 *233*
6.1 *233*
10.1 *37*

DEAD SEA SCROLLS AND RELATED TEXTS

(1QapGen) *Genesis Apocryphon*
21.13 *90*

(1QH) *Thanksgiving Hymns*
12.27–37 *96*

(1QM) *War Scroll* *197*
6.4–6 *36*
17.7–8 *38*

(1QpHab) *Pesher Habbakuk* *153*
12.8–9 *234*

(1QS) *Community Rule*
3.4–5 *139*
5.6 *271*
8.2–6 *248*
8.3–10 *271*
9.4–5 *271*
10.17–18 *133*
11.20 *89*

(4Q174) *Florilegium*
1.6–7 *248*

(4Q246) *Aramaic Apocalypse* *95, 192*
ii 5–10 *36*

(4Q400) *Songs of the Sabbath Sacrifice*
1 ii 1 *38*

(4Q404) *Songs of the Sabbath Sacrifice*
23 ii 11 *38*

(4Q405) *Songs of the Sabbath Sacrifice* *72*

(4Q419c) *Self-Exaltation Hymn* *83, 95, 192*

(4Q504) *Words of the Luminaries*
frag. II 4.6 *282*

(4Q521) *Messianic Apocalypse*
2.1–10 *102*
2.7–12 *36, 48*

(4QMMT) *Halakhic Letter*
92 *192*
C 4.9–11 *234*
C 7–8 *164, 170, 191*

(4QpNah) *Pesher Nahum*
234

(11QMelch) *Melchizedek*
2 *61*

ANCIENT JEWISH WRITERS

Philo
On the Migration of Abraham *134*

On the Special Laws
1.97 *210*
2.163 *210*

Josephus
Jewish Antiquities *76*
4.219 *293*
8.46–49 *79*
10.267–280 *72*
13.288–296 *165*
13.372 *166*
13.409 *166*
14.22–24 *79*
14.142 *183*
17.345–347 *73*
18.23 *255*
18.63 *79*
18.64 *276*
20.167–168 *40*
20.199 *181*
20.208 *184*

The Jewish War
1.112 *166*
1.479 *185*
2.117 *286*
2.118 *255*
2.202–203 *287*
2.258–260 *40*
2.259–262 *286*
2.261–263 *40*
2.411 *179*
2.56 *286*
2.57 *286*
2.60–62 *286*
5.532 *184*
6.250 *246*
6.290–291 *184*
6.303–304 *286*
7.410 *40, 255*

The Life
110 *149*
196–197 *163*
374–384 *23*

RABBINIC WORKS

Amidah
11 *37*

Babylonian Talmud
Bava Batra
9b *78*

Sanhedrin
43a *80, 264*
67b *80*

Jerusalem Talmud
Berakhot
2.3 *259*

Mishnah
Abot
1.1 *134*
1.2 *228*
2.2 *185*
2.4 *179, 192*
3.9–10 *79*
3.13 *134*

Berakhot
2:2 *143*
5.5 *79*

Megillah
2.5 *174*

Middot
1.1 *236*

Sanhedrin
4.1 *280*
7.5 *281*

Sotah
9.15 *79*

Yoma
8.6 *135*

Midrash Tanhuma
Beshallah
4.7 *117*

Tanna Debe Eliyahu
16 *175*

Targum Exodus
15.18 *37*

APOSTOLIC FATHERS

1 Clement
23.4–5 *109*

Index of Scripture references and ancient sources

2 Clement
11.2-3 *109*

Ignatius
To The Ephesians
17.2 *262*
20.2 *90*

Shepherd of Hermas
Similitudes
50 – 114 *109*

NEW TESTAMENT APOCRYPHA AND PSEUDEPIGRAPHA

Gospel of Peter
5 *290*

Gospel of the Ebionites
6 *131*
7 *241*

Gospel of Thomas *18, 76, 107*
1 *295*
3 *41, 49*
9 *161*
27 *135*
37 *88*
44 *96*
62 *87*
64 *237*
65 *87*
65 – 66 *116, 260*
71 *250*
86 *88, 91*
106 *88*
111 *152*
113 *49, 87*

CLASSICAL AND ANCIENT CHRISTIAN WRITINGS

Cicero
Against Verres
2.5.165 *287*

Dio Chrysostom
Orations
8.5 *77*

Diogenes Laertius
6.13 *76*

Epistle to Diognetus
3.1-5 *242*
6.1 *210-211*

Eusebius
Ecclesiastical History
2.23.13 *92*
3.39.11-12 *109*

Hesiod
Works and Days
724-726 *175*

Horace
Epistles
1.16.48 *291*

Juvenal
Satires
14.77-78 *291*

Lucian
Demonax
65 *77*

The Passing of Peregrinus
76

Origen
Against Celsus
1.38 *80*
2.59 *293*

Pliny the Elder
Natural History
5.15.70 *228*

Tacitus
Annals
12.60 *286*

Histories
2.61 *83*
5.9 *195*

Tertullian
Against Marcion *92*

FURTHER SOURCES

Cairo Genizah copy of the *Damascus Document*
11.13-17 *135*

Codex Bezae (D) *267*

Egerton Papyrus
2 *160*

Oxyrhynchus Papyri
1224 *77*

Index of modern authors

Ådna, Jostein 242n, 244n
Allison, Dale C. xiii, 1n, 3, 4n, 6n, 7n, 10, 11n, 14n, 16n, 31n, 42n, 44n, 45n, 72n, 74n, 83, 94n, 103, 106n, 109–110, 152, 249n, 282
Anderson, Paul N. xiv, 6n
Andrade, Nathanael 286
Andrejevs, Olegs 92n, 94n, 96n

Barber, Michael 11n, 240
Barrett, C. K. 240
Bauckham, Richard 4n, 97, 201
Billings, Bradly S. 268
Blomberg, Craig xiv, 129n
Blumhofer, Christopher M. 243n
Bock, Darrell L. 97n, 258–259
Bockmuehl, Markus 118, 131, 134n, 228n, 280n, 300n, 303n
Bond, Helen 217, 264n, 274n
Borg, Marcus J. 140n
Bornkamm, Günther 22n, 47, 100n, 186n, 264n, 275
Bryan, Steven M. 239n, 244n
Bultmann, Rudolf 12, 17n, 30n, 58n, 94n, 234n, 267, 274, 292n, 302
Burridge, Richard A. 2n

Cadbury, Henry J. 2n, 5n, 7–8, 132n
Cahill, Michael 88n
Caird, George B. 57–59, 240
Camponovo, Odo 30n
Casey, Maurice 86n, 90n, 91, 94n, 97n, 223n
Chancey, Mark A. 22n
Charlesworth, James 231, 237n

Chilton, Bruce 31, 42n, 49n, 202, 258, 292
Collins, Adela 97
Corley, Kathleen 262, 293n
Court, John M. 1n
Crossan, John Dominic 1n, 2, 237n, 291, 292n
Crossley, James G. xiv, 2n, 6n, 18n, 139n
Crump, David M. 126n

Dahl, Nils Alstrup 6n, 11n, 163n
Dalman, Gustaf 88n, 89n, 91n, 96n
de Jonge, Marinus 95n, 217n
de Lacey, D. R. 176
Deines, Roland 163n, 169, 171n
Dugard, Martin 3n
Dunn, James D. G. xiv, 4n, 17n, 83n, 87n, 98n, 140n, 274n

Ehrman, Bart 8n
Elliott, John H. 18n
Evans, Craig A. 4n, 46–47

Feldmeier, Reinhard 11n
Ferda, Tucker S. 217n
France, Dick 252
Fredriksen, Paula 198, 226n, 258
Frey, Jörg 302–303
Freyne, Sean 198, 240

Gärtner, Bertil 248
Gnilka, Joachim 14
Goldingay, John 31–32

Hahn, Ferdinand 8n

Index of modern authors

Harrington, Hannah 136
Havukainen, Tuomas 10
Hengel, Martin 4n, 7n, 13n, 18n, 68n, 78n, 94n, 96n, 101, 106n, 111, 272n
Hofius, Otfried 100n
Holtzmann, H. J. 99
Horsley, Richard 27n, 80n, 163n, 168n, 184n

Jeremias, Joachim 13–14, 30n, 159

Kähler, Martin 1n, 14n
Käsemann, Ernst 13
Kazen, Thomas 140
Keck, Leander 106
Keener, C. S. 69n, 226n
Keith, Chris 6n, 16n, 185, 187
Kinman, Brent 226n
Klawans, Jonathan 140n, 267
Kloppenborg, John S. 259n
Knight, Jonathan 2n
Kvalbein, Hans 31, 44n, 120

Ladd, George Eldon 37n
Lessing, G. E. 193
Levine, Amy-Jill 18n
Levine, Lee I. 232
Loisy, Alfred 302

McKnight, Scot xiv, 4n, 8n, 29n, 50n, 151, 225, 269n
Manson, T. W. 86n
Martin, Dale B. 197n
Maslen, Matthew W. 288
Mason, Steve 172n
Meggitt, Justin 7n
Meier, John P. xiv, 25, 42n, 54, 78n, 110, 119n, 131n, 134, 142, 203, 231n
Merz, Anna 2n, 107n, 111n, 174, 279
Meyer, Ben F. 56n, 143, 246
Mitchell, Piers D. 288
Moule, C. F. D. 186n

Neusner, Jacob 169n, 173, 175n, 176n

O'Grady, Selina 3n
Oman, Kraig 116n
O'Reilly, Bill 3, 3n
Owen, Paul 92n

Park, Wongi 2n
Perrin, Nicholas 30n, 37n, 42n, 250–251, 265n
Philip, Tarja 141n
Pitre, Brant 263n–264n
Porter, Stanley E. 5n

Reed, Jonathan L. 77, 292n
Regev, Eyal 231
Reimarus, H. S. 193
Reimer, Andy 80n
Reinhartz, Adele 18n
Rowlands, Jonathan 4n

Saldarini, Anthony J. 170n
Sanders, E. P. xiv, 1n, 11n, 24n, 82, 100n, 123n, 169n, 173–174, 175n, 182n, 195, 225, 227n, 229n, 241, 271, 276n
Schiffman, Lawrence H. 148n
Schmithals, Walter 82
Schnabel, Eckhard J. 215, 242n, 253–254, 280n
Schnelle, Udo 6n, 11n, 14, 23n, 80, 296n
Schröter, Jens 4n, 7n, 8n, 10n, 14n
Schwartz, Daniel R. 133n, 175n
Schweitzer, Albert 1n, 16n, 151, 259
Schwemer, Anna Maria 4n, 7n, 13n, 18n, 96n, 106n
Scott, Bernard B. 111n, 112
Segal, Alan 232
Shepherd, David 92n
Smith, Barry 265, 272
Smith, Mitzi 4n

Snodgrass, Klyne 111n, 117n, 118n, 236n
Spieckermann, Hermann 11n
Stauffer, Ethelberg 12n
Stemberger, Günter 166n, 173n
Stendahl, Krister 144
Strecker, Georg 12n
Stuhlmacher, Peter 11n, 14n

Theissen, Gerd 2n, 11n, 107n, 111n, 174, 197n, 229, 279
Thiessen, Matthew 140n, 141
Thoma, Clemens 18n
Tomson, Peter 104
Twelftree, Graham 81
Tyrell, George 1n

van Henten, J. W. 231, 249n
Vermes, Geza 18n, 91, 92n, 94n, 100n, 119n, 158, 178n, 186n, 212n, 227n, 234n, 262, 281n, 294

Wassen, Cecilia 160n
Watson, Francis B. 6–7n, 17n
Webb, Robert L. 284n, 285n
Wenham, David 113, 270
Williams, Logan 137n, 139n
Williams, Peter J. 91n
Willitts, Joel 4n
Winter, Dagmar 11n
Witherington, Ben 75, 94n, 226n
Wrede, W. 99–100
Wright, N. T. xiv, 18n, 25n, 46n, 47n, 106n, 118n, 149n, 152, 160n, 174, 176, 228n, 229–30, 273, 287

Yinger, Kent L. 163n, 174
Young, Brad H. 78n